Between the Temple
and the Tax Collector

Between the Temple and the Tax Collector

The Intersection of Mormonism and the State

SAMUEL D. BRUNSON

© 2025 by the Board of Trustees
of the University of Illinois
All rights reserved
1 2 3 4 5 C P 5 4 3 2 1
⊗ This book is printed on acid-free paper.

Library of Congress Cataloging-in-Publication Data
Names: Brunson, Samuel D., author.
Title: Between the temple and the tax collector : the intersection
  of Mormonism and the state / Samuel D. Brunson.
Description: Urbana : University of Illinois Press, [2025] |
  Includes bibliographical references and index.
Identifiers: LCCN 2024034048 (print) | LCCN 2024034049 (ebook)
  | ISBN 9780252046322 (cloth) | ISBN 9780252088391
  (paperback) | ISBN 9780252047602 (ebook)
Subjects: LCSH: Church and state—Latter Day Saint churches—
  History. | Church and state—Church of Jesus Christ of Latter-
  day Saints—History. | Latter Day Saints—Taxation—Law and
  legislation.
Classification: LCC BX8643.P6 B78 2025 (print) | LCC BX8643.P6
  (ebook) | DDC 261.7088/289373—dc23/eng/20240911
LC record available at https://lccn.loc.gov/2024034048
LC ebook record available at https://lccn.loc.gov/2024034049

Contents

Acknowledgments   vii

Introduction   1

PART I. FRONTIER RELIGION, FRONTIER TAXATION

1   Mormon Origins   9

2   Funding a City   25

3   Collecting Taxes in Nauvoo   46

4   The Mormons' Utah Home   55

5   Brigham Young and Federal Taxation   63

6   Enlarging Mormonism's Borders   81

7   A Corporate Church in Brooklyn   90

PART II. TINKERING AROUND THE EDGES OF TAX AND RELIGION

8   Mormon Protest Against Taxation   107

9   Polygamy and . . . Taxes?   127

10 The Mormon Church's Lobbying 149

11 Volunteer Missionaries and Paid Clergy 159

12 Tax Exemption as a Lever for Change 179

Conclusion 199

Notes 203

Index 261

Acknowledgments

I wrote a good portion of this book on my bed, my sofa, and at my kitchen table during the COVID-19 pandemic. That means that my writing time was interspersed not just with teaching and meetings, but also with helping with math homework and making sure kids were at class, troubleshooting computers, petting cats, and all of the other things that working at home with a spouse also working from home and kids schooling from home entails.

Writing a book, like practicing a religion, is simultaneously a solitary and a deeply communal endeavor. I could not have produced this book without the generosity of friends and colleagues. I am especially grateful to Ardis Parshall and Johnathan Stapley, who, when in the course of their own research came across documents touching tax law, spontaneously and generously sent them my direction.

I am also immensely grateful for all of the people who helped transform my several Word documents into the actual book you are holding. That includes Tamira Butler-Likely, Leigh Ann Cowan, Jennie Fisher, Denise Peeler, Tad Ringo, and Alison Syring at the University of Illinois Press. It also includes Joseph Stuart, who put together the book's index.

I also want to thank Stephen Bainbridge, Victoria Haneman, Fred Karger, Jeffrey L. Kwall, Lloyd Hitoshi Mayer, Ajay K. Mehrota, Brian Mittendorf, Nathan Oman, Anne-Marie Rhodes, Michael Stanger, Shirley Tillotson, John Turner, and Spencer Weber Waller, all of whom read draft chapters and offered

viii · *Acknowledgments*

invaluable insights and suggestions for how I could improve the book. A big thank-you as well to the anonymous Proposal Reviewer A, who suggested a title far better than the one I had originally proposed.

After speaking to a colleague who is also writing a fascinating history (albeit one unrelated to Mormonism), I'm also immensely grateful for the vast digitizing efforts of the Church History Library and the Joseph Smith Papers Project. Given the travel restrictions (both externally and internally imposed) attendant to a worldwide pandemic, if I had to travel to archives in Salt Lake, I could not have written this book, at least not in the timeframe I did.

I also need to thank my sister, Charity Wyatt. Late in the game writing this book, I did a random search of the Church History Library catalogue and discovered that they had a box of corporate documents for the Eastern States Mission that could help me flesh out Chapter 7. And then I looked at plane tickets from Chicago to Salt Lake, tickets that had a surprisingly steep price tag in the timeframe I had available. As I debated spending the money, I called my sister, who agreed to take time out of her Saturday afternoon and scan the documents for me. Along with that, I'm grateful to Jeff Thompson, a librarian at the Church History Library who helped me over email and the phone, and then helped my sister in person.

Additionally, I need to thank my employer, Loyola University Chicago School of Law, for supporting me as I wrote this book. My scholarly and teaching focus are on tax and nonprofit law; a history of Mormonism and taxation is, at best, tangentially related to what my Jesuit-affiliated employer hired me to do. And yet it has been entirely supportive of the time and effort I have taken to write.

Finally, I want to thank my wife and children (and cats and guinea pig) who shared my workspace as I wrote from home. Thank you Jamie, Jane, Mary, and Miles (and also Rainbow Brite, Lemonade, and Mabel)!

Introduction

Jefferson's famous "wall of separation between Church & State"[1] has largely dominated the academic, legal, and popular discourse around the relationship between religion and the state. A 2023 search for "separation of church and state" on the legal database Westlaw came up with more than 7,000 law review articles that include that phrase, the oldest from 1892 (the sixth volume of the *Harvard Law Review*) and the most recent, as of December 2023, from 2023. Much of this legal scholarship wrestles with the questions of how much (if any) aid the government can give to religious endeavors and under what circumstances (if any) religious individuals and organizations can be excused from generally applicable laws that violate their religious beliefs.

This scholarly focus on separation and its limits reflects the contemporary legal landscape, with some religious organizations asking for government support[2] and with some religious individuals and organizations asking for exemption from generally applicable laws.[3] The judicial decisions adjudicating the requests have proven controversial, perhaps because a clear majority of Americans support the legal separation between church and state.[4] Americans are not ready to tear down the wall dividing the two.

And yet that wall is necessarily and inevitably porous. Religious individuals and institutions are not only geographically located within secular society, they participate in civic life. This is not to deny the separation enshrined within the Establishment Clause, either as a legal matter or a normative goal. But there

2 · Introduction

is an emerging corner of church-state scholarship that is beginning to explore the ways in which the formal legal separation of church and state does not and, in fact, cannot wholly separate religion from law.[5]

The Mormon Church learned this in the mid-nineteenth century. In the aftermath of the murder of Mormonism's founding prophet, mobs threatened—and at times committed—violence against the Mormons living in Nauvoo, Illinois.[6] A year and a half after Smith's death, the governor of Illinois threatened to expel Mormons from the state, using federal troops if necessary. Faced with violence from their neighbors and the government, the majority of Illinois's Mormon residents fled the frontiers of the United States for the Great Salt Lake Basin. They attempted to separate their church from the state, not with a wall, but with more than 1,000 miles. As they traveled beyond the frontier, though, the frontier moved to catch up with them. In 1848, shortly after the Mormons arrived at their new home, Mexico ceded more than half of its territory—including the territory where the Mormons had settled—to the United States, spoils to the victor of the Mexican-American War.[7] While Utah provided the Mormons with some autonomy and some distance, they remained interconnected with and subject to the non-Mormon United States government.

In the world of the twenty-first century, absolute separation between church and state is even less plausible than the early Mormons' attempt at physical separation. The framers of the Constitution could not have anticipated today's globally interconnected world or the modern regulatory state's size.[8] The breadth of the modern regulatory state means that church and state will interact, sometimes peaceably and sometimes not, irrespective of either side's preferences. While it has likely always been the case, today religion is inextricably entangled with the society in which it finds itself situated. That is not to say that religion is indistinguishable from the broader society, but it is to say that it operates within the constraints of society.

And that society includes civil government. While authors have spent plenty of pixels analyzing how this relationship between church and state fits within the boundaries of the US Constitution, constitutional questions are only one of the issues raised by the relationship. Many of the interactions between church and state raise no constitutional questions, either because the constitutional question has been answered or because the interactions are quotidian and necessary.

This book is interested in these quotidian interactions. But because these interactions happen in an abundance of spheres and areas, I am narrowing the inquiry along two axes: taxation and Mormonism.

Introduction • 3

The idea of looking at the interaction of religion and taxes may initially feel like an inapposite subject to explore. After all, separation suggests that religion and taxation inhabit separate and unrelated spheres. That separation is a relatively recent occurrence, though recent scholarship by Dr. Anna Grzymała-Busse makes the provocative argument that while the modern state largely emerged in conflict between the authority of the Roman Catholic Church and secular rulers, the secular rulers "also *emulated* the church." Among other things, rulers learned from the church how to efficiently collect taxes.[9] The connection between religion and taxation, in other words, is neither new nor unique to Mormonism.

Still, in the modern United States (and many other countries), churches are exempt from taxation. But exemption is a relative state; exempt churches do, in fact, pay some taxes, though the specific taxes they face differ by jurisdiction.[10] Moreover, even where churches are exempt, their members are not. And critically for a book that wants to look at the daily, regular interaction of church and state, in the United States, questions of tax raise no constitutional issues to bog down the analysis. US courts have made clear that the importance to government of raising revenue means that the government does not have to accommodate religious belief or practice as it designs its tax regime.[11] A focus on taxation will serve as a microcosm for government, and narrowing the focus to taxation allows us to see how church and state interact without introducing fraught constitutional questions and conflicts.

On the second axis, focusing specifically on how the Mormon Church interacts with taxation also provides a productive area of inquiry. In many ways, the interaction between Mormonism and taxation will reflect the relationship between religion and the state broadly, but in many other ways, the Mormon experience with taxation is unique. Mormonism and taxation are particularly well-suited for this exploration. Mormonism emerged less than two centuries ago, in 1830. Its emergence and growth line up well with the rise of the modern state and, with it, the modern tax systems that allow democratic states to flourish.[12] The opaque, partisan, regressive taxes of the nineteenth century had transformed into a "direct, transparent, centralized, and professionally administered, graduated tax system" by the end of the 1920s.[13] Mormonism grew up alongside modern progressive taxation.

The relationship between taxation and Mormonism goes beyond mere timing, though: Mormonism has played several different roles in its interaction with taxation. At times it (and its members) has been a taxpayer. Twice in its history, Mormonism has established theocratic governments, where Mormon

4 · *Introduction*

leaders had to decide not only how to run and fund the church, but how to run and fund the civil government. At yet other points, Mormonism has used the political or judicial system to try to achieve or prevent changes in the tax system. The interaction of Mormonism and taxation, then, provides a useful window into the ordinary entanglements between church and state that happen every day.

These connections between Mormonism and taxation have largely, though not entirely, gone unexamined in the academic study of Mormon history. In *Mormon Hierarchy: Wealth and Corporate Power*, historian D. Michael Quinn provided an overview of the types of property tax and some questions of tax exemption that the Mormon Church dealt with in the twentieth century.[14] Similarly, economic historian Leonard Arrington mentioned church leaders in the Utah territory considering the impact of territorial taxes on the poor and, eventually, their shift from funding public works through taxation to funding them through tithing.[15] While Quinn and Arrington mention taxes, though, they do so in passing, without exploring how the taxes work, why they were implemented, or how they impacted the church. To the extent that Mormon history looks at taxes, it tends to take this type of high-level approach. Similarly, Mormonism is virtually absent from academic discussions of tax. Though Mormonism has helped shape various tax regimes both legislatively and judicially, as we will see in later chapters, tax researchers have given virtually no consideration to its impact on the development of taxation in the United States or elsewhere.

Because tax and Mormonism have rarely been combined in the same article or book, the language of tax may be opaque to people familiar with Mormonism, and the history of Mormonism may be obscure to people who know tax. And both disciplines may be daunting to people unfamiliar with either. My goal in the following pages is to provide history and analysis that is not contingent on prior knowledge of either taxation or Mormonism. I hope that the content of this book will teach tax people more about taxes and Mormon Studies people more about Mormonism. But I also hope it will teach tax people more about Mormonism and Mormon Studies people more about taxes. And I have written it to be accessible and informative for people who are unfamiliar with either taxes or Mormonism.

Founded by a poorly educated farm boy on the new country's western frontier and peopled by religious radicals,[16] early Mormonism was quintessentially an outsider religion. Time and again Joseph Smith and his followers were driven further west, following the edge of the country's expanding borders and running from both disastrous economic decisions (in Ohio) and hostile neighbors and governments (and, sometimes, violence) in Missouri and Illinois.[17]

After the assassination of their founder and prophet, the majority of Mormons fled violent persecution and attempted to leave the United States. The country ultimately refused to let them leave, though, and then—even isolated from their fellow citizens (albeit on stolen Native American land)—they again caught the attention of their fellow citizens and the federal government as they publicly adopted polygamous marriage.

The Mormon practice of polygamy led to escalating federal intervention as polygamists were jailed, Mormons lost fundamental rights (including the right to vote, sit on a jury, and hold public office) irrespective of their marital status, and finally, the federal government disincorporated the church and seized the majority of its property.[18]

But today, 130 years after this nadir in Mormon history, the Church of Jesus Christ of Latter-day Saints has become a quintessentially American church. Its members serve in the highest reaches of government, the business world, and even academia. In 2020, Mormons made up about 1 percent of the US population.[19] The following year, there were nine Mormons in Congress, three in the Senate, and six in the House of Representatives. At 1.7 percent, Mormons are overrepresented; moreover, those nine Mormons are the smallest Mormon contingent in Congress in more than three decades.[20] Mormons are overrepresented in business and the legal profession.[21] Church leaders testify in Congress and file amicus briefs with the Supreme Court. Mormonism today is almost unrecognizable as the outsider it was for its first three-quarters of a century or more.

While this book focuses on the intersection of taxation and Mormonism, it is critical to not overread that relationship.[22] Taxes are important, but they are not the sole driver of decision-making, as a colleague of mine likes to emphasize.[23] But as I will show, taxes were continually in the background of Mormon development, and at times broke through to the forefront of decision-making. Similarly, at some distinct moments, Mormonism affected, directly or through the judicial system, the broader reach of taxes.

With that in mind, over the following pages, we will follow Mormonism's path from outsider to insider. We will see how religion and the state, inextricably intertwined, interact outside the spotlight of constitutional conflict. And we will follow that path through the lenses of the Mormon Church and of the tax law.

The first half of the book runs roughly chronologically, following the relationship between the Mormon Church and taxes from the late eighteenth century (before the birth of the church's founding prophet) through the end of the nineteenth century. Then, beginning with chapter 8, the organization of the book

6 · *Introduction*

shifts. Instead of running chronologically through the twentieth and into the twenty-first centuries, the book will look at tax issues that appeared, in varied forms, across Mormonism's history and, to some extent, across international geography.

Where the chapters of the book evince some degree of progression and increased sophistication, the second half allows a certain amount of the *ad hoc* approach the church takes to taxation to emerge. Tax, after all, played a role in the church's formation, but not the central role, and at a remove of decades, the Mormon Church sometimes approached the same question differently.

Over time, too, tax regimes became more complicated, more sophisticated, or sometimes just different. By looking at how Mormonism reacted to similar tax issues in the nineteenth, twentieth, and twenty-first centuries, we will be able to understand just how pervasive the relationship between church and state continues to be, and just how inevitably permeable the wall separating them is.

PART I

Frontier Religion, Frontier Taxation

Mormonism was born into a newly and rapidly changing world. Western New York, where Joseph Smith grew up and where he founded his Church of Christ, had, between his birth and the establishment of the church he founded, shifted from the country's frontier to a rudimentary market economy.[1] The church was born at the tail end of states disestablishing their established churches.[2] And it was born into the liminal frontier between premodern and modern taxation.

In fact, in 1799—just six years before Smith's birth—Great Britain had instituted a national income tax.[3] But the United States was far behind in establishing a modern, transparent tax system. In fact, in 1817, the federal government repealed its excise tax on alcohol, raising the bulk of its revenue through indirect tariffs. While Americans bore the economic incidence of tariffs through the increased cost of imported goods, the actual tariff burden they bore was invisible to the American public.[4] Tariffs' opacity meant that the funding of the federal government could be incredibly political and incredibly regressive.[5]

The taxes most Americans actually felt were state and local taxes. But state and local taxes tended to be *ad hoc* and at least as political as federal tariffs. States had not yet developed a regime of universal property taxation that attempted to identify and tax all property within a jurisdiction at a constant rate.[6] Rather, individual tax collectors would evaluate each

8 · FRONTIER RELIGION, FRONTIER TAXATION

taxpayer and assess a specific amount of tax due based on that particular taxpayer's situation, a far cry from today's almost automatic, largely objective tax assessment.[7]

But from its birth (and even before), Mormonism had to navigate this wild west of taxation. Members had to comply with the developing and inconsistent tax law, and within less than a decade and a half, Mormon leaders had to actually design, enact, and enforce tax policy. The first eight chapters of this book will follow chronologically as the (sometimes incoherent) tax law influenced and was influenced by Mormonism. Over the course of the nineteenth century, with experience, both became more sophisticated and more capable of interacting. And, while taxation did not fundamentally form Mormonism, and while Mormonism did not fundamentally alter the broader system of taxation in the United States, both left their marks on the other. So for the first half of this book, we will follow the chaotic developments as tax authorities and the Mormon Church navigated the Jeffersonian wall of separation between church and state, and as they trailblazed the tax gaps in that wall.

1

Mormon Origins

Mormonism emerged from the American frontier. Formally founded in 1830, the Mormon Church traces its origins to a vision founder Joseph Smith Jr. experienced ten years earlier. Immersed in the world of the Second Great Awakening, fourteen-year-old Joseph Jr. walked some distance from his family's home in upstate New York and, alone, vocalized a prayer asking which church was true. Consistent with Methodist practice at the time, he felt gripped by a spirit but, unlike the traditional Methodist experience, he identified the spirit as Satan, not as God. Pushing through, he had a vision of God and Jesus Christ, who told him not to affiliate with any of the extant churches because none was true.[1]

In the aftermath of his vision, during breaks between laboring with his family for sustenance, Joseph Jr. received angelic instruction. Eventually, he also received a book made of golden plates that he translated into the Book of Mormon. After translating and publishing the Book of Mormon, Joseph Jr. organized the Church of Christ, the precursor to the modern Mormon Churches.

This origin story is, naturally, incomplete, treating the foundation of the new Mormon Church as sui generis, largely divorced from the society surrounding it. Scholars have explored the interaction between Joseph Jr.'s vision and his family's religious seeking, between the church and New England practices of folk magic, and between early Mormon converts and religious dissent. Largely, though, they have not explored the place of taxation in the origins of the Mormon Church.

10 · FRONTIER RELIGION, FRONTIER TAXATION

This oversight is not surprising; taxes seem at best tangential to the development of a new religious movement. And yet the origins and the development of the Mormon Church intersect frequently with questions of taxation, in part because the nineteenth century introduced not only Mormonism but also modern systems of taxation. England introduced its first national income tax in 1799; the United States adopted a federal income tax about six decades later. Mormonism and modern taxation are intertwined in part because they have both grown and evolved together, in response and dialogue with the same social, economic, and political developments.

Critically, the way that the Mormon Church engages with taxes serves as a microcosm of its interaction with the secular state. While taxation is not the proximate cause of Mormonism, church taxes certainly played an important role both in launching the Great Awakenings and in cementing the Smiths' history of religious dissent and religious seeking.

Church, Tax, and the American Founding

From colonial days through the beginning of the nineteenth century, a number of colonies and states used church taxes to support their established church or (eventually) Protestant churches in general. Of the thirteen original American colonies, ten had an established church. In New York, New Jersey, Maryland, and the Southern colonies, the established church was the Church of England, while most of New England (other than Rhode Island) recognized the Congregational Church as the established church.[2]

Early religious dissenters faced persecution until 1689's Act of Toleration[3] relieved religious dissenters of official state persecution. Under this law, Protestant Christians enjoyed some degree of political autonomy. That political autonomy did not always relieve them of duties, though: for instance, even after the passage of the Act of Toleration, dissenters had to pay church taxes.[4]

Church taxes provided an important source of revenue for established churches during colonial times. The early colonies provided for governmental support of the established church; in Virginia, the Church of England benefited from that support, while in Massachusetts, the Congregational Church received state money. In fact, three months after the first meeting of the Massachusetts colonial legislature, it imposed a tax explicitly to support ministers and houses of worship.[5] Colonial governments treated the established church as an arm of government. In its quasi-governmental role, it made sense both that the established church would be treated differently from other religions and that it would receive public funding.[6]

Still, by the 1720s, facing pressure from England, several colonies exempted dissenters from church taxes, provided the dissenters actively participated in and provided financial support to some other church. If a dissenter did not actively participate in and support a non-established church, that dissenter had to pay the ecclesiastical taxes that ended up supporting the established church.[7] This exemption was far from universal, though. Some colonies—particularly Southern colonies that had established the Church of England—did not exempt other Protestants from their church taxes until after the Revolutionary War. And almost no colony exempted Catholics or Jews from colonial church taxes.[8]

After the United States declared its independence from England, states began to disestablish. Disestablishment occurred on a state-by-state basis, starting with New Jersey and Delaware in 1776 and ending with Massachusetts in 1833. Even after disestablishment, though, eliminating the church tax proved controversial. In Maryland, for instance, the new state constitution disestablished the Church of England. But while the Church of England was no longer the established church, the new state's constitution allowed the legislature to enact taxes to support churches generally. In practice, that meant that Maryland allocated the proceeds raised by the church tax to churches according to their membership. The legislature's ability to enact church taxes continued until the state changed its constitution—fourteen years after disestablishment—to prohibit church taxes.[9]

The Smith Family and Church Taxes

As a boy, Joseph Jr. likely knew nothing about church taxes. Joseph Jr. spent his childhood in Vermont and moved to New York as a teenager. Vermont, Joseph Jr.'s birthplace, did not disestablish the Congregational Church until 1807, two years after he was born. At the same time, Vermont did away with the church tax used to support the Congregational Church, forcing even the established church to find private support.[10] Similarly, by the time the Smith family moved to New York, the state had long since revoked its church tax. Prior to disestablishment, New Yorkers paid taxes to support the Church of England. Dutch Reformed congregations were exempt from the church tax, but dissenters paid taxes to support the established church. In 1777—almost thirty years before Joseph Jr.'s birth—New York formally disestablished the Anglican Church and ended taxes supporting it.[11]

While Joseph Jr. never would have paid the church tax—and while church taxes likely never occurred to him—the history of his family's religious seeking and dissent intersected tangibly with Vermont's church tax. More than three

12 · FRONTIER RELIGION, FRONTIER TAXATION

decades before Smith broke permanently with Protestant Christianity, his grandfather Asael Smith broke with the established Congregational Church in his home of Tunbridge, Vermont, for Universalism.

Breaking with the established church was a big deal. Early New Englanders did not have the same vision of a separated church and state that American society and jurisprudence later adopted. In fact, New England had both the longest and deepest support for its established churches of the colonies-turned-states. For almost two centuries, the Congregational churches in New England received state support, on the belief that church and state not only could, but should, be connected.[12]

Vermont was emblematic of this New England history with publicly supported churches. Until disestablishment, the public supported religious worship in a significant portion of Vermont towns.[13] In 1781, the Vermont legislature formally gave towns the authority to levy property taxes to support bridges, schools, and church meetinghouses. Two years later, the legislature updated the law, providing even broader legal support for religious taxation.[14] The 1773 law provided that two-thirds of a town's voters could authorize the town to build a church building and hire a minister. At the same time, the voters could authorize poll and real property taxes to fund these expenses.[15]

While the law allowed a supermajority of a town's voters to establish a church tax, it also provided a safe harbor for religious minorities. A resident who wanted to be excused from paying the tax had to bring a certificate, signed by "some minister of the gospel, deacon, or elder, or the moderator in the church or congregation to which he, she or they pretend to belong, being of a different persuasion." The law presumed that all town residents belonged to the Congregational Church until they presented the certificate. Up until the day a resident presented the certificate, that resident owed their share of the church taxes. Upon providing the certificate, the religious dissenter no longer owed any church tax.[16]

Sometime before moving to Vermont, Asael Smith left the Congregational Church of his birth and became a Universalist, a move viewed as heretical by many of his Congregationalist neighbors.[17] In 1797, the Tunbridge Universalist Society requested an exemption from the town's church taxes.[18] The Society had seventeen members, including Asael, who acted as the moderator of the group, his brother Jesse, and his son Joseph Sr.[19] Some combination of religious dissatisfaction and desire to avoid paying ecclesiastical taxes led them to formally affiliate with the Universalist church.

By the time Joseph Jr. was born in Sharon, Vermont, in 1805,[20] his father and grandfather were no longer formally Universalists. Within a year of Asael

Mormon Origins · 13

delivering his certificate to the town clerk, the Tunbridge Universalist Society was defunct. Asael had a pew in the newly built Congregational Church while, a year later, one of the putative members of the Tunbridge Universalist Society denied having ever signed the request for exemption.[21] By the time Joseph Jr. was two years old, Vermont no longer imposed a church tax. Still, taxes had played a role in the religious nonconformity of Joseph Jr.'s father, uncle, and grandfather.

Disestablishment, Taxes, and the Great Awakening

The same church tax that motivated Asael to formally establish a Universalist society also played an indirect role in Joseph Jr.'s 1820 vision. Joseph Jr. reported that after his family's move to New York, the region experienced "an unusual excitement on the subject of religion." Methodists, Presbyterians, and Baptists vied for converts, encouraged by clergy who wanted to ensure that everybody was converted. Several members of the Smith family joined the Presbyterians, but teenage Joseph Jr. was attracted to Methodism. Confused by the vying doctrines, in 1820 he prayed his fateful prayer and experienced a vision in which Jesus Christ told him not to join any church.[22] Mormonism traces its roots to that vision.

Joseph Jr.'s vision did not emerge, contextless, from out of nowhere: it came out of the religious marketplace of the Second Great Awakening. The Second Great Awakening began in the late eighteenth century and climaxed around 1820.[23] A populist revival movement stressing both the Bible and the simplicity of understanding its text, the Second Great Awakening was characterized by "spiritual regeneration, itinerant preachers, revivals and camp meetings, and a restoration ideal."[24] Western New York, where Joseph Jr. spent his early adolescence, was fertile ground for this religious fervor, with successive religious revivals eventually leading to the sobriquet "The Burned-Over District." Coming of age in this environment, religion would naturally have been a critical topic in Joseph Jr.'s teenage years.[25]

The religious revivalism that characterized the Second Great Awakening largely came in reaction to disestablishment. Disestablishment cut the formal ties between state and church; government could no longer formally employ religion as a tool to ensure public morality. To combat potential immorality and to ensure that the frontier's newly mobile, increasingly consumerist society remained tied to religious values, Protestant ministers held revivals.

But revivalism was not solely to reinstitute religious values among a newly created religious marketplace. Without an established church—and without

14 · FRONTIER RELIGION, FRONTIER TAXATION

the tax revenues the state collected and provided to the church—clergy needed to find money elsewhere. Not only were Americans suddenly free to join any church or no church at all, but their dollars followed them. Without a church tax, ministers had to compete for congregants and for funding.[26]

Indirectly, then, taxes played a role in paving the way for Joseph Jr.'s Church of Christ. While he would have had no personal memory of ecclesiastical taxes, they played a not-insignificant role in the religious nonconformity that he inherited from his father, uncle, and grandfather. And ecclesiastical taxes—or, rather, their elimination—were a salient underlying motivation for the revivalism that made up the Second Great Awakening. The Second Great Awakening, in turn, provided the context and impetus for Joseph Jr.'s eventual founding of the Church of Christ.

Joseph Jr. and New York Taxes

Still, while taxes underlay some of the important foundations for the emergence of Mormonism in the early nineteenth century, Joseph Jr. likely would not have personally recognized the role that taxes played in this restorationist religion. (Often, in fact, the pressures that taxes exert on decision-making are subtle and go unrecognized by the individuals making decisions.) And it was not just church taxes that would not have been salient to Joseph Jr.: few if any federal taxes would have directly impacted the Smiths' everyday lives. The federal government raised revenue almost exclusively through tariffs.[27] Tariffs ultimately fell on consumers and, in that way, raised the prices the Smith family paid for goods. But the government collected tariffs from shippers when products were brought into port.[28] As a result, the amount of the tax was already built into the price of goods by the time the Smith family purchased them.

New York taxes would have been scarcely more salient to the Smiths. Like most states in the post-Revolutionary era, New York initially relied principally on property taxes to raise revenue. Northeastern states were able to reduce their property tax during the first decades of the nineteenth century, replacing them with other streams of revenue.[29] New York had low expenses, and could largely raise the revenue necessary to pay those expenses through the sale of public land, indirect taxes carried over from colonial times, and investment returns.[30] For instance, New York was one of the earliest states to charter a state bank, and by 1810 was receiving substantial dividends from its bank investments.[31] Still, New York did impose taxes on its citizens and two—a general property tax and a road tax—would have played a part in the annual life of the Smiths.

For the first year and a half that they lived in New York, the Smiths would not have paid property tax. The Smith family had not owned real property since

Mormon Origins • 15

they left Vermont in 1803. Throughout Joseph Jr.'s young life, his family stood on the precipice of economic oblivion. At the very beginning of the nineteenth century, Joseph Jr.'s father, Joseph Smith Sr., was cheated out of his return on a speculative investment in ginseng. To cover his debts, Joseph Smith Sr. sold his farm, while his wife Lucy contributed the $1,000 she had received as a wedding gift. The Smith family turned to tenant farming, with help from family to smooth their economic valleys.[32]

When the Smith family moved from the upper Connecticut Valley to Palmyra, New York, the whole family had to work. Soon they bought a farm, which Joseph Sr. and his sons cleared and worked. The farm put additional economic pressure on the family, though, and they all had to work to meet their mortgage obligations and to support themselves.[33] As new landowners in New York, they also owed property tax.

New York's property tax season encompassed nine months. Between May and June, the assessors from each assessment district went through their districts and wrote the value of the houses and land owned by residents on their assessment rolls. They also assigned a value to each resident's personal property, which they reduced by the resident's debt. Residents who disagreed with the assessed values (which were determined using "the best evidence in [the assessor's] power") could, by sworn affidavit, affirm a different value for their property. If a resident did so, the law required the assessor to accept the sworn value.[34]

In July, assessors had to post their assessment lists in at least three places in their town or ward. Residents then had ten days to inspect the lists and challenge the assessments. After ten days, the assessors gathered to review the challenges. Once finished, the assessors would sign the assessments and deliver them to supervisors of their respective towns.[35]

The board of supervisors would then take the valuations and use them to determine how much tax each property owner owed. With the amount of tax determined, the board of supervisors delivered the assessment rolls to collectors by November 1. The collectors were then responsible to collect the assessed taxes and deliver the taxes (less the 5 percent the law awarded them as compensation for their services) by February 1 of the following year. If a property owner refused to pay, the law authorized the collector to sell that recalcitrant owner's property to meet their unpaid tax obligations.[36]

Between 1820 and 1825, the Smith family would have participated in this annual dance of tax assessment and collection. In 1825, though, after the death of eldest son Alvin, the family lost its ability to meet its mortgage obligations. Rather than lose the land altogether, they sold it to a local Quaker landowner and became tenants on the land that had once been theirs.[37] Upon losing their

16 · FRONTIER RELIGION, FRONTIER TAXATION

land, they also lost their obligation to pay property taxes and no longer took part in the nine-month tax season they had participated in for the previous half decade.[38]

While the loss of their farm removed them from the property tax rolls, it did not affect their obligation to pay the road tax. New York imposed a road tax on all free male residents over the age of twenty-one (other than ministers and priests), irrespective of property ownership. The road tax was primarily an in-kind tax: overseers of the road districts would assign each eligible taxpayer a certain number of days he had to work on the highways. The number of days was to be determined based on an individual's "estate and ability." The law allowed the overseer to require every male subject to the tax to work at least one day, but not more than thirty days, each year. Overseers had to provide road taxpayers with at least twenty-four hours' notice of the time and place they were to work on the highways, and then the individuals had to show up and do their work. In certain circumstances, the road overseer could also require a taxpayer to bring a "team, cart, waggon or plow, with a pair of horses or oxen, and a man to manage the same." Anybody furnishing these things would get a triple credit toward his road tax obligation; that is, one day providing a team would qualify as three days of road tax labor.[39]

While the road tax was nominally an in-kind tax, individuals with enough money could avoid physically laboring on the highways. The law allowed taxpayers to choose between showing up in person or sending "an able bodied man as a substitute." An individual could also pay the overseer of the roads sixty-two and a half cents for each day he was assessed in lieu of working, and the overseer would use that money to improve the roads and bridges.

The law also provided a stick to enforce these taxpaying duties: failure to work or pay the assessed road tax (or "hindering others" from meeting their road tax obligations) resulted in a $1 fine for each offense. (People who were supposed to provide teams, carts, wagons, or plows faced a trebled fine.)[40] Road tax lists from 1817 show Joseph Smith Sr.'s name and, in 1820, his son Alvin's name appears as well.[41] Given the family's poverty, it is likely that they would have provided in-kind labor to meet their obligations. The road tax, then, would have played a regular part in the Smith family's life while they lived in Palmyra.

Joseph Jr. did not turn twenty-one until December 1826 and would therefore not have been subject to the road tax until 1827. In the years between the Smith family's sale of its farm and the year Joseph Jr. became subject to the road tax, he followed a number of pursuits, including financial endeavors to help his family. With the death of their oldest son, the Smith family was in a dire financial situation. Joseph Jr. and his brother Hyrum looked for work around the countryside. Joseph Jr. took a job digging for treasure, he helped his family with farming, and eventually, he returned to a previous job doing farm chores for Josiah Stowell and perhaps working in Stowell's sawmills.[42]

The year after he turned twenty-one proved to be an important year in Joseph Jr.'s life, not because he began to pay the road tax but because, in January 1827, he married Emma Hale. Emma's family contrasted with Joseph Jr.'s in many ways. For one thing, the Hales had no history of tax protest. In fact, after returning from the War of 1812, Emma's oldest brother Jesse had worked as a tax assessor and collector in Harmony, Pennsylvania, for several years. After Jesse, Emma's brother David served in the role of tax collector.[43] While neither Joseph Jr.'s nor Emma's familial experiences with taxation had a direct effect on the founding of the new church, they represent the various backgrounds members of the soon-to-be-established church brought with them as they joined.

At the same time that Joseph Jr. worked to help support his family and prepare for his financial future, he also engaged in significant religious endeavors. His visions did not end in 1820; he reported visits with Moroni, the long-dead final editor and writer of the Book of Mormon, in September of every year between 1823 and 1827. At the last visit, the angelic visitor delivered the golden plates he had helped inscribe to Joseph Jr.[44] Joseph Jr. spent the subsequent two years translating the plates and, in 1829, published the Book of Mormon.[45]

Exempting Churches in New York

On April 6, 1830, in the presence of around fifty people, Joseph Jr. formally organized the Church of Christ. This new church was probably not incorporated under New York law; rather, it likely came into existence as an unincorporated religious society. While incorporation provided (and continues to provide) certain benefits, its benefits would have been relatively unimportant to the fledgling church. The main benefits incorporation offered included perpetual succession and the easier management of property. Joseph Jr.'s new church did not own property, and at this early point in its existence, was not tremendously worried about succession. Also, incorporation would have had costs to the new church, including requiring an organization foreign to what Joseph Jr. envisioned.[46]

Formal organization, albeit as an unincorporated entity, provided the fledgling religion with some benefits, including with respect to taxes. Without property, New York's exemption of property belonging to churches and "places of public worship" from its property tax would have provided no benefit to the newly organized church. But New York tax law also provided personal benefits: it exempted all personal property belonging to "any minister of the gospel, or

18 · FRONTIER RELIGION, FRONTIER TAXATION

to any priest of any denomination whatsoever" from the state property tax. It also exempted up to $1,500 of real property owned by ministers and priests from property taxation.[47]

While twenty-four-year-old Joseph Jr. had little formal education and even less experience with reading and interpreting law, this exemption was not lost on the new church's members. Within months of the church's organization, *The Reflector*, a Palmyra newspaper, reported that at least one (unidentified) member formally requested the state's ministerial exemption:

> A disciple of the "Gold Bible," lately called upon an assessor and demanded an exemption from taxation, to the amount of $1500—alledging that he was a Minister of the Gospel, at the same time producing a certificate, signed by Jo. Smith, and Oliver Cowdry, by way of proof—the course to be taken in this matter has not as yet transpired.[48]

Case law interpreting this exemption for ministers is sparse, and none of it predates 1830. Later judicial opinions did shed some light on the exemption's requirements, however. In 1849, a New York court stated that to qualify for this exemption, a taxpayer had the burden of proving that he or she was a minister.[49] At least one taxpayer cited favorably by a New York court established that he was a minister by presenting the assessor with "his certificate of ordination"; he then "demanded to be exempt from taxation."[50] The unidentified Mormon followed precisely the same process of getting an exemption.

The formal organization of the church was important in this process. New York courts in the nineteenth century consistently looked at the denomination of ministers claiming the exemption. Moreover, with the organization of the church, Joseph Jr. and Oliver Cowdery issued licenses, which could be (and were) used as evidence that one qualified as a minister. On June 9, 1830, Joseph Jr. and Cowdery issued a license certifying that John Whitmer was an apostle of Jesus Christ and an Elder of the Church of Christ "established & regularly organized in these last days AD, 1830 on the 6th day of April."[51] The same day, they issued a license to Christian Whitmer certifying that he was a "Teacher in this Church of Christ"[52] and a license to Joseph Smith Sr. certifying that he was a Priest in the church.[53]

In 1830, this exemption was unlikely to have any significant benefit for the Smith family. At this point they did not own any real property; while they undoubtedly owned some taxable personal property, the exemption for ministers would likely have had little value to them personally. (It is worth noting, though, that in 1830, Hyrum Smith, Joseph Jr.'s older brother, was taxed on fifteen acres in Manchester that he lived on, although he did not own the land.[54])

The property tax exemption was not the only exemption enjoyed by ministers of the gospel and priests of any denomination. New York law also exempted ministers and priests from New York's road tax obligation.[55] The formal organization of a church—and especially a church with lay ministry—could thus significantly affect both institutional and personal tax obligations. While it was not organized for tax benefits, the leaders and members of the fledgling church evinced awareness of the interaction between their positions in the church and their tax obligations and understood how to obtain the tax benefits that flowed from that interaction.

Mormonism Moves to Ohio

Though the nascent Church of Christ originated in 1830 in New York, by the end of the year it had begun to shift west. In December, Joseph Jr. received a revelation directing the church to move to Ohio. Within another six months, while in Missouri, he designated Jackson County, Missouri, as the location to which the church would assemble and build its city of Zion, a frontier settlement and millenarian city of safety and opportunity for the young church.[56]

Over the next seven years, the church operated on parallel tracks in Ohio and Missouri. These parallel tracks ended in January of 1838 when Joseph Jr. and more than 800 of his followers left Ohio for the last time and joined with church members in Missouri.[57] The church would stay in Missouri until 1839 when violence forcibly expelled the church and its members from the state.[58]

While those years proved critical in the development of the church and its theology, the church's interaction with taxing authorities likely proved routine. For the most part, the members of the church in Ohio and Missouri faced the same taxes members faced in New York.

The state of Ohio raised revenue from its residents primarily through property taxation. Among other things, Ohio taxed land and "dwellinghouses of the value of two hundred dollars." It also taxed the capital of merchants employed in the state and all "horses, mules, and asses, and neat cattle of three years old and upwards."[59] Like New York, then, members who moved to Ohio would have primarily owed taxes on whatever property they owned.

Many would have owed little or no property tax, though. Ohio's property tax, with its exemption for homes with a value of less than $200, would likely have excluded the majority of the young church's members from paying the tax. In 1833, when Kirtland had about 150 Mormon residents, Mormons only owned about 400 acres total, half of which belonged to Joseph Jr. and John Johnson. By 1836, the now 3,000 Mormons only owned 1,700 acres, and only thirty plots

20 • FRONTIER RELIGION, FRONTIER TAXATION

were larger than twenty-five acres. Between 1832 and 1837, the average value of an acre of land in Kirtland rose from $7 to $44, meaning that on average, only Kirtland residents with more than four-and-a-half acres would even be subject to property tax.[60]

Like New York, counties in Ohio also employed a road tax.[61] The tax applied to all males who had lived in the state for at least three months and were between twenty-one and sixty years old. Unlike New York, each person subject to the road tax had to perform two days of service each year.[62] Ohio did not exempt ministers from its road or property tax; the only exemption was for people whom the town supervisor deemed unable to perform the required service.[63]

While members of the young church faced a similar tax landscape in Ohio to that they had known in New York, as the church grew and expanded, it faced an expanded array of taxes. For instance, while the church never built standard meetinghouses during Joseph Jr.'s life, in Ohio it built its first temple.[64] Between 1833 and 1836, the church built a two-story stone and plaster building that melded classical and Gothic architecture. When completed, the Kirtland temple's size rivaled the largest buildings in northern Ohio.[65]

The temple proved financially costly to the mostly impoverished members of the church, with the price of its construction ultimately reaching between $40,000 and $70,000.[66] This price tag does not include members' donated labor to help build the temple.[67] When completed, the church used its temple as a meetinghouse, as well as for other purposes.[68] With the construction of its temple, the church held property potentially subject to property taxation.

The church's use of the temple as a meetinghouse likely saved the church from the ongoing cost of property taxation. While Ohio's property tax was expansive, it provided for a limited religious exemption: Ohio law exempted from tax up to fifteen acres of land owned on behalf of a religious society and used as a meetinghouse or a burying ground.[69] The Kirtland temple sat on a lot slightly smaller than two acres, meaning it fit comfortably within the property tax exemption.[70] Thus, Ohio's property tax would not have impacted the institutional church in Ohio, where it owned a temple, any more than it did in New York, where the church owned no land.

By the middle of the 1830s, Joseph Jr. and his church—now known as the Church of the Latter Day Saints—were in desperate need of money. Between the costs of building the temple and the collapse of the United Firm, which had been the financing vehicle for the church and its publications, the church carried significant debt. Its members had lost their land in Missouri, so the church had little potential revenue to pay that debt.[71] These church-specific financial woes were compounded by the Jacksonian termination of national currency and the lack of silver and gold in Ohio.[72] Without a national currency, and without adequate precious metals, people on the frontier had to find other means of exchange. The state could not help—the US Constitution foreclosed states from issuing their own currency.[73] As a result, in antebellum America, banks became the primary source of currency. Like the states, banks could not issue legal tender, but banks could issue notes and these banknotes circulated locally as if they were currency.[74]

In 1836, Joseph Jr. and other leaders of the church decided to take advantage of the ability of banks to issue notes and attempted to charter a bank they called the Kirtland Safety Society.[75] If it wanted to receive a banking charter in Ohio, the church had to convince the state legislature to pass a law incorporating the bank.[76] The Kirtland Safety Society failed to obtain a charter from the legislature and, instead of an incorporated bank, church leaders renamed their endeavor the Kirtland Safety Society Anti-Banking Company, a joint stock company rather than a corporation.[77]

Although the Kirtland Safety Society's failure to obtain a banking charter ultimately led to its doom, that failure shielded it from taxation. In 1825, Ohio imposed a tax on banks equal to 4 percent of the dividends they paid. In 1831, it increased the tax rate to 5 percent. The Kirtland Safety Society Anti-Banking Company, however, would not have been subject to the dividend tax because the tax applied to banks "incorporated by law of this state."[78]

The failure of the church to obtain a banking charter not only saved the Safety Society from this ordinary dividend taxation but also shielded the Safety Society from a significant penalty tax. In 1836, Ohio enacted a law that would impose a 20 percent tax on any bank that did not give up its right to issue notes with denominations of less than three dollars after July 4, 1836, and with denominations of less than five dollars after July 4, 1837.[79] The Safety Society issued notes in "denominations of one, two, three, five, ten, twenty, fifty, and one hundred dollars, all signed by various members of the Church, the majority bearing the names of Joseph Jr. as cashier and Rigdon as president."[80] Had the Safety Society obtained a state charter, it would have been subject to a 5 percent tax on its dividends as well as a 20 percent penalty tax.

Though the Kirtland Safety Society's lack of a banking charter protected it from taxation, its inability to obtain a charter also presaged its economic failure. The Mormons' timing in creating a bank could not have been worse—the Kirtland Safety Society soon ran up against the Panic of 1837, which decimated banks throughout the country. Losses on loans and other failures reduced the value of state-chartered banks' book assets by nearly 50 percent, and a little over one in four chartered banks closed their doors in 1837 alone.[81]

22 · FRONTIER RELIGION, FRONTIER TAXATION

The Panic did not spare banks (or non-bank financial institutions) in Ohio, including the Kirtland Safety Society. But the Safety Society faced other problems as well. Disgruntled church members began to leave the church. Some of those who left had been significant investors in the Safety Society. Notably, John Johnson had pledged real property as collateral for his 3,000 shares but, when he left the church, he transferred that property to family members. This loss of this and other capital further impaired the Safety Society's ongoing viability.[82]

The economic fallout of the failure of the Kirtland Safety Society ultimately led to dissidents forming their own church. Dissidents also began threatening church leaders with both violence and lawsuits. Members in Ohio felt pressure to choose sides.[83] By 1838, this combination of "internal dissent and financial turmoil" drove the Mormon community from Ohio to join their coreligionists in Missouri.[84]

The Mormons' brief stay in Missouri has little of interest from a tax perspective. Missouri taxes looked almost identical to Ohio taxes, with the addition of a capitation tax.[85] The state's primary source of revenue, though, was its property tax. Like Ohio and New York, Missouri provided a limited religious exemption: the state did not include buildings used for public worship, including their furniture and connected land, in its property tax base, provided the building, furniture, and land were in fact used for public worship.[86] In theory, this exemption could have been tremendously valuable to the church. Joseph Jr.'s plan for the church's Jackson County, Missouri settlement included twelve temples. Ultimately, though, the church never built the temples; rather, when the Ohio-based Mormons fled to Missouri in 1836, they built a log tabernacle in which they could hold their religious services. Joseph Jr. was furious that they built a tabernacle before a temple.[87]

Before they could begin building even their first Missouri temple, though, the so-called Missouri-Mormon War began. The conflict started in August 1838 and ended in early November with the Mormons' surrender. The state of Missouri expelled its Mormon residents, forcing them to leave their homes and much of their property.[88]

Missouri's expulsion of its Mormon population proved financially costly to the now-homeless Mormons. The most obvious cost was that Mormon landowners lost their land, forced to sell it quickly as they fled or, in some instances, abandon it altogether. The lucky ones managed to sell their land to speculators, who purchased Mormon property at significantly deflated prices. But those who sold their land for a fraction of its value ended up better off than others, whose property was expropriated, in some cases by the same people who forced them to flee.[89]

The loss of property stung. At least three times, the Mormons appealed to the federal government for compensation of the costs they bore as a result of their expulsion from Missouri.[90] They appealed to the state of Missouri. Failing to find satisfaction at either level of government, they appealed to the populations of at least six other states requesting either that the state legislature or the state population help them appeal to the federal government for redress of their injuries.[91]

And in at least one of those appeals, tax made a rhetorical appearance. Joseph Jr. wrote to the Green Mountain Boys of Vermont requesting their aid in receiving compensation for the Mormons' loss of property. The Green Mountain Boys were a semi-formal militia formed in Vermont to protect residents' landholdings from incursion by New York.[92]

Joseph Jr. hoped his plea would appeal broadly to the militia and that the injustice of unrecompensed injury and crimes against the body of the Mormons would move them to use their influence to aid the Mormons. But his appeal did not rest solely on an inchoate sense of injustice: he also grounded his request for aid in a rhetorical appeal to the militia in his capacity as a fellow taxpayer. The injured Mormons, he explained, were free citizens whose "wealth went freely into [Missouri's] treasury for lands, and whose gold and silver for taxes, still fills the pockets of her dignitaries, 'in ermine and lace'."[93] As taxpayers, Joseph Jr. implied, the Mormons had a specific and special claim to fair treatment by the government. By ignoring their pleas, Missouri sanctioned injustice and sanctioned that injustice specifically against citizens who contributed to its ability to function. As such, Joseph Jr. suggested, Mormon taxpayers had a special claim to the government's help and protection.

In grounding the Mormons' right to fair treatment in their status as taxpayers, Joseph Jr. and his church placed themselves in a rich tradition of demanding civil rights by virtue of a group's taxpayer status. Early suffragists demanded that women who owned property refuse to pay their taxes until they received the right to vote.[94] In the late nineteenth and early twentieth centuries, African Americans similarly demanded equal rights—including the right to schooling for their children—in part because of their status as taxpayers.[95]

Ultimately, Joseph Jr.'s plea failed. The Missouri judicial system refused to compensate the Mormons for their losses. The Green Mountain Boys lent no aid. The Mormons' appeal to the federal government landed on the desk of the Secretary of War. Secretary Cass declined to help them, explaining that they had been injured by *state* law. As such, the federal government had no constitutional authority to intervene.[96] While the Mormons failed to obtain justice or compensation for their expulsion, Joseph Jr. and the Mormons had begun to characterize themselves as citizens and rightsholders, not merely because of their place of birth, but because their contribution to the state's coffers as taxpayers meant they had *earned* their citizenship and rights.

* * *

While there is no reason to believe that Joseph Jr. consciously considered taxes as he founded and organized his church, it is clear that taxes played a role in his religious heritage and his and his followers' lives. That role was not a quotidian one—taxes then, as today, were largely a seasonal consideration—but that role would have been constantly present in the background patterns of daily life. While taxes were not a top consideration, from its earliest days, the church was willing to accommodate taxes in its organization and practices. During its first eight years, the church did not display any particularly sophisticated engagement with questions of taxation, but even in its earliest years, the church demonstrated an awareness of taxation and proved willing to engage with questions of tax on their own terms.

2

Funding a City

As they fled from Missouri, the Mormon refugees found asylum and even welcome in Quincy, Illinois. While Quincy would not serve as the Mormons' permanent home, they purchased nearly 700 acres of land from speculators in nearby Commerce, Illinois, located roughly fifty miles north along the Mississippi River. In Illinois, they hoped to finally establish a permanent city that would both welcome and protect Mormons from a hostile world.

Smith and his family moved to Commerce in May and encouraged his followers to join them.[1] Soon, Smith renamed the city "Nauvoo," based, he said, on the Hebrew word for "beautiful."[2] In the Mormons' new Illinois home, Smith understood that achieving his religious vision would ultimately depend not on his creation, ex nihilo, of a new society, but on his ability to function within the existing political system.[3] In December 1840—less than two years after the Mormons began settling in Nauvoo—the state of Illinois ratified a charter for Nauvoo, making it the sixth city chartered in the state. Its charter was largely based on the charter of Springfield, Illinois's capital city, and was similar to other Illinois cities' charters.[4]

With its newly chartered city, the Mormon Church found itself in an unprecedented situation. Even before the charter's ratification, church leaders considered themselves "tantamount to the recognized government of the area."[5] Suddenly, far from being merely citizens and taxpayers, church leaders were also government officials, responsible, among other things, for imposing and collecting taxes.

Nauvoo: The Sacred and the Profane

Most of the time, the new leaders of the City of Nauvoo seemed to distinguish between their dual roles as religious and political leaders. That delineation required affirmative effort by the political and religious leaders. In Nauvoo, most city leaders also held ecclesiastical leadership positions in the Mormon Church. For example, between Nauvoo's incorporation in 1841 and Smith's death in 1844, the city had two mayors. From February 1841 until May 1842, John C. Bennett, an assistant president in the First Presidency of the LDS church, served as mayor of Nauvoo.[6] During the last four months of Bennett's mayoralty, Smith served as vice mayor, then succeeded Bennett as mayor until Smith's death in June 1844.[7]

In addition to Nauvoo's two mayors, the city council read as a who's-who of Mormon leadership. Smith himself served on the city council during Bennett's time as mayor. Sidney Rigdon, an assistant president in the church's First Presidency, and William Law, a counselor in the presidency, were city councilmembers. Four of Smith's brothers—William, Don Carlos, Samuel, and Hyrum—spent time on the city council. Future church presidents Brigham Young, John Taylor, and Wilford Woodruff held office on the city council. In addition to the three future church presidents who served on the city council, an additional eight current and future members of the Quorum of the Twelve—which would develop into the second-highest ecclesiastical body in Mormonism—also spent time as councilmembers.[8] In fact, of the twenty-six men who served on the city council between the city's incorporation in 1841 and Smith's death in 1844, only four—Sylvester Emmons, Benjamin Warrington, John T. Barnett, and Hugh McFall—were not members of the Mormon Church.

Prominent Mormon hierarchs also filled other civic and governmental roles in Nauvoo.[9] In spite of the significant identity between city and church leaders, though, the mayor and city council recognized that city functions did not always overlap with church functions and were often, though not always, able to separate their political roles from their religious ones. That became clear with the city's approach to raising revenue. The city leaders treated taxes as separate and distinct from the tithing that funded the church.

There was no guarantee that the Mormons would separate their civic and religious roles in Nauvoo. In founding and moving to Nauvoo they were trying to create their Zion. To Mormons, "Zion" was an aspirational home where the Mormons would find refuge from the persecution and mob violence that had driven them out of their previous homes, but its government would ultimately be that of a "theocratic, militaristic city-state." That theocracy stood in stark contrast to the Jacksonian democracy that was ascendant in the United States at the time.[10] In designing and running a theocratic city, Mormon leaders could have easily elided the difference between religious and civic expenditures and between tithing and taxes.

Religious Revenue in Early Mormonism

Church leaders had more experience thinking about and implementing religious revenue regimes than they did secular ones. As an ecclesial matter, the church had experimented with different techniques to raise revenue, both to support the activities of the institutional church and to redistribute wealth to the poor. Shortly before Missouri drove out its Mormon residents, the church organized a committee to develop and adopt a plan that would allow it to financially support its poor members. The committee consisted of Bishop Edward Partridge and his two counselors, Isaac Morley and Isaac Corrill. In December 1837, the committee presented its recommendation. It believed that support for the poor should come from voluntary free-will offerings. Members would determine the amount of those offerings based on a percentage of their net worth, which the committee considered a fairer system than "the tithing of what a man raises or his income from year to year." At the same time, the committee recommended exempting widows and families with assets worth less than $75 from these free-will offerings. The church, they said, should allow these members to keep their "honorable standing in the church" even if they did not make payments to support the poor. (While the committee did not talk about consequences to the rich for non-payment, its statement implies that wealthier members who did not voluntarily support the poor would lose that standing.)

To implement its plan, the committee recommended taking three steps. First, each man in the church would provide to Bishop Partridge or his successor an annual inventory of his financial worth less "his honest debts." Second, the bishop, along with the high council (another governing body of the church) would determine the percentage of their net worth members would pay the following year, a procedure similar to the way New York determined landowners' property tax liability each year. Finally, members would pay the amount they owed either by deeding property to the church or signing a "subscription paper" listing the amount they owed. In addition, members who agreed to pay the amount would formally acknowledge that "voluntary titheing is better than Forced taxes."[11]

Less than four years after the committee's proposal, the church was already exploring new ways to raise revenue. In 1841 Smith assigned the role of organizing church finances to the Quorum of the Twelve. The Quorum of the Twelve

28 · FRONTIER RELIGION, FRONTIER TAXATION

encouraged members to donate (or, in the church's terminology, "consecrate") their property to the church with the end goal of building a temple in Nauvoo.[12] In addition to this consecration of property, in 1841, Smith instituted a tithe to fund the church.[13] And, as church leaders grappled with governing and running a city, they began to walk back their earlier disparagement of "Forced taxes."

The Nauvoo Charter and Taxes

Given the theocratic governance of Nauvoo, it would make sense for the city's revenue regime to reflect the presiding bishopric's skepticism of taxation or possibly the church's radical ideas for raising funds. But that was not the direction Nauvoo's Mormon leaders chose. Rather, the regimes they implemented to fund the city proved distinctly indistinct. The same church leaders who wanted their members to voluntarily consecrate their property to the church also implemented taxes that would not have felt out of place in any other city in Illinois or, for that matter, in the United States. Radical religious movements were fine, but the church appeared uninterested in remaking secular taxation.

The Nauvoo Charter, approved by the Illinois state legislature, underlay all of the political authority Nauvoo's leaders claimed. That charter, the Mormons boasted, was "one of the most liberal charters, with the most plenary powers, ever conferred by a legislative assembly on free citizens." It provided Nauvoo's residents with extensive civil liberties, in contrast, they said, to the denial of "liberty and our sacred rights" they had endured in Missouri.[14] Famously, the charter made it possible for the city to enact extraordinarily broad habeas corpus laws that it used to protect Smith from arrest and to create the Nauvoo Legion, a "standing army controlled by the leaders of Nauvoo."[15]

While some powers granted by the Nauvoo Charter proved extraordinary, most were relatively standard, including the authority to collect taxes to fund city government. The city charter expressly granted the city council authority to "levy and collect taxes for city purposes" on all real and personal property within the city borders. It authorized the city council to set tax rates of up to 0.5 percent of taxable property's assessed value.[16]

This taxing authority in the Nauvoo Charter was substantially identical to tax provisions in the laws incorporating the cities of Springfield[17] and Quincy,[18] down to the maximum rate of 0.5 percent. Likewise, the act incorporating the city of Chicago allowed for property tax at a rate of up to 0.5 percent, though the Chicago charter went further than Springfield or Nauvoo, stating specifically that the city would use this tax revenue to pay for lighting and repairing streets, highways, and bridges, for supporting a night watch, and for defraying other city expenses.[19]

The Nauvoo Charter explicitly granted the city council authority to tax property and to license, tax, and regulate nine professions ("auctions, merchants, retailers, grocers, hawkers, peddlers, butchers, pawnbrokers, and money-changers").[20] At the same time, it implicitly allowed the city council to impose other unenumerated taxes. On top of the Nauvoo Charter's express grants of power, it empowered the city council to "exercise such other legislative powers as are conferred on the City Council of the City of Springfield."[21] In short, Nauvoo's city council could do anything that Illinois permitted its capital city to do. Springfield (and thus Nauvoo) had the power to tax carriages, wagons, and other vehicles. In addition, the cities could "tax, restrain, prohibit and suppress, tippling houses, dram shops, gaming houses, bawdy and other disorderly houses."[22]

This final set of provisions looks suspiciously like Springfield anticipated using some of its taxing power as a regulatory, rather than revenue-raising, mechanism. It did not have to use taxes to regulate establishments that served alcohol, allowed gambling, and provided prostitutes of course: it also had explicit authority to restrain, prohibit, and suppress them. But the ability to tax, rather than prohibit, these undesirable businesses was not merely a superfluous option for the city. While the Springfield charter granted the city council the authority to license and regulate porters and to license and regulate theaters, shows, and amusements, it did not provide authority to tax porters or amusements.[23] With the authority to ban or tax these disfavored businesses, the cities of Springfield and Nauvoo had a wide array of tools with which to deal with potential nuisances. The city councils could ban them or it could countenance them and use them as a source of revenue. They had the option to employ whatever tool best served their cities.

Designating Tax Rates and Base

Though Illinois granted broad explicit and implicit taxing authority to the Nauvoo city council, city leaders had limited theoretical guideposts in creating a tax regime. Mormon leaders had some experience with finance, but their financial experience had generally run counter to the prevailing individualistic economics of the American frontier, sometimes disastrously so. For instance, in 1831, Smith received a revelation that included an economic plan for Zion, his millennial New Jerusalem. That plan centered "frugality, industry, virtuous living, and certain core management principles of consecration and stewardship."[24] His communitarian experiments, based on the post-Resurrection Apostolic community of the New Testament,[25] all ended up falling apart. Similarly, Mormon leaders' 1830s foray into printing banknotes had ended with the bank's collapse,

30 • FRONTIER RELIGION, FRONTIER TAXATION

a victim both of the Panic of 1837 and of the general distrust of their unchartered Kirtland Safety Society Anti-Banking Company.[26]

Even if the Mormons had more extensive experience with finance, however, that experience would likely not have prepared them for establishing a tax system from scratch. While state and local governments necessarily possessed and exercised the power to tax, there was little theoretical discussion in the nineteenth century about principles underlying taxation (beyond perhaps tariffs). Even at the end of the century—decades after the Mormon leadership designed a local tax regime for Nauvoo—an American political economist asserted that the state of English-language literature on finance was "shabby in the extreme."[27]

Between their limited experience with municipal finance and the general ad hoc nature of taxation in the nineteenth century, the founders of Nauvoo were forced to feel their own way through the design of revenue-raising regimes. They could—and, as we have seen, did—give themselves the ability to impose and collect taxes in the same ways that similarly-situated cities did, but they ultimately had to choose both what to tax (that is, the tax base) and how much to tax it (the tax rate). How did they decide what specific contours taxation should take in Nauvoo? Mormon leaders' philosophy on taxation appears to have been influenced significantly by their and their converts' experience in England with high and regressive taxes.[28]

Mormon missionaries first visited England in 1837, led by church apostle Heber Kimball. These missionaries proved enormously successful. Kimball and his six companions converted about 1,500 people during their first year in England. In 1840—shortly before Nauvoo received its state charter—Brigham Young led the church's Quorum of the Twelve Apostles on a second mission to England, where several thousand more people joined the young church. By the end of the decade, about 50,000 Britons had affiliated with Mormonism. When the main body of the Mormons moved to Utah, roughly one in three members of the church were emigrants from England.

These British converts to Mormonism overwhelmingly came from England's urban poor.[29] And they had experience directly bearing the brunt of regressive taxation in a way that their American counterparts did not. While Americans faced some state-level taxation, that taxation primarily fell on property that they owned. Prior to the Civil War, the vast majority of federal revenue came from customs taxes.[30] Americans bore the economic burden of these tariffs, but that burden was indirect, disguised in higher prices for the imported goods they purchased. Like their British counterparts, Americans bore the burden of taxation but had no way to determine the amount of taxes they indirectly paid.

Funding a City • 31

Even though the government could disguise American consumers' tariff burden, Americans were aware that they were bearing a burden and sometimes pushed back. In 1830, the tariff rate peaked at 62 percent. Such high tariffs stoked backlash, though the backlash came largely from southern states. Sky-high tariffs protected New England manufacturers' interests as well as the interests of Midwestern producers of raw materials.[31] Mormons had their roots in the Northeast and their feet in the Midwest and, as such, likely felt the protectionist advantages of tariffs more than they felt the pricing increases. At the very least, there is no evidence that the Mormons felt burdened by the increased costs that tariffs imposed.

By contrast, British taxation felt remarkably salient to British church members and, by proxy, to Mormon leadership. The experience of British Mormons with taxation may have left church leaders beyond the Far West committee wary of taxes, especially of taxes that were overly burdensome and regressive.

Upon arriving in England in 1840, Young was shocked at the formal class structure he encountered. Writing to their comrades in Nauvoo, Young and Willard Richards described what they perceived as a once-prosperous society now in decay. Young and Richards traced that decay directly to the higher classes that were becoming more "avaricious, & are trying to get all they can themselves, & will hardly let the poor live."

This avaricious and decaying world, Young and Richards seemed to believe, largely resulted from the Industrial Revolution. People employed in manufacturing earned 6 to 10 shillings per week. Out of their earnings they paid two or three shillings in rent and another for coal. With the money they had left after paying for these necessities, they also had to pay "taxes of *every kind*, we might say, for smoke must not go up chimney in England without a tax, Light must not come in at the window without paying duties, many must pay from 1 penny to 6 pence per week for water, & if we should attempt to tell all we should want a government list, after paying all taxes what think you will a family have left for bread stuff?"[32]

On top of taxes on smoke and light, the poor in England had to pay taxes on grain, on spices (which, as a result of taxes, cost four times what they cost in the United States), and, if they could afford dogs, on those dogs. "There are taxes for living, & taxes for dying," Young and Richards reported. "We scarce recollect an article without tax except cats & mice & fleas."[33]

Two years later, an article in *The Latter-day Saints' Millennial Star* underscored the place of the bread tax on English converts' experience emigrating to Nauvoo. Emigrants, the article claimed, could not only find ample work in Nauvoo (in implicit contrast to their un- or underemployment in England): the cost of

32 · FRONTIER RELIGION, FRONTIER TAXATION

living was about one-eighth of the cost they had faced in England. Why were Nauvoo prices so much lower? Once emigrants were on a ship under the U.S. flag they could "completely and practically NULIFY THE BREAD TAX. They eat free bread, free tea, free sugar, free everything" and, as a result, expended the same amount on their journey from England to Nauvoo that they would otherwise have spent on food in England.[34]

The "bread tax" that *The Millennial Star* mentioned referred to England's regressive, and increasingly unpopular, Corn Laws. In the eighteenth century, England had become a net exporter of grain. The country not only dropped its export duties, it also subsidized its farmers' exportation of grain. At the same time, it took an aggressively protectionist approach to the importation of grain, banning it entirely (with limited exceptions for years of bad crops) until 1773. In 1773, the country reopened its doors to the importation of foreign grain. Its consumption of foreign grain steadily increased until, in 1791, the country began to impose significant tariffs. These tariffs ensured that cheaper foreign grain would not supplant expensive local grain. At the same time, it ensured that English consumers had to pay more for their bread. Though the rate of the tariff varied over the years, its effect on English consumers—and particularly poor English consumers—did not.[35]

While tariffs are often invisible to consumers, these corn taxes proved anything but invisible to English consumers, especially to the poor. Although the tariffs on grains reached their pinnacle in 1815, sporadic anti-Corn Law agitation popped up during the subsequent two decades. That agitation tended to arise primarily when food prices were high, but protests tended to be local and unorganized. That changed in 1836 with the founding of the Anti-Corn Law Association in London. Still, while leading Radicals affiliated with the Association, it proved ineffective at combating tariffs on grains. Two years later, Manchester Radicals formed the Anti-Corn Law League. The League had more success, as it channeled Radical Party energies toward a single, politically-salient topic.[36]

Radical Party members were not alone in their opposition to the Corn Tax. In 1841, 650 Christian ministers of various denominations attended a conference in which attendees painted a dystopian picture of England. "The people of England," the editor of the *Anti-Bread Tax Almanack* wrote, "still cry in vain for food—the poor are pining for lack of nourishment—hunger has taken possession of the peasant, and the cellar of the operative—crime fills our prisons—disease rages in our hospitals—and starvation hurries its victims to a premature grave!" And what led to this collective and widespread hunger? Do not blame the stars, the editor wrote. This poverty and hunger came from "the selfish or ignorant inventions of men." The suffering of England's poor could be placed directly at the feet of the bread tax, an "impious interference with the bounteous dispensations of divine providence."[37]

While this history of regressive taxation occurred an ocean away from Nauvoo, British converts and the missionaries who taught them brought their lived experience of high and regressive taxation with them. Church and civic leaders in Nauvoo would have experienced (or, at least, been aware of) the milieu of controversy over regressive English taxes. That experience and awareness must have factored into church leaders' decisions about how to enact taxes in the Mormon-led City of Nauvoo. While the historical record does not describe any explicit references to these British taxes, in designing taxes, the Nauvoo city council had to grapple with questions of tax fairness. They had to collect enough revenue to make Nauvoo a desirable city in which to live while not putting the burden of taxation primarily on the backs of the poor.

With the memory of taxes they had paid at their other homes, the examples of other tax regimes in Illinois, the parameters provided in the Nauvoo Charter, and their experience with high and regressive British taxes, the Mormon leaders in Nauvoo designed and implemented a series of taxes to fund the city. And the questions that this implementation raised—who to tax? what? at what rate?—did not admit to theological answers. Rather, the city council minutes reveal that the leaders of Nauvoo grappled with these questions as practical issues that they had to solve through political means.

Exempting Farmers?

While the Nauvoo Charter provided a broad framework for taxation, the city council had to address questions of how to implement the taxes its charter authorized. It had to choose the specific tax design and tax base it would use. On November 6, 1841, for example, John Barnett, one of the non-Mormon members of the city council, proposed that the city tax all real and personal property located within the city limits. Mayor Bennett preferred a narrower tax base and proposed that only that property already subject to state tax would be assessed and taxed and that it be taxed "to the full amt contemplated in the Charter."

The proposed amendment led to a lively debate. Barnett asked the mayor's intentions in making his proposal "as he c[ould] not see its object." John Taylor also asked about the necessity of the amendment. The mayor explained, but his explanation (which was not recorded in the meeting minutes) appears to have proven unsatisfying because Alderman Gustavus Hills proceeded to demand yet another explanation. The city council tinkered with the language of the mayor's proposal, with a special emphasis on excising language suggesting that property would be taxed to the full extent of the charter.

34 • FRONTIER RELIGION, FRONTIER TAXATION

At this point, Alderman Daniel Wells mentioned that the farmers on the outskirts of Nauvoo—who had supported chartering the city—assumed the city would not tax them on their land. As such, they had not sent in any objections to taxation. If, however, the city council were to tax their land, the farmers would seek redress.[38]

In the American imagination, farm life holds a special place. Thomas Jefferson considered a nation filled with independent farmers to be critical to the country's virtue and morals and believed that agricultural work was central to the success of American democracy.[39] Though his vision did not ultimately materialize, this lionization of an agrarian lifestyle has nonetheless proved an important force in the development of the country, including its tax laws. The modern federal income tax has an abundance of provisions that provide preferential treatment for farmers and Congress has proven willing to pass tax provisions to alleviate farmers' concerns.[40] In political debates, farmers have often emerged as the winners.[41]

Early in their tenure, then, policymakers in Nauvoo had to confront this agricultural exceptionalism. Barnett asked directly whether the city council intended to tax farmers. Charles Rich pointed out that land values—including the value of farmers' land—had doubled with the incorporation of the city. Wells responded that he did not want to tax land that had not been laid out into lots. He proposed an amendment to that effect.

Ultimately, notwithstanding the American solicitude to farmers, Wells and the farmers lost. The city council adopted the original resolution with minor changes, rejecting Wells's proposal to exempt farmers.[42] But passing the resolution did not end the city council's debate over its taxing power. A week later at the council's subsequent meeting, Willard Richards asked that the city council reconsider the tax resolution. He laid out his reasoning for such reconsideration (though again, the minutes do not describe his explanation). After Richards spoke, Mayor Bennett explained the "rights & powers given by the City Charter, & the right of the City [Council] to Tax the Citizens." Joseph Smith followed up, speaking "at considble length on the Subject of the right of Taxn, & the Taxes laid on by the County &c." Mayor Bennett spoke again and Richards withdrew his motion to reconsider.[43]

Building a Comprehensive Property Tax

The following year, the city council made changes to its tax law, ultimately arriving at a relatively comprehensive property tax regime. Under the October 1842 ordinance, virtually all "Lands, tenements, & hereditaments, situated in

Funding a City · 35

this City, claimed by individuals, or bodies politic or corporate" would be subject to property tax. The ordinance exempted only land owned by the city itself, land used for burying the dead, the Temple Lot, unimproved church land, and land used by literary institutions. The city also taxed certain types of personal property: "Stud Horses, Asses, Mules, Horses, Mares, Cattle, Clocks, Watches, Carriages, Waggons, Carts, money actually loaned, Stock in trade, & all other description of personal Property, & the Stock of incorporated companies." The city council intended to tax all residents in proportion to the "true value" of the property in their possession.[44]

The property tax base chosen by the city council followed the state's tax base closely but did not adopt it wholesale. In 1839, Illinois had enacted a property tax that, like Nauvoo, taxed all "lands, tenements, and hereditaments" located in the state. The state law provided a similar list of exemptions, albeit with a handful of differences. Like Nauvoo, the state exempted land held for burying grounds, land used by literary institutions, and land owned by the state. In addition, Illinois exempted church grounds and land owned by the United States.[45] While Nauvoo did not expressly exempt land owned by the federal government, more than two decades earlier the Supreme Court had held that states could not constitutionally tax federal property.[46] Even without an express exemption in Nauvoo law, then, had the federal government owned land within Nauvoo city limits, the city could not have taxed that land.

Illinois took the same broad approach toward taxing personal property as it took with respect to real property. The Nauvoo city council largely adopted the state's list of taxable property in the order state law listed that property. Illinois's list of taxable property included stud horses, asses, mules, horses, mares, cattle, clocks, watches, carriages, wagons, carts, money actually loaned, and stock in trade, as well as a catch-all provision including "all other description of personal property, of the stock of incorporated companies." As in Nauvoo, all of this taxable property was taxed based on its "true value."

Notably the Nauvoo property tax did not include in its base two classes of property expressly taxed under Illinois law: "slaves, and servants of color."[47] How could Illinois, a purportedly free state, tax residents on the value of enslaved persons? In the early nineteenth century, the question of slavery was deeply contested in Illinois. The first Europeans to settle in the state were French and brought enslaved persons with them. Most of Illinois's English settlers came from the South and brought their proslavery views. The state's first constitution protected existing slavery and allowed for the limited introduction of new enslaved people into the state. By 1823, proslavery Illinoisans were calling for a constitutional convention to legalize slavery in the state, a move only defeated

36 · FRONTIER RELIGION, FRONTIER TAXATION

because of an influx of northerners.[48] Even without considering the de facto slavery permitted in Illinois, the state was hostile to Black people, enacting onerous discriminatory Black Codes on free Black people from moving to Illinois. It was not until the adoption of its 1848 constitution that Illinois definitively prohibited slavery within its borders (though the same constitution prohibited free people of color from entering the state).[49]

The majority of Mormons who settled in Nauvoo came from northern states. As northerners they generally opposed slavery. Smith "had been consistently opposed to slavery" even though he never embraced immediate abolition and his opposition to slavery generally lacked urgency.[50] One of the main planks of Smith's 1844 third-party presidential campaign was the elimination of slavery by compensating white slaveholders, a program he expected would lead to the end of slavery in the United States by 1850.[51]

In spite of the Mormons' anti-slavery background, Mormon leaders proved willing to countenance, and even sometimes embrace, the practice. While Smith envisioned Nauvoo as a city of God, welcoming all, irrespective of their race or nationality, the city never housed more than a handful of free Black residents. The Nauvoo city charter only allowed free white men to vote, hold elective office, and belong to the Nauvoo Legion, the city's militia. The city banned interracial marriage.[52] And, although Smith encouraged slave owners who converted to Mormonism to free their slaves, at least a few Mormons moved to Nauvoo and, taking advantage of the uncertainty of Illinois law, refused to follow Smith's recommendation.[53]

Against this background of not-quite-illicit slaveholding, it is worth asking why the Nauvoo city council, when it enacted its property tax, chose to adopt most of the language of the state property tax but did not mention "slaves, and servants of color" as taxable property. There is no record of its decision-making, so any evaluation is conjecture. Whatever the reasoning, though, the exclusion of enslaved persons from the property tax base made the ownership of slaves in Nauvoo less expensive. If slaveholders did not have to pay taxes on the people they enslaved, the tax law provided at least some subsidy to slaveholding, at least compared to owning taxable property.

Of course, it is possible that slaveholders were taxed on enslaved persons under the catch-all "all other description of personal Property" and that including an explicit provision taxing slaveholders on the value of enslaved persons would have been mere surplusage. That logic ultimately feels unconvincing, though: if following the lead of the state and explicitly including "slaves, and servants of color" as property subject to taxation would have been surplusage, other types of property listed in the law would also have been. Whatever the reason, the Nauvoo city council largely adopted Illinois's property tax law but deliberately excluded enslaved persons from the city's list of taxable personal property.

The Temple Committee as Taxpayer

While there is no record that the exclusion of enslaved persons from the property tax base led to any debate or controversy in Nauvoo, the city council's attempt to enact a comprehensive property tax did generate some controversy. Perhaps the most unexpected was that a theocracy might tax religious property owned by the dominant religion. In fact, Nauvoo's property tax did reach temple property, albeit temporarily and probably inadvertently.

The temple in Nauvoo played a critical part in the Mormons' 1840s ecclesiology. In October 1840—months before the state granted Nauvoo its charter—Mormons voted to build a temple.[54] Three months later, Smith dictated a revelation which, among other things, commanded church members to build "a house to [God's] name, for the Most High to dwell within. For there is not a place found on earth that he may come to and restore again that which was lost unto you, or which he hath taken away, even the fulness of the priesthood."[55]

It took another three months to lay the cornerstone of what would become the Nauvoo temple. Even laying the cornerstone failed to jumpstart construction, the result both of competing priorities and a general lack of financial resources.[56] Though they would not complete construction of the temple until after Smith's 1844 death, within a few years "the temple dominated the Nauvoo landscape."[57]

In many ways, the temple also dominated the theological landscape of Nauvoo. In Smith's theology, temple rites promised that "[a]ll Mormon men . . . could become priests in the kingdom, all spread along a hierarchical dynasty."[58] In Nauvoo, all of his religious innovation—ideas of "religious power, insight, teachings, and ritual"—focused on the temple.[59]

With its theological importance, it is no surprise that the city council excluded the Temple Lot from its property tax base. In the nineteenth century—and even through today—real property owned by religious organizations and used for religious purposes commonly enjoyed exemption from state property tax. With the temple as the only explicitly religious building in the city, it makes sense that Nauvoo's tax law focused on exempting it and not churches broadly.

While the city's property tax exempted the Temple Lot itself, the exemption proved narrower than the council members anticipated. The city's tax on personal property did not include any corresponding exclusions. This mismatch underscores that, while Mormons were creating tax policy in the 1840s, they

38 · FRONTIER RELIGION, FRONTIER TAXATION

were not yet sophisticated drafters of law. It also shows what happened when civic and religious needs diverged.

Though the city council did not explicitly exempt personal property associated with the temple, the Temple Committee believed that the city council intended to exempt its property from taxation. It was thus surprised when "sundry kinds of property which has been consecrated for the building of the Temple have been taxed while in the hands of the Temple Committee." In December 1843, William Clayton explained to the city council that the Temple Committee had been forced to pay taxes on its personal property for 1842. Clayton was both the Recorder of the committee and the city treasurer. After presenting his case to the city council, Clayton proceeded to petition the city council to pass a new ordinance exempting not only the Temple Lot but "all kinds of property in the hands of the Temple Committee which is consecrated & designed for the building of the Temple in said City of Nauvoo" from city taxation.[60]

The city council proved sympathetic to Clayton's request. They granted his petition and instructed Orson Spencer, a city alderman, to draft an amendment to the law fixing the (apparently inadvertent) taxation of Temple Committee property.[61] While the exemption for Temple Committee property mirrors the exemption for the Temple Lot, it also represents a narrowly targeted tax benefit for the church itself. While Mormon leaders treated their civic roles separately from their religious roles, they were not above using their civic power to benefit the church.

Dog Taxes and Public Nuisance

Even the Mormons' Zion refugee was not exempt from controversies that swept the country. And sometimes, the question of what to tax was a controversy that swept the country. Property taxes were easy and common, but cities, including Nauvoo, debated whether they should tax other things, too. One surprisingly fraught debate surrounded the dog tax. Immediately after setting aside his objection to the first iteration of the property tax, Richards proposed a relatively common, if somewhat controversial, tax: dogs within the city limits of Nauvoo, he proposed, would be taxed at a rate of five dollars each.[62] Dog taxes such as the one Richards proposed had been debated and implemented throughout the English-speaking world for at least the previous half-century. As early as 1796, John Dent, a member of the British Parliament, proposed a new tax on dogs, a measure he hoped would not only raise revenue but would also halve the number of dogs in Great Britain. Why would a member of Parliament want to dramatically reduce the number of dogs in the country? Because, he believed, dogs were a nuisance and their burdens fell disproportionately on the poor. Dogs transmitted rabies, they killed sheep (reducing both farmers' income and the food supply), poor people "squandered their money on useless pets," and the resources expended to feed dogs could better feed people.

As a result of Dent's dog tax proposal, newspapers painted him as a villain and described the tax as a measure meant to exterminate dogs in Great Britain.[63] Still, dog taxes managed to cross the Atlantic and quickly became a relatively common color in the palette of US tax law. In 1843, for example, the town of Ottawa, Illinois, enacted a law prohibiting dogs within town limits unless the dog had a collar with the owner's name on it. In addition, owners had to pay a 50-cent annual tax on each dog they owned.[64] Similarly, in 1846 Iowa imposed a tax on dogs. Dog owners did not have to pay the tax on their first dog but paid fifty cents annually for each additional dog.[65] Three years later, the city of Burlington, Iowa, reported that between April 1848 and April 1849 it had raised $41 from its dog tax, which represented almost half a percent of the city's revenue.[66]

As in Britain half a century earlier, some Americans supported the dog tax while others opposed it. Passions often ran high with respect both to dogs and the dog tax. In response to a proposed increase in the Alexandria, Virginia dog tax, a resident wrote to his local paper that

> I keep a dog, and several individuals that I know keep them, as a safeguard to their property. I have been paying a tax of nearly one hundred dollars per annum, which tax is more than I can conveniently pay already, without increasing my dog tax: because the dogs happen to bark of a night, and disturb my neighbor, who having no employment, must commence writing communications in the newspaper in order that he may have all the dogs killed, that he may get a better sleep. I recommend "A" to seek employment or exercise, and then he will sleep sound, and not hear dogs bark when thieves are about.—The present dog tax is unjust and oppressive enough already and ought not to be increased.[67]

While the letter writer's opposition to the proposed increase in the dog tax reflected both animosity toward his neighbor and toward an increased tax burden, others opposed the dog tax for more romantic reasons. When Virginia proposed a dog tax to protect merino sheep, John Randolph responded, "[M]y dog always loves me. No sir, the dog is *faithful*, don't tax him, but tax man, Colonel!—tax man, he is *perfidious*."[68]

Others objected not to the tax itself but to its enforcement. A letter writer in Springfield, Illinois, claimed that between the city tax on dogs, the Register's fee, and the collar marking, each dog cost at least $1.50 in government fees and taxes. Dog owners had to pay the fees and taxes, though, because the city

40 · FRONTIER RELIGION, FRONTIER TAXATION

marshal would kill unregistered dogs on a specified date. When the day came, the letter writer complained, the Marshal came to town "firing pistols and guns around our premises, endangering the lives of women and children, frightening horses, calling puppies from our very yards and mutilating them in such a manner that it sickened all good feeling persons to behold them." Ultimately, the day ended with thirty dogs "MURDERED" and fifteen registered. But, the letter writer claimed, a majority of dogs in town were neither killed nor registered; in fact, the Marshal only registered enough dogs to pay for his time. The letter writer found this unfair—while the dog tax, well administered, would provide revenue to the city, "to make a few pay for the masses is a little too strong under a democratic administration."[69] While the letter writer believed that a dog tax could be fair, selective enforcement allocated the burden of funding government in an unjust and undemocratic manner.

Though the dog tax had fierce opposition, it had equally fierce support. Two years after the *Sangamo Journal* published the letter condemning the Marshall's murder of dogs, it published an editorial advocating for a state-wide dog tax. Growing wool had become an important industry in Illinois, but dogs were killing sheep. The editorial explained that while "hundreds of these worthless animals [dogs] are suffered to prowl about the country the farmer has no security for this species of property. Within the last year thousands of dollars worth of sheep have been killed by dogs in this country." The newspaper believed that a tax on dogs would, at the very least, "have a tendency to lessen the number of worthless animals which prey upon the property of our enterprising farmers."[70]

In fact, much of the support for dog taxes focused not on its revenue-raising abilities, but on its regulatory benefits. The *Chicago Prairie Farmer* printed a letter decrying dogs as "very troublesome and destructive enemies of sheep." The writer claimed he didn't know of any "remedy which would probably prove more effectual than a tax of one dollar per head per annum, or more."[71] In Richmond, Virginia, a newspaper situated the dog tax starkly: the legislature needed to "[t]ax the dogs out—let the sheep in."[72] The next year, the same newspaper reported that the legislature had introduced a bill to tax male dogs $1 each and female dogs half that. The revenue from the dog tax would compensate farmers whose sheep had been killed by dogs.[73]

In addition to raising the issue of dogs killing sheep, proponents of a dog tax brought up their significant concern over hydrophobia (that is, rabies). In 1834, a Pennsylvania newspaper reported that a horse had died of rabies after being bitten by a rabid cat. Given the significant risk that rabies constituted, it asked, "[w]ould not a tax on dogs be advisable?"[74] (How the paper got from rabid cat to a dog tax is not altogether clear, but the fear of rabies and desire to reduce its incidence is.) Almost two decades later, an Illinois newspaper reported the death of several head of cattle resulting from rabid dog bites, which, it reported, had become a common occurrence. If "our laws are too inefficient to reach the evil" of controlling rabid dogs, the paper advocated relatively brutal self-help ("As a sure preventative against the further spread of this disease, we would recommend the cur-tailing of their tails by severing them just behind the ears."). That said, the paper reported satisfaction in learning that the county trustees were drafting a dog tax.[75]

In this milieu of pro and anti-dog fervor, how did the Nauvoo city council respond to Richards's proposed dog tax? As with the property tax, they began to debate. In immediate response to Richards's proposed five-dollar tax, Smith suggested that the tax be levied at twelve and one-third cents per dog.

After Smith's counterproposal, several council members, including Barnett, Wilson Law, and Brigham Young, expressed their opposition to Richards's proposal. Orson Pratt joined the tax's opponents and added that if the city were to tax dogs, it needed to tax dogs according to the dogs' value, in accordance with the authority granted them by the city charter.

At this point, Barnett expanded on his opposition. He was willing, he explained, to pay taxes on his dog, and even to value his dog at $500, but he was unwilling to allow anybody to "be privileged to kill his dog." Moreover, he did not want to pay a dog tax if the city used dog tax revenue to support the poor. His refusal to use a dog tax as a redistributive tool suggests that he viewed the dog tax primarily as a measure to regulate dogs rather than as a source of municipal revenue.

Smith spoke next (again at length) to say, in essence, that he opposed the dog tax. Young agreed but argued that if the city council were to enact a dog tax, it should base the amount of tax on the value of the dogs being taxed. Smith's brother Hyrum interjected that he could "go for killing Sluts."[76] (Though "slut" has a long history as a misogynistic pejorative, by the nineteenth-century, Americans could use "slut" synonymously with "bitch" in referring to female dogs.[77])

John Taylor pointed out that assessing the value of a dog could be difficult, and Vinson Knight opposed the tax, arguing that laws already in place were sufficient.[78] (Several months earlier, the city council had enacted a fine of between one and ten dollars on any dog that "is set upon Cattle or Hogs &c, or molests any Person."[79]) Knight's statement provides a second indication that the city council understood the proposed dog tax to function more as a tool to regulate dogs in the city than a provision intended to raise revenue.

With virtually no support, Richards's proposed dog tax was dead. But that was not the last the Nauvoo city council saw of dog taxes. On January 13, 1844, a little more than two years after the city council rejected a dog tax for the first time, seventy-three residents of Nauvoo—including prominent Mormons—delivered

42 · FRONTIER RELIGION, FRONTIER TAXATION

a petition to Mayor Smith, the aldermen, and the city councilors requesting that "all dogs be Taxed one dollar a head, and all bitches five dollars a head" annually. The petitioners argued that a dog tax would meet both the revenue and regulatory functions of taxation. City revenue would increase and, at the same time, "bad dogs would decrease."[80]

This time around, the proposal had more support: Samuel Bennett spoke in favor of it, and Brigham Young, in a reversal of his prior opposition, moved that the city council grant the petition. But Smith objected. In 1834, Samuel Baker had given Smith a dog. The dog, Old Major, had become like family to Smith, even staying with him while he was incarcerated in Liberty Jail.[81] Smith "said he would never pay a tax on his dog in this city." With Smith objecting, the petition was tabled.[82] The minutes do not make it clear whether Smith's objection came in his capacity as mayor of the city or prophet of the Mormon Church but, either way, his rejection of a dog tax sealed the tax's fate.

Give and Take

While the Nauvoo city council rejected the dog tax, it did implement other, less controversial taxes in addition to its property tax. For example, the city imported the road tax its members and leaders had been subject to in New York and Ohio. As with the dog tax, the first time the city council considered implementing a road tax, members engaged in an extensive debate about whether and how to assess it. Barnett, who had opposed the dog tax, moved that the city set the road tax in 1841 at three days' labor. Smith's brother Samuel followed up, underscoring the current importance of "making Roads & Lanes good."

John Greene cautioned that in setting the road tax, the city council should not "go to the greatest extent of Taxation." After all, he said, the citizens of Nauvoo had a lot of other work they needed to accomplish in 1841.[83] Then, after Smith, Wilson Law, and Vinson Knight expressed their support for Barnett's motion, the council voted in favor of a tax of three days' labor.[84] The following year the city council also assessed the city's road labour tax at three days.[85]

The road labour tax was not a panacea for the problem of transportation. In New England, citizens' payment of their road tax obligations often resulted in "halfhearted labor," the result of their indifference about the quality of their forced labor.[86] In at least some cases, the residents of Nauvoo appear to have had the same indifference about their obligations under the road labour tax. In October 1842, the city council instructed the Supervisor to recover arrears from those who had been delinquent in meeting their 1841 road labour tax obligations.[87] Then, in January 1843, the city council resolved that road labour tax delinquents would have until April 30, 1843, to "work out their road labour tax."[88]

Funding a City · 43

Again in 1844 the city council had to deal with delinquency and again gave road labour tax delinquents until April 30 to comply with their 1843 liabilities.[89]

Although many city council members were also ecclesiastical leaders in the deeply hierarchical Mormon Church, Nauvoo's Mormon citizenry did not passively accept the taxes they imposed. And they did not just protest taxes individually. In May 1842, thirty-five citizens signed a petition requesting a change to the assessment of Nauvoo's road tax. Instead of assessing every person the same amount of labor, the petitioners wanted a progressive road labour tax which would "tax every man according to the property he possesses."[90]

While basing the road labour tax on citizens' wealth would have represented a significant change in Nauvoo's law, this shift would not have been unprecedented. By 1800 many New England towns had replaced their flat-rate road tax assessments with a wealth-based tax.[91] Nauvoo's Committee of Ways and Means considered the petition but, while there was precedent for a progressive road labour tax and desire among at least some citizens, ultimately rejected the change. The city continued to require all residents subject to the road labour tax to provide the same amount of labor.[92]

While the city council rejected the road labour tax petition, some tax-related petitions succeeded. On the same day that the city council received the road labour tax petition, twenty-nine men signed a different petition requesting that the city repeal its licensing fee on stores and groceries. A licensing fee is an amount a person must pay the government to engage in certain businesses or professions. Though licensing fees are not precisely the same as taxes, they have many similarities. Importantly, like taxes, licensing fees raise revenue for governments. Unlike taxes, their revenue features are secondary to their regulatory features. But where the revenue component of a licensing fee gets too comparatively large, that fee may become a tax for all practical purposes. One court has explained that a licensing fee is meant to "reimburs[e] the sovereign, in whole or in part, for the necessary expense of" regulating the occupation. If the fee exceeds the costs of regulation by too much it "would become a tax for revenue and cease to be a valid license fee."[93]

Although licensing fees are not precisely taxes, then, they often function in similar ways and thus it is worth exploring how the citizenry and the city council of Nauvoo engaged with licensing fees. The petitioners claimed that the design of the fee imposed on grocers and other retailers was deeply unfair and regressive. City law imposed a fee of $10 on the privilege of selling in the city. The petitioners said that they could not "Discover the most perfect Wisdom or Equity" in the fee; unless they misunderstood the law, a merchant had to pay the $10 fee whether the merchant had $10 or $100 of goods to sell. By their calculation, then, someone selling $10 of goods was subject to a licensing fee of 100 percent, while someone selling $100 of goods paid a licensing fee of 10 percent.

The petitioners argued that in light of the fact that "[a]ll men are born free and have Certain Equal privileges and unalienable privileges among which are Life Liberty and the pursuit of happines," the city should amend the fee to make it proportional to the value of merchants' goods.[94] The Committee on Municipal Laws recommended that the city council grant the petition's request. After some discussion by Smith, Lyman Wight, and William Law, the city council went beyond the citizens' request. Rather than simply amending the fee to make it proportional, the city council eliminated its licensing fee on stores and groceries.[95]

Monetizing the Mississippi

The Mormons in Nauvoo saw the Mississippi River as a potential source of revenue, critical to the development of the city and its economic flourishing. Smith had found Nauvoo attractive in part because of its location on the Mississippi. Situated about twenty miles below rapids, Nauvoo's location would prove "of incalculable advantage to this place, as steamboats can only ascend the rapids at a high stage of water."[96]

Early in the city's life, the Mormons operated a ferry that provided steady revenue to the city.[97] They planned to profit from the city's proximity to the Mississippi River in other ways as well. As part of his inaugural address, Mayor Bennett proposed that the city build a shipping canal. Such a canal would ensure that the "future greatness of Nauvoo would be placed upon an imperishable basis."[98] The city council formed a committee, which recommended investigating the feasibility of building a canal.[99] In general, the city leaders, led by Smith, were in favor of determining the practicality of building such a canal and ultimately authorized a survey. But Sidney Rigdon objected; he believed that a canal would prove impracticable, both as a matter of expense and a matter of taxation. Rigdon believed that "the People have the right to Consent to Taxn, but representatives not to put it on, of themselves."[100] In spite of their early excitement, though, in the end, Nauvoo's leaders abandoned the idea of building a canal, whether because of expense, taxation, or because the "prospect of chiseling through a layer of stone more than a mile long must have been uninviting to most."[101]

While the city abandoned its attempt to build a canal, it did not abandon its desire to raise revenue from its proximity to the river. On March 5, 1844, Smith called an emergency meeting of the city council. He reported that steamboats had been declining to pay wharfage fees because Hiram Kimball and Arthur Morrison claimed that they owned the land and that the captains owed no wharfage. Smith explained to the city council that if the captains did not pay the wharfage "he should blow them up" along with anybody who assisted in resisting the city ordinances. The city council agreed that, as mayor, Smith was responsible for enforcing the city ordinances and debated the best way to continue to collect revenue. They landed on the idea of deputizing the owners of wharves to collect a city boat tax.[102]

Two days later in a public discourse (ostensibly aimed at deciding whether the city should tolerate and support lawyers in their midst), Smith claimed that the city was losing revenue to which it was entitled. He recounted to his audience the story of a rogue Mormon—"the two first lettrs of his name are Hiram Kimball"—who attempted to undercut the city's revenue from the wharves. According to Smith, after the city council had enacted a tax on steamboats, Kimball went to the steamboat captains and told them that he owned the landing so they did not need to pay the tax.

Smith vehemently denied Kimball's claim. The city, he said, owned the wharf from the printing office to the northern limits of the city. Moreover, federal maritime law had given incorporated cities the authority to collect tolls and wharfage. As a logical matter, he continued, it would make no sense to allow private interests to collect these fees and taxes: "no vessel could land anywhere, if subjct to individual laws." So for the same reasons cities had the right to tax "citizns to make roads," they had the right to "tax the Boats to make wharfs."[103]

Two days after Smith's public excoriation of Hiram Kimball, the city council began to consider a formal wharf tax. It instructed the Committee on Municipal Laws to research and eventually report a bill for the city council to enact.[104] There are no records, however, of the city enacting a wharf tax or even considering it after March 9, 1844.[105] While the city did take advantage of its convenient and important location on the Mississippi to raise revenue, it appears to have ultimately left wharf taxes out of its revenue arsenal.

*　*　*

Nauvoo's leaders lacked a technical background in tax policy. This governance blind spot is unsurprising, though: tax policy was at best a nascent field in 1840. While they lacked a technical understanding of issues of tax design, they did not have to create a city tax system from nothing. They had their previous experiences as taxpayers. They had other cities' tax systems, which they adopted in their charter. They had a strong sense that however they designed their tax system, they needed to be careful that it did not primarily burden the poor. While they may not have spoken the language of progressive taxation, they understood its moral necessity.

3

Collecting Taxes in Nauvoo

While critical to the implementation of a revenue regime, designing taxes is only one part of raising governmental revenue. Equally important is determining how to collect and enforce the enacted taxes. As the political authority of Nauvoo, the Mormons on city council had to establish these mechanisms. After all, taxes were not self-executing and citizens were not always eager to calculate or pay their taxes. Here, as with the decision of what to tax, Mormons in Nauvoo did not break new ground. Rather, they assigned tax assessors and collectors to administer their tax collection system—the same collection mechanism used broadly throughout the country. The assessors and collectors compiled lists of taxable property, determined the value of that property, and then proceeded to collect the tax due and turn it over to the government.[1]

Sometimes, the roles of assessor and collector were filled by two different individuals.[2] In Nauvoo, this was a dual role—a single person functioned as both assessor and collector. Beginning in 1842, the city council assigned one assessor and collector to each city ward. Before they could begin their official duties, they had to provide a bond of $1,000 to the city. After posting the bond and taking an oath of office, the city recorder gave each assessor-collector a list of all taxable property in his ward. The assessor-collector would then go to each property owner in the ward and request a list of all of their taxable property. Together with the property owner, the assessor-collector would value the

Collecting Taxes in Nauvoo • 47

property. If a property owner refused to cooperate, that individual faced a $20 fine.

After collecting information and assessing property, the assessor-collector delivered his assessments to the Clerk of the Municipal Court. At that point, the law gave property owners an opportunity to contest their tax assessments. Once the contestation period ended, the Clerk returned the tax list to the assessor-collector, who proceeded to collect taxes from property owners. In 1842, the city council set a tax rate of fifty cents per $100 of property.[3] To formally implement this collection regime, as part of the city council's creation of the assessor-collector administration, Hyrum Smith formally moved that the "Citty Collector be authorized to Collect the Citty tax." His motion carried on March 5, 1842.[4]

As with assessment, tax collection in Nauvoo was an in-person affair. While he had already gone to each property owner to assess tax, after the Clerk returned the tax list, the assessor-collector went to each property owner to collect the tax due. When a property owner paid their tax, the assessor-collector provided them with a receipt. If a taxpayer was not home when the assessor-collector came, Nauvoo law required him to leave a written notice that included both the amount of tax due and where the taxpayer could pay the tax.[5]

After collecting taxes, an assessor-collector's final responsibility was to deliver the taxes he had collected to the city. For example, in November 1842, the city council formally required the assessor-collector to "lodge all Funds received by him for City Taxes, & now in his Hands, with the City Treasurer, & lay a statement of the Arrears due due [sic] for City Taxes, before the City Council."[6] For their efforts, Nauvoo paid assessor-collectors two dollars per day.[7] In September 1844, their pay dropped to one dollar per day.[8] In Nauvoo's first year as a city, Lewis Robinson served as the city collector. That year, he collected $700.67 in taxes. As compensation for his collection efforts, Robinson received $39.24.[9] (While the system was in place, it did not always work smoothly. In June 1842, Robinson wrote to the city council requesting an extension to collect the 1841 taxes. The city council granted him until the second Saturday in September.[10])

While the position of assessor-collector was critical to the function of the city of Nauvoo, the men who filled that role did not always do their job. In 1842 Horace Hotchkiss, a land speculator who sold a good portion of Nauvoo to Smith, wrote to Sidney Rigdon about lots in Nauvoo that he still owned. His letter hints at a breakdown in the tax collection system; he wrote that taxes had not yet been paid on his lots. "This of course must be attended to by somebody," he concluded.[11]

48 · FRONTIER RELIGION, FRONTIER TAXATION

Two years later, assessor-collector Jonathan Hale appeared in front of the city council. Though he had been reelected assessor-collector for 1844, as of October he had not yet started "on account of sickness." He suggested that the city council appoint a new assessor and collector, inasmuch as "the Twelve wishes me to go away." (Interestingly, while he is speaking to the city council about his civic duties, "the Twelve" refers to a governing body of the Mormon church; here Hale explicitly conflates religious and political leadership with respect to his tax collection duties.) The city council declined. Rather, they unanimously agreed that he should continue as the assessor and collector until he formally resigned.[12]

Tax Sales

Throughout history, being the person who collects taxes could be a dangerous profession. In the late eighteenth century, opponents of the excise taxes in Wales attacked, beat up, horsewhipped, and robbed tax collectors. Protestors cut one tax collector's nose off, while they dragged another out of his bed and murdered him in front of his family.[13]

While Nauvoo never saw tax-related violence on this scale, even in Nauvoo, tax collectors could elicit powerful negative reactions. In March 1841, the *Times and Seasons*, a Mormon newspaper, published a letter from Walter Bagby, the tax collector for Hancock County, Illinois (which included Nauvoo). "Pay up forthwith," he wrote, "if you would save the cost of my second coming!"[14] In 1842, Bagby tried to collect taxes due on real property Smith owned. Smith paid county and state taxes but refused to give Bagby money for Commerce city taxes.[15] The city of Nauvoo had subsumed the lots in question and Smith would not pay taxes he believed he did not owe. To collect the taxes, then, in July 1843, Bagby instructed the sheriff to auction a lot to satisfy the putatively delinquent tax.[16]

On August 1, Smith met with Jacob Backenstos and William Clayton about the seized lot. Bagby approached the three and they began arguing. A week later, describing the incident, Smith claimed Bagby had used abusive language and had picked up a rock to throw at Smith. Before he could throw it, Smith grabbed him by the throat and began choking him.[17] Smith subsequently pleaded guilty to assault and battery and paid a fine.[18]

The next year, Smith risked a second tax sale of real property he owned. And again, his reaction demonstrated his deep antipathy toward tax sales. After Smith left Kirtland, Ohio, he leased land he owned there to Joseph Coe. By 1844,

Coe requested that Smith let him have the land. Smith, however, was "tired of hearing the report of its liability to be sold for taxes." He wanted Coe off the land, replaced by a new tenant who would pay rent and "keep all the Taxes regularly paid." That new tenant should post enough security that "there is no further trouble, or anxiety about the danger of losing either rent, or having it sold for Taxes."[19]

Smith accused Coe of knowingly neglecting to pay taxes on the leased land. That knowing neglect was, in Smith's mind, inexcusable. "It is astonishing," he wrote to Coe, "that any man can be so wicked and corrupt as to suffer the property of his benefactor and best friend to be sold in order to defraud him out of it by getting a Sheriffs Deed, surely the shades of darkness prevail over such a man; his heart must be hard as the nether-mill-stone, and virtue have no place in him."[20] Ultimately, Reuben McBride, who managed Smith's property in Kirtland, reported that he had "hired the money to pay the tax on the farm." (While it is no longer a common phrase, to "hire money" means to borrow.) McBride then managed to collect the money from Coe in time to repay the borrowed tax money.[21]

In spite of Smith's misgivings about tax sales for delinquent property tax payments, Nauvoo law allowed the city to seize delinquent taxpayers' property and auction it off to satisfy their unpaid taxes.[22] The risk of losing one's land to tax sales was understandably unpopular. At the same time, though, the Mormons who ran Nauvoo had little choice. Illinois state law authorized sheriffs to advertise for sale the property of taxpayers who neglected or refused to pay their taxes. The sheriff was to sell enough property to cover the delinquent taxes. The law directed the sheriff to first sell personal property and, if the proceeds proved insufficient to pay the taxes owed, to then sell real property.[23]

The Nauvoo city council complied with state law, notwithstanding Smith's bad experiences with and the general unpopularity of tax sales. And they did so in part to demonstrate that they were not subverting state law through the broad authority of their city charter. In 1845, Mayor Daniel Spencer explained the city's strategy, speaking of individuals who were "dissatisfied with their lands being advertized for sale for taxes—on account of a law that has been passed by the Legislature." Because the state, not the city, required the tax sales, Daniel Wells recommended that the landowners bring the issue up at the Municipal Court. The Municipal Court, he explained, was the appropriate venue for this kind of complaint. Beyond being the appropriate venue, allowing the court to hear the question would demonstrate that Nauvoo complied with state law.[24] The city's acceptance of state tax law, residents' preferences notwithstanding, was one example of the city's broader acceptance of the civil law.

Money to Pay Taxes

Other than the road labour tax, Nauvoo did not accept in-kind tax payments. Residents had to pay their taxes with currency or precious metals. But currency was scarce on the frontier and, after the church's disastrous experience attempting to charter a bank in Kirtland, church leaders had given up on banking as a way to escape their debt problems. To facilitate economic activity, the city of Nauvoo issued $1 notes called "scrip." The city expressly provided that holders of scrip could use it to pay any debts they owed to the city. In addition, a holder of scrip could present it to the city treasurer, who would redeem it with unappropriated money from the city treasury.[25] Effectively, then, this scrip was meant to facilitate ordinary commercial transactions in a city that had limited access to state-issued currency.[26] It also provided a way to pay taxes: Nauvoo initially permitted residents to pay their taxes in gold, silver, or, if they did not have gold or silver, city scrip.[27]

By 1843 the city began to run into problems with scrip. As a result of these problems, the city council decided to stop accepting scrip in payment of taxes. Residents had to pay in gold or silver coins. The city would no longer issue scrip (though holders could still redeem previously issued scrip).[28] Notwithstanding this new ordinance, the city council made occasional exceptions to the rule, sometimes allowing residents to use scrip to meet their tax obligations. On March 9, 1844, Henry Sherwood and Jonathan Hale petitioned the city council to order the Treasurer to accept his endorsement on city scrip to fulfill tax obligations. The city council granted the petition, ordering that "all the assessors endorsemets on scrip shal be allowed by the Treasurer."[29]

People's lack of confidence in Nauvoo-issued scrip was not merely an inconvenience for the city's collection of revenue. It had a real impact on public employees. In August 1844, members of the city police force delivered a petition to the city council. The city paid its police in scrip. But, the petition complained, the public had no faith in the city's ability to redeem the scrip. As a result, those merchants who accepted scrip did so at a discount to its face value. Often they would not accept scrip at all, leaving the police unable to purchase "anything that will feed or clothe them." The petition requested that the city council do something to bolster public confidence in scrip. "[W]e are of the opinion," the petition concluded, "that no man among us who considers our situation will object to paying a tax to meet the wants of the city."[30]

Two days later, the city council considered the complaints in the petition. City councilors were sympathetic to the plight of the police. City finances were, however, in relatively dire straits. Brigham Young said that he would be willing

Collecting Taxes in Nauvoo • 51

to pay the police with gold and silver rather than scrip, except that the city lacked the gold and silver with which to pay. John Greene, the city marshal, pointed out that not only was the city treasury empty, but he had personally loaned the city $70 to help pay the police. In an attempt to solve the policing problem in light of the city's lack of resources, Young suggested either that the city council find individuals to buy scrip to prop up its value or that the city try to raise money through a "voluntary tax." The proposed voluntary tax, he said, could be collected by Mormon bishops, an express (and unusual) conflation of the religious and civic worlds of public revenue in Nauvoo.

The city council was on board with Young's proposal. Because the city already collected all of the taxes it was authorized to collect, mandatory taxes were not an option. Orson Pratt suggested that the city council go to the public and request that they pay a voluntary tax to fund the police. Young proposed that the voluntary tax start with the city council itself.

While the voluntary tax appealed conceptually to the members of the city council, it was not clear that such a program would prove successful. The city council had already told Greene to go to the city wards and try to raise money to fund the police. He had tried, with no success. With the potential failure of a voluntary tax, the city council also explored alternative ways to deal with the revenue shortage. Orson Spencer, for instance, thought that Nauvoo could replace its police with a rotating voluntary watch. Heber Kimball proposed lowering police salaries. Young thought that maybe they could continue to pay in scrip but offer interest on the scrip. While his idea garnered some support, Police Captain Jonathan Dunham pointed out that interest on worthless scrip would not provide any substantive relief to the police.[31]

Still, the city council went as far as drafting a bill authorizing the mayor to issue $1,000 of scrip bearing 10 percent interest for a year and using that scrip to pay the police.[32] Orson Pratt objected to the bill and Daniel Spencer suggested that the council defer voting on the bill until they tried requesting money from the public. With that, the city council tabled the bill. Instead, at the mayor's recommendation, they turned to Mormon bishops to "offere the subcriptin to the diffrnt wards."[33] Instead of increasing taxes, the city council decided to conscript to the city's ecclesiastical structure to raise money to pay its police force.

Police funding was not the first time Nauvoo had considered a voluntary tax. Years earlier, the political elites of Nauvoo had temporarily implemented a voluntary tax among themselves. In February 1842, Smith assigned the fees he earned as a city council member to the city indefinitely. Brigham Young, Willard Richards, Heber Kimball, and Wilford Woodruff followed suit. Smith's

52 · FRONTIER RELIGION, FRONTIER TAXATION

younger brother Samuel did not assign his fees to the city indefinitely but did turn over the fees he had earned for his prior year's work. Wilson Law, the city collector, also gave up his right to fees he had earned up until that time. Law had a specific vision for his money and requested that the city divide his forgone fees equally between the blind inhabitants of the city's Fourth Ward.

The city council then began to discuss the propriety of paying city councilors at all. Some, including Young, argued that city councilors should not receive compensation. Law agreed, believing that their pay should be "appropriated to the Poor." George Washington Harris did not "wish it to be said that the Citizens are Poor." Following up on that theme, John Taylor went even further, asserting that members of the city council were rich.

Other city councilors disagreed. While Samuel Smith had been willing to give up his previous year's fees, he also believed that the city should pay councilors. Hyrum Smith and John Barnett sided with Samuel. Barnett explained that if the city did not pay its councilors, he could not continue as a city councilor, by implication disagreeing with Taylor's assertion that members of the city council were uniformly rich.

While the city council did not come to a conclusion on pay at this meeting, Law continued his push for a social safety net, proposing that to the extent members of the city council declined their pay, that money be used to create a "poor Fund," earmarked to benefit Nauvoo's poor. The city council approved the proposal and Law declined the money due to him from the prior and current year (other than the amount of any fines that he might incur).[34]

A year later, Brigham Young exercised his right to revoke his assignment of city council fees. He requested that he receive pay equal to his assessed taxes. The city council accepted his retraction and gave him a certificate to present to the city collectors when they came to demand payment. The certificate would constitute payment of Young's taxes.[35] With his tax obligation satisfied, Young continued to donate the rest of his pay to the city. In essence, the city of Nauvoo received the same net amount from Young whether it taxed him or not.

The End of Nauvoo

The Mormons' experiment with overlapping religious and civic authority proved both tenuous and short-lived. Neighbors increasingly saw the Nauvoo Legion, a militia authorized by Nauvoo's charter, as a threat and, in his inaugural address to the Illinois legislature, Governor Thomas Ford suggested rolling back some of the extraordinary rights granted in the city's charter. The next day, Representative James M. Davis went further than the governor, introducing a

Collecting Taxes in Nauvoo • 53

resolution to revoke the city's charter altogether.[36] In response, one of Smith's brothers argued to Democrats that they should support the Mormons and the Nauvoo Charter because "all the Mormons had voted, at the last election, for the Democratic ticket."[37] The motion did not come to a vote in January but in March the House voted to revoke the Nauvoo Charter. The Mormons managed to preserve their self-government, though, with the bill failing to pass the Senate by a single vote.[38]

The death of the bill notwithstanding, the Mormons saw this legislation as a shot across their bow. *The Wasp*, a Nauvoo newspaper edited by Smith's brother William, expressed shock that the same legislative body that had granted Nauvoo "PERPETUAL SUCCESSION" would, mere years later, "take it away." While the Mormons in Nauvoo continued to exercise their rights of self-governance under the Nauvoo Charter, they had "no thanks to give to that honorable body; for they would have deprived us of them if they could."[39]

The failure of the Senate to act did not put to rest the question of the future of Nauvoo's autonomy. In 1844, the "opponents of *Joe Smith*" announced that they planned to start a new newspaper in Nauvoo. The *Nauvoo Expositor*'s prospectus disclaimed any focus on religion. Rather, it would go "in for the repeal of the Charter of Nauvoo City, and against all political revelations and unconstitutional ordinances." Notwithstanding its claim that it would not discuss religion, the editors of the *New York Daily Tribune* appear to have believed that Mormonism was intimately connected with the Nauvoo city charter. If the *Nauvoo Expositor* "conducted [itself] with candor and ability," they wrote, "the 'Decline and Fall of Mormonism' will be the title of the next chapter in the History of Modern Superstition."[40]

By the beginning of 1845, the *Expositor* had achieved its goals. On January 29, 1845, months after the murder of the Mormon's prophet-mayor Smith and his brother Hyrum, the Illinois legislature revoked the Nauvoo Charter.[41] With that, the Mormons' first experiment with creating their own tax system ended. And, for a group of people without formal experience designing and implementing taxes, it appears to have been largely successful. Problems with scrip notwithstanding, the city raised sufficient revenue to function, and the city council (mostly) separated its secular duties from its members' concurrent religious duties. Running the city gave church leaders experience that would be critical in their soon-to-be western home.

* * *

With the dissolution of the Nauvoo Charter, the Mormons' Illinois experiment with building and funding a theocratic city ended. When they left the

54 · FRONTIER RELIGION, FRONTIER TAXATION

city, they left with a better understanding of taxes than they had brought with them—where before they had been taxpayers, now they were also tax-writers. The Mormons did not decamp for Utah immediately upon the revocation of the Nauvoo Charter, though. Even without a formal charter and with a legally disbanded legislature, the *New York Daily Tribune* reported that "[t]he Nauvoo Government continues. . . . The whole municipal affairs proceed as usual."[42]

In fact, the post-revocation city council still had to deal with a question of taxation that had bedeviled it almost from its first days. On February 8, 1845, George Smith and Daniel Wells submitted a petition "pray[ing] your Honorable Body that the tax on Lands in the City of Nauvoo and not laid out in City lots, and which have not been paid for the years 1843 and 1844 may be abated."[43] Though the city council had decided in 1841 that property within the city boundaries that had not been laid out in formal lots was subject to property taxation, in 1845, after Alderman Charles Rich "spoke in full on the . . . petition," the city council of the no-longer-incorporated Nauvoo granted the tax abatement.[44] In the declining days of the Mormons' experiment with their own city, owners of land that had not been laid out in lots retroactively escaped their obligation to pay taxes to the city.

4

The Mormons' Utah Home

By the end of 1845, the Mormons found themselves without a prophet and without the protection of the city they had spent the previous half-decade building. At the same time, conflict with their non-Mormon neighbors continued, with some of those neighbors calling for their expulsion. It had become clear that the Mormons would yet again be forced from their homes.[1]

The Mormons' external conflict with their neighbors was compounded by internal conflict with their fellow saints. Joseph Smith's death left a vacuum in the church's leadership, with no clear plan for succession. A number of people claimed the right to succeed Smith, including members of the Smith family and other hierarchs in the church. These competing claims ultimately split the young movement. Some Mormons, including Smith's widow Emma, stayed in Nauvoo, while others left Nauvoo in favor of other Midwestern locations. The bulk of church members, however, followed Brigham Young and the Quorum of the Twelve.[2]

Young recognized the inevitability of the Mormons' departure from Nauvoo. The relationship between Mormons and their neighbors had devolved into violence; in an attempt to quell that violence, Young announced his intention to lead the Mormons out of Illinois.[3] By the beginning of 1846, Young had decided not only to leave the state of Illinois but to leave the United States entirely.[4] The Mormons looked at several western destinations, ranging from Texas to Oregon to Vancouver Island. By August 1845, they had narrowed their search to focus on the Great Salt Lake.[5]

56 · FRONTIER RELIGION, FRONTIER TAXATION

The Mormon exodus from Illinois began in earnest in February 1846. As the Mormons left Nauvoo, they sold or abandoned their real property and much of their personal property. They had lost the Nauvoo Charter and the self-governance it provided, but they took with them the knowledge and experience they had gained through their experiments with governance in Nauvoo during the first half of the 1840s.

In 1847, the first wave of Mormon settlers arrived in the Salt Lake Valley. A month after his initial arrival, Young recommended that the settlers appoint a president and other officers to govern the settlement. Ultimately, Young appointed John Smith, uncle of Joseph, as the initial president. He also appointed a new High Council to function as both an ecclesiastical and a legislative body with the dual mandate to institute the church organization in the Mormons' new home and to pass necessary laws and ordinances.

John Smith arrived in Salt Lake in September and a week later, on October 3, church members ratified all of Young's proposed civil and religious appointments.[6] The High Council immediately began its work, dividing into committees to handle various governmental duties. In its early days, the High Council enacted regulations governing land ownership and water rights, as well as rules governing mills, timber, and fences.

With civil government again came civil taxes. On October 24, three weeks after it began its work, the High Council enacted its first tax law in Salt Lake, "when it was decided that 'every man in the Old Fort should be taxed sufficient to pay for gates for the same.'" In addition to creating a tax, the High Council appointed William W. Willis to assess and collect the Old Fort tax, following the same tax process the Mormon-dominated city council had used in Nauvoo.[7]

Regulatory Taxes and Fines

As in Nauvoo, the High Council in Salt Lake enacted laws to raise revenue, but it also used taxes and fines to regulate residents' behavior. For instance, in their new inhospitable desert home, Mormon (civic) leadership wanted to prevent price-gouging. In December 1847, the High Council set prices for various goods and services. Lumber, for instance, could cost $2 or $3 per hundred feet, depending on the quality of the logs. Laborers could charge $1 per day. The High Council also set prices for various commodities, including beef, wheat, corn, and sugar.

The High Council enforced these price-setting laws through fines. To the extent that a laborer overcharged, the laborer forfeited their work. The same with a merchant who overcharged for goods. Moreover, the laborer or merchant had to bear the expenses of investigating the case. If any Salt Lake resident sold

The Mormons' Utah Home • 57

"bread stuff to the Indians," they had to disgorge the money they received to their ward bishop who used the amount to support the poor and to pay for the investigation.[8]

On June 10, 1848, the High Council had an extensive discussion about fence-making. Members of the High Council were especially concerned about residents who did not build or maintain fences. To ensure that landowners in Salt Lake enclosed their property with fences, the High Council authorized captains of pioneer companies[9] to build fences for those who had not and to collect the costs for the fences from the delinquent property owners. Where the captains were unable to build fences, the High Council authorized them to "collect a dollar per day from each delinquent" with an unbuilt fence, effective four days after the High Council's meeting.[10] This escalating fine provided a strong incentive for landowners to comply with the city's fence laws.

Two months after the High Council authorized fining those who failed to build fences, Charles C. Rich, who would soon become the stake president of the Salt Lake Stake, reported that the city needed twenty men to work on the roads. While it is not clear that the church had yet instituted a formal road tax in their new home, Rich, perhaps remembering the road taxes in Nauvoo, suggested that men who owed taxes could pay off those taxes by working on the road. If they declined, "men would be hired & those who owed taxes would have to pay in grain &c."[11]

Governing Deseret

While in many ways the governance of the Mormons' new home reflected what they had established in Nauvoo, in other ways it varied. Unlike Nauvoo, city government alone would be insufficient to meet the Mormons' needs. Upon the signing of the Treaty of Guadalupe Hidalgo, the Mormons' new mountain home became part of the United States. To maintain their independence and self-rule, they needed to live not only in a city but in a state.[12]

The first step toward statehood was organizing a provisional state government. In the early months of 1849, the Mormons formed a government for the prospective State of Deseret;[13] they planned for this provisional government to last until Congress formally adopted their proposed government or appointed a new one. This government, like the governments of Salt Lake City and Nauvoo, was deeply Mormon. Church president Brigham Young was appointed governor. Willard Richards, one of Young's councilors in the church's First Presidency, served as secretary of state while Heber C. Kimball, the other member of the First Presidency, became chief justice.[14] The Council of Fifty—a political organization of Mormon leaders—controlled the legislature while bishops, who led geographically defined congregations, "were elected magistrates over their respective" congregants.[15] In this way, the Mormon Church would "practically [control] the Territory of Utah from 1850 to 1858." Its members would continue to "[dominate] the territorial legislature" for another thirty-three years.[16] In its first four decades, Utah's governance would be created and maintained largely according to Mormon principles and preferences.

The government of the provisional state started its work almost immediately. In its first official action, the government incorporated the "Perpetual Emigrating Fund for the Poor," an entity that collected donations to provide financial assistance to poor Mormons moving to Deseret.[17] A little more than a year later, the General Assembly incorporated Salt Lake City. The city's charter was "almost a verbatim copy of that for Nauvoo."[18] The Salt Lake government thus found itself possessed of the same powers as the city council had in Nauvoo, including the power to lay and collect taxes.

The Provisional State of Deseret also exercised its ability to create taxes. On January 9, 1851, the same day the government of Deseret incorporated Salt Lake City, it enacted a formal road tax. The new road tax was similar to the road taxes Smith and his family had been subject to in New York and the road taxes in Nauvoo, but the Mormons' understanding and implementation of road taxes had shifted over the years.

The Deseret road tax applied to all males who were eighteen years or older and who had lived in the proto-state for at least three months. (Unlike many road taxes, there was no age ceiling on Deseret road tax liability.) Those subject to the tax had to work on the roads or highways one day each year. In addition, the Deseret government added a property tax component to the road tax. Owners of taxable property paid an additional road tax of up to half a percent of the value of property or one day of labor for every $300 of property. Each county court would assess property value for this tax during its regular March session.

Both the poll and the property tax components of the road tax could be paid in labor or in money. If a taxpayer chose to pay his road tax in labor, he was responsible for providing "ten hours good & faithful labor for each day assessed." Alternatively, he could pay $1.50 per day in lieu of providing physical labor. Anybody who refused to labor or pay would be liable for a fine of twice the delinquent tax. The law rested enforcement in the supervisors of the road districts; to the extent a supervisor failed "to prosecute all delinquents in their respective districts," the supervisor himself would be "liable to pay twice the amount lost, by or through his or their neglect."[19] By making the supervisor liable for double the unpaid road tax, the legislature provided a strong incentive for the supervisor to take his collection responsibilities seriously.

The Deseret government earmarked revenue and labor from its road tax to building and maintaining roads. To raise money for its general fund, Deseret relied largely on a property tax. On the same day it enacted the road tax, the territorial government enacted a 2 percent tax on property, including money, held by territorial residents. The government appointed Horace S. Eldridge as its assessor and collector.[20]

Utah Territory

Though the Mormons established a government in their new western home and though they enacted laws, the Mormons' provisional government was never truly official. Notwithstanding their hope for statehood, in September 1850, the federal government formally organized the Utah (not Deseret) territory. In the transition from Deseret to Utah, the Mormons formally lost their theocratic control of the territory; still, they were not entirely shut out. President Millard Fillmore appointed Brigham Young as governor of the territory, a post Young held until 1857. Mormons and non-Mormons split the other territorial offices.[21]

In its first session, the new territorial government adopted the laws passed by the government of Deseret. While the Mormon Church no longer formally controlled the territory, then, the new secular Utah embraced the tax laws passed by a theocratic Deseret. This wholesale adoption is not surprising: while the Mormons had developed their facility with taxes governing the theocratic Nauvoo, the tax policies they adopted were rooted in common secular US practice. The Mormons' experiences enacting tax law in Nauvoo and Deseret underscore that intersections between religion and the state are not always antagonistic. Religion, they discovered, can use secular tools to achieve secular ends.

The creation of the Utah territory did not immediately supplant Deseret. The Deseret government continued to meet, effectively a ghost government in the Utah territory, until 1870.[22] This ghost government lacked the ability to enact laws, however, and as a result, had no continuing influence on the territory's tax system. With the death of Deseret, the church formally slipped out of its unique secular role and into a purely religious sphere. Still, the Utah territory maintained its unique relationship between the dominant Mormon faith and the civil government. Mormons relied on church courts to resolve disputes with their coreligionists even after the country established a federal judiciary in Utah. While church courts had no civil authority to enforce their judgments,

60 · FRONTIER RELIGION, FRONTIER TAXATION

a church member who sued a fellow member in a civil court risked losing his or her church membership.[23] The threat of ecclesiastical discipline ensured that church courts could exert coercive enforcement authority over Mormons who used them to resolve nonreligious conflicts.[24]

The existence of church courts also proved relevant to the civil government's collection of taxes. Even after the federal government metaphorically built its Jeffersonian wall between the Utah territory and the Mormon Church, at times the Utah government used the Mormon Church to collect taxes. For example, in 1861, the tax assessor and collector complained to the Salt Lake High Council— an explicitly and exclusively religious body by this time—that some Mormons had refused to pay their taxes. The High Council ordered these delinquent taxpayers to pay their taxes on penalty of religious excommunication.[25]

Of course, the church did not automatically enforce civil laws on behalf of the government just because the government asked. Rather, it exercised its own legal and practical judgment. On one occasion, when asked to enforce a school tax, the Salt Lake High Council declined because, it explained, "the district trustees were not properly bonded and could not legally assess the tax." The High Council's decision here seems to have been largely procedural, though: five years later, it was again asked to assist the Salt Lake school district in collecting taxes. This time it agreed to help.[26] Whether the church chose to enforce the tax law or not, however, the civil government recognized that the church had soft authority over its members and saw the church as a potential locus of tax enforcement.

The Mormon Church's interaction with territorial Utah tax law went beyond mere questions of whether to help collect. In the post-theocratic era, the church became a sometimes-taxpaying, sometimes-tax exempt organization, and sometimes-lobbyist on its members' behalf. Mormons and Mormon leaders continued to pay (or sometimes refused to pay) taxes.

In 1871, just a year after the Deseret ghost government ended, the civil collection of taxes ran into conflict with the church's antipathy toward civil courts. Mormons could not entirely avoid nonreligious courts, of course. Church courts had no jurisdiction over criminal matters and, to the extent they heard civil cases, their jurisdiction existed only because litigants voluntarily submitted to the church courts' jurisdiction. Church courts could only hear disputes with non-Mormons with the consent of the non-Mormon party, and, to avail themselves of the Mormon court system, non-Mormons generally had to post a bond.

While the church could not *legally* enforce the exclusive jurisdiction of its courts, in predominantly Mormon Utah their exclusive jurisdiction proved enforceable nonetheless.[27] In 1878, President John Taylor counseled church members to settle business disputes between themselves with "a little charity and

The Mormons' Utah Home · 61

benevolence." Where that failed and a Mormon found him- or herself on the receiving end of a civil suit, Taylor recommended a solution to the defendant:

> I tell you what you should do, whenever a man would attempt to "pop" you through the courts of the law of the land, you should "pop" him through the courts of our Church; you should bring him up for violating the laws of the Church, for going to law before the ungodly, instead of using the means that God has appointed.[28]

Church members who disregarded the church's exclusive jurisdiction rule were, in the church's mind, guilty of "unChristianlike conduct" and could face disfellowship for suing fellow members in civil courts.[29]

The exclusive jurisdiction rule mapped poorly onto the enforcement of the tax law, however. Even after the church no longer formally ran the government, in Utah the majority of residents and a significant portion of government bureaucrats belonged to the Mormon Church and, as such, the exclusive jurisdiction rule demanded that they resolve any tax disputes through the church court system.

Tax collectors—including Mormon tax collectors—did not necessarily view church courts as the appropriate venue to enforce the tax law. On January 5, 1871, the church's Presiding Bishopric confronted the question of whether a Mormon tax collector needed to resort to the church court system to collect unpaid taxes. Edwin Rushton, a Salt Lake County tax collector, sued Brother Bailey, a member of Rushton's ward, in civil court for nonpayment of tax. The ward member followed Taylor's advice and sued Rushton in a church court.

Rushton explained to the Presiding Bishopric that he had instructed Bailey to show up on a particular day to work off his tax liability but Bailey failed to show up. Bailey came the following day but Rushton had all of the laborers he needed and sent Bailey home. Rushton subsequently attempted to collect the tax but Bailey refused to pay, claiming the tax was unconstitutional.

At an impasse, Rushton summoned Bailey before a justice of the peace and, in return, Bailey sued him in a church court. Stuck between two judicial systems, Rushton asked Presiding Bishop Edward Hunter what he should do about Mormon taxpayers who refused to pay their taxes.

The Presiding Bishopric discussed the matter. Daniel H. Wells explained to his colleagues that he believed Rushton was justified in suing delinquent taxpayers in civil courts after "other means had failed." The tax law, Wells reminded them, had been "made by ourselves and administered by our own brethren." Administering these laws through justices of the peace and probate judges "was a very different thing to summoning a brother to a Gentile Court."

62 · FRONTIER RELIGION, FRONTIER TAXATION

"Every man in Israel," he concluded, "ought to honor the law by living above it, and not give the Collector of taxes so much trouble, but pay them cheerfully, and at the proper time."[30] And with that, the church acknowledged that different rules governed personal lawsuits between members and lawsuits filed by Mormons in their capacity as government officials. Members *should* pay their taxes cheerfully but, if they did not, the tax collector—even if the tax collector was a member of the church—had the church's blessing to take delinquent taxpayers to secular courts to collect their unpaid taxes.

* * *

The Mormon experience in Deseret and early Utah built on the understanding of taxation the Mormons had developed in Nauvoo. They made marginal changes and advancements, but, during the years they governed, made few innovations. Their time governing the territory without the intervention of the US government was short, though, which limited the amount they could advance.

The principal change in the early years of Utah was that the church learned to accommodate taxation by a secular government. Rather than chafing, church leaders acknowledged the legitimacy of the government's taxing authority and, at times, helped with its administration, even where such help required modification to the church's distaste for secular courts. When the federal government replaced their theocratic government with a purely civil one, they figured out how to function within that government. Their experience accentuated the idea that civil and religious governance were separate spheres; while one could intrude upon the other on occasion, those intrusions were the exception.

5

Brigham Young and Federal Taxation

The Presiding Bishopric's 1871 decision allowing Mormon tax collectors to take their coreligionists to civil court when they failed to pay their taxes removed an important barrier to Mormons' practical ability to serve as tax collectors. Without this concession, a Mormon tax collector would be toothless in the face of recalcitrant Mormon taxpayers. The Presiding Bishopric, in granting this concession, seemed to recognize questions of tax as special, standing in contrast to members' normal religious obligations. Still, their decision was narrow and did not represent a broad repudiation of the church's exclusive jurisdiction rule.

The Presiding Bishopric's exception to church courts' exclusive jurisdiction also did not reflect an unequivocally positive view of taxes. In fact, in the same meeting in which church leaders granted Mormon tax collectors limited access to civil courts, Daniel Wells also characterized the federal government as an "enemy who is trying to rob us of our means for income tax." The church, he explained, had, in the past, used its tithing revenue to aid the poor, build tabernacles, and fund public works. With the imposition of a federal income tax, though, the church would have to cease collecting tithing. Still, it would "carry on our public works and sustain the poor through some other channel, rather than that heretofore paid in as Tithing."[1]

The Presiding Bishopric—and likely Mormons in general—would not necessarily have seen the Presiding Bishopric's positive view of the poll tax as contrasting with its disapproval of the income tax. The poll tax was a local tax,

64 · FRONTIER RELIGION, FRONTIER TAXATION

enacted, enforced, and paid by Mormons in Utah. The income tax, by contrast, was a federal tax, one that the Mormons had no input in designing or enacting. Moreover, and critically, certain non-Mormon federal income tax assessors and collectors had spent the previous eighteen months pursuing church president Brigham Young for an income tax deficiency, not just on his income, but on church tithing revenue.

In many ways, Brigham Young's experience with taxation encapsulates and highlights the myriad ways in which Mormonism interacted with tax laws in the nineteenth century. As with so many things, Young spoke of taxes extensively and inconsistently. His rhetoric was informed by his experience as a government official, as a religious leader, and as a taxpayer. As a government official, Young had debated and voted on tax provisions. As a religious leader, he had seen taxes that he considered unfair and oppressive. As a taxpayer, he had paid (and contested the payment of) taxes. These experiences helped shape his view of taxation, including the importance taxes played in building a civil community.

We have already seen some of Young's experiences with taxes, both in England as a missionary and in Nauvoo on the city council. We saw that he acted as governor in Deseret and in the early days of the Utah territory. In this chapter we will drill down on how he talked about taxes as well as how he fought them.

Sermonizing Taxation

As the Mormons fled Nauvoo and searched for a new home, Young had plenty on his mind, including, at times, taxes. As with Young's views on other topics, his rhetoric surrounding taxes proved at times inconsistent, often reflecting the specific situation in which he found himself.[2] At times he recognized the obligation his people had to pay taxes. In Winter Quarters, Nebraska, a waystation for the Mormons' flight to Utah, Young excoriated members of the church who complained about, and evaded paying, taxes and tithing. Those people, he said, should leave the body of the Mormons. Anyone who stayed should "both help support the poor and pay their tax."[3]

This obligation to pay taxes was not absolute, however. Young believed that if the church settled on Indian land, the government did not have the legal right to tax them. Because it was Indian land, he believed, the Native Americans who possessed the land were sovereign. Young's belief in Native American sovereignty appears more instrumental than deep-seated, however. While he believed Mormons living on Native American land should escape the obligation to pay taxes to the federal government, he also believed that the Mormons could claim and settle on Pottawatomie land without regard to those Native Americans who already called it home.[4] In fact, Mormons believed that the dislocation of Native peoples represented a step in the Native peoples' eventual redemption.[5]

Young believed that taxes were a civil, not a religious, obligation. As a religious leader, he was also confident that religious obligations were more important than civil ones. In Nebraska, as the Mormons fled Nauvoo for Utah, he asserted that "there was A great difference between the tithing & taxes." Tithing, he explained, was a perpetual law, one that required heads of household to pay 10 percent and would likely continue until Jesus returned to earth. By contrast, "taxes was levied according to circumstances."[6] At times, though, Young muddled this divide between civil and religious obligations. In the early days of Deseret, when Young acted as both church president and territorial governor, he charged the church's bishops with the responsibility to "see that every man pays his tithing and his taxes."[7] At one point in the late 1850s, he even proposed dropping taxation altogether and using labor tithing to build roads and bridges.[8]

In his dual role as a religious and civic leader, at times Young had to deal both with his people's religious and civic recalcitrance. For most of the last half of the nineteenth century, Utah faced a significant shortage of cash.[9] Less than 1 percent of the assets of Utah's national banks was represented by coins and other specie.[10] In the context of this lack of liquidity in Utah, Young (no longer acting as governor) addressed complaints that Utah taxation fell heavily on the people. He assured them that "your legislators are very easy—their hand is very light upon you, in the matter of taxation." To those who thought that the territory's five-mill (0.5 percent) tax was heavy, he asked how much they thought the territory had raised in taxes. Of the 15,000 men who were taxpayers, and of the roughly $20,000 they owed in taxes, the territory had raised $1,200 in coin. The rest was paid in-kind, in "wheat, chickens, eggs, butter, city scrip, county and territorial scrip, auditor's warrants, labour, &c., &c."[11]

Moreover, Young suggested that those complaining about the heavy burden of territorial taxation should look at the taxes in other territories like New Mexico, Nebraska, and Washington. Young confidently asserted that they imposed higher territorial taxes than Utah. And the heavy burden of Salt Lake taxes? Take a look, Young said, at Chicago, St. Louis, and New York.[12]

Was Young right that Utahns and residents of Salt Lake City paid uncharacteristically low taxes? It is hard to say with any certainty. The 1840s saw states enact a flurry of taxes in reaction to the elimination of canal toll revenues after the Panic of 1837, a severe financial panic that eventually led more than one in four banks to close.[13] Around that same time, as a result of the added emphasis on taxes as a revenue source, states began enacting constitutional provisions mandating uniform taxation.[14] Prior to these state constitutional limitations,

66 · FRONTIER RELIGION, FRONTIER TAXATION

state legislatures had exercised essentially unfettered discretion in deciding who, what, and how much to tax.[15]

This pre-uniformity variation existed in many territorial revenue regimes. Nebraska's territorial property tax, for instance, could be anywhere between 0.15 and 0.65 percent depending on how much revenue counties needed. Utah's 0.5 percent tax fell on the high end of the permissible range for Nebraska taxes.[16] But the tax rate was not the only determinant of tax liability in a system that depended largely on property tax. The assessor—who determined the value of taxed property—was equally critical. And here, the statutory language governing property taxes becomes entirely unhelpful. Even if Nebraska imposed the lowest tax rate its laws permitted—meaning the rate fell 0.35 percentage points below Utah's—as long as Utah assessors assessed property at a lower value than Nebraska assessors assessed property in Nebraska, Utahns may have paid less in taxes notwithstanding their higher rate.[17] At best, then, we can see Young's assertion as having rhetorical value, encouraging Mormons both to live in Utah and to pay their taxes.

At the same time, Young countered Utahns' complaints that they paid too much in taxes, he also addressed some legislators who opposed taxes. These legislators, Young said, "rise up and say, 'Considering that we pay such a tax in tithing, we think the Church should make all our public improvements.'" Those legislators who "would vote down every tax, if they had the power," were conscientious, Young said. But they were not wise.[18]

So how were cash-poor Utahns supposed to pay their taxes? Young pointed to the money Utahns paid for "ribbons, ruffles, fringes, gewgaws, and baubles in general." These discretionary purchases were unnecessary, he argued. (It is telling that his examples of conspicuous and unnecessary consumption focused solely on *women's* consumption.) Young liked to see "women prettily dressed" as much as anybody, but he told women to "save a portion of the money that is laid out for useless articles and pay your taxes."[19]

Along these lines, Young was generally skeptical of those Mormons who claimed poverty as an excuse for their tax delinquency. "If you ask people to pay their tithing," he said, "some of them answer they are too poor; or if you ask them to pay taxes to build bridges and keep them in repair, they are too poor even to do that." In his characteristic way, he went on to say that "some cannot even go to Utah when they are wanted—but they can go very well to the gold mines, because that is their God."[20] In his paradigm, then, taxpaying (at least where those taxes stayed local and funded infrastructure) was a sign of wealth and divine favor. Refusal to pay, by contrast, was merely an excuse. Worse, refusing to pay taxes could result in collective poverty.[21] If the Mormons really

Brigham Young and Federal Taxation • 67

wanted to pay their tithing, pay their taxes, or move to Utah, Young believed they could find the means to do so.

Young was not just skeptical of his people's claims of poverty, either. He was equally skeptical of his people's wealth. The Mormons would not always be poor. Someday "we will get so rich by and by that we will refuse to pay our taxes; we have got so rich now that we cannot pay our tithing. The rich do not pretend to pay any tithing, or but very few of them."[22]

Complaints against taxation were, in Young's telling, not merely a sign of selfishness. The widespread neglect of tax obligations could "run a nation into barbarism." In fact, he attributed the "destitute and degraded condition" of Native Americans to "their fathers being opposed to principles of tithing and taxation."[23] (While Mormon cosmology conflated Native Americans with the Lamanites of the Book of Mormon, both Young and his nineteenth-century Mormonism took a decidedly dim view of Native Americans. Young considered most unable to "'leave off their habits of pilfering and plundering' and work like civilized white people." Those few who were redeemable, he explained, would eventually be assimilated into "the growing Mormon kingdom."[24])

Ultimately, while Young's focus on taxes had a practical bent—the territory needed to support itself and its people—he viewed taxes as representing more than merely a civic obligation used to fund public goods. Mormons' payment of their taxes reflected the divine favor with which they had been blessed. Taxpaying provided evidence of the superiority of Mormons over those people who had driven them out and who denigrated them. "Who pay their taxes as well as the Latter-day Saints?" Young asked in 1877. "No people. Who honor so well the laws of our government? No other people."[25]

While Young touted the Mormons' taxpaying on the one hand, he decried secular overtaxation on the other. In 1853, he directed remarks toward British and Irish immigrants who had come to Utah. Some of these immigrants appear to have chafed at the obligations they faced in Utah; after arriving, some even left Utah to settle in California. Young accused these emigrants of forgetting their lives prior to Utah. "The people in England who earn five pounds have to pay three of it for taxes," he said. If they owned carriages or other property in England, they would owe the government half the value in taxes. In Utah, by contrast, people paid five dollars a year in taxes. But they complained when asked to stand guard one night in four to protect themselves and their families.[26]

Taxpaying also separated the Mormons in Utah from their non-Mormon neighbors. Young related that a Utah bishop had tried to collect school taxes from some non-Mormons. Those non-Mormons refused to pay and the courts sided with the tax objectors. By refusing to pay their taxes, Young explained,

68 · FRONTIER RELIGION, FRONTIER TAXATION

those non-Mormons avoided building their local community. To protect the community, Young encouraged church members to buy from merchants who paid their taxes.[27] While it was unfair that Mormons bore the brunt of funding local government, Young reminded his people that they had the responsibility to render unto Caesar, paying their taxes and otherwise complying with the law.[28]

At times, Young even reminded the Saints that their obligation to pay taxes applied not only where the government supported them but also where their taxes funded an antagonistic government. Perhaps Mormons did not need to be excited about paying taxes to the federal government. Still, Young said, "I don't know but the Lord will let us pay a little money tax to the Devil. The Government requires a direr tax of some $27,000 dollars."[29]

While Young acknowledged his people's obligation to help fund the federal government, he was not always eager to comply. In 1862, the federal government instituted the first national income tax to help pay for the Civil War.[30] Young responded to this new tax with deep sarcasm. He was sympathetic, he said, to the poor government's plight. "We feel much for our Government, their situation is lamentable; they are poor and needy, and destitute, and soon will be in a starving naked condition, and will find themselves in a great peril they now think not of." Still, the Mormons' hands were tied. Other territories had become states, but Utah remained a territory. As a result, "we do not own a particle of real estate here and cannot lawfully pay one dollar of this income tax." (Here Young seems to be conflating the new income tax with more-familiar property taxes.) To the delight of his followers, Young suggested that, while the Mormons would not illegally pay a tax, the federal government could take that amount of money from the territory by eliminating the salaries of the federal judges and the federally-appointed territorial marshal, state attorney, and governor.[31]

Taxing Tithing

While the Mormons in Utah applauded Young's sarcastic take on federal income taxes, his sarcasm ultimately ran into the reality of the assessed income tax. In 1869, John P. Taggart, the Assessor of Internal Revenue for the District of Utah, determined that the church owed almost $60,000 in unpaid taxes and penalties.[32] Over an eighteen-month period during the close of the 1860s, in spite of rhetoric that was generally at least grudgingly positive toward taxpaying, Young and the church were forced to battle this tax assessment.[33]

In 1869, newly-elected President Ulysses S. Grant appointed a number of new Internal Revenue assessors, including Taggart. Taggart replaced Augustus L. Chetlain, Andrew Johnson's appointee from three years earlier.[34] Many of

Grant's Treasury appointments were patronage appointments, meant to reward those Republicans who helped him gain and maintain power.[35] Taggart appears to have been one of these patronage appointees: while he had no particular expertise in the collection of revenue, he had a long history with President Grant, having served as an assistant surgeon on Grant's Civil War staff years earlier.

Taggart arrived in Utah amid enormous animosity between Mormons and the Eastern establishment and he did nothing to calm this animosity.[36] Within months of his appointment, he testified at a hearing in front of a House of Representatives committee on how to best enforce laws against polygamy. In his testimony, he claimed that "Mormons recognize and observe no law except such as they are compelled to observe. So far as my own department is concerned, I know they do not scruple at any means they can to contrive to evade the revenue law." He further told the House committee that he had investigated six assistant assessors who were Mormon and determined that they were unduly partial toward their coreligionists; he fired them and doubled the income tax assessments in Utah.[37]

The Mormons, in turn, disliked and distrusted Taggart. Brigham Young wrote to the Commissioner of Internal Revenue that Taggart had made himself "extremely unpopular among our citizens." The Mormons in Utah saw him as bitter and prejudiced, an "officious meddler" in matters that did not concern him.[38]

In mid-1869, Taggart instructed Francis Lyman, a Mormon and an assistant assessor, to assess the Mormon Church's income. Lyman wrote to Young, warning him about the impending assessment. A month later, Taggart demanded that Young appear at his office to declare the church's income. Young responded that the church had already made its return.[39]

To the extent that the church filed a return, that return no longer exists today, about a century and a half after the dispute. However, later discussions between Young and the territorial collector of internal revenue suggest that the church had filed a return, but that the government considered the return fraudulent. Collector O.J. Hollister argued that the church's 1868 return included less income than the church had in tithing revenue in 1850 even though church membership and resources had increased by five- or tenfold.[40]

Hollister's assessment of the return may well have been accurate. In a conversation with a former assistant assessor, Young expressed his belief that, under the Internal Revenue law, charitable donations did not represent income to the recipient. In 1850 there was no federal income tax, so the church would not have filed a tax return. And in 1868, if the church believed that tithing revenue was not income for tax purposes, it would not have included tithing on its return, even if that revenue had more than quintupled over the intervening years.

70 · FRONTIER RELIGION, FRONTIER TAXATION

Whether the church refused to make a return or Taggart refused to accept its return, eventually Taggart instructed his son Edwin (an assistant assessor) to put together a tax return on behalf of the Mormon Church. (The Internal Revenue law allowed assessors to file a return on behalf of a taxpayer if the taxpayer refused to do so.) While Edwin estimated that the church had tithing revenue of between $2 million and $5 million a year, he ultimately decided that the church had $791,180.22 of taxable income. At a 5 percent tax rate, the church owed about $40,000 in taxes. On top of that, he assessed a 50 percent penalty for the church's refusal to file a return (or, at least, an acceptable return).[41]

As trustee-in-trust for the church, Young was personally liable for the church's taxes if the church failed to pay. Though he would have been aware that a tax assessment was coming, it is unlikely that he anticipated the size of the assessment. The previous several years, Young had paid taxes of about $1,000 per year on about $20,000 of annual income. This new assessment was a sixty-fold increase.[42] (For context, a tax liability of $60,000 in 1869 would be the equivalent of a tax liability of a little over $1.2 million in 2021.[43])

Though Young had been forewarned to expect an assessment, any assessment against the church would have been uncharacteristic. Congress had not explicitly exempted churches from the Civil War income tax, but with very few exceptions, the tax only applied to natural persons, not to entities.[44] Moreover, while Congress had not exempted churches, it had delegated regulatory authority to the Secretary of the Treasury. And the Treasury had issued regulations that exempted charitable institutions, including churches, from tax.[45]

So if the Civil War federal income tax was mostly a tax on the income of individuals *and* the Secretary of the Treasury had issued regulations explicitly excluding churches, why did Taggart think he could tax the Mormon Church on its tithing revenue?

Because of a Shaker community in New Lebanon, Ohio. The United Society of Believers in Christ's Second Appearing, popularly known as the Shakers, believed in the communal ownership of property. As a result of these communal beliefs, the community in New Lebanon filed a single tax return in the name of a single community member. That return included the combined income of all of the members of the community.

At the same time, the community deducted $46,000 from its income. The Shaker community calculated this amount by deducting $1,000 for each of the community's forty-six male members. (The Civil War federal income tax allowed each taxpayer a $1,000 deduction, thus ensuring that nobody who earned less than $1,000 had to pay income taxes.)

Brigham Young and Federal Taxation • 71

To determine whether to accept the New Lebanon Shakers' tax return, the Commissioner had to answer two questions. First, he had to decide whether the Shaker community at New Lebanon was an appropriate taxpayer. If so, he had to decide whether it could take a $46,000 deduction against its income. The Commissioner first decided that, while the tax law generally did not reach entities, in extraordinary circumstances it could. The case of the New Lebanon Shaker community, in which no individual Shaker had a right to the community's money, qualified as one of those extraordinary circumstances. The Commissioner further decided that the tax law provided a single $1,000 exemption per taxpayer. Because the Shaker community, and not the forty-six male members, was the taxpayer, the Commissioner allowed the community only a single $1,000 exemption to offset its communal income.[46]

While significant differences existed between the Mormon Church in Utah and the Shaker community in New Lebanon, Taggart viewed this ruling as justification for invoking the extraordinary circumstances exception. He believed the ruling gave him authority to treat the Mormon Church as a taxpayer in spite of the general rules against churches and other entities paying income tax. He also viewed it as authority to conflate Young and the church and to collect the tax he believed the church owed from Young personally.

Still, even with the Shaker precedent and the government's skepticism toward the Mormons in Utah, it was far from clear that the Mormon Church should be taxed on the tithing it received. The new federal income tax applied to "profits, gains, and incomes." In mid-nineteenth-century America, tithing was still a new and uncommon practice and Taggart largely elided the question of how tithing fit into the scheme of profits, gains, or incomes. Rather, he baldly asserted that the Mormon Church had large profits, gains, and incomes.[47]

In doing so, Taggart followed the instructions he received from his superiors. The Commissioner, worried that the statute of limitations would bar the government from collecting taxes from the Mormon Church, directed Taggart to quickly make an assessment. As long as the assessment was made in time to fall within the statute of limitations, the church and the government could fight over whether the Mormon Church owed taxes and, if so, how much it owed later.[48]

Once Taggart made the assessment and delivered it to the Mormon Church, his role ended. The law treated his assessment as presumptively correct. If the church disagreed, it had the burden of proving that the assessment was wrong. But the church would not approach Taggart—the federal system separated the roles of assessor and collector. With his assessment complete, Taggart handed the baton to O.J. Hollister, the collector of internal revenue for the Territory of Utah. Hollister, not Taggart, was responsible for collecting the amount Taggart had assessed against the Mormon Church.[49]

Hollister was under national pressure to successfully collect the church's taxes. The whole country watched the tax drama in Utah. And the country expected Hollister to prevail and collect the tax by whatever means necessary. An example of the pressure imposed on Hollister came in a *Chicago Tribune* story about polygamy and the federal government's control of the Utah territory. In the middle of the story, the *Chicago Tribune* asked whether Hollister intended to seize Mormon property if the church failed to pay its taxes.[50]

Even if the rest of the country had ignored Hollister's collection attempts, the law would have put plenty of pressure on him to collect the church's taxes. The Civil War income tax law made collectors personally liable for the taxes on the assessment lists they received.[51] If Hollister failed to collect the taxes Taggart had assessed on the Mormon Church, he would personally owe the government nearly $60,000.

In spite of these pressures, the differences between Hollister and Taggart could not have been starker. Where Utahns and Taggart evinced mutual antipathy, church leaders believed that Hollister was reasonable, and perhaps even on their side. At the very least, he showed respect and courtesy toward the Mormons, who in turn described him as "gentlemanly."[52]

While Taggart had to rush to make his assessment within the statute of limitations, once he had completed his assessment, the urgency around the Mormon Church's tax bill dissipated. Young requested an extension of time in which to pay the assessed tax. The Commissioner told Hollister to determine whether such an extension would prejudice the government's ability to collect the tax. If not, he instructed Hollister to grant the extension and to assist Young in his request for an abatement of the tax.

Hollister decided that an extension would not prejudice the government and granted Young's request. He promised that he would not make any move toward collecting the tax without notifying Young first but nonetheless instructed Young to hurry with his request for abatement.[53]

About a week after Hollister granted the church its extension, Young formally requested the abatement of the tax. In his request, Young highlighted two flaws in the $60,000 the government said he owed. First, he *had* filed a return and that return had been accurate. And second, tithing was a voluntary donation by church members, not a taxable quid pro quo. The church used the tithing money it received for charitable, not speculative, purposes and ultimately earned no profits or gains from its tithing.[54]

Brigham Young and Federal Taxation • 73

Hollister notarized Young's request for abatement. He declined, however, to sign an accompanying certificate testifying that he believed Young's statements to be true. Consistent with the Mormons' regard for Hollister, Daniel Wells, an apostle of the church and, at the time, mayor of Salt Lake City, explained that Hollister refused to sign because of a technicality. The certificate, Wells said, was labeled "Assistant Assessor's certificate." Because Hollister was the collector of internal revenue, not an Assistant Assessor, he could not sign.[55]

Wells was almost certainly wrong about Hollister's reasons, though. While Hollister remained congenial, in a letter to Young he explained that he could not agree with Young's assertion that tithing represented a free-will offering to the church or that it did not represent profit or gain. He explained his view

> that the tithing has been devoted to laudable enterprises in general, perhaps always, saving & excepting, begging your pardon the perverting of Christians to Mormonism. But I cannot see it to be in the nature of a voluntary contribution, nor a fund from which neither the Church nor individuals derive gain or profit.[56]

Two considerations underlay Hollister's skepticism. First, he explained, the church had refused to show him its tithing accounts for 1868. As a result, he believed Young's statements were partial and incomplete at best.[57] The church resolved this particular concern to Hollister's satisfaction, inviting him to the Tithing Office to examine the church's 1868 tithing accounts.[58]

But that did not resolve his second concern. Based on previous statements by Young, Hollister did not believe that tithing was voluntary. Both Mormon scripture and Young in his capacity as church president had referred to tithing as a "law." And violation of that law, Hollister said, subjected Mormons to significant penalties. At the most extreme, nonpayment could lead to excommunication which, in isolated Utah, he believed could lead to both spiritual and financial ruin and, ultimately, death.

Hollister acknowledged that not everybody who failed to pay their tithing was excommunicated (though he insisted that at least some had been) but said that nonenforcement was ultimately irrelevant. Whether or not the church exercised an enforcement mechanism, tithing was enforced by the sting of Mormons' consciences. Critically, in Hollister's mind, that sting had been placed in their consciences through the unflagging effort of the church, which was supported by the tithing revenue.[59]

In addition, the church's expectation that its members tithe was not merely an inchoate desire. The church, Hollister explained, treated members' tithing obligations as an account due. That account ran with members throughout their lives. Tithing, then, was not a voluntary offering—it was a mandatory part of

74 · FRONTIER RELIGION, FRONTIER TAXATION

Mormon life, enforced through both intrinsic and extrinsic pressure. And the church did not merely hope that members would pay; in its financial documents, it expected and tracked members' payment. In Hollister's opinion, that made tithing look less like a free-will offering and more like an obligatory payment.

Hollister also dismissed the idea that the federal disincorporation of the church impacted its tax liability. In 1862, as part of its anti-polygamy legislation, Congress had "disapproved and annulled" the laws "incorporating the Church of Jesus Christ of Latter Day Saints."[60] Whether or not it existed as an entity, the church continued to *act* as if it existed and continued to elect Young as trustee-in-trust of the church every year. That role authorized Young to act on the church's behalf, and Young in fact acted on the church's behalf. As a result, whatever the church's status for legal purposes, Hollister believed that it existed as a potential taxpayer for purposes of the federal income tax.

But while Hollister believed that the church owed taxes, he also believed that it owed a lot less in taxes than Taggart had assessed. After examining the church's books, Hollister believed that the church had about $85,000 in net income. With a 5 percent tax rate and a $1,000 exemption, he believed the church needed to pay about $6,300 in taxes, a nearly 90 percent reduction in the amount Taggart had assessed.[61]

While church leaders were pleased with Hollister's recommendation that the government substantially reduce its tax assessment, they were not entirely placated. After all, Wells pointed out, other churches also raised money. But, pursuant to the exemptions in the tax law, those other churches did not pay taxes.[62]

Moreover, even the lower tax assessment may have proven difficult for the church to pay. Payment of taxes, church leaders argued, was incompatible with the type of revenue the church received. Of the more than $143,000 its Tithing Office received in 1868, only about $25,000 was in cash.[63] The vast majority of tithes the church received were paid in labor and in goods. T.W. Ellerbeck, Young's clerk, argued to Hollister that "if delivering potatoes to the Church was Church income—then the tax should be paid in potatoes, as they were disbursed to the poor & the work-men in kind & no money was realized at all."[64] If the government wanted to collect these types of in-kind taxes, Ellerbeck sarcastically suggested, it needed to build storehouses to receive them.

Ellerbeck's argument that income paid in kind was not taxable fell on deaf ears. Income is income, whether received as cash, property, or even services.[65] If the church wanted to get the final $6,300 in taxes erased, it needed to convince the Bureau of Internal Revenue that tithing did not constitute income taxable to the church.

Young tried to do just that. In a letter to Internal Revenue Commissioner Columbus Delano, he laid out five reasons why the government should disregard Taggart's assessment and not tax the church on its tithing revenue. He started with a legal argument: gifts, under the federal income tax, were excluded from income. And what was tithing, if not a gift to the church? (Young disputed Hollister's allegations that non-tithepayers faced ecclesiastical discipline and, in fact, claimed that half of the members of the Mormon Church did not pay tithes and even he paid "a little, but not as much as I should."[66])

He followed his legal argument with a policy argument. Tithing, he explained, had already been taxed in the hands of the donor. If it were also taxed in the hands of the church, that would create double taxation of the same income.[67]

Young also renewed his objection to Taggart's enormous assessment, while reiterating his objection to taxing in-kind receipts. He elaborated on the problem the church faced in paying taxes on in-kind tithing—the problem was not *just* that the church and the Mormon people were cash-poor. There was also a problem with the valuation of in-kind tithing. A bishop might collect twenty gallons of molasses in satisfaction of a ward member's tithing obligation. The church would record the value of that tithing as $40 on its books. Using that valuation, the church would owe $2 in taxes.

But it would cost the church more than $13 to transport the molasses to Salt Lake. And when it sold the molasses, it might bring in less than a dollar per gallon, rather than the $2 per gallon the church had credited to the tithepayer. So while the church marked the donation as satisfying $40 of tithing, it might sell the molasses for less than $20. After transportation costs, the church would pay $2 of taxes on less than $7 of net revenue. Given the vagaries and difficulties of collecting and valuing in-kind donations, even using the church's financial records risked significantly overstating the church's actual income.

To conclude, Young disputed Taggart's characterization of the church's use of its tithing revenue. The church used tithing primarily to build houses of worship and pay the salaries of church employees, he explained. It did not, as Taggart believed, use its tithing revenue for speculative investment purposes. Finally, Young argued that Taggart's penalty had been assessed inappropriately. The church had filed an honest and timely tax return and should not have faced the 50 percent penalty.[68]

Even if the Commissioner of Internal Revenue rejected the church's arguments, though, Young had one final argument up his sleeve. In July 1870, Congress amended the tax law. Prospectively, it raised the exemption amount from $1,000 to $2,000, specifying that each family would only receive a single exemption. At the same time, it provided (perhaps in reaction to the earlier Shaker

76 · FRONTIER RELIGION, FRONTIER TAXATION

decision) that religious societies holding their property jointly and severally would get one exemption for every five members.[69]

Young latched onto this change in the tax law. At various times in its history, the Mormon Church had held property communally and Young believed the church should qualify for this new provision (albeit prior to its effective date). He got provisional support in this from the Bureau of Internal Revenue, which instructed Hollister to ascertain how many members the church had. Unless the church owed more than $1,000 for every five members, Hollister could assist Young with his request for abatement.[70] Young reported that the church had 50,000 members. If the new exemption applied, the church would get 10,000 exemptions. Using the $1,000 exemption amount that had applied in 1868, it would only owe taxes on income in excess of $10 million.[71]

Somewhere along the line, however, the Bureau of Internal Revenue got its priorities crossed. In spite of the instruction to Hollister that he help Young with the tax abatement, on July 15, 1870, the Bureau told Hollister that he had ninety days to collect all of the assessments made against the Mormon Church. If he did not deliver the money to the federal government by mid-October, he would be personally liable for the $60,000 tax debt.[72]

Two weeks later, the church got yet another temporary reprieve. Hollister informed Young that the Bureau had reinstated the suspension on collection.[73] The reinstatement delayed, but did not end, the government's collection of the tax. After some consideration, the government decided that the Mormons in Utah did not hold their property jointly and severally and, as a result, could not take a $1,000 exemption for every five members. Young was going to have to pay the government. And he was going to have to pay $60,000.[74]

Not only would Young have to pay $60,000 for 1868, but if tithing was, in fact, taxable, the church would owe taxes for 1869, 1870, and into the future. The cash-poor church needed to figure out both how to find the money to pay the taxes Taggart had already assessed *and* how to come up with money to pay its future taxes.

While Young remained hopeful that the church could convince the Commissioner of Internal Revenue to abate its taxes, he tempered his hope by preparing for a future in which he failed. He pursued two strategies to minimize the church's future taxes. First, he asked William H. Hooper, Utah's territorial delegate to Congress, for his help.

The Mormon leader asked Hooper to determine whether John W. Douglass, the new Commissioner of Internal Revenue, had instructed Hollister to drop the penalties but, at last, to collect the assessed taxes.[75] Young also asked Hooper to examine the tax returns of liquor manufacturers in Utah. While he had no

Brigham Young and Federal Taxation • 77

evidence that Taggart was in partnership with them, he had heard rumors.[76] Such rumors would not have been entirely unfounded. While there is no evidence that Taggart personally was corrupt, the Bureau of Internal Revenue was plagued by corruption, in part the result of the low wages it paid. And nowhere did employees of the Bureau face more temptation to commit fraud than with the liquor tax.[77]

Nothing came of Young's initial requests to Hooper. Finally, though, toward the end of 1870, Young decided to ask the charming Utah delegate to do what he did best: lobby Congress and convince its members that the church did not owe taxes. Young did not request that Hooper take any particular tack, but instead provided him with the church's position and asked him to use that information as he saw best. In December, Hooper took advantage of a meeting with Senator John Sherman of the Senate Committee on Finance to argue (unsuccessfully, as it turned out) that the Mormon Church was not subject to tax and the collection should be suspended.[78]

While Hooper lobbied in Washington, Young also took steps at home to minimize the future impact of taxes. In his first move, he declined to give Hollister a security interest in church property while they waited to see if the Commissioner abated the church's tax. If Hollister wanted the church's property, he would have to take it under protest. Young hoped that the spectacle of the federal government seizing church property would be offensive enough to Congress that it would take the church's side. Hollister agreed with Young's assessment of the optics of seizing church property.[79] After Wells told Hollister that the church would not provide security but would also not obstruct any attempt Hollister made to seize it, Hollister replied that he did not want to take the church's tabernacles or organ because "it would raise a howl about persecution that they would not get over for 50 years."[80]

Although Young hoped to sway public, and particularly congressional, opinion, he did not count on success. At the beginning of December, Commissioner Douglass largely rejected the church's request for abatement. While he waived the 50 percent penalty after determining that the church had neither failed to file a return nor filed a fraudulent one, he also decided that the church's tithing revenues represented taxable income. As a result, he authorized Hollister to immediately collect the $40,000 the church owed.[81]

By the middle of December, the Bureau of Internal Revenue had again changed course. Young received a telegram informing him that he had been given an additional ninety days before he had to actually pay the tax.[82] The respite, while undoubtedly welcome, did not solve the church's biggest problem: future taxes on tithing. In light of the Acting Commissioner's ultimate decision

78 · FRONTIER RELIGION, FRONTIER TAXATION

that the church owed taxes on its tithing, Young began to explore how the church could reimagine its revenue to ensure that church revenue fell outside of the reach of the income tax. He ultimately landed on two possibilities and was prepared to implement either one.

First, as he pointed out to other Mormon leaders, while tithes represented donations to the church itself, local bishops actually collected tithing. In many cases, the bishops also dispersed the tithing. Perhaps the church could decentralize its collection of tithing, devolving its tax liability to each bishop outside of Salt Lake County. If each bishop were assessed on the tithing, that would do more than just free Young from the crushing burden of taxation he faced. Taggart had granted the church a single $1,000 exemption. If each bishop in the church shouldered the taxpaying responsibility for the tithing he collected, presumably each bishop would enjoy an individual exemption.[83] This flowering of exemption amounts would substantially reduce the church's collective tax liability, albeit at the cost of losing some degree of financial centralization.

Young was also prepared to take a far more drastic step: on January 3, 1871, he proposed ending tithing altogether.[84] Ending tithing had the potential to be financially ruinous. At the time, tithing made up more than half of the church's revenue.[85] In addition, the end of tithing posed a theological problem; after all, in revelation, the Lord had announced to Joseph Smith that tithing would be "a standing law unto them forever."[86]

In spite of its place in Smith's revelations and in canonized Mormon scripture, Young made immediate moves toward ending the practice. Wells agreed and, the following day, began preparing a notice to the church detailing the new policy.[87] That same day, Young himself wrote a letter to the bishops in Utah, instructing them that church leaders "wish the people to pay no more tithing, nor you to make any more returns to the General Tithing Office, until further notice."[88]

While Young was trying to figure out the future of Mormon revenue, the national press reported on Douglass's decision almost gleefully. Ten days after Young announced to the church's bishops that tithing was no more, *Harper's Weekly* simultaneously mocked Young's taxpaying and his polygamy, informing its readers that

> Brigham Young thought his income tax too large last year. He declared it was erroneous and asked to have it abated. Not being so successful as he desired, the venerable householder revenges himself by complaining of the extravagance of his family. Perhaps if he had only the usual quota of wives and daughters, he might find it required less cloth to clothe them.[89]

Brigham Young and Federal Taxation · 79

While its import was unknown to the Mormons or, for that matter, to a gleeful national press, on the same day that Young initially proposed ending tithing, something momentous for the church's eighteen-month battle occurred across the country: Alfred Pleasonton began his short-lived term as Commissioner of Internal Revenue. (By the middle of 1871, Pleasonton had been suspended and, in December, was replaced as Commissioner by Douglass.[90])

Pleasonton had served as a general in the Civil War and an income tax collector in New York. He was also staunchly opposed to the federal income tax. Shortly after his appointment as Commissioner, he wrote to the House Committee on Ways and Means to describe the evils of the income tax. In his letter, he recommended its immediate and unconditional repeal.[91]

At the same time, he revisited the Mormon Church's appeal of its tax assessment. Upon further reflection (and probably consonant with his desire to minimize or eliminate the federal income tax), he concluded that the church's return on speculative investments was income subject to tax. Its tithing, by contrast, represented voluntary donations to the church and, as such, was exempt from tax. He instructed Taggart to make a new assessment consistent with his conclusions.[92]

With Pleasonton's decision, church leaders abandoned their plan to eliminate tithing. Members of the church who wanted to pay tithing would "have the privilege of paying their Tithing & donations."[93]

In spite of Pleasonton's orders, Taggart remained intent on taxing the church. But when he requested the church's tax return for 1870, Young replied that he could not find any evidence that the church's tithing had produced a speculative (and thus taxable) return.[94] And at that point, questions of federal income tax largely dropped out of church leaders' correspondence. By the time Douglass replaced Pleasonton, he seemed to have other things to worry about than collecting taxes from the Mormon Church in Utah. And then, a year later, the federal income tax disappeared, sunsetting according to the original terms of the law.[95]

And with that, the church's 18-month ordeal as a taxpayer ended. In response to the potential fiscal crisis the church faced as a result of the application of the federal income tax to its tithing revenue, Mormon leaders discovered that they were willing to change their doctrinal practices to avoid potentially ruinous financial consequences.

*   *   *

In some ways, Young's decision to sacrifice tithing, a practice Joseph Smith's revelation had declared a standing law to the church forever, presaged the

80 · FRONTIER RELIGION, FRONTIER TAXATION

church's abandonment of polygamy two decades later. Like tithing, LDS plural marriage in the latter half of the nineteenth century was not just a peripheral practice. It was central to Mormonism. Men in the church had a religious duty to practice polygamy if circumstances permitted, and those who failed to comply faced damnation in the eternities.[96]

And yet, in the face of a sustained attack by the federal government on Mormon polygamy, in 1890 the church formally renounced its practice (though it continued, often with implicit church approval, for another fourteen years).[97] Unlike the church's brief flirtation with ending tithing, the end of polygamy came after a sustained federal campaign of criminalizing polygamous marriages, disenfranchising Mormons who practiced polygamy, and dissolving the church's corporate existence and seizing its assets.[98] As he formally ended the practice (for the first time), church president Wilford Woodruff explained that because the Supreme Court had found the laws forbidding polygamy constitutional, he intended to submit to those laws.[99] A year later, Woodruff justified the doctrinal change, asking his people whether they preferred to continue practicing polygamy and risk the confiscation of all temples, the end of the religious ordinances in the temples, the arrest of church leaders and other polygamous Mormons, and the loss of personal property. Or maybe they preferred to "leave our prophets and apostles and fathers free men, and the temples in the hands of the people, so that the dead may be redeemed."[100]

Following Young's lead from two decades earlier, church leaders decided that it was better to change their religious practices in response to federal pressure than to defy the federal government and give up their assets. While Congress had not enacted an income tax to pressure religious change, the church nonetheless proved susceptible to the influences of legal pressures in the nation in which it existed.

The federal income tax would not reemerge in the United States until the early twentieth century and, when it returned, it expressly exempted the income of churches from taxation.[101] But for this brief period in the 1860s and 1870s, the church, which had previously and occasionally functioned both designing and administering taxes, learned what it felt like to be in the shoes of those subject to the obligation to pay taxes. And it learned flexibility in the face of legal regimes inconsistent with its preferences, a lesson it would revisit in the future.

6

Enlarging Mormonism's Borders

While a significant portion of Mormons moved to Utah after their expulsion from Nauvoo, not all would remain in Utah. The church sent proselyting missionaries around the world. It sent colonists to neighboring states and neighboring countries. Its members moved away and its converts did not always gather in Utah.

As the church expanded into new places where it was less well-known, the church and its members lost both their home-court advantage and their majority status. They began to face taxation in an increasing number of jurisdictions. These different state taxes could be similar to the taxes the church had helped implement in Utah, but they could and did also differ substantially. In these new homes and locations, Mormons and the Mormon Church faced, for the first time in decades, generalized tax rules and ordinary tax procedures that were not tailored to their experience. They had to learn to comply with their tax obligations or use ordinary grievance procedures to challenge them.

This chapter will illustrate the Mormons' experience with expanded taxation in two eras and locations. First, it will look at nineteenth-century Nevada, where Mormons faced actively hostile tax collectors. Then, following the church's expansion from its United States home, it will look at how Mormons experienced taxation in Hawai'i in both the nineteenth and twentieth centuries. In both places, as well as others that Mormons began to call home, the church and its members faced generally applicable tax laws that sometimes worked in their favor and sometimes did not.

Muddy River Colonies

Though Utah offered the Mormons much of what they wanted in a home—particularly security and autonomy—they did not stay put in the Salt Lake Valley. Within a handful of years after their arrival, church leaders began sending groups of Mormons to colonize other parts of the West. In 1852, church leaders established the first of its many colonies, about 300 miles south of Salt Lake. Colonists at Harmony assisted with the church's nearby ironworks. The church established other colonies to convert Native Americans, help with traffic to California, and raise crops. In establishing these and other colonies, the Mormon Church aimed to achieve a higher degree of economic self-sufficiency and to support a higher standard of living among its members.[1]

While the church established its colonies to create a higher collective standard of living for the body of the Mormon Church, colonists themselves endured hardships and deprivations. Living in isolated and remote areas, colonists had to import many of their necessities across significant distances and at significant expense. And colonists generally did not choose to move to the colonies—rather, church leadership called them to move. From the church's perspective, assigning Mormons to move to the colonies ensured that colonies had people with the right mix of skills both to survive and, with luck and hard work, to prosper.[2] To establish that mix, though, the church often disregarded individual Mormons' preferences.

The potential for prosperity proved tremendously important to church leaders. In the late 1850s, after learning that the US government was exploring the navigability of the Colorado River, Brigham Young decided it would be in the church's economic interests to strengthen Mormon colonies in Southern Utah, especially around the Great Basin. In 1861, he traveled to Southern Utah and discovered that, despite the colonization efforts, only seventy-nine families, spread between eight small towns, lived there. To increase the Mormon presence and better exploit the resources of Southern Utah, Young called 309 families to establish the city of Saint George. Three years later, the church called a number of missionaries to form colonies along the Muddy River.[3]

The Muddy River Valley was located about fifty miles from Las Vegas. During the first year of the Muddy River mission, Thomas S. Smith, along with more than forty families, founded the town of St. Thomas along the river. Eight miles upstream, Joseph Warren Foote founded St. Joseph. The Muddy River mission proved tremendously successful, with the settlers growing hot-weather crops like wheat, corn, and cotton year-round. Additional families poured in and, by

Enlarging Mormonism's Borders • 83

the late 1860s, the Muddy River colonies were sending thousands of pounds of agricultural products northeast to the main body of the Mormons.[4]

Soon, though, the Muddy River colonists ran into problems. As they established their cities along the Muddy River, they assumed they were residents of the territory of Utah. They would soon be disabused of that idea. On October 31, 1864, President Abraham Lincoln proclaimed neighboring Nevada a state.[5] Almost immediately, Nevada's first two senators worked to expand the new state's boundaries at the expense of the Utah and Arizona territories. In 1866 Congress authorized the extension of Nevada's eastern boundary one degree of longitude eastward, provided the state approved the expansion. Arizona objected and sent a memorial to Congress protesting its loss of territory. Congress rejected Arizona's objection and in 1867, the Nevada legislature voted to accept the new territory.[6]

Nevada believed that its new boundaries encompassed the Muddy River colonies. The Mormon colonists disagreed. They continued to pay their taxes to Utah, rather than paying Nevada's higher taxes. When the Lincoln County, Nevada, assessor presented them with a tax bill, church leader Erastus Snow advised residents to bring their tax receipts to the courthouse in Lincoln County. In case that failed and Nevada still demanded taxes, Snow further suggested that colonists "arm, and defend your property if necessary."

The Muddy River colonists followed his advice. The Nevada authorities proved unimpressed, though, and in August, a tax collector from Nevada walked into a Mormon cooperative store in Panaca and demanded a list of the store's inventory. When the clerk refused, the collector locked the clerk and bystanders out of the store. In response, the Mormon men in town "armed themselves and sent the town constable after the key."[7]

As we have seen, this kind of potential for violence was an occupational hazard for frontier tax collectors in the United States. As early as 1786, a state excise tax officer went to western Pennsylvania to collect the excise tax. A mob approached him and he pulled out his pistols. The mob seized his pistols, broke them into pieces, and proceeded to punish him by, among other things, shaving half of his head and parading him through the three counties in which he was supposed to collect the excise tax.[8]

A century later, frontier tax collectors faced much the same resistance when they attempted to fulfill their duties. In 1873, a Louisiana newspaper wrote that it had "never advised its people to pay taxes to the Durell-Kellogg usurpation." But, it said, peaceful resistance would not suffice. Were its readers "ready for revolution? If they resist, they should by no means fail."[9]

84 · FRONTIER RELIGION, FRONTIER TAXATION

In 1882, a tax collector went to the Coeur d'Alene reservation to collect taxes from the Native American inhabitants. They refused to pay and, when he threatened to return with a posse, they told him they would "resist to the bitter end, and shoot the first man who attempted to enter the reservation."[10] In 1888, the Chickasaw people in Gainesville, Texas, warned tax collectors that they would not pay a new cattle tax. They explained that they would resist "peaceably if possible, but forcibly if necessary, and therefore civilly warn all officers to abstain from trying to collect any more of the cattle tax."[11]

As late as 1895, a deputy tax collector in Kentucky went to Carter County to collect a railroad tax that had been in dispute for four decades. He levied a farmer's property for the tax and, as a result, a mob of about 500 men came after him. He "escaped being lynched . . . only by slipping off in the night as they approached."[12]

The Mormons at Muddy River adopted this violent frontier response to Nevada's tax collector. But while they had temporarily driven the tax collector off, they could not postpone his visit forever. In 1870, the United States made an official survey of the Utah-Nevada border. The survey placed the Muddy River towns comfortably within Nevada's Lincoln County.[13] The colonists were in a bind. While they had paid taxes, they had paid to Utah and to Arizona—the wrong jurisdictions.[14] Nevada, which, it turned out, had a right to that tax revenue, intended to collect its back taxes. In February 1871, Joseph Young wrote to his brother Brigham that on February 15, 1871, the deputy sheriff of Lincoln County went to St. Joseph and served a summons on all of the men there to appear at his office a month later "and to answer to a charge of delinquent tax for the years 1869 & 70." In total, the sheriff intended to collect $12,000 in gold.[15]

Nevada's demand for tax payments made in gold represented the culmination of nearly a decade of controversy in the United States. Beginning in 1862, the federal government had put about $500 million of paper fiat currency—called "greenbacks"—into circulation. The government did not set aside a gold reserve to support the greenbacks and it did not announce a date for their redemption. To ensure that the greenbacks kept their value, Congress legislated that the greenbacks would be legal tender to pay all debts, public or private, within the United States.[16]

In 1866, the Nevada Supreme Court addressed the question of whether taxes were debt and thus payable in greenbacks. The two judges who heard the case disagreed about whether taxes themselves fit within the federal definition of "debt." They both agreed, though, that *judgments* for taxes constituted debt. Justice Cornelius Brosnan, who did not believe that the definition of debt included taxes, nonetheless wrote,

Enlarging Mormonism's Borders • 85

If the state will disrobe herself of sovereignty, and enter the forensic arena with her subject, to collect a paltry tax of one dollar by the ordinary process of a suit at law, and at a cost to the delinquent taxpayer of from twenty to thirty dollars, which is of no benefit to the state, as is now the patent fact; and if in doing this the state recovers judgment, I can perceive no satisfactory reason why such a judgment may not be satisfied by payment of the amount in legal tender notes of the United States.[17]

Two months after the court's decision, the Nevada legislature codified the court's conclusion. Effective as of 1866, all "costs, fines, licenses, taxes and salaries may be paid in any currency made, by the laws of the United States, a legal tender."[18]

Two years later, the United States Supreme Court adjudicated a challenge to an Oregon law that required citizens to pay their state taxes in gold or silver coin. The taxpayer challenging the law argued that greenbacks were legal tender to pay taxes (echoing the Nevada Supreme Court's decision). The Supreme Court disagreed. "[T]he clause making the United States notes a legal tender for debts," it explained, "has no reference to taxes imposed by State authority, but relates only to debts in the ordinary sense of the word, arising out of simple contracts or contracts by specialty."[19]

The Supreme Court's decision did not *mandate* that states only accept tax payments in gold and silver. But it opened the door for them to refuse greenbacks. In 1869, the Nevada legislature took advantage of the Supreme Court's permission and again changed course. On February 2, it passed a law requiring Nevada taxpayers to pay any state, county, or municipal taxes in United States gold or silver coins.[20]

The Muddy River colonists did not have gold or silver to pay the tax. In fact, the prior year more than 100 of them had signed a petition requesting that the Nevada legislature abate their taxes and create a new county that encompassed the Muddy River settlements. The petition proved unsuccessful and, when Nevada officials threatened to seize Mormon property to satisfy their tax liabilities, the church appears to have decided it would be fruitless to fight. Instead, it released the settlers from their missions and allowed them to return to their Utah homes if they chose to do so.[21]

As a result, when the sheriff arrived in 1871, he encountered people in the process of leaving Nevada. Angry and concerned that the tax revenue would disappear with them, the sheriff announced that he would "return and make oath to the facts and get attachments on personal property and to return with sufficient posse to enforce the attachment of property."[22] Again, this was common in frontier tax collection: the sheriff often served as tax collector and assessor and, when the sheriff "encountered violent resistance, the sheriff summoned

86 · FRONTIER RELIGION, FRONTIER TAXATION

the *posse comitatus* (power of the county)—able-bodied adult males in his jurisdiction—to his assistance."[23]

His threat proved largely toothless. By March 1871, most of the Mormons on the Muddy River had abandoned their Nevada homes, "not caring to live in and pay taxes to Nevada."[24] Brigham Young, displeased with the Muddy River towns, reportedly announced that if "the Gentiles wanted that country they were welcome to it."[25] For the residents of the Muddy River, even without paying Nevada taxes, their time proved an economic disaster. They returned to Utah impoverished. After six years of work, settler Warren Foote "left the Muddy with two old horses, one old wagon, and two cows."[26]

Though taxes were higher in Nevada than in Utah, tax burden is rarely the only factor that goes into individuals' decision-making process. While the higher Nevada taxes drove Mormon colonists out of the Muddy River colonies, they did not drive all Mormon colonists out of Nevada. Snow told those who lived near Pioche, a mining town, that, while they might find Nevada's taxes oppressive, the "advantages of market afforded by your proximity to the mines would enable you to pay the Nevada taxes much easier than the brethren of the Muddy can do." Some chose to stay. Those who stayed benefited from the mining boom and were able to funnel cash into the cash-poor Mormon economy.[27] And, while they paid Nevada taxes going forward, they fought Lincoln County's attempt to collect back taxes. After several court cases, Lincoln County officials dropped their attempts to recover the delinquent taxes that had been erroneously paid to Utah.[28]

Hawai'i

While church leaders called some Mormons to establish colonies hundreds of miles from the main body of the church, they called others to leave their Utah home and travel even further. For example, the church called Henry P. Richards to preach and proselyte in Hawai'i. In some respects, Richards's trip to the islands was unexceptional; the church had first sent missionaries to the Hawaiian Islands in 1850 in hopes of converting white men who had traveled there as whalers.[29] In many ways it was not even exceptional for Richards—his arrival in Honolulu on January 12, 1877, marked his second mission to the islands.[30]

When Richards arrived for his second mission, the Kingdom of Hawai'i was still a sovereign nation. It would not become part of the United States until 1893, when a group of white American residents, backed by 160 US Marines, overthrew the monarchy and claimed temporary sovereignty of the islands. Four years after this coup, the US annexed Hawai'i as a territory, and in 1956 it became a state.[31]

Enlarging Mormonism's Borders · 87

While Richards's mission was, on its surface, unexceptional, it proved important for the Mormon Church in several regards. He became the first Mormon to receive from the Minister of the Interior a license to solemnize marriages as a religious minister. He also managed to get an audience with Their Majesties Kalakana and Kapiolani, where he presented a copy of the Book of Mormon to Queen Kapiolani.[32]

The Kingdom of Hawai'i imposed a number of taxes that residents—including Richards—had to pay. To begin, the Kingdom imposed an annual $1 tax on virtually all male inhabitants between the ages of 17 and 60, whether they were Hawaiian citizens or not.[33] In addition, every male resident between the ages of 21 and 60 owed a $2 tax to support schools.[34] Male residents between the ages of 17 and 50 owed $2 of road taxes on top of the other personal taxes.[35] Hawai'i also taxed property owners on the real and personal property they owned.[36]

Hawaiian law provided exemptions from these personal taxes, exempting, among others, individuals with age, health, or wealth problems. In addition, Hawaiian law explicitly exempted "[a]ll clergymen of any Christian denomination regularly engaged in their vocation."[37]

Richards declined to pay the $5 in personal taxes that the Kingdom assessed against him, believing that the exemption for Christian clergy encompassed Mormon missionaries. The Kingdom sued to collect these taxes, and, at trial, Richards testified that he was a "minister or clergyman" for the Church of Jesus Christ of Latter-day Saints. As a Christian minister, he asserted that he qualified for an exemption from the personal taxes that the Kingdom had assessed against him.

The Crown argued against his qualification for the tax exemption on three grounds. First, they said, his title was "Elder," not "Reverend." By disclaiming the title "Reverend," the Crown argued, he disclaimed being a minister. The Crown also argued that he was not Christian because Mormonism accepted revelation beyond those contained in the Holy Scriptures. Finally, Mormons should not qualify for the tax exemption because of their practice of polygamy.

The court disagreed. In the first instance, it said, the title he chose was not determinative of his status as a minister. Other Christian clergy—notably Baptists and Methodists—also often claimed the title "Elder." And the Roman Catholic Church denominated its clergy "Father." What mattered was not whether Richards called himself a minister—it was whether he *acted* as a minister. The court found unequivocally that he did follow that vocation.

The court used similar reasoning in deciding that belief in revelation outside of the Bible did not disqualify someone from being Christian. Roman Catholics were unquestionably Christian, but they accepted authority from outside the canon of Christian scripture. The court reasoned that if Mormons accepted the

Bible, believed in Jesus, "and believe[d] also in the revelations of Joseph Smith, they must equally as Roman Catholics be considered a Christian denomination."

Finally, Richards testified—and the court believed—that Mormons were not authorized to practice polygamy in Hawai'i. While the court acknowledged that in Utah Mormons engaged in plural marriage, "until it is shown by proof that the Mormons of this Kingdom are affected in their conduct by this doctrine, it will not be a ground for excluding them from the privilege accorded to other denominations professing Christianity." Again the court referenced Catholicism; the Catholic Church had authorized an inquisition, the violence and coercion of which would be unacceptable under Hawaiian law. But that practice outside of Hawai'i did not impact its categorization as Christian *in* Hawai'i.

The court understood that the Kingdom had exempted Christian ministers because Christian ministers had to be supported by some portion of the community. Taxing them would impose an additional cost on the public "in the support of religion and morals." To the extent that this was the goal of the tax exemption, that goal supported exempting Richards—and, by extension, other Mormon missionaries in the Kingdom of Hawai'i—from personal taxes.[38]

Richards's securing exemption from tax as a Christian minister marked the only major interaction between Mormonism and taxation on the islands for the next century. But in the last half of the twentieth century, questions of taxation and Mormonism reemerged in Hawai'i. In 1963, the church opened the Polynesian Cultural Center on Oahu, a forty-acre "ethnic theme park" showcasing "'authentic reproductions' of traditional Polynesian villages." The Polynesian Cultural Center is staffed largely by Polynesian students at the adjoining Brigham Young University-Hawai'i.[39]

The Mormon Church initially established the Polynesian Cultural Center to provide employment to the students at BYU-Hawai'i.[40] Even today, more than one in five BYU-H students are native Hawaiians or Pacific Islanders.[41] While the church opened the Polynesian Cultural Center primarily to provide financial support for Polynesian students, the Polynesian Cultural Center proved tremendously profitable.[42] Tickets currently range from about $70 to about $243 per adult, with children receiving a slight discount.[43] In 2019, the Polynesian Cultural Center's admissions revenue totaled nearly $38.7 million. On top of its admissions revenue, the Polynesian Cultural Center received more than $21 million in other revenue.[44]

This massive stream of revenue nearly undercut its federal tax exemption. In 1975, the IRS attempted to revoke the Polynesian Cultural Center's exemption on the basis that it was "too profitable and too professional" to be a tax-exempt organization. By 1981 it had grossed $125 million and, if the IRS successfully revoked its exemption, it could have faced a $9 million bill for back taxes.[45]

Enlarging Mormonism's Borders • 89

The Polynesian Cultural Center appealed the IRS revocation. After a pro-tracted ten-year battle, the Center prevailed and kept its federal tax exemption.[46] (The idea that a theme park could be exempt from taxation is not unique either to the Mormon Church or to the Hawaiian Islands: the Holy Land Experience, which operates a Bible-themed theme park in Florida, is also exempt from federal income tax.[47])

Almost a decade after it prevailed against the IRS, though, the Polynesian Cultural Center lost its state property tax exemption. In 1992, the Land and Tax Appeal Court of Hawai'i held that the Polynesian Cultural Center was not charitable under Hawaiian law. Rather, it was a "commercial enterprise and business undertaking."[48] The court disagreed with the Polynesian Cultural Center's argument that they operated as a "living museum[]." Rather, it believed that they were tourist-oriented businesses operated for commercial purposes.

Upon losing its tax appeal, the Center had to pay $375,000 in taxes for the years 1987–1989 and it faced an additional $900,000 tax bill for 1989–1992.[49] While the loss of its state tax exemption did not affect the Center's federal exemption, it created real tax liability, as well as a constant interaction with the state of Hawai'i. That real tax liability has proven ongoing: In spite of the Mormon Church's increasing sophistication when it comes to questions of tax, it has proven unable to reobtain state property tax exemption for the Polynesian Cultural Center. Rather, it has to pay its property taxes and, if it disagrees with the state's assessment, it must operate through the same dispute mechanisms available to any for-profit business. For instance, in 2016 the Polynesian Cultural Center filed a tax appeal with the state. It did not argue that it was exempt from tax but, instead, disputed its liability for $2.3 million of excise taxes it had paid the state.[50]

*   *   *

The Mormon Church's expansion through its various missionary endeavors introduced it to tax regimes—and with them, questions of taxation—it had never encountered before. When it faced tax consequences it deemed incorrect, the church had to choose how to engage with the incorrect results. Sometimes, it withdrew its members from the taxing jurisdiction. Other times it suggested that the benefits of staying were worth the additional tax cost. And as it became more sophisticated and more integrated into new communities, it found itself using the judiciary to argue for the tax result it believed most apposite to its situation.

7

A Corporate Church in Brooklyn

On February 16, 1919, Reed Smoot—apostle of the LDS church and Senator from Utah—dedicated a chapel in Brooklyn. At the time, about 400 members of the church lived in New York City (with about 350 "members and friends" at the dedication) and about 750 members in the state of New York. The chapel at Gates and Franklin Avenues in Brooklyn was the first chapel the church built in New York State.[1]

Two years before its dedication, though, this Brooklyn chapel caused the Mormon Church's East Coast operations to run headlong into the Brooklyn tax assessor. The assessor determined that under New York law, the church needed to pay property tax on its new Brooklyn building. For the rest of the year, the church tried to figure out how it could eliminate this tax, whether through the courts or through some sort of corporate reorganization. Ultimately, the tax assessment caused the church to make a fundamental change to its corporate structure that it did not want to make.

While we rarely think of churches changing their behaviors in response to taxes, it should be unsurprising that they would. Most taxes provide incentives for taxpayers to act differently than they would have made in the absence of a tax. Sometimes the alteration in behavior is the point of the tax. As we saw in Nauvoo, some citizens (unsuccessfully) lobbied for a dog tax in an attempt to reduce the number of dogs in the city. Today many cities and states look to sin taxes to regulate behavior: for instance, a number of cities have considered taxes on sugary drinks as a way to combat obesity. As a simple economic matter, it makes sense. As prices rise, demand falls. A sin tax is one way to raise prices, which means that fewer people will consume the taxed product and that those who do will consume less.[2]

Sin taxes differ from most types of taxes in one significant respect. While sin taxes *can* raise revenue, their principal purpose is to change behavior. If they raise revenue, that is a happy accident, secondary to their main goal. By contrast, for revenue-focused taxes, changing behavior is a bug, something to avoid where possible. Tax policymakers try to minimize distortions in taxpayers' decision-making. Taxes that change taxpayer behavior are inefficient. Inefficient taxes are bad for two reasons. First, they discourage taxpayers from making the decisions they otherwise would have made. Second, they make it economically rational for taxpayers to engage in tax-evasive behavior, behavior that does not provide an economic benefit (outside of reducing taxes) to the taxpayers but which reduces the amount of revenue the government collects.[3]

Of course, there is often a tradeoff between efficiency and equity in designing taxes. The most efficient tax is a head tax, where every taxpayer pays a set amount by virtue of being alive. Head taxes are efficient because no matter what a taxpayer does, the taxpayer owes the same amount of taxes. The one way to avoid the tax is deeply unpleasant.[4] As such, a head tax does not distort taxpayer decisions. This type of tax is thoroughly inequitable, though. A head tax of $2,000 per person would be disastrous for a family of five earning $15,000, while it would be nearly unnoticeable to a single individual earning $250,000. Progressive taxes that increase with income are less efficient than head taxes because behavioral change can reduce a taxpayer's tax bill, but by reflecting a taxpayer's ability to pay they are also significantly more equitable.

It should come as no surprise that the same distortionary pressures that taxes impose on individuals can be felt by entities, including tax-exempt entities. And that type of pressure is illustrated well by the Mormon Church's response to the assessment of property tax on its new Brooklyn building in 1917. In short, the church changed its preferred corporate structure in response to the tax. While it would not have made the decisions it ended up making in the absence of a tax, the church decided that reducing its New York property tax was worth compromising its preferred legal form.[5]

Church leaders in Salt Lake learned about the potential property tax in early 1917. On January 5, 1917, Walter Monson, the president of the church's Eastern States Mission, wrote a letter to Joseph F. Smith, the president of the church. Monson reported that in December 1916 he had hired an attorney to "get our Brooklyn property on the tax exemption list."

The attempt had failed, though. Absent an exemption, Monson estimated that taxes would cost the church between $800 and $900 per year.[6] In light of the expected cost, he wondered whether it would be consistent with church policy to incorporate the Eastern States Mission. He hoped that "the benefits of the law might be enjoyed by the Church as well as by other religious organizations. It is not only for one year that the tax exemption would benefit the Church, but for all time to come."[7]

In the early twentieth century, New York had a relatively broad property tax. Unless the law contained an explicit exemption, all real property located in the state was taxable, as was all personal property "situated or owned" within New York.[8] This broad property tax did not mean that *all* property located in New York was subject to tax, however. The state granted a number of exemptions to the property tax. The availability of these exemptions largely depended on the identity of a property's owner. For the Mormon Church's purposes, the tax law excluded the property of a "corporation organized exclusively for . . . religious . . . purposes." (If the religious organization used the property for purposes not associated with its religious mission, though, it would lose its property tax exemption on that property.)[9]

The tax assessor believed that only churches incorporated in New York could benefit from this property tax exemption. Since the Mormon Church was incorporated in Utah, its property was not, in his mind, eligible.

Monson was understandably puzzled about why the Brooklyn tax assessor declined to exempt the church's Brooklyn property from the tax rolls. After all, it met the statutory requirements—it was owned by a corporation organized for religious purposes and was used for those religious purposes. The law said nothing about applying only to New York corporations. Still, in spite of the lack of statutory support for the assessor's position, Monson immediately entered into problem-solving mode. He believed that because the benefit of tax exemption to the church would be perpetual, the church might want to form a corporate entity in New York to hold the Brooklyn property.[10]

Four days after his initial letter, Monson again wrote to his church's First Presidency. He updated them on his search for a new mission office, then reiterated the importance of the church qualifying its property for the New York property tax exemption. "[E]very effort," he explained, "should be made to get our property on the tax exemption list." Achieving exemption would be hard, in his opinion, "were the City officials to discover we are handling our commissary on the premises."[11]

The First Presidency forwarded Monson's letter to Franklin Richards, the church's attorney.[12] In his response, Richards emphasized that the New York property tax situation did not warrant any change to the church's corporate structure: it had already made a decision about how to hold property. In states like New York that did not recognize corporations sole, the church's preferred corporate form, and where the church had no permanently organized stakes or wards, church property was owned by the Corporation of the Presiding Bishop of the Church of Jesus Christ of Latter-day Saints,[13] itself a corporation sole.[14] (A corporation sole is a corporation that consists of one person. It was originally envisioned and created as a legal vehicle to prevent church property from being treated as the property of a religious officeholder for legal purposes. Corporations sole largely entered United States law through nineteenth-century lobbying by Catholic bishops.[15])

The Corporate of the Presiding Bishop currently owned the Brooklyn property and, because the state had already assessed property tax for 1917, Richards did not see any advantage in immediately changing the property's ownership. There would, he believed, "be plenty of time during the year in which to consider whether or not it would be advisable to adopt the method suggested by Brother Monson, before another tax becomes due."

In the meantime, he had corresponded with attorneys in various states about transferring property to the Corporation of the Presiding Bishop. In doing so, he planned to determine whether property so held would qualify for property tax exemption. He believed that in most cases it would but, in states where property owned by the "Bishop's corporation" would not qualify, "we will consider in each case whether there is any other way of holding the title that would seem to be more advantageous to the Church." Richards also reported that he had begun lobbying the Utah state legislature to amend its corporation sole law. Under his proposed bill, Utah corporations sole would have the legal ability to hold title to property located outside of Utah and would also have the right to dispose of that property without requiring formal church approval.[16]

Franklin's preference for corporations sole did not exist in a vacuum. A California lawsuit from twenty-five years earlier illustrated the risks of failing to hold religious property through a formally organized corporation sole. In 1886, Lydia Rebbeck had executed a deed conveying real property to Bishop George A. Blakeslee of the Reorganized Church of Jesus Christ of Latter Day Saints (a sister church to the Salt Lake-based Mormon Church Franklin and Richards belonged to) and to Blakeslee's successor as bishop. When Rebbeck died, others claimed the land and Bishop Blakeslee sued for possession.

During the pendency of the litigation, Bishop Blakeslee died and E.L. Kelly, who had been elected to replace Blakeslee, tried to step into the litigation. The court determined that the word "successor" in the deed was meaningless if

Rebbeck had conveyed the property to Blakeslee in his personal capacity or in his role as bishop. It was only meaningful—and Kelly only had standing to substitute into the case—if the conveyance had been made to Blakeslee as a corporation sole. However, Blakeslee had not demonstrated to the court that he had taken the requisite steps to form a corporation sole, either in California or in Illinois. As a result, neither his heirs nor the Reorganized Church had any ownership interest in the land.[17]

The lesson? Holding religious land without having a corporation sole could prove dangerous to a church's ability to hold its property in perpetuity. In light of that judicial history, it made sense that Richards emphasized the need for the church to hold its property through its corporation sole.

Still, widespread anti-Catholic sentiment caused some legislators to balk at allowing corporations sole. Because the Catholic Church was lobbying for states to approve corporations sole, some legislators believed that the legal form provided them with too much power.[18] In short, while corporations sole provided an important mechanism for hierarchical churches to hold property, there was also public distrust of the form.

That public distrust manifested itself in New York law. Although New York allowed for religious corporations, its Religious Corporations Law made no mention of corporations sole. Rather, the law provided specific rules for the corporate form of various denominations. A Roman Catholic or an Eastern Orthodox church that wanted to incorporate had to be governed by trustees. The archbishop or bishop was a trustee by virtue of his office, as were the vicar-general of the diocese and the rector of the church. But in addition, New York law required that an incorporated Catholic or Eastern Orthodox Church have two lay trustees who were members of the church.[19] New York used this lay trustee requirement to undermine clerical authority in an attempt to protestantize the Catholic Church. A corporation sole would have allowed the bishop to decide how to use church property unilaterally. Lay trustees, by contrast, could push back against clergy on both doctrinal and property matters.[20]

Against the background of state law that did not provide for corporations sole and, in fact, that was hostile to hierarchical religions with centralized control of property and doctrine, it would have been fruitless for the Mormon Church to create a corporation sole—its preferred corporate form—in New York. To qualify for tax exemption, the church would need to either win its court case or create a corporate structure with which it was uncomfortable. In that context, Richard's recommendation that the church wait until it knew what the court would decide made perfect sense.

Church leaders seem to have taken his advice and stopped worrying about the New York property tax exemption while their New York attorneys fought for exemption in court. That fight ultimately proved unsuccessful. Six months after Monson had raised the question of property tax exemption with the Mormon leadership, the *Brooklyn Daily Eagle* reported that "the Mormon congregation at Gates and Franklin Avenues has lost its action to have its property at that location declared exempt from taxation on the ground that it was a religious corporation." In ruling for the city, Justice Thompkins of the New York Supreme Court explained his belief that "the tax law provision exempting the real property of a corporation used exclusively for religious purposes must be deemed to refer to New York State corporations and not foreign corporations." Because the Mormon Church was incorporated in Utah, Justice Thompkins held that the city was justified in not granting it an exemption.[21] (Counterintuitively, in the New York court system, the Supreme Court is the trial level court, not the court of final appeals, as it is in the federal and most other state judicial systems.)

Shortly after Justice Thompkins's ruling, Monson sent a letter to the First Presidency reporting that the church had lost its case and enclosing a clipping of the *Daily Eagle* article. The church's New York attorneys, he added, had appealed Justice Thompkins's ruling. They argued that it was "unjust to tax one church because of having been incorporated in some other State, while another church is exempt because of having been incorporated in this State." The attorneys planned to base their argument on a hypothetical situation where a New York-incorporated church had to fight for tax exemption in New Jersey, Utah, or another state, hoping to convince the court of the potential harms to New York-based churches if it upheld this discriminatory exemption rule.

In the meantime, Monson reiterated his request that church leaders think about incorporating the Eastern States Mission or the Brooklyn congregation as a New York corporation. His estimate of the amount the church might owe in New York taxes if it failed to qualify as exempt had grown significantly; now, rather than $800 to $900, he estimated that the church could owe between $1,200 and $1,500 each year. While the appeal would cost the church $25, he reported, the attorneys had volunteered to incorporate the church in New York for no additional cost.

To ensure that the Salt Lake-based church maintained control of the Brooklyn property, Monson proposed that church leaders appoint a General Authority as an officer of the to-be-formed corporation. Before the church's New York corporation could transfer title in any property it held, the General Authority would have to affirmatively approve the transfer.

96 · FRONTIER RELIGION, FRONTIER TAXATION

Monson believed that the denial of a tax exemption was a case of persecution against the Mormons, given that the Catholic Church and various Protestant churches—"all of which are foreign importations"—qualified as exempt while the Mormon Church, also foreign, did not. In the name of fairness and justice, then, he was "anxious to defeat the ends of a Priest-ridden Justice and secure the advantages of tax exemption to which we are entitled."[22]

Monson's sense of persecution was not necessarily unwarranted: in 1916, he received an anonymous letter warning that "you had better not build a Mormon temple in New York. If you do it will be dynamited and I hope you are in it at the time."[23] At the same time, though, while he felt the sting of discrimination, he was willing to discriminate himself: in early 1917 he had written to Salt Lake about his search for a new mission office. A Mr. Haviland, who had also helped him acquire the Brooklyn property, "graciously directed me from that section of Brooklyn inhabited by Jews and Italians, to suitable places on Bedford Avenue," which, while not the "leading business district" was, at least, a fashionable residential neighborhood.[24]

Richards, in his role as the church's attorney, agreed with Monson that the church should pursue an appeal of the New York Supreme Court's ruling. He underscored that it was worth the $25 expense to get a final determination of whether property owned by a church incorporated in Utah in fact did not qualify for property tax exemption under New York law. "[I]t is much more desirable," he explained, "to have the titles [to New York property] held by the Presiding Bishop's Corporation if it is practicable to do so." But if the appellate court agreed with the trial court, he believed, church leaders should "seriously consider" creating a New York corporation.[25]

The First Presidency took their attorneys' advice. They approved their New York counsel's pursuit of the appeal in hopes of exempting their Brooklyn property from tax. In an odd postscript, though, the church leaders proved slightly confused about the issues the church faced. They wrote that their attorneys should "bear in mind that the Church of Jesus Christ of Latter-day Saints is not a corporate body."[26] If true, that would have severely undercut their argument for exemption. Whether or not the property tax exemption applied to foreign or only domestic religious organizations, New York law was clear that to be exempt, property had to be owned by a religious *corporation*.[27] If the Brooklyn property were owned by an unincorporated religious entity, it would clearly be taxable.

The church leaders were wrong, though. The Corporation of the Presiding Bishop of the Church of Jesus Christ of Latter-day Saints, not an unincorporated church, owned the Brooklyn property.[28] So, while their reminder about the unincorporated nature of the church was puzzling, it was not germane to the question of taxability. If New York law permitted the exemption of property owned by a religious corporation incorporated outside of New York, the church's Brooklyn property would qualify.

The New York attorneys moved quickly; by July 19, 1917, they had filed their briefs with the appellate court. Stuart Kohn, who led the case, felt confident in their chances. The question, he said, was novel: no court had before ruled on whether a foreign religious corporation qualified for exemption from New York property tax. The answer seemed obvious to him, though: the plain language of the law only specified that the owner needed to be a "religious corporation." The trial court had "read into it the word 'domestic corporation,'" an extra-statutory condition that Kohn did not believe the text of the law supported.

If they won, he informed Monson, it would not only prevent them from paying taxes in the future but it would also "save this year's taxes." Still, in spite of his confidence in winning, Kohn recommended that the church move forward in forming a New York corporation. Alternatively, Kohn informed Monson, property "held for the church by a religious officer of a religious corporation" was also exempt; if the church did not want to create a new corporate entity, it could also transfer the property to an individual. Whichever it chose, it needed to move quickly. The court would not hear their appeal until the fall, while the next year's property tax would be assessed in October. If the church lost its appeal, any delay in restructuring the ownership of the church's Brooklyn property beyond October would mean the church had to pay two years' worth of property taxes.

If the church transferred its Brooklyn property to a New York corporation before the next year's assessment, though, even if the church lost its appeal, the property would be exempt in the current *and* future years. As long as the church moved quickly enough, at most it would owe taxes on the property for a single year. To ensure that the church was ready to move forward should it lose its appeal, Kohn requested a name for the proposed corporation and at least three directors and officers. One of those three people had to reside in New York.

In addition to the tax benefits a New York corporation would provide the church, Kohn believed that it could also give the church positive publicity. The corporation's articles of incorporation would be public record, he explained, "and the newspapers will undoubtedly make some comments thereon." If Monson provided him with a statement of the purposes of this new religious corporation, and made the statement as fulsome as possible, the church could take advantage of the public nature of the articles of incorporation to "bring to the attention of the public fully what it stands for and its purpose."[29] Incorporating in New York would not merely provide the church with tax benefits (though it

98 · FRONTIER RELIGION, FRONTIER TAXATION

would clearly provide those benefits): by the public nature of incorporation, this tax-efficient move would also help the church in its proselyting goals.

Monson forwarded Kohn's letter and legal briefs to the First Presidency. He believed that Kohn's letter laid out clearly the church's situation. He also reiterated to them that the church had to pay its 1917 property tax and again ask for exemption for 1918.

Monson also added his own analysis to Kohn's. He worried that the denial of exemption the church faced in New York might repeat itself in Pennsylvania, in Massachusetts, in Vermont, or in another state with tax laws similar to those of New York. To avoid that possibility, he again asked that they approve the incorporation of the New York Branch of the Eastern States Mission. Alternatively, if they preferred to avoid creating an additional corporation, Monson volunteered to hold title personally in his capacity as president of the mission. He promised them that "the responsibility and confidence entailed in such action will not be betrayed"[30] (though even without betrayal, reposing ownership of the property in an individual complicated the church's perpetual holding of the property and put it at some risk of forfeiture).

On August 10, Monson again wrote to Salt Lake. He informed the church leadership that he had spoken with Kohn the day before and that Kohn had reiterated the need to move quickly. If the church wanted to ensure a property tax exemption for 1918, it had to receive its state charter by October 1. Before it could receive a state charter, the attorneys would need to draft and file articles of incorporation with the state. He reminded the church leaders that Kohn would not require any additional payment to draft and file the articles of incorporation but also emphasized that Kohn wanted instructions about what to do as soon as possible.[31]

Four days later, George Gibbs, secretary to the First Presidency, responded to Monson's letter. Church counsel Richards was on vacation on the coast, Gibbs informed Monson. But Smith had recently seen him and Richards had assured Smith that he was thinking about whether the church should form a New York corporation. Gibbs assured Monson that Richards and the First Presidency would confer and decide on a course of action "in ample time for Messrs. Kohn and Koch to prepare and file the articles of incorporation before October 1st."[32]

Upon receiving a forwarded copy of Gibbs's letter, Kohn wrote back emphasizing the need for immediate action. It was not good enough for the church to file articles of incorporation before October 1, he explained. If the church wanted to ensure that its New York property would be exempt from taxation in 1918, it needed the state to issue the charter, it needed title to the property to pass to the new corporation, *and* it needed the title to be recorded, all before October

1. To ensure that all of the steps occurred in time, Kohn requested that Gibbs "ask Mr. Richards to give me an early reply to my communications."[33]

Richards arrived home on August 25[34] and took Kohn's timeframe to heart. By the end of the month, the First Presidency had decided on the strategy they wanted to pursue. The church had always considered it "inadvisable" to fracture its corporate identity, creating different corporations in different states to hold property. Similarly, it did not believe that vesting title to church property in a single person was a good idea.

Still, church leaders believed it was in their best interest for the church's New York property to be exempt from state property tax. Thus, the First Presidency decided to pursue the same type of ownership it had adopted in some other states: New York property would be "held by three church officials as Joint Tenants." The church leaders proposed that the property be held by church president Joseph F. Smith, Presiding Bishop Charles W. Nibley, and—so that there was at least one New York resident—Walter Monson.[35] Because New York law exempted religious property held by an officer of the religion on its behalf from property tax, transferring title to the three men would effect the exemption the church was so eager to achieve.

Owning property as joint tenants would give Smith, Nibley, and Monson equal rights to use the property during their lifetimes, as well as allowing the survivors to automatically inherit the property rights of the joint tenant who died.[36] In the first days of New York's legal history, two or more people who held property automatically held it as joint tenants, but New York quickly ended the default rule. By 1917, if people wanted to hold property as joint tenants, the conveyance of the property had to expressly provide that it would be held as joint tenants.[37]

To make it happen, the First Presidency sent Monson the executed deeds transferring title in the property to the three men. They instructed him to have Kohn inspect the documents to make sure that they met New York's requirements and, if they did, to have the deeds recorded.

Along with the executed deeds, the First Presidency sent a number of other documents to ensure that New York recognized the transfer. They sent a copy of the title insurance, a copy of the law under which the Corporation of the Presiding Bishop had been incorporated, and a copy of the Corporation of the Presiding Bishop's articles of incorporation. They hoped that these documents would provide evidence to New York of the Corporation of the Presiding Bishop's legal right to both acquire and transfer property.

Upon receiving the church leaders' letter, Monson immediately went to the church's New York counsel. He thoroughly discussed the transaction's

100 · FRONTIER RELIGION, FRONTIER TAXATION

implications with them. In the end, Kohn agreed to go to the tax collector to ask whether the change in legal ownership would allow the church to take its Brooklyn properties off the tax rolls. The church's New York attorneys explained that the tax collector appeared to have "discretionary powers beyond the letter of the law" when it came to determining what property was taxable.

Monson's outrage and sense of persecution had not diminished, even with an end in sight. Earlier he had complained that other foreign churches, similar to the Mormon Church, qualified for property tax exemption in New York. He had since learned that these other churches' property qualified not because of the general tax exemption but because of special legislation explicitly granting them exemption.[38]

The type of targeted tax exemption Monson complained of had been common until the mid-nineteenth century. Prior to the Civil War, state taxation was often ad hoc, uncontroversial, and ungrounded in any type of policy considerations. States did not have general incorporation laws, so corporations were chartered by special legislative action and, in many cases, the legislation that chartered a church would also explicitly grant the church a property tax exemption.

By the middle of the nineteenth century, however, states began to move toward a norm of universal taxation. Under this modern norm, people began to worry that "the contractualizing of tax exemptions would create a permanent limitation upon government flexibility and authority and enshrine the dead hand of the past." While property tax exemptions granted in organizations' charters did not entirely disappear, after the Civil War they became increasingly rare.[39]

Even if New York had still been granting special legislative property tax exemptions in 1917, Monson did not believe that the church should pursue that avenue. In his opinion, it would be "folly to attempt to get by the New York Legislature with a bill favoring the 'Mormon' church in that we are so unpopular." Still, his perception was that New York law specifically favored some select churches rather than treating all alike, a state of affairs he considered "strange."

For all his perception of discrimination against the Mormon Church, Monson also recognized that the church enjoyed some local support. He reported that some of his neighbors were so outraged by the court's determination that the Mormon Church's property did not qualify for tax exemption that they had petitioned the state asking that "this injustice based upon pure technicality be set aside."

Monson also requested that the church send Richards to New York indefinitely. He believed that, as the church's attorney and as a member of the church, Richards understood both the church's legal and spiritual affairs and that his

A Corporate Church in Brooklyn · 101

presence would help sway New York officials. At the same time, though, he did not want to alienate the church's New York counsel. So, in addition to asking that the church send Richards to New York, Monson asked that church leaders not tell Kohn that it had been his idea.[40]

Richards appears to have declined Monson's invitation to relocate to New York. He did, however, quickly provide advice to Smith and his counselors in response to Monson's letter. In the past several weeks, his opinion about the best course of action had changed. While in August the church had been moving toward having the property held personally by three joint tenants, now Richards advised church leaders that they should take Kohn's advice and form a New York corporation.

He still felt that as a general rule, the church should not form corporations under the laws of states other than Utah unless the state had permanent Mormon wards or branches *and* state law allowed for corporations sole. In spite of his strong preference for corporations formed under Utah law, though, Richards could "not see any other way of saving the large amount that would be required annually to pay taxes on this property." To ensure that the church's Brooklyn property qualified for the property tax exemption, Richards agreed that the church could form a New York religious corporation to hold title to the Brooklyn property in spite of New York's lack of corporations sole. He felt confident that the arrangement would be safe; after all, two of the three board members of the new corporation would be comprised of the church president and the Presiding Bishop of the church. He did, however, want to ensure that the articles of incorporation permitted board meetings to occur outside of the state of New York.

In anticipation of the First Presidency's approval, Richards had prepared a deed to transfer the property to a to-be-formed New York corporation.[41] At 8:00 p.m. on September 24, Monson presided over a meeting to incorporate the Eastern States Mission of the Church of Jesus Christ of Latter Day Saints. Thirty-seven members in good standing with the church attended and voted unanimously to form the New York corporation.[42] The church's New York attorneys forwarded the articles of incorporation and an application for a corporate charter to the Secretary of State.

In light of the creation of a New York corporation, Monson also returned the deed that (indirectly) conveyed land from the Corporation of the Presiding Bishop to himself, Smith, and Nibley as joint tenants. (Interestingly, the deeds had been drafted so that the church would convey title to Arthur Winter who, in turn, would convey the land to the three church leaders.) In its place, Monson had received a deed conveying title to the Brooklyn property to him personally.

102 · FRONTIER RELIGION, FRONTIER TAXATION

In turn, he had immediately executed a deed transferring title to the property to the newly-formed corporation.[43]

New York law required a staggered board, so Monson was elected to a three-year term, Smith to a two-year term, and Nibley to a one-year term.[44] With all of this done, Monson reported, the church's New York attorneys believed that the property would qualify for tax exemption for 1918 and for subsequent years. Monson agreed, writing, "I trust that this action will ensure our rights to the benefits of tax exemption law."[45]

Monson seems to have been correct. Creating the corporate Eastern States Mission of the Church of Jesus Christ of Latter Day Saints and transferring title to the Mormon Church's New York property allowed the church to avoid paying property taxes going forward. But while the property tax exemption forced the Mormon Church to adopt a corporate structure it would have preferred to avoid, it did not effectively create the protestantizing effect that the New York law intended. With two of the three board seats filled by top church hierarchs, the church managed to largely avoid lay control over its New York property. The primary function of the New York corporation was to manage real property in New York, and the president of the board could acquire and dispose of real property provided he got the written approval of one other trustee.[46] Because two of the trustees were church leaders based in Salt Lake, essentially, the by-laws circumvented the lay control New York tried to impose on Catholicism and other hierarchical religions.

Kohn was also correct that acting quickly was critical to the church if it wanted to avoid property taxes for 1918. True to his word, Kohn pursued an appeal of Justice Thompkins's ruling that the Mormon Church, as a foreign entity, did not qualify for a New York property tax exemption. In May 1918 the Appellate Division upheld Justice Thompkins's ruling. The court accepted, for the sake of its ruling, both that the Corporation of the Presiding Bishop of the Church of Jesus Christ of Latter-day Saints was a religious corporation and that it used its land exclusively for religious purposes.

In spite of the fact that the church met these two statutory criteria, the Appellate Division agreed that, based on prior court decisions, New York's property tax exemption was only available to corporations formed under New York law. Because the church's property had been held in 1917 by a non-New York corporation, property tax had properly been assessed on its property.[47]

Forming a New York corporate entity before October 1, 1917, then, had saved the Mormon Church from having to pay property taxes for 1918 and subsequent years. In spite of its preference for a single, integral corporate identity and for corporations sole, the church chose to act against its preferences for the sake of tax benefits.

A Corporate Church in Brooklyn · 103

Ultimately, this move had little substantive impact on how the church operated. While the New York corporation had one director who lived in New York, the board was dominated by its Salt Lake members. Central church leadership continued to control the operations of the church and its property in New York.

Adding a new corporation did add some degree of complexity and cost to church operations, though. The church now had to be aware of and comply with New York's laws and rules regulating corporate behavior. It was willing to do so to eliminate its property taxes, though, demonstrating the power of tax to alter even religious behavior.

While necessary to avoid New York property tax, the change proved temporary. In 1949, New York courts reassessed the state's requirements for church property tax exemptions. The Williams Institutional Colored Methodist Episcopal Church challenged a property tax assessed against real estate it owned on West 130th Street in Harlem. The parent church, incorporated in Arkansas, financed the purchase and, for a period of time, held title to the Manhattan real property. Like the Mormon Church, several years after it bought the property, the Williams Institutional Colored Methodist Episcopal Church formed a New York corporation to hold the property. But it also challenged the property tax assessment for the period of time the property was owned directly by the Arkansas corporation.

The trial court acknowledged the precedent set by the Mormon Church's litigation thirty years earlier. But it also believed that the earlier courts had been wrong. Subsequent precedent had clarified that "where the exemption in the statute is express, as it here is, an institution within the exemption is mandatorily exempt and the courts may not insert qualifying clauses or add conditions not contained in the Act." Furthermore, where property falls squarely within an express exemption to property tax, "assessors in making an assessment are without jurisdiction and act illegally and not merely erroneously."[48] The next year, the court of appeals agreed.[49] As of 1950, a church that owned property in New York could qualify for a property tax exemption on that property even if the church was incorporated in another state.

Still, the Mormon Church did not immediately dissolve the corporate Eastern States Mission of the Church of Jesus Christ of Latter Day Saints. In 1952—two years after New York courts determined that a foreign church could own exempt property in New York—the church called Delbert G. Taylor to preside over the Eastern States Mission.[50] A couple years later, he wrote to the church's First Presidency and told them that when he arrived, the minutes and other corporate documents were a mess and the bylaws and other governing documents were "cumbersome and difficult to keep in order." To modernize the corporation and keep up with legal developments, he amended the articles of incorporation and revised the corporation's bylaws.[51] The corporation adopted the amended certificate and revised bylaws on April 23, 1955, five years after the courts had rendered the original need for a New York corporate identity superfluous.[52]

* * *

Again the church had proved its willingness to adapt in the face of tax law hostile to its preferences. Its change in corporate form in Brooklyn was less drastic than its temporary abandonment of tithing. While church leaders preferred the church to be a single entity incorporated as a Utah corporation sole, it had no scriptural or doctrinal commitment to the form, just familiarity and comfort. Still, to procure tax advantages, the church was willing—indefinitely—to abandon its familiarity and comfort.

But while the church's New York corporate entity existed longer than the church's brief abolishment of tithing, in the end, it too went away. In 1959, the Eastern States Mission sold property it held in Elmira, NY to John Lyon and William Davis. A court had to approve the sale, though, and needed a corporate resolution authorizing it.[53] Gerald G. Smith, president of the Eastern States Mission, quickly provided that resolution.[54] But the sale hit a second roadblock: when the buyers' attorney requested a certified copy of the certificate of incorporation, the New York Secretary of State replied that it had no record of the Eastern States Mission of the Church of Jesus Christ of Latter Day Saints.[55] Smith forwarded the question to the First Presidency,[56] which responded in January 1960, with the date of incorporation, the name of the clerk who had accepted it, and the certificate number.[57]

Around this time, the church had also begun a push to eliminate ward and stake corporations, except where they served a necessary legal purpose.[58] Pursuant to this policy, and with the ability of the church to hold tax-exempt property without a New York corporation, the church eventually dissolved the corporate Eastern States Mission of the Church of Jesus Christ of Latter Day Saints.[59] It again held its New York property in its Utah corporate solution.

In addition, as a coda to its tax experience in New York, it no longer owns the chapel at issue in Brooklyn. At some point prior to the 1980s, the church sold its Brooklyn building to the Evening Star Baptist Church.[60] Still, it owns many other properties in New York. And as long as it uses those properties for religious purposes, they are exempt from New York taxes even though they are owned by a Utah corporation.

PART II

Tinkering around the Edges of Tax and Religion

On February 3, 1913, Delaware, Wyoming, and New Mexico ratified the Sixteenth Amendment, breaking the three-quarters threshold necessary to amend the US Constitution and expressly allow for an unapportioned federal income tax. Eight months later, President Woodrow Wilson signed the first federal income tax act of the twentieth century, ushering in the modern era of taxation.[1]

The new federal income tax was part of a Progressive Era shift from funding government through a partisan, regressive system of tariffs and excise taxes to a professionalized regime of taxes focusing on income and wealth transfers.[2] Even the professionalization of federal taxes did not automatically reform the chaotic series of state taxes though. After all, the federal government has done little to constrain states in their adoption of state and local tax rules.[3] Nonetheless, today state income taxes share the general structure of the federal income tax, including its objective and professionalized nature.[4] And while the Sixteenth Amendment did not affect states' ability to impose taxes, states also adopted the ethos of this new era of professionalized tax regimes. New federal tax practices often found their way into state tax law.[5]

The early decades of the twentieth century also saw the professionalization of many non-US tax regimes. By the 1920s, as national economies began to both collide and depend on each other, a number of supranational organizations began to collaborate on tax policy; while each country remained sovereign and controlled its own internal tax policy, many began to draw from the same collection of experts and aim toward the same tax results.[6]

The Mormon Church's post-1920s relationship to taxes reflects this professionalization of national and international tax regimes. Instead of trying to comply with—and design—various ad hoc tax systems, based more on tradition than economic theory, the question became how to operate within a routinized and "scientific" fiscal regime. No longer on the physical or metaphorical frontier, no longer operating within a tax system of radical creation and discovery, the church had to exist within a broad, far-reaching bureaucratic state.

The following chapters, then, move from the chronological development of the first half of the book to a topical development. In the modern tax systems of the twentieth and twenty-first centuries, the Mormon Church began to explore the boundaries that the state placed on members' tax obligations and on its tax exemption. Similar questions would come up periodically and frequently would result in similar consequences.

While the following chapters deal largely with issues that arise after 1920, the same issues the church engaged with in the latter half of its existence also, at times, predated the establishment of modern taxation. On occasion, then, the chapters will dip back into the late nineteenth and early twentieth centuries, highlighting both the ways church-state interaction differed and remained constant between the different time periods and tax regimes. Ultimately, these chapters will illustrate the ways religious organizations find themselves enmeshed in and engaged with the modern administrative state, and how that entanglement plays out in both state and church policy.

8

Mormon Protest Against Taxation

The United States has a long history of pushing back against taxes. One of its foundational myths depicts colonists rebelling against a British tax on tea. (In fact, the Boston Tea Party was in response to the British government undercutting other tea suppliers by dumping cheap tea into the colonies.) Irrespective of the underlying causes of the Boston Tea Party, however, it has entered the collective memory of the nation as a protest against unfair taxation.[1]

The Boston Tea Party was not the last time Americans objected to taxes. Tax protest has a long and storied history in the United States. Until the twentieth century, objection to taxes led from "one rebellion to another."[2] By the twentieth century, violent tax revolts had largely (though not entirely) subsided. But the anti-tax rhetoric continued, potentially compromising the legitimacy of both taxes and the government itself.[3]

Mormons were not immune from this anti-tax sentiment. Like other Americans, they pushed back against their obligation to pay to support the government. Mostly, that opposition remained at the theoretical level; like other Americans, Mormons might object to their taxpaying obligations, but they nonetheless pay their taxes. Mormon discomfort with taxes grew throughout the twentieth century, though, peaking in the 1970s. Faced with widespread tax rebellion among its members, the Mormon Church had to decide whether and how to respond. The buildup to this inflection point was slow, though, and mirrored general American arguments against taxes.

On Taxation without Representation

On February 12, 1870, S.A. Mann, the acting governor of the Territory of Utah, signed legislation granting women in the territory the right to vote. The rest of the country was deeply interested in how suffrage would affect the Mormons' peculiar institution of polygamy. In fact, before the Territory enfranchised its women, Congress had considered granting the vote to the women of Utah. Indiana Representative George Washington Julian believed that his bill to grant Utah's women the right to vote would empower them to eliminate polygamy.[4] The *New York Times* agreed, writing that women's suffrage in Utah would mark the end both of polygamy and, perhaps, of Mormonism.[5]

Representative Julian, the *New York Times*, and any other Americans who expected women's suffrage in Utah to signal the end of polygamy (and perhaps Mormonism) found, instead, disappointment. Utah women immediately took advantage of the franchise, actively participating in the public affairs of Utah. They did not, however, end polygamy. With Utah women unwilling to eliminate Mormonism's plural marriages, Congress would have to address polygamy directly. In 1882, it passed the Edmonds Act. Among other things, the Act disenfranchised all polygamous women and men. And then, in 1887, Congress amended the Edmonds-Tucker Act. One provision of the updated law disenfranchised *all* of the women in the Utah Territory, polygamous or not.[6]

The loss of Utah women's seventeen years of voting undoubtedly left a sour taste in Emmeline B. Wells's mouth. Wells spent decades of her life working on behalf of women; among other roles she played in advocating for women, she headed the Utah Women's Suffrage Association in the mid-1890s.[7]

Wells also had experience with polygamy. In 1852, shortly after her second husband died, she became a plural wife to Daniel H. Wells. While she and her children lived separately from her husband and his other wives, her marriage to Daniel Wells lasted until his death in 1891.[8] On September 5, 1894, three years after her husband's death, Wells recorded in her journal that she had visited the courthouse and paid her taxes for the first time. While her home had belonged to her, her late husband had previously paid the property taxes she owed.

As befitted a suffragist, she was torn about paying the taxes. She wrote that she "felt very much like protesting against Taxation without Representation but in view of so soon having Statehood and perhaps Woman Suffrage I am willing to bide the time."[9]

Her reference to *taxation without representation* alluded to the famous Revolutionary War motto, but it also had a more recent antecedent. The slogan had been adopted sporadically by suffragists in their calls to grant women the right

Mormon Protest Against Taxation • 109

to vote, especially during the centennial celebrations of the country's independence. In 1873, the "women of New England who believe that 'TAXATION WITHOUT REPRESENTATION IS TYRRANY'" invited the public to a commemoration of the Boston Tea Party. The celebration would feature speeches, poetry, music, and refreshments. The New England Woman Suffrage Association would use all proceeds to "secur[e] for Woman the application of the principle which made the Tea Party, a hundred years ago, so worthy of celebration to-day."[10]

Three years later, the organizers of the country's centennial celebration in Philadelphia denied members of the National Woman Suffrage Association a place on the celebration's program. Susan B. Anthony and four others nonetheless stormed the stage and presented the Declaration of the Rights of the Women of the United States.[11] The Declaration laid out nine articles of impeachment. The fourth again invoked the Revolutionary slogan, reading:

> TAXATION WITHOUT REPRESENTATION, the immediate cause of the rebellion of the colonies against Great Britain, is one of the grievous wrongs the women of this country have suffered during the century. Deploring war, with all the demoralization that follows in its train, we have been taxed to support standing armies, with their waste of life and wealth. Believing in temperance, we have been taxed to support the vice, crime and pauperism of the liquor traffic. While we suffer its wrongs and abuses infinitely more than man, we have no power to protect our sons against this giant evil. During the temperance crusade, mothers were arrested, fined, imprisoned, for even praying and singing in the streets, while men blockade the sidewalks with impunity, even on Sunday, with their military parades and political processions. Believing in honesty, we are taxed to support a dangerous army of civilians, buying and selling the offices of government and sacrificing the best interests of the people. And, moreover, we are taxed to support the very legislators and judges who make laws, and render decisions adverse to woman. And for refusing to pay such unjust taxation, the houses, lands, bonds and stock of women have been seized and sold within the present year, thus proving Lord Coke's assertion, that "The very act of taxing a man's property without his consent is, in effect, disfranchising him of every civil right."[12]

Suffragists in several US cities also formed taxpayer associations and anti-tax leagues. Those activists who refused to pay taxes without access to the ballot box could, however, pay a steep price. As Anthony highlighted, the state often seized their property, including their homes and cattle, and sold it at foreclosure sales to cover suffragists' unpaid tax obligations.[13]

110 • TINKERING AROUND THE EDGES OF TAX AND RELIGION

Ultimately, in spite of its rhetorical salience and occasional invocation, the *no taxation without representation* slogan played a minor role in suffragists' demands for granting women the right to vote.[14] Similarly, the slogan played a nonexistent role in Wells's work for woman suffrage. While she considered not paying her tax in 1894, she decided better of the impulse. In 1895, she again recorded in her diary that she "called at the City & County building and paid my taxes."[15]

So she was shocked a month later when she was informed that a portion of her taxes were due. She knew she had already paid and, though she was leading a meeting, she immediately stepped away, upset, to figure out what had happened. She talked to John D. Spencer, the Salt Lake County tax collector,[16] but found him "very unsatisfactory, and not at all courteous." Ultimately, she discovered that the tax was on property owned by Emeline *Young* Wells that had been misattributed to her, and she delivered the news to the other Emeline's husband.[17]

While Wells had absorbed the suffragist indignation at paying taxes without access to the ballot box, her indignation never materialized into action. It existed purely as an entry in her journal, a reflection on the unfairness of unrepresented taxpaying. She did not, however, want to lose her home, and she studiously complied with her property tax obligations.[18]

Reed Smoot and the Modern Income Tax

After the Civil War federal income tax expired in 1873, federal income taxation disappeared for forty years. While those who believed that tariffs fell too heavily on the poor and too lightly on the rich made some noise about replacing tariffs with a permanent federal income tax, it took until 1894 for Congress to actually enact one.

But the Supreme Court struck that income tax down as unconstitutional.[19] It took another fifteen years for Congress to enact a corporate income tax (styled an *excise* tax to elide any potential constitutional problems).[20] The corporate excise tax tipped Utah Senator (and Mormon apostle) Reed Smoot's hand as an opponent of income taxation. While he could not prevent its passage, he joined with Senator John Kean in procedurally delaying the Senate's vote on the tax.[21]

Four years later, in 1913, Congress expanded the reach of income taxation beyond corporations. That year, the states ratified the Sixteenth Amendment, which authorized Congress to enact an unapportioned income tax.[22] With that explicit constitutional permission, Congress immediately enacted the first modern federal income tax.

The federal income tax found support through an "uneasy coalition of Democrats and western Republicans."[23] But while western Republicans broadly supported federal income tax, there was a notable exception: Utah was one of the three states that rejected the Sixteenth Amendment and never subsequently ratified it.[24] A decade after the ratification of the Sixteenth Amendment and the implementation of the income tax, Utah Senator William H. King, a Democrat, excoriated Republican Senator Smoot's record. King reminded his audience that

> [i]n 1893 the Democrats proposed an income tax law intended to tax the incomes of such men as J. P. Morgan and John D. Rockefeller, who were making 50 to 75 million a year, yet they paid no tax on that excessive income. When the constitutional amendment was offered to make that bill a law the state of Utah (Smoot and Spry) voted against it to our everlasting shame.

While the Amendment—and the federal income tax—eventually passed, King noted that Smoot continued to try to undermine the ability of the income tax to reach the wallets of the wealthy. The previous year, Smoot had "voted to reduce the excess profits tax which the rich had to pay from 65 per cent down to 20 per cent." He also voted to remove a tax on large estates and, by doing so, he "added $155,000,000 to the poor man's burden."[25]

When Smoot arrived in Washington, DC in 1903 as a Senator-elect from Utah, he was entering the second of two leadership roles he filled. Three years earlier, he had been elevated to the Quorum of the Twelve Apostles.[26] As such, during his time in the Senate, he was both a religious and a political leader. In spite of his dual roles, when he acted as a Senator, he generally was not acting as a Mormon apostle. He did not take direction from church leaders, largely because he felt no need to. In Smoot's mind, stand-pat Republicanism was entirely compatible with Mormonism. Moreover, church presidents Joseph F. Smith and Heber J. Grant "made no definite requests of Reed Smoot in respect to general legislation. Similarity of economic and social philosophy among the three as a general rule made such action unnecessary."[27]

Though Smoot opposed the income tax, once it passed, church leaders counted on his expertise to guide them in understanding the church's obligations under the new law. Smoot was sensitive to the church's needs with respect to the tax law. On January 22, 1914, the church's First Presidency wrote to Smoot asking him about the Mormon Church's exempt status. Church leaders were particularly concerned about language in the statute that allowed an exemption for organizations "organized *and operated* exclusively for religious" purposes.

Their concern? They had heard rumors that the government had assessed taxes against Trinity Church on that church's income from investments and business endeavors. At the time of the letter, the church held interest coupons on Utah Light and Railway Company bonds. (Corporations borrow money by

112 · TINKERING AROUND THE EDGES OF TAX AND RELIGION

issuing bonds. At the end of the bond's term, the corporation is responsible for paying back the face amount of the bond. And during the life of the bond, it also pays holders interest, called "coupon payments." In the early twentieth century, bonds literally came with perforated coupons attached to them. When each coupon became due, bondholders could detach it and deliver it to a bank in exchange for the interest payment.)

The church stood to collect $14,225 in coupon payments, but it ran into a hiccup in collecting the money: while it had sent the coupons to New York, the bank refused to make the payment without certificates of ownership and exemption. The tax law required any corporation that made payments of certain types of passive income, including interest, to both withhold the normal tax amount and make a tax return for the payee.[28] The church had received—and filled out—the necessary forms and sent them, along with the letter, to Smoot.

The First Presidency believed that other churches had already asked similar questions; in fact, they said, they had waited to ask to allow time for the question to percolate through the system. But at this point, they were in a hurry—to the extent they had to file a tax return, they had to do it by March. And if they wanted to collect the church's coupon interest without any amount being withheld, they had to deliver the church's certificate of exemption by February 1. Thus, they enclosed the certificates and asked Smoot to deliver them to New York as soon as he had considered the question and come to an informed decision.[29]

Five days after the First Presidency sent their letter, Smoot reached out to the Treasury Department to ask whether the church was exempt from taxation. After explaining the church's income and expenditures to the Treasury representative and providing him with portions of the letter from the First Presidency, Smoot requested that the Treasury write an opinion confirming the church's exemption.[30] He did not, however, record in his diary whether the Treasury official provided that opinion. We therefore have no record of whether the coupon payment on the Utah Light and Railroad Company bonds ended up being tax-free in 1914.

In their letter, the First Presidency presciently explained that they had heard that there would be test cases surrounding the question of the taxation of churches' passive income. And on that point, they were absolutely correct. The courts did not, however, provide a definitive answer until a decade after the church wrote to Smoot when the US Supreme Court decided that the relevant question was the use of funds, not the source. Congress deliberately exempted churches from the income tax, and that included an exemption of a church's passive (and even active) endeavors that were necessary to fund its charitable mission.[31] Still, the Supreme Court's eventual decision left a decade during which, in the face of uncertainty, the church had to convince payors not to withhold taxes on payments of passive income.

It is hard to disaggregate Smoot's views on income taxation from the church's, at least in part because generally, the church's interest lined up with Utah's. While Smoot was perfectly willing to break with his region and oppose income taxation, he was a great proponent of tariffs. Tariffs are taxes on imported goods. While the importers nominally pay the tax, they pass the cost of tariffs on to consumers through higher prices. The idea that consumers bear the burden of tariffs is not new—people generally understood it in the nineteenth century. While tariffs may have been harmful to US consumers, though, producers supported not only maintaining, but increasing, the tariff burden on imported goods.[32] By increasing the cost of imported goods, tariffs protect the profits of US producers (who are not subject to domestic tariffs) by increasing the price of imported goods.

Why did Smoot, presumably with the approval of the Mormon Church, support tariffs? The Mormon Church was invested in sugar beets, which competed with imported sugar. In 1890, church president Wilford Woodruff sent members of the Quorum of the Twelve to raise money for the Utah Sugar Company. He had also caused the church to invest in the company, claiming a revelatory injunction to help build a sugar factory. Over the next two decades, church-supported sugar companies began to sprout around Utah and Idaho.

In 1907, three of the largest merged to form the Utah-Idaho Sugar Company, a $13 million company that, together with the Mormon Church-supported Amalgamated Sugar Company, dominated the Western sugar industry. The fortunes of these companies were tied closely to the Mormon Church, with church presidents serving as corporate presidents and with other hierarchical church leaders sitting on the companies' boards of directors.[33]

Federal policy aided the church's production of sugar beets. In 1909, the tariff on sugar represented the country's largest source of tariff revenue. Congress worried that the tariff-free importation of sugar from the Philippines and the explosive growth of Western beet sugar threatened that revenue.[34]

The tariff on imported sugar meant that Mormon beet sugar could undercut—or at least compete with—imported sugar, a position that Smoot understood well. In fact, it is possible that protectionist concerns about sugar beets played a role in his opposition to income taxation. In 1912, Congress passed a Free Sugar bill, substantially reducing the tariff on imported sugar. To make up for the lost revenue (estimated to be as high as $50 million), Congress intended to pair it with a 1 percent tax on corporate and individual incomes in excess of $5,000.[35]

114 • TINKERING AROUND THE EDGES OF TAX AND RELIGION

The desire to replace the sugar tariff with an income tax went back at least to the middle of the 1890s when Senator Anthony Higgins argued that a proposed sugar duty would "rest more heavily upon the poor people of the country than the income tax, for the incomes of the poor are not to be taxed."[36] While Smoot did not point to this link between the reduction of sugar tariffs and the imposition of income taxes as a justification for his opposition to income taxation, their connection was obvious.

Like Smoot, church leaders, including President Smith, supported tariffs on sugar to protect the church's beet sugar interests.[37] The confluence of church and Senator did not go unnoticed by the public. While the church lacked the ability to control the Senate or fix sugar prices by itself, the national press nonetheless pointed out Smoot's self-interest as a leader in the Mormon Church as he voiced support for sugar tariffs. In 1910, *Hampton's Magazine* published an extensive article about the church and its sugar trust. It pointed out that Smoot had pleaded with the Senate to maintain a high tariff on sugar. "Smoot," it wrote. "Smoot the apostle; Smoot the representative of the Mormon Church in the Senate; Smoot the spokesman for this marvelous partnership of Mormonism and the Sugar Trust; that is the man who was pushed to the front to handle the sugar schedule in this year of grace 1909."[38]

As *Hampton's Magazine* pointed out, Smoot undoubtedly felt some pressure from the church to support tariffs. Presiding Bishop Charles Nibley was close friends with Smoot. In addition to his prominent role in the Mormon Church, Nibley served as a member of the board of directors of the Utah-Idaho Sugar Company and, in 1914, became the largest shareholder of the company. Nibley frequently contacted Smoot about issues affecting beet sugar; in 1913, in fact, Smoot shared a detailed description of the Democrats' tariff plan with Nibley.

Still, Smoot vehemently denied accusations that the church influenced his stance on tariffs. He asserted that, when he was in Washington, DC, he represented all of the people in Utah, Mormon or not. He supported tariffs not because the church did, but because they raised workers' wages and contributed to American industry.[39]

The *Salt Lake Tribune* questioned Smoot's assertion that he represented Utahns at large and that he was not beholden to the Mormon Church. At the same time, though, the *Tribune* disputed the idea that an "insidious lobby" approached the Senate "and unduly influenc[ed] members of that body in regard to the Wilson-Underwood tariff bill." The very idea was "futile" and "absurd."[40] (The Wilson-Underwood tariff bill would have reduced or eliminated a number of tariffs, including the tariff on sugar.[41]) Even if Smoot was in the pocket of the church, the *Tribune* believed, his support of tariffs was in the best interest of his constituents. Supporting tariffs did help the Mormon Church, but the protectionism also benefited a significant Utah crop that provided income and wealth to Utahns irrespective of their religious beliefs.[42]

Smoot continued to support tariffs throughout his political career. Perhaps his crowning achievement was the enactment of the Smoot-Hawley Tariff in 1930, which "helped push the average tariff on dutiable imports to near-record levels just as the economy was sliding into the Great Depression,"[43] an inauspicious coda to a career spent, in part, supporting protectionist legislation.

He also continued to oppose excessive taxation and especially higher income tax rates. In 1913, Republican Smoot joined with Democrats in opposing a proposed increase in the tax rate on high-income taxpayers.[44] A year later, in "one of the most forceful speeches of his public career," he decried the administration's war revenue bill, arguing that "no additional levy would have been necessary if the protective tariff law had remained in force." He also found the excuse that the war in Europe made additional taxation necessary baldly pretextual and dishonest.[45] In a church general conference, he boasted that since "the close of [World War I] I have exercised all my power to eliminate every unnecessary expense of our government with a view of lightening the burden of taxation upon the institutions of our country and individual taxpayers."[46]

That said, Smoot was not opposed to all taxes. In addition to his fierce advocacy for protective tariffs, in the early 1920s, he proposed a national sales tax as a simpler way to raise federal revenue.[47] He estimated that a sales tax of 1 percent on all consumer purchases in excess of fifty cents would bring in $1.25 billion annually.[48] But though Smoot found some support for his national sales tax in the Senate, by 1921 it was dead. Smoot remained hopeful that he could pass a national sales tax, but he was the only person who still believed in it. For everybody else, "the longer it was discussed, the more embarrassed became those who had the job of defending it."[49]

In the end, Smoot's preferred vision of federal revenue, a vision he propounded both in the Senate and in his church, never materialized. The federal government shifted from relying primarily on tariffs—which had protected the church's sugar interests—to relying on income taxation. It failed to adopt a national sales tax. And tax rates continued to rise through the middle of the twentieth century, first exclusively targeting the wealthy but, in short order, reaching the pocketbooks of most Americans, wealthy or not.[50]

Mormon Leaders and Opposition to Progressive Taxation

While Smoot opposed income taxation on policy grounds, preferring protective tariffs and sales taxes, once enacted as law, he did not encourage his constituents or coreligionists to disobey the law. During the first half of the twentieth century, there was no organized movement of Mormon tax protestors. In fact, until World War II, it is unlikely that a significant portion of Mormons even had to pay federal income taxes.

Why not? Because in its original iteration, Congress designed the federal income tax to apply to the wealthy; it was not a tax on the middle-class or the poor. That changed with the fiscal exigencies of World War II. When the war started, fewer than eight million Americans (roughly 6 percent of the population) paid federal income taxes. By 1945 the number had more than sextupled to 49.9 million. By the end of the war, nearly 90 percent of employed Americans filed tax returns annually and about 60 percent owed the government some amount of income tax.[51]

In less than a decade, the income tax became relevant to a majority of Americans. And its sudden relevance meant that more people felt its burden.[52] Within twenty-five years of the end of World War II, the country experienced a resurgence of anti-tax sentiment. Tax protests became a significant movement, especially among white middle-class taxpayers in the American West and South.[53]

Mormons were not immune from this new anti-tax movement. But the Mormon tax resisters who emerged could draw on more than the general sense of grievance of other Western tax resisters: Ezra Taft Benson, a high-ranking and deeply politically conservative leader in the church provided them with a religious justification for their objections to tax. Beginning in 1943, Benson served in the Mormon Church's Quorum of the Twelve Apostles. His tenure in that body lasted forty-two years, until, in 1985, he became the church president. His service in church leadership began with the close of World War II and ran throughout the Cold War years, with their fear of encroaching communism.[54]

In 1952, a decade into his service in the Quorum of the Twelve Apostles, Benson received a call from President-elect Dwight Eisenhower offering him a cabinet appointment as Secretary of Agriculture. With the blessing of church president David O. McKay, he accepted the offer.[55]

During his eight years on Eisenhower's cabinet, Benson's already-conservative politics shifted even further rightward. He began to see the rise of communism as part of a worldwide conspiracy, a conspiracy that included prominent members of all three branches of the US government, the civil rights movement, and the United Nations, among others. As he resumed his apostolic duties after

Mormon Protest Against Taxation · 117

his term in government, he also embraced conservative conspiracy theorists and ultra-right-wing organizations, including the John Birch Society, the All-American Society, and the Freemen Institute. He considered unions, welfare, and federal educational aid to be essentially socialistic, putting the United States "on the 'royal road to Communism.'"[56]

Benson believed that the endpoint of this royal road was supremely dangerous. Communism intended to "deprive men and women of their agency, weaken the home and family, and deny the existence of God."[57] Benson's distrust of communism, both religiously and secularly, fit comfortably within the mainstream of twentieth-century Mormonism. In 1936, the church's First Presidency wrote that communism was a "system of government that is the opposite of our Constitutional government" and that supporting communism would be "treasonable to our free institutions." Underscoring the fundamental Americanness of the Mormon Church at the time, the First Presidency went on to declare that "no faithful Church member can be a Communist."[58]

Benson viewed the welfare state as the equivalent of socialism and communism and was not shy about condemning government spending and regulation.[59] In his mind, the appropriate role of government was limited to the protection of its citizens. To actively aid them (for example, through redistributive policies) fell outside of the government's role and was both inappropriate and socialist.[60]

Benson generally focused his condemnation on government spending and regulation. Occasionally, though, he turned his focus to the mechanisms the government used to raise revenue. By the mid-twentieth century, that mechanism was primarily the federal income tax. Since its enactment (over Smoot's objection) in 1913, that income tax had been a progressive tax, meaning higher-income individuals pay taxes at higher marginal tax rates. And during Benson's ministry and government service, high-income individuals faced significant tax rates. During the Eisenhower administration, the top marginal tax rate fluctuated between 91 and 92 percent. It did not fall below 70 percent until the early 1980s, and even then it only dropped to 50 percent. Finally in 1987—two years after Benson became president of the Mormon Church—the top marginal tax rate fell below 50 percent for the first time since 1931.[61]

(It is important to keep in mind that this does not mean that high-income taxpayers paid 91 or 92 percent of their income in taxes. In 1951, for example, the top rate applied to that portion of a taxpayer's income in excess of $200,000; income below that amount was subject to taxes at a far lower rate. In fact, in the 1950s, notwithstanding the high marginal tax rate, the wealthiest 1 percent of Americans paid income taxes at an *average* rate of about 17 percent.[62])

118 · TINKERING AROUND THE EDGES OF TAX AND RELIGION

Benson had a remarkably low view of using taxes to redistribute wealth. During a church general conference, he asserted that the government "providing so-called 'benefits' for some of its citizens" was just a "means for legalized plunder."[63] Frequently he labeled progressive taxation Marxist.[64] And in 1977, he told an audience at BYU, the church-owned university, that many people "are now advocating that which has become a general practice since the early 1930s: a redistribution of wealth through the federal tax system. That, by definition, is socialism!"[65]

Though Benson laid the religious groundwork for Mormon opposition to income taxation, like Smoot he did not suggest that Mormons refuse to pay their taxes. While his rhetoric painted redistributive taxation as a sign of impending communism, Benson's recommendations focused on telling members to avoid communism, to defend the Constitution, and to defend capitalism. So while future Mormon tax protestors may have embraced his view that progressive taxation was indistinguishable from communism, to the extent those tax protestors decided to defy the law, they went beyond any actions he advocated.

Wolves Among the Flock

Soon, what may have been an inchoate (and nominally religiously motivated) opposition to progressive taxation in the hands of Smoot and Benson blossomed into a full-fledged anti-tax movement in the hands of lay Mormons. By the 1960s, American tax resistance had taken a decidedly "western and southern turn."[66] That Western turn included the largely Mormon population of Utah.

These protestors were not, of course, solely Mormons opposed to paying their income taxes. Tax protestors included a broad swath of Americans, from "scripture-quoting Mormons" to "atheistic followers of novelist Ayn Rand." Irrespective of their religious beliefs, these tax protestors acted under the banner of a "strictly interpreted Constitution, minus the 16th Amendment which authorized the income tax they abhor."[67]

The Mormon tax protestors added a distinctly Mormon gloss to this frivolous Constitutional anti-tax movement. In the Doctrine and Covenants, a canonized work of Mormon scripture, God speaks of the "laws and constitution" that "I have suffered to be established." The revelatory voice goes on to explain that God "established the Constitution of this land."[68] On this foundation, subsequent church leaders built a theology that included a divinely inspired US Constitution.[69]

Mormon tax protestors used this idea of a divinely established Constitution to justify their refusal to pay taxes. John Grismore, a church member from Bountiful, Utah, and author of an anti-tax book, claimed that he had a "deep

Mormon Protest Against Taxation • 119

religious conviction" that laws conflicting with his interpretation of the Constitution were "null and void." And, notwithstanding the Sixteenth Amendment, he viewed the federal income tax as in conflict with his Constitution. Francis Maloney, another Mormon from Mesa, Arizona, claimed during his trial for tax evasion that his membership in the Mormon Church obligated him to refuse to pay his taxes.[70] Karl Bray, a precious metals dealer in Salt Lake City, made the exceptional claim that Utah was at the heart of the tax protest movement. He estimated that the state, with its population of about 1.2 million,[71] was home to 14,000 tax protestors.[72] (The IRS disputed his numbers, claiming that fewer than 100 Utahns had filed tax protest returns.[73])

Mormon tax protestors' claim that their religion forbade them from paying taxes was belied by the history of the church's interactions with taxation. Even if those protestors did sincerely believe that the taxpaying violated their religious principles, though, that belief did not shield them from the consequences of their refusal to pay. For instance, on his 1972 tax return, Bray claimed more withholding exemptions than he qualified for and, rather than filling out the required fields on his return, he wrote, "5th amendment. Go to Hell; Do not pass Go, do not collect $200." A jury convicted him of failure to file a tax return and falsifying a tax withholding statement, both misdemeanors.[74]

While these Mormon tax protestors believed paying federal income tax was inconsistent with their religion, their church disagreed. L.S. Brown, a Richfield, Utah, dentist and member of the Church of Jesus Christ of Latter-day Saints, was convicted of tax crimes and sentenced to three concurrent one-year terms in prison. He believed that there were "many things worth going to jail for," though he regretted the hardship his trial and imprisonment imposed on his wife and six children. Brown's religious leaders told him that, if he lost his appeals, he would face a church court proceeding and would probably be excommunicated. (By this point, church courts had shifted from being a substitute for civil courts to a site for religious disciplinary actions. Facing a church court was standard procedure for members convicted of a felony.) Brown was less concerned about the church court because he believed he would get a fair hearing for his side of the story in the church proceeding, something he claimed that the trial court did not allow him.[75]

But perhaps Brown should have had less confidence in his chances at the ecclesiastical level. The widespread Mormon tax protests proved an embarrassment to the church. In the church's October 1972 General Conference, new church president Harold B. Lee warned his listeners about "wolves among the flock, trying to lead some who are weak and unwary among Church members, according to reports that have reached us, who are taking the law into their own

120 · TINKERING AROUND THE EDGES OF TAX AND RELIGION

hands by refusing to pay their income tax because they have some political disagreement with constituted authorities." To those who preached law-breaking through tax evasion, Lee underscored that Mormon scripture demanded obedience to the law.[76]

The next year, the church followed up on Lee's address, issuing a "Priesthood Bulletin." In that Bulletin, the church reaffirmed its opposition to tax protestors who claimed the church supported their refusal to comply with their federal income tax obligations. It instructed local church leaders that they should "be on guard against such persons." The church would not give them a platform to spread their anti-tax ideology. "They are not to be invited to speak in priesthood or sacrament meetings, firesides, or other Church meetings in attempting to spread their propaganda."[77]

These condemnations of illegal tax protests proved unsuccessful at stemming the tide of anti-tax protestors in the church. So in 1976, church leaders increased the religious pressure on members to comply with their tax obligations. The church announced that conviction for tax evasion or tax fraud would automatically lead to a church court proceeding which could impose ecclesiastical penalties, up to and including excommunication. Moreover, church leaders instructed bishops and stake presidents to ask known tax protestors about their tax payments during temple recommend interviews. (At the time, members who wanted to participate in liturgical ceremonies in the temple had to interview annually for a "recommend" that allowed them to enter the temple.) Church president Spencer Kimball and his counselors underscored the importance of tax compliance with local Mormon leaders in "closed door 'solemn assemblies' throughout the country."

This time, the church's condemnation of tax evasion proved more effective. In 1976, Roland Wise, the Utah director of the IRS, reported that, while Utah had previously been home to a disproportionate share of tax protestors, "there seems to be a turnaround now in this area." Between the risk of jail time and the church's renewed push for tax compliance, Wise described a "surge" in taxpayer compliance, as well as a desire among Utahns to "square away with the law,"[78] sometimes literally. In 1978, the Utah State Treasurer received an anonymous letter, accompanied by a $3,000 cashier's check. The letter writer admitted that they had not paid all of their income taxes for more than twenty years, rationalizing that the government would have wasted the money "by sending it to foreign governments." The writer had since "repented and paid an honest tax for many years." But, according to Mormon practice, "true repentance requires restitution," and the letter writer sent their unpaid taxes, anonymously, to truly repent.[79]

Still, Mormons are not automatons, inevitably and invariably following the mandates of their religious leaders. While the church's crackdown on tax evasion

Mormon Protest Against Taxation • 121

increased members' compliance with the tax law, it did not eliminate tax evasion by Mormons altogether. The same year the Utah Treasurer received an anonymous cashier's check, the IRS determined that James and Jean Smith had underpaid their taxes between 1971 and 1973 and, as a result, owed the government $5,715.53. The Smiths disagreed and sued the IRS in the Tax Court. They made a number of frivolous arguments for why they did not owe taxes.

Their two principal arguments were common among tax protestors and had no particular religious valence. First, they claimed, the Sixteenth Amendment was not properly ratified and as such did not authorize the federal government to impose an income tax. But even if the Sixteenth Amendment had been ratified, they claimed that it only applied to corporations and, because the Smiths were not corporations, the federal government could not tax them. Second, the Smiths argued, they "never received any income in 'constitutional dollars.' The only income they received was in unredeemable Federal Reserve notes which do not constitute income until redeemed."[80]

Not content to merely parrot common and frivolous tax protestor arguments, the Smiths also invoked their Mormonism. Among a "plethora of other contentions" that the Tax Court dismissed as baseless, the Smiths claimed that they had been "singled out and selectively prosecuted by the Internal Revenue Service because they are members of the Church of Jesus Christ of Latter-Day Saints (Mormons) and because of the false belief that members of the Church of the Latter-Day Saints constitute what Federal officials call the 'Tax Rebellion Movement.'"[81] Irrespective of their sincerity in making these secular and religious arguments, the Tax Court dismissed their suit.

Four years after the Smiths invoked a Mormon "Tax Rebellion Movement" and a decade after Lee first spoke about the anti-tax wolves among the flock, the church renewed its attempt to quash Mormon tax evasion and fraud. In January 1983, the church's First Presidency sent a letter to all of the stake and mission presidents in the United States. (Stake presidents in the Mormon Church are lay leaders over a geographic region not unlike a diocese in Catholicism. Mission presidents oversee missionaries serving in a particular geographic mission.[82]) In its letter, the First Presidency reiterated the constitutionality of the federal income tax. Unless and until the Supreme Court reversed its position, income taxation represented the law of the land, and refusing to pay was "in direct conflict with the teachings of the Church."

Apparently, some Mormons decided that the church's guidance on members' *federal* income tax obligations did not apply to state taxes; the First Presidency incredulously reported that some members of the church "also refuse to pay state income taxes." In response, the church leaders not only repeated their counsel on federal income taxes but also "now apply that counsel and

122 • TINKERING AROUND THE EDGES OF TAX AND RELIGION

instruction to state income tax laws." Members who opposed federal or state income tax laws could challenge them in court or could challenge them through legislative means. But, the First Presidency announced, a Mormon who deliberately refused to pay their federal *or* state income taxes was "out of harmony with basic teachings of the church" and ineligible for a temple recommend or a high-profile calling within the church.[83]

That same year, the church added a section on taxpaying to its *General Handbook of Instructions*. In the modern LDS Church, most local ecclesiastical offices are held by lay members who receive no pay for their services and have no formal training in running a congregation. Recognizing the limitations this type of lay leadership represented, in the late nineteenth century, the church began issuing formalized printed guidance to provide its leaders with standardized guidelines. In 1899, the church began to issue a pamphlet entitled "Instructions to Presidents of Stakes, Bishops of Wards and Stake Tithing Clerks" that it updated periodically.

Initially, these pamphlets dealt almost exclusively with tithing. By the 1913 version, though, they had broadened their scope to represent a general leadership handbook. The Presiding Bishopric and the First Presidency issued the first sixteen editions; starting in 1944 the First Presidency alone took on the responsibility for the *General Handbook of Instructions*. After 1983, the Handbooks ceased to credit a particular body; instead, they were issued by the Church of Jesus Christ of Latter-day Saints.[84] The church continued to issue a periodically-updated printed version of its General Handbook of Instructions until 2020 when it shifted to an online-only version.[85]

The last chapter of the 1983 edition of the *General Handbook of Instructions* was entitled "Church Policies." It was a catch-all of policies, ranging from the use of copyrighted material at church to the use of birth control. And between a section on "Business Schemes and Political Causes" and a section on "Fraudulent Claims of Sales Agents" was a section on income taxes. The section read as a direct rebuke to members asserting that they were not subject to the income tax, whether for religious or other reasons:

> All Church members in the United States are obligated by the twelfth article of faith to obey federal and state income tax laws (see also D&C 134:5). If a member disapproves of income tax laws, he may attempt to challenge them in the courts or to have them changed by legislation or constitutional amendment.
>
> A member who refuses to pay federal or state income taxes or to comply with a final judgment in an income tax case is in direct conflict with the law and with the teachings of the Church. Such a member may be ineligible for a temple rec-

ommend and should not be called to a position of principal responsibility in the Church. A member who is convicted of willfully violating federal or state income tax laws should be disciplined by a Church court to the extent warranted by the circumstances.[86]

Given the timing of the First Presidency letter and of the new section, it is hard to read it as anything less than a final, formal rebuke of the 1970s Mormon tax protestors. And largely it appears to have worked. While Mormons may have claimed a central role in tax resistance in the 1970s, since the 1980s, there has not been an identifiable connection between the Salt Lake-based church and criminal tax noncompliance.

Subsequent versions of the *General Handbook of Instructions* have continued to lay out the necessity of members complying with their tax obligations. For many years, the language surrounding Mormons' obligation to pay taxes changed very little. In 1989, the *Handbook* expanded its injunction from members in the United States to "Church members in any nation."[87] In 1998 the language again shifted to church members being obligated to "obey the tax laws of the nation where they reside."[88] Finally, in 2020, as the *Handbook* shifted online, the church's explanation of members' duty to pay their taxes became far more explicit and detailed, expanding the injunction beyond merely income taxes and condemning both refusing to pay taxes and making frivolous arguments:

> Church members are to obey the tax laws of the nation where they live (see Articles of Faith 1:12; Doctrine and Covenants 134:5). Members who disagree with tax laws can challenge them as the laws of their countries permit.
>
> Church members are in conflict with the law and with Church teachings if they:
>
> - Intentionally fail or refuse to pay required taxes.
> - Make frivolous legal arguments to avoid paying taxes.
> - Refuse to comply with a final judgment in a tax proceeding that requires them to pay taxes.
>
> These members may be ineligible for a temple recommend. They should not be called to leadership positions in the Church.
>
> A Church membership council is required if a member is convicted of a felony for violating tax laws. . . .[89]

The church's explicit pro-taxpaying policy seems to have had at least some impact on members, though not always the impact the church intended or anticipated. In rare cases, the church stating its policy could even backfire. For instance, in 1992, prominent church member James "Bo" Gritz wrote to the

First Presidency. Gritz had converted to Mormonism in 1984. After joining the church, he ran for vice president and then for president as part of the far-right Populist Party.[90] In his campaign speeches, Gritz borrowed heavily from church president Benson's earlier conspiracy-laden sermons.[91]

Two years after his failed attempt at the presidency, Gritz formally disaffiliated from the Mormon Church.[92] What triggered his resignation? Among other things, he complained that his stake president refused to approve his temple recommend after Gritz said he did not plan to file his 1993 tax return. Gritz asked his stake president, "Where in the equation of salvation does the (Internal Revenue Service) fit?" but his stake president insisted on seeing Gritz's tax return before approving his temple recommend. Gritz claimed that he had never before failed to file his return and that in 1994 "it made me a little angry that he would place my temple recommend in review because of this damnable IRS situation . . . so I told him I wasn't going to file."[93]

The stake president's zealous enforcement of the church's income tax policy is not universal, of course. Not all members have heeded the church's call to comply with their tax obligations, and not all of those out of compliance have faced any immediate church consequences. For instance, George Thompson, a resident of New Jersey, had been a member of the church his entire life. In the early 2010s, he volunteered in the church's Manhattan temple with several Mormon Church-affiliated Boy Scout troops. Professionally, he served as the president of Compliance Innovations, Inc. He and his wife owned the company through a trust. In 2008, the IRS assessed penalties against Thompson because Compliance Innovations, Inc. had failed to pay its employment tax liabilities in 2004, 2005, and 2007. (Under tax law, the IRS can collect unpaid employment taxes, as well as interest and penalties, from an officer of a corporation that fails to withhold and pay over those taxes.[94])

This was not the Thompsons' first failure to pay taxes, either. Compliance Innovations, Inc. had previously failed to pay its employment taxes in 1999 and 2000 and the Thompsons had failed to pay at least a portion of the income tax they owed in 1992, 1995, 1996, 1999, and 2000. While they had entered into installment agreements with the government to pay their taxes over time, as of 2013 the penalties and taxes remained unpaid.

In spite of his unpaid taxes, local church leaders had done nothing to prevent Thompson from attending the temple and serving in other church callings. He had not, it appears, faced any of the church discipline or ecclesiastical consequences laid out in church policy.

Or rather, he faced no limitations on his church participation *as a result of his failure to pay taxes*. Thompson tried to negotiate an installment agreement with the IRS under which he would pay his various tax liabilities over time. The tax law permits installment agreements but wants to maximize the amount delinquent taxpayers pay and minimize the amount of time over which they pay it. To accomplish this, in calculating the amount a taxpayer can pay the IRS looks at the taxpayer's income and reduces it by the taxpayer's "necessary" expenses.[95]

Thompson reported that he earned $27,633 per month and had necessary expenses of $24,416. His necessary expenses included a budget of $2,680 a month for food, clothing, and other miscellaneous expenses and $4,619 a month for housing and utilities. Under his calculations, he could afford to pay about $3,000 per month toward the nearly $900,000 he owed the federal government.

The IRS allowed most of his claimed expenses but denied three. It disallowed his monthly tithing of $2,110, other church service expenses of $232, and college expenses for his children of $2,952. Without those expenses, the IRS determined that Thompson could afford to pay $8,389 a month toward his tax liability.

Thompson challenged the IRS's determination in court. Among other things, he argued that by refusing to include tithing as a necessary expense, the IRS violated his First Amendment rights. If he did not pay tithing, he explained, the church would require him to resign his ministerial roles.

The court did not accept his First Amendment argument. It reminded Thompson that "it is *his Church* who is requiring him to resign his positions if he does not tithe. The settlement officer did not require petitioner to resign his positions nor did she pressure the Church to require petitioner to resign." The First Amendment does not prohibit a *church* from requiring its members to tithe if they want to hold ministerial roles, but that internal church policy had nothing to do with the state.[96]

The court's opinion marks the end of public access to Thompson's ecclesiastical standing. While he and his church leaders know whether he lost his church roles in the temple and with the Boy Scouts, there is no public record of the end of this story. It is worth noting two things, though. First, if he lost his church roles for failure to pay tithing, that essentially represents the tardy application of church policy. Under the policies laid out in the *General Handbook of Instructions*, he should have lost his positions when he first refused to pay his federal income taxes.

Second, as both a practical and a legal matter, his installment agreement did nothing to prevent him from paying tithing. After allocating the necessary expenses, the IRS does not ensure that taxpayers actually spend their money in the ways laid out. To the extent Thompson wanted to pay tithing, he could have reduced other expenses or earned additional income. He had to pay the

IRS $8,389 each month. Once he did that, how he used the rest of his money was up to him.

* * *

By the twentieth century, the church no longer had any direct involvement in the creation of tax law or its enforcement. Since losing control of the territory of Deseret, the church had formally and finally separated from the state. As a result, it played no formal role in collecting tax. Informally, though, when tax noncompliance became widespread among its members and threatened to tarnish its reputation, the church attempted to backstop the state's tax collection with its own soft power. It added ecclesiastical incentives to the legal incentives that already encouraged Mormons to pay their taxes. Those ecclesiastical incentives do not carry the power of the state, but for a believing member, they carried significant weight. Notwithstanding its initial skepticism of the federal income tax and its skepticism of redistributive taxation during the Cold War, the Mormon Church ultimately accepted the necessity of lawfully enacted taxes as the appropriate realm of the state.

9

Polygamy and . . . Taxes?

Between the 1840s and the 1890s, the Mormon Church sacralized polygamous marriage, a practice deeply inimical to American society at large. Because it is a titillating practice (sex! religion!), discourse surrounding Mormon polygamy rarely looks beyond the marital practice itself. Mormonism's historical practice of polygamy seems incongruous with modern conservative Mormonism and this juxtaposition is salacious in its own right. When polygamy comes up, discussions tend not to stray far from that subject matter.

Mormon polygamy did not occur in a vacuum; polygamous Mormons had to interact with the outside world. The general American disapproval of polygamy meant that interaction was often strained and risky. Mormons' reactions to the risk and to the fraught nature of publicly practicing polygamy impacted both where they lived and how they structured their economic lives. Ultimately, where polygamists lived and how they lived economically impacted how and how much they owed in taxes. In a surprising and unexpected twist, then, the Mormons' countercultural marital practices, followed by its disavowal of plural marriage, raised unexpected questions related to taxation.

Restoring, then Abandoning, Polygamy

Joseph Smith's restorationist impulses, combined with his reading of the Bible, impelled him toward polygamy perhaps as early as the 1830s.[1] During Smith's

128 · TINKERING AROUND THE EDGES OF TAX AND RELIGION

life, though, the practice of polygamy remained a tightly guarded secret. By the time of his death, Smith had introduced "celestial marriage" to a handful of close associates, but he denied the practice publicly.[2] (While there may be technical differences between *polygamy, celestial marriage,* and *plural marriage,* in this chapter I will use all three terms interchangeably.) In fact, it would only be in August 1852—when the Mormons were safely established in Utah—that the church publicly acknowledged its practice of polygamy.

The practice proved deeply unpopular outside of Mormonism.[3] It led to increasingly draconian federal legislation aimed at stamping out the practice among the Mormon people. These federal statutes criminalized polygamy and imprisoned men who married multiple women. They disenfranchised those found guilty of polygamy and, eventually, disincorporated the Church of Jesus Christ of Latter-day Saints, escheating much of the church's property to the federal government.[4]

As a result of the significant legal jeopardy for church members and the church as a corporate body that polygamy entailed, in 1890, church president Wilford Woodruff ended the church's embrace of polygamy.[5] A decades-long practice is hard to reverse instantly, though. While the church had putatively eliminated polygamy, polygamous families continued to live together and, in fact, some Mormons entered into new plural marriages after Woodruff's 1890 manifesto.[6]

This continued polygamy became an issue when Utah elected Reed Smoot—a monogamous hierarch in the church—to the Senate. In spite of his not being a polygamist, several Senators sought to block him from being seated. In the hearings that followed, they called church president Joseph F. Smith—nephew of church founder Joseph Smith—to testify. Smith's testimony revealed "fatal inconsistencies" regarding the continued practice of Mormon polygamy and led an embarrassed church to crack down on the practice.[7]

During the following decade, the church began to impose ecclesiastical discipline on members and leaders who insisted on continuing to practice and preach polygamy. As the church began to purge polygamy's most zealous advocates, it laid the groundwork for splinter Mormon groups that continued to sanction polygamous marriages.[8] Deeply unpopular among the mainstream Mormon Church, in many ways, these polygamous Mormon groups "occupy much the same legal and political space with regard to Mormons as Mormons did to the rest of the country in the late nineteenth century."[9]

In this book, I have dealt primarily with the Salt Lake-based Church of Jesus Christ of Latter-day Saints. As the largest of the Mormon movements, its interactions with the tax law have been the most salient and most obvious.

Polygamy and . . . Taxes? • 129

But the Salt Lake-based church's interactions with the tax law have not been the only interactions between Mormonism and taxes. They have also not been representative of the experiences of all of the Mormon movements.

In spite of early opposition, by the mid-twentieth century, the Church of Jesus Christ of Latter-day Saints had become a culturally mainstream religious organization, especially in the United States. Members of the church participate in politics and business at the highest levels.[10] Not all of the branches of Mormonism have commanded such power and influence, though. The polygamous Mormon religions in particular have remained unpopular and largely powerless outside of their own distinct communities. These polygamous Mormon movements demonstrate another side to the relationship between religion, the state, and taxation.

These polygamous Mormon groups have a fraught relationship both with the Salt Lake-based Church of Jesus Christ of Latter-day Saints and with legal authorities in the states in which they operate. The Fundamentalist Church of Jesus Christ of Latter-day Saints, one of the largest polygamist Mormon churches, illustrates this fraught relationship. The mainstream Mormon Church excommunicates any member who practices polygamy. And its distaste toward polygamy is not limited to people engaged in the practice. Prior to 2019, the Church of Jesus Christ of Latter-day Saints refused to baptize the children of polygamists until those children turned eighteen. (Other children could be baptized at the age of eight.)[11]

On top of the disfavor polygamist Mormons faced from the mainline church was the disfavor they faced from the state. In 1935, Utah changed unlawful cohabitation (its law against polygamy) from a misdemeanor to a felony. Polygamists faced up to five years' imprisonment. In 1953, more than 100 Arizona law enforcement officers raided the polygamous town of Short Creek, Arizona.[12] Just over fifty years later, Texas authorities raided the Fundamentalist Church of Jesus Christ of Latter-Day Saints' (or FLDS's) Yearning for Zion Ranch and seized more than 400 children based on an anonymous tip that turned out to be a hoax.[13]

This double rejection by the state and their ancestral church has led many polygamous Mormon groups toward insularity. Not all live in secluded homogeneous communities, but a substantial portion of polygamist Mormons do.[14] Many of these groups have no particular love for the state. Nonetheless, in spite of their insularity and separation, members of the various polygamous Mormon groups are as enmeshed in the broader American legal systems as members of any other group. One of those legal interconnections comes with respect to the tax law. Whatever dim view the FLDS Church and its members hold of the government, they, like other American citizens, are subject to its taxing power.

130 · TINKERING AROUND THE EDGES OF TAX AND RELIGION

The government reciprocates polygamists' dim view. In 2008, the Senate Judiciary Committee held a hearing on Mormon polygamy and crime, a connection the hearing assumed and witnesses were happy to confirm. Witnesses in the hearing alleged crimes ranging from forced marriage (and sex) for underage girls to tax evasion. There seemed to be an implicit assumption that, because they rejected American norms of marriage and sexuality, polygamists also rejected American norms of taxpaying. The importance of tax allegations was not merely an aside during the hearings—several former polygamists testified of the importance to the community of tax fraud.

One witness was Carolyn Jessop, a woman who had been born into the FLDS church and who made a dramatic escape from the community. Jessop testified that the FLDS community engaged in "systemic abuse and disregard for the law." Part of this disregard, she said, could be illustrated by their religious doctrine of "bleeding the beast." The "beast," she explained, was the federal government, and bleeding it consisted of a two-part strategy: first, members tried to "avoid paying taxes at all costs" and second, they applied "for every possible type of government assistance that is available, whether they qualify or not."[15] Sara Hammon, a former member of another polygamous Mormon group, also testified that polygamous groups encouraged crime including tax evasion and welfare fraud.[16]

While these assertions of tax evasion and welfare fraud were powerful, they were also vague, not describing the mechanisms that polygamist Mormons used to avoid taxes or request welfare benefits. In fact, in his testimony, Dan Fischer, also a former polygamist member of the FLDS church, testified that "there are probably some who pay their taxes fairly and for sure there are some who are eligible for welfare and should be the recipients of its benefits."[17] In an affidavit filed following the testimony, Dan Fischer's brother Marvin Fischer contested a number of claims made during the hearing. He asserted, among other things, that he—a member of the FLDS church—paid thousands of dollars annually in local, state, and federal taxes.[18]

In fact, the most specific assertion of polygamous tax evasion presented by witnesses was not actually tax evasion: it was polygamist women complying with the tax law. Because no state in the United States recognizes polygamous marriages as valid, a polygamist Mormon man typically marries his first wife legally. Subsequent wives are "spiritual wives," married in religious ceremonies not recognized for civil purposes.[19]

Dr. Fischer reported that it was standard practice for these spiritual wives to "list themselves as 'head of household' on their income tax returns for the benefit of the tax credit."[20] Dr. Fischer's implication that this represented fraudulent

Polygamy and . . . Taxes? • 131

behavior underscores his lack of familiarity with federal tax law. Congress created "head of household" status specifically for unmarried individuals who have children and whose children live with them for at least half the year. A polygamous spiritual—but not legal—wife would, in most circumstances, qualify for the special rates available to heads of households. By claiming that status, polygamous wives do not attempt to cheat the tax law—they in fact comply with it.[21]

Nonetheless, polygamist Mormons probably cheat on their taxes more than the average American, though not for reasons connected to their practice of polygamy. Polygamous Mormons are more likely than the general population to work in the agricultural industry and other less formal employment. On average, those industries have lower tax compliance rates than jobs in the formal economy with wage withholding; naturally, then, polygamists, like other workers in their fields, will be less likely to pay taxes.[22]

Still, even if polygamous Mormons are more likely than the average American to cheat on their taxes (because they are more likely to work in less formal industries), the focus on them filing as heads of household, underpaying their taxes, and overclaiming welfare is likely a distraction, albeit a common one in American politics. Polygamists tend on average to be poorer than the surrounding community—the median family income in Hildale-Colorado City, home of the FLDS church, is significantly lower than the median family income in Utah generally. Women in the community are less likely to have paid employment.[23] Poorer families and unemployed heads of household are not a robust source of uncollected revenue.

That said, looking to poorer taxpayers—polygamous or not—for unpaid taxes is a relatively common move by the IRS. The top 1 percent of income earners in the United States are responsible for at least 30 percent of unpaid income taxes. Yet the residents of the five counties in the United States with the highest audit rates are disproportionately low-income (and disproportionately Black).[24] With less-complicated tax situations, poorer taxpayers are easier to audit and, without access to attorneys, more likely to lose in court.

The popular portrait of polygamist tax evasion features polygamists as small-time grifters, trying to marginally reduce government revenue as a result of countercultural marriages that do not fit comfortably in the familial model envisioned by the tax law. In this story, their small-time grifting is accentuated by a feeling of persecution and isolation from the government. By treating Mormon polygamists as unsophisticated outsiders whose tax evasion derives from their marital practices, the government failed to anticipate or plan for the Kingstons, who perpetrated one of the largest tax fraud schemes in US history.

132 · TINKERING AROUND THE EDGES OF TAX AND RELIGION

In the late 1990s, the *New York Times* described the Kingston family as a "wealthy but secretive polygamous clan based in a Salt Lake suburb."[25] About a quarter century later, in April 2023, four members of the Kingston family received prison sentences ranging from six to eighteen years for their parts in a long-running scheme to fraudulently claim more than $1 billion in biofuel tax credits. (Lev Dermen, the fifth member of the scheme, was not part of the polygamous Kingston clan. He received a sentence of forty years for his part in the fraud.)[26]

Beginning in 2010, the Kingstons faked paperwork so that they could claim tax credits for biofuels. Over time, the fraud became more and more complicated, as they continued to create fake paperwork and started to ship fuel internationally, recertify it, and reuse the same fuel for new tax credits. At some point, they even claimed tax credits without any paperwork or underlying transactions.[27]

The Kingstons' tax fraud had nothing to do with their polygamy, however. Most polygamists could not have engaged in the fraud even if they were aware of the biofuel tax credit and wanted to claim it fraudulently. The scheme required money and connections, and the Kingstons had both.[28] But their tax fraud—one which cost the US government an enormous sum of money—looked nothing like the specter of tax evasion raised in congressional hearings on polygamy. Instead, it looked like the type of tax evasion wealthy *monogamous* fraudsters would perpetrate if they had the idea, the means, and the lack of scruples.

The allegation that Mormon polygamists are inherently dishonest when it comes to taxes appears, in part, a placeholder for society's continued distrust of polygamists. Because they live in the shadows of society, and because they reject societally accepted familial norms, they must, in the popular imagination, also reject their obligation to help fund the society that largely rejects them. While that line of thinking makes some intuitive sense, there is no evidence that polygamous Mormons are more likely to cheat on their taxes than other similarly-situated Americans and, for those who do cheat, no evidence that their imagination is so constrained that they can only cheat in ways related to their polygamy.

Polygamy, Communitarianism, and State Taxes

Most analyses of polygamy among Mormons understandably focus on their countercultural marriages. In many ways, though, Mormon polygamists' marital relations are not the most interesting thing about them. In addition to rejecting monogamous marriage, many polygamist Mormon groups reject the economic

Polygamy and . . . Taxes? • 133

system of private ownership that underlies American society. That rejection, which puts them out of step with the individualistic capitalism that surrounds them, creates friction with American society that is just as important as, if less visible than, their familial structures.

Modern polygamist Mormons did not invent their communitarian economics out of whole cloth. Rather, they inherited it—along with polygamy—from nineteenth-century Mormonism. And even nineteenth-century Mormonism did not invent communitarianism. It joined a large number of utopian restorationist Christians in experimenting with communitarian economics. These communitarian Christians wanted to recreate the apostolic community of the New Testament, a community in which new members sold their property upon joining and gave the proceeds to the apostles. The apostles, in turn, used that money to support their religious flock according to people's needs.[29]

Throughout the nineteenth century, the Mormon Church tried to implement this communalism at various times and in various ways. By the twentieth century, though, the Salt Lake-based Mormon Church had largely abandoned its communitarian past. The polygamous Mormon movements that peeled off from the mainstream church, by contrast, not only continued to embrace the church's nineteenth-century plural marriage; they also continued to embrace these communitarian economics.[30] With this economic disconnect from the surrounding American society, these groups' communal property ownership puts them out of step with the capitalism of the society that surrounds them and, at times, puts them in uncomfortable and odd tax positions.

These uncomfortable and odd tax positions occur at both the state and the federal level. In 1942, the FLDS church created the United Effort Plan Trust, a legal entity it used to hold its communal property. Members of the FLDS church "consecrated" (or donated) their property to the UEP Trust. While they appear to have had some kind of possessory interest in the property during their lifetime, at death the property fully reverted to the UEP Trust.[31]

Church leaders managed the Trust's property. They determined "where members lived, when they moved and what properties they could build on."[32] Over the years, the UEP Trust acquired the bulk of the land in the twin towns of Colorado City, Arizona, and Hildale, Utah, where the FLDS church was based.

The UEP Trust's ownership of the land raised unique issues when it came to paying property tax. The UEP Trust did not subdivide the land it owned. Rather, church leaders calculated what portion of the total tax its various members owed. The members then paid their share to the bishop who, in turn, paid property taxes to the county government. Where there was a shortfall, wealthier members and businesses stepped in to pay any outstanding tax.

134 · TINKERING AROUND THE EDGES OF TAX AND RELIGION

Not all residents of Colorado City and Hildale belonged to the FLDS church. Nonmembers who lived on UEP Trust property received tax notices and sent their payments to a post office box. To the extent they underpaid, the FLDS church grossed up their payments. Doing so ensured that the state did not seize and sell the UEP Trust's property for unpaid taxes.[33]

In 2005, several former members of the FLDS church sued the UEP Trust and asked the court to appoint new trustees. The plaintiffs alleged that without reconfiguring the Trust management, the "homes and livelihoods of thousands of people in Utah, Arizona and Canada could be endangered."[34] The FLDS church leaders who managed the trust did not hire attorneys to defend the suit; because of their failure, Utah courts removed them as trustees and replaced them with a court-appointed special fiduciary.[35] Among other things, the newly-appointed trustee reorganized the trust to allow beneficiaries to get deeds to their houses. The deeds forbade members from transferring the property back to the FLDS church, even if the church formed a new trust.[36]

FLDS leadership was not happy with the state stepping in and taking over the trust, viewing it as an infringement of their religious rights.[37] Warren Jeffs, the president and prophet of the FLDS church, instructed his members to refuse to cooperate with the Trust or the trustee.[38] Many followed his instructions and did not pay the property tax they owed.[39] Like many states, in Utah and Arizona, failure to pay property tax creates a lien on the property.[40] The state can then sell tax liens to investors and, if property owners fail to pay the taxes and interest they owe for a certain amount of time, the investors can foreclose on the property, forcing the residents to leave. In fact, about 150 homes in Colorado City were at risk of foreclosure as a result of about $124,000 in delinquent taxes for 2007. The following year, the amount of unpaid taxes on UEP Trust properties in Colorado City nearly quadrupled. Residents of UEP Trust property in Hildale also followed FLDS directives to not pay taxes.[41]

In most circumstances, a tax lien would only affect property owners who failed to pay their taxes. In Colorado City and Hildale, though, because the UEP Trust did not subdivide its property, most tax parcels contained more than one housing unit. If the residents of one housing unit failed to pay their property taxes, all of the people living on that parcel could face interest, penalties, and potentially loss of their homes to a tax sale. This risk was not just hypothetical: because many FLDS residents refused to pay their property taxes, the UEP Trust came close to losing almost all of its Hildale property (which, in turn, would have caused residents to lose their homes).

The loss of their homes would have been devastating to community members, whether they had paid their share of property taxes or not. Either way, families would have to leave their homes and find a new place to live. This

Polygamy and . . . Taxes? · 135

potential housing crisis was averted at the last possible moment when, literally days before a tax sale was scheduled, the state received several large property tax payments which cured the default.[42] Polygamous residents of Hildale and their nonpolygamous neighbors alike could remain in their homes.

Polygamy, Communitarianism, and Federal Taxes

While the Utah-based Mormon Church preached and practiced polygamy for decades, its communitarian experiments proved far shorter-lived. Joseph Smith's experiment with communalism only lasted two years between 1831 and 1833. Not only did the courts prove wary of this radical departure from the familiar individualistic norms of private ownership, but also the broad poverty of the Mormon people, combined with their expulsion from Jackson County, proved fatal to the economic experiment. Smith tried again with a modified form of communalism in Jackson County but abandoned it by the time the Mormons moved to Nauvoo.[43]

Brigham Young tried to reimplement Joseph Smith's abortive attempts at communitarianism in the 1850s and then again in the 1870s. Ultimately, though, they broke down and the Utah-based Mormon Church again abandoned its attempts at creating an economic system that contrasted with the broader capitalism surrounding it.[44] Even that institutional abandonment did not end all Mormon attempts at communitarianism. Polygamist Mormon groups again reinstated communitarianism. But the polygamist communitarians had to deal with a legal issue that had never bedeviled earlier Mormon attempts at communitarianism: a federal income tax.

The income tax reflects the economics of the society at large. Specifically, the US federal income tax assumes that taxpayers (generally) act selfishly and that they own private property. As a result, communitarian societies fit poorly with the assumptions underlying the income tax. This poor fit is not limited to polygamist Mormons: in the early twentieth century, the Israelite House of David, a communitarian religious group that, among other things, operated an amusement park in Michigan and sent baseball teams and bands around the country, believed that, if no tax accommodation were made for communitarian religious groups, it would go out of business.[45]

How would the income tax drive a communitarian religious organization out of business? With members of communitarian organizations owning property collectively, the communitarian organization itself owned the property; it could not make distributions to members. Generally, corporate income is subject to two levels of taxation. A corporation pays taxes when it earns money, and then shareholders pay taxes when the corporation distributes its earnings to them.[46]

136 · TINKERING AROUND THE EDGES OF TAX AND RELIGION

To prevent the evasion of the second level of taxation, Congress imposed a surtax on corporations that did not distribute their earnings to shareholders. That surtax, imposed on top of the corporate tax, could be substantial, potentially crushing the Israelite House of David or other early twentieth-century communitarian religions.[47]

In recent decades, the law has become more comfortable with corporations that do not pay dividends. Even today, though, members of communitarian organizations face higher taxes than would an individual who engaged in the same enterprise directly. Today, a communitarian entity that owns the property would pay taxes on its income, then members, who did not own the property and who often worked on behalf of the religious organization, would pay taxes on the value of distributions made to them, whether the distributions come as salary or as room, board, and other support. Unlike a corporate employer, however, these two layers of taxation created a burden on communitarians that non-communitarians did not have to bear.

For example, a farmer who owns their own farm and earns $100 of profit by selling produce must include that $100 in their income and pay taxes on it. If, however, the farmer belonged to a communitarian religious group, the farmer would not own their own farm. Instead, the communitarian organization would earn the $100 of profit and pay taxes on that profit. Then whatever money it had after taxes it could pay to its member-farmers. They, in turn, would owe taxes on the amount they received.[48]

In the first decade of the modern income tax, courts determined that religious groups that also engaged in business—essentially, all communitarian religious organizations—did not qualify as exempt from tax. Because their economic activity was significant, it undercut the argument that they were primarily religions.[49] Communitarian religious groups found themselves trapped: if they practiced their religiously dictated communitarianism, they owed significantly more in taxes. If they wanted to avoid a second layer of tax, they had to give up their communitarianism.

Fortunately for the Israelite House of David and other religious communitarian groups, Congress proved sympathetic to their plight. In 1936 it enacted special tax rules for "religious and apostolic organizations." While it did not define precisely what qualified as a religious and apostolic organization, the legislative history made clear that Congress intended the new provision to apply to communitarian religious groups like the Israelite House of David. In the single paragraph of recorded legislative history for the new tax provision, Senator David Walsh said:

Polygamy and . . . Taxes? · 137

It has been brought to the attention of the committee that certain religious and apostolic associations and corporations, such as the House of David and the Shakers, have been taxed as corporations, and that since their rules prevent their members from being holders of property in an individual capacity the corporations would be subject to the undistributed-profits tax. These organizations have a small agricultural or other business. The effect of the proposed amendment is to exempt these corporations from the normal corporation tax and the undistributed-profits tax, if their members take up their shares of the corporations' income on their own individual returns. It is believed that this provision will give them relief, and their members will be subject to a fair tax.[50]

This new tax regime exempted religious and apostolic organizations from tax, instead taxing members on their pro rata share of the organization's income. To ensure that somebody paid taxes on the organization's income, members had to include their pro rata share of communal income irrespective of whether the religious organization distributed that income to them.[51]

While Congress enacted the provision in the tax law for religious and apostolic organizations in 1936, polygamist Mormon communities apparently failed to notice it until the 2010s. Sometime in 2012, the FLDS church appears to have requested that the IRS treat it as a religious or apostolic organization so that its members could benefit from the single level of taxation.

I say it *appears* that this happened because in letter rulings such as the one the IRS issued rejecting this request, the IRS is supposed to excise identifying information. It redacts names, locations, and other identifying details, replacing them with algebraic variables and other anonymous descriptions. So, for instance, in talking about the origin of the religious organization that requested exemption as a religious or apostolic organization, the IRS writes:

All your officers, religious leaders and members are members of Y. Y follows the beliefs and practices that were the original beliefs and practices of Z Church established and set forth by Founder. When Z Church departed from many of these beliefs, practices and teachings of Founder, some members separated from Z Church and established Y. You believe that Y is the continuation of Z Church established by Founder and has authority of the true successor to the divine authority of Founder.

The ruling goes on to mention that the beliefs and practices include "polygamy or plurality of wives."[52] While that strongly suggests that the ruling is aimed at a Mormon polygamist church, it does not, of itself, necessarily implicate the FLDS church. There are several different fundamentalist Mormon churches, after all.

138 · TINKERING AROUND THE EDGES OF TAX AND RELIGION

But the IRS, whether deliberately or negligently, did a shoddy job of hiding the identity of the ruling's subject. Nowhere was its negligence clearer than its mention of a "news article from Examiner.com on Date 3 [that] reported that a court in your state found a leader of Y with three wives under 'celestial marriages' guilty of bigamy."[53] With that level of specificity, it merely requires a Google search to find the *Standard-Examiner* story reporting that a Texas jury found Wendell Loy Nielsen, a former president of the FLDS church, guilty of three counts of bigamy for taking three wives in "celestial marriage."[54]

This carelessness and lack of respect for the FLDS church's privacy foreshadowed the IRS's substantive conclusion. In analyzing the FLDS church, the IRS acknowledged that it met the statutory requirements of a religious or apostolic organization. A qualifying group had to be religious or apostolic, it had to have a common treasury, and members had to include their pro rata share of the organization's income on their tax returns, whether or not the organization distributed that income to them.

The IRS acknowledged that the FLDS church-connected organization was a religious organization—it was formed as a religious trust, it advanced FLDS doctrine, and the only members of the organization were members of the FLDS church. It also acknowledged that the organization had a common treasury which included both assets consecrated by members and income the trust earned from its businesses. Finally, the trust agreement provided that members would include their pro rata share of the trust's income on their tax returns.

In spite of the FLDS church meeting all of the statutory requirements to qualify for the tax benefits available to religious or apostolic organizations, the IRS denied the FLDS church its tax-exempt status as a religious or apostolic organization.[55] It did so on the grounds of nonstatutory rules that were not originally intended to apply to religious or apostolic organizations. In fact, the IRS could only apply these rules as a quirk of how the Internal Revenue Code was organized.

In short, in the early 1970s, in reaction to racially discriminatory private schools, the IRS added an extra-statutory requirement to qualify as an exempt public charity under section 501(c)(3) of the Internal Revenue Code. On top of the statutory requirements, an organization had to also qualify as a charitable trust under the common law. The common law forbade charitable trusts from engaging in illegal activities and activities that violated public policy. The Supreme Court eventually blessed the IRS's exegesis. Notably, the Supreme Court found the common law charitable trust rule applied particularly to entities exempt under section 501(c)(3), in spite of there being no statutory mention of the law of charitable trusts.[56]

Polygamy and . . . Taxes? · 139

While section 501(c)(3) is probably the most well-known section of the Internal Revenue Code, it is not the only provision that exempts organizations from paying taxes. Congress ultimately codified the exemption for religious and apostolic organizations in section 501(d). Other than sharing the same section of the Internal Revenue Code, though, religious and apostolic organizations have little in common with 501(c)(3) public charities. Critically, donors to religious and apostolic organizations cannot take a charitable deduction for their donations, while in many cases donors to public charities can.

Still, the IRS denied the UEP trust an exemption as a religious or apostolic organization on the basis of the common law of charities. The IRS asserted that because the organization promoted polygamy, which was an illegal purpose, it could not qualify as a charitable trust. And because it could not qualify as a charitable trust, it could not benefit from the provision that eliminated double taxation for communitarian organizations.[57]

Principle Voices of Polygamy faced a similar (if more legally justifiable) result. Principle Voices of Polygamy was an advocacy group, formed to bridge the gap between polygamous Mormons and non-polygamists by, among other things, educating the public about polygamous families and cultures, empowering polygamists, and providing polygamists with crisis referrals.[58] In 2012 it too requested a tax exemption, albeit as a public charity under section 501(c)(3) rather than as a religious or apostolic organization.

The IRS treated Principle Voices of Polygamy's privacy as carelessly as it had treated the FLDS's. In its ruling it quoted language from the organization's (now-defunct) website.[59] And like the FLDS request, the IRS denied the Principle Voices application for tax exemption. Again, it based the rejection on the fact that Principle Voices of Polygamy advocated polygamy and that polygamy violated both public policy and the law. Because Principle Voices of Polygamy "operated to condone and support those engaging in the illegal act of polygamy," the organization did not meet the (still extra-statutory) requirement that a tax-exempt public charity comply with the common law of charities.[60]

In many ways, the IRS's carelessness and dismissal of the fundamentalist Mormon claims to tax exemption reflected the sentiment of a South Carolina newspaper about the Utah-based Mormon Church in the nineteenth century. While the newspaper believed that "[a]ll religions are guaranteed by the Constitution, . . . whenever a system goes beyond common morality, it ceases to be a religion, and should be unceremoniously stopped."[61] While the mainstream Mormon Church's reputation has changed substantially since the South Carolina newspaper decreed that it was not a religion, both law and society continue to be skeptical of the practice of polygamy. Even the tax system, to

140 · TINKERING AROUND THE EDGES OF TAX AND RELIGION

which polygamy would have no obvious connection, looks at religiously motivated polygamy with a skeptical eye and disfavors its practitioners and their
institutions.

Mormon Polygamy in Mexico

In reaction to the federal government's crackdown on polygamy in the nineteenth century, some Mormon polygamists left the country entirely. As they
took their familial practices with them, they faced new tax regimes, regimes that
had also failed to anticipate polygamy. Like their Nauvoo progenitors, in the
1880s these polygamist expatriates looked again to Mexico. In 1885, John Taylor,
the president of the church, negotiated the purchase of 100,000 acres in Mexico
and sent a group of about 350 polygamist Mormons from Arizona to the Casas
Grandes Valley in Mexico.[62] While polygamy was illegal in Mexico, the government of Porfirio Díaz turned a blind eye to the Mormons' marital practices.[63]

During the next decade, Mormon colonists established nine farming communities in Chihuahua and Sonora. These communities raised sheep, cattle,
wheat, and fruit, among other things.[64] Especially in the early years, the colonists were desperately poor, facing "hunger, scant clothing, wretched dwellings
(scarcely adequate for beasts), disease without medicine, sickness without
doctors, labor unremitting, none of the amenities of civilization."[65]

When it came to civil authority, the Mormon colonists functioned in a dual
role, similar to Mormons in Nauvoo and in the State of Deseret. They were both
sovereigns in their communities and subject to the Mexican government. As
sovereigns, the colonists imposed and collected taxes and paid for public goods.
When they first moved to Mexico, the settlers of Colonia Juarez wanted to provide an education for their children. They began building an adobe schoolhouse
in 1888. The schoolhouse cost $1,400, which the colonists raised by assessing
a tax of $50 on each married man and $25 on each unmarried man older than
twenty-five.

Eight years later, the settlers converted the school into an academy so that
young men and women could stay in the community and receive an education. The Juarez Stake Academy opened with 291 students in 1897. To fund the
academy, colonists levied an income tax on male residents. (The rate varied by
year; in 1900, for example, the tax amounted to 4 percent of family income.)
Nonresidents of Colonia Juarez—who would not have been subject to the income tax—paid tuition of between $5 and $15.[66]

While the Church had officially ended plural marriages in 1890, the Mexican
colonists continued to practice polygamy until 1904, when the church reiterated
its termination of polygamy and expressly told the Mexican colonists that they

Polygamy and . . . Taxes? • 141

could no longer enter into polygamous marriages. Nonetheless, those already in polygamist marriages continued their families for another half decade.[67]

The Mormon colonists in Mexico proved insular, rarely interacting with their native Mexican neighbors. In part, this insularity allowed them to continue with their polygamous families even while polygamy violated both Mexican law and church rules. While they were subject to the laws of the municipalities where they lived, practically they continued to be self-governing. By 1912, their population had grown to about 4,000,[68] but the Mexican Revolution of 1910 marked a significant change in the colonists' relationship with Mexico.

Mormon officials formally remained neutral in the revolution. But as a result of anti-American and anti-Mormon sentiments, the Mormons in Mexico faced threats and robberies. Ultimately, the Mexican Revolution triggered an exodus of Mormons from the Mexican colonies back to the United States. After the Revolution, fewer than one in four Mormon colonists remained in or returned to the Mexican colonies.[69]

The Mormon colonists' experience with robbery and threats bled into their experience with state taxation. In May 1912, Jose Randall, the tax collector for the district of Montezuma, claimed that, as he tried to collect taxes from the Mormons of Colonia Morelos, they "beat him and ran him out of the colony." He asked the commander of the military zone for troops to allow him to levy cattle and personal belongings to settle the amounts Mormons owed the government.[70]

The colonists disputed Randall's story. They claimed that he showed up in the colony and, without identifying himself or mentioning taxes, began taking colonists' livestock. From one he "seized a fine team of work mules." From another, he demanded money and provisions and told the colonist to "charge it up to the government's account."[71]

A week later, while the church's First Presidency in Salt Lake had received reports of what was happening in the colonies, they had still not received any official notice about the conflict between the Mormon settlers and the Mexican government. They were inclined to believe the church members, though, as they had instructed members in Mexico to "avoid unnecessary friction." Church leaders believed that it was a misunderstanding that would ultimately be corrected.[72]

Two years later, the issue of taxes came up again. This time, there was no informal collection and no violence toward the tax collector. Rather, for the first time since the Mormons had been driven out of their homes by revolutionaries, the municipal officers of Casas Grandes demanded taxes on all property belonging to Mormons in the state of Chihuahua. Because the Mormons had become refugees "residing in the intermountain country," officials sent the tax

142 · TINKERING AROUND THE EDGES OF TAX AND RELIGION

notices to church leaders in Salt Lake. They offered to reduce the amount due by half if colonists paid the taxes by December 31, 1914 (that is, about a week after Salt Lake received the tax notices). Taxes were due in Mexican currency, which traded for about twenty cents to the US dollar, meaning that if colonists could raise the money quickly enough from United States sources, they could cut the real cost of their Mexican taxes significantly.[73] The church advised colonists to pay the taxes.[74]

Three years later, the Mexican consul announced that Mexico would treat Mormons the same way it treated other citizens, using the same procedures to collect taxes from Mormon colonists as it used to collect taxes from Mexican citizens and other property owners in Mexico.[75] In 1918, though, Anthony Ivins of the church's First Presidency wrote that Mormon colonists in Mexico were still subject to a type of double taxation. While "[m]ost people feel the pincers of the tax collector once a year," he wrote, Mormon colonists were different. They paid their regular tax to the Mexican government annually. But they also "hand[ed] over any available surplus to Villa and his band of expert and lawless collectors now and then."[76]

At this point—and, in fact, every point in the story of Mormon colonists in Mexico—the imposition of taxes is at best attenuated to their practice of polygamy. Their polygamy may have made them less popular and easier targets, but it did not formally factor into the amount of taxes they paid. Still, the fact that polygamy sent them to Mexico and kept them insular is relevant to the story of their taxes.

While most of the Mormon colonists left Mexico, a handful of their descendants remain. These descendants of Mormon colonists are Mexican citizens who speak Spanish and participate in mandatory Mexican military service. They also remain outsiders, descended from United States Mormons with some decidedly US traditions and practices. To the criticism that these US-descended Mormons are invading and stealing, they respond with a taxpayer-citizenship argument. In their nearly century and a half in Mexico, they say, they not only have title to their land, but they pay taxes on it.[77] As taxpayers—an identity that we see was both contested and uncertain in the early decades that Mormons lived in Mexico—they claim belonging and legitimacy.

Polygamy in Canada

In trying to escape US laws, polygamous Mormons did not put all of their hope in Mexico. Two years after the Mormon Church purchased land in Mexico, it sent a small group of polygamous members to Alberta, Canada. The settlement in

Polygamy and . . . Taxes? • 143

Alberta became a "haven for polygamous Mormons fleeing persecution in the United States."[78] These new polygamous settlers initially faced a hostile reception from the Canadian public. As in the United States and Mexico, polygamous marriage was illegal in Canada. Canadian authorities warned Mormon men that they could only live with one wife or they risked prison time.[79]

In spite of Canada's laws against polygamy, the Canadian Mormon colonies ended up thriving. While public opinion opposed the Mormon settlers, the Dominion's government both tolerated and aided them. For instance, Mormon settlers benefited from an 1890 Department of Agriculture program that paid $15 to each head of a family who settled in Canada, with an additional $7.50 for each member of the family who joined him. Settlers could claim free hay and timber from government supplies and, in addition, the Canadian government provided $250 of aid to agricultural societies annually.[80]

In addition to Dominion programs that helped Mormon settlers in Canada, the settlers received financial support from Salt Lake. The church sent experienced leaders to Alberta to lead the Mormon communities there. It also "provided manpower for the colony by 'calling' Church members in the Mormon heartland of Utah and Idaho to serve a mission in the Alberta colony." The church entered into agreements with land companies to jointly develop irrigation. It even bought land to alleviate a land shortage among Mormon settlers.

The church's growing sophistication in the world of politics led it to send a delegation to Ottawa requesting that the Dominion legalize polygamy. Several Cabinet ministers met personally with the delegation.[81] While the Canadian government did not legalize polygamy, Mormon polygamists nonetheless faced no criminal prosecution for their practice.[82]

With the formal end of polygamy at the turn of the twentieth century, the question of polygamy and taxes in Canada could also have ended with no notable consequences. The end of polygamous communities in Canada was forestalled, however, when a small group of FLDS members moved to Lister, British Columbia in 1947. They renamed their settlement Bountiful and reintroduced Mormon polygamy and Mormon communitarianism to Western Canada.[83]

The settlement grew to about 1,000 people and, in 2002, split into two roughly equal-sized factions. One remained loyal to Warren Jeffs and the FLDS church. The other followed Winston Blackmore, an excommunicated former member of the FLDS church.[84]

While Blackmore admitted to having faced police investigation since the 1990s, he managed to avoid prosecution for his polygamy. However, he, like Al Capone, proved less fortunate when it came to his tax crimes. Auditors accused him of underreporting $1.8 million of income over five years and of laundering

144 · TINKERING AROUND THE EDGES OF TAX AND RELIGION

personal and family expenses through J.R. Blackmore & Sons, a business he owned.

Blackmore responded that his income had rarely exceeded $30,000 per year. As for the rest of the $1.65 million the government said he had earned? He claimed that, for tax purposes, it belonged to the religious group he led.[85]

Canada, like the United States, has a special tax provision for communitarian religious organizations. The Dominion enacted its communitarian tax provisions in 1977 in response to litigation by Hutterite communities. The Hutterites are a communitarian Christian religion. They, like other Christian communitarians, founded their economic lives on the economics of the apostolic church. Hutterites collectively live and work in a colony; the colony owns all of the property and provides members with basic sustenance.[86]

Until the 1960s, Hutterite colonies in Canada paid no Canadian income tax in spite of operating successful agricultural businesses. In the 1960s, the tax authority levied taxes against some Hutterite colonies. After negotiation, a number of Hutterite colonies and the Minister of National Revenue agreed that Hutterite individuals would pay taxes on their share of colony income. While the majority complied, at least one colony refused to be bound by the agreement and, when the government assessed taxes on its members, sued.[87]

The government enjoyed initial success in the trial court but it lost on appeal. The appeals court held that the colony's income and profits were in no way attributable to individual members. The government could only tax members on the direct benefits they received from the colony. Income and profits that the colony did not distribute to members could not be taxed either to the members or to the Hutterite colony itself.[88]

In response to this litigation, the Canadian legislature enacted a special tax provision to govern the taxation of religious communitarian organizations. The Hutterite Rule provides that where a congregation carries on a business to support or sustain the congregation's members, that business is treated as a trust for tax purposes. The tax law treats the trust as owning all of the congregation's property and, by default, the trust must pay taxes on its income each year. A congregation can opt out of this default rule by making an election under which participating members of the congregation must pay taxes on their share of the congregation's income.[89] (Some contemporaneous discussion at the enactment of the provision suggests that the law was enacted solely to benefit the Hutterites; the law did not say so explicitly, though, and the Advisor to the Senate Committee believed it also applied to the Amish.[90])

If the Hutterite Rule applied to Blackmore's income, he would shift his tax burden to the members of Bountiful. That shift would potentially impose a real

Polygamy and . . . Taxes? • 145

financial burden on Blackmore's followers. Lynn Burch, a Justice Department attorney, claimed that many of the members of Blackmore's church worked for his company "for a pittance" in logging and wood-processing plants.[91] But in the quarter century between its enactment and Blackmore's case, the Hutterite Rule remained obscure, largely unknown even among Canadian tax attorneys. Blackmore's litigation was the first time Canadian courts had been asked to address what the law meant or how widely it applied.[92]

To determine whether the Hutterite Rule applied to Blackmore's 450-member church, the court grappled with the definition of a "congregation." The tax law includes a four-prong definition of *congregation*. The first prong requires that members of the community live and work together. The second requires that the members adhere to the practices and beliefs, and follow the principles, of the religious organization of which the congregation is a constituent part. The third prong requires that the community prohibit members from owning property individually. Finally, the fourth prong demands that members "devote their working lives to the activities of the congregation."[93]

The court noted that, in many ways, the community at Bountiful functioned like any other community. For instance, it held hockey games, rodeos, and barbeques. In other ways it differed: members of the Bountiful community eschewed private property, instead holding all things in common. People who joined had to contribute all of their property to the community and were in turn given enough to meet their needs. Members also paid 10 percent of their income in tithing (though sometimes they provided labor in lieu of cash). Before the schism in the community, they also engaged in "famine calls," where the church told members to live on their stored and canned food for three months and contribute as much cash as they could to the church.

In 1980, Blackmore's father formed J.R. Blackmore & Sons Ltd., a company that engaged in logging, the manufacture of fenceposts, and farming. By the 2000s, the company employed about sixty people, with an additional thirty during the summer. It paid its employees and owned a number of properties.

To determine whether Blackmore's group qualified for the Hutterite Rule's special tax treatment, the court looked carefully at the language of the law and of the four prongs. While the court acknowledged that a group did not *have* to look like a Hutterite colony to qualify, it also pointed out that the Hutterites were the only clear example of a group that the law unquestionably applied to and, as such, the structure of Hutterite colonies became a guidepost in the court's analysis.

Blackmore's Mormon fundamentalist community, the court decided, did not look enough like the Hutterites to qualify under the Hutterite Rule. In reaching

146 · TINKERING AROUND THE EDGES OF TAX AND RELIGION

this conclusion, the court evaluated each individual prong in the definition of "congregation." Did members live and work together? The court decided that, unlike the Hutterites, who lived in a geographically defined area, the Bountiful members lived across provinces and even in the United States. Likewise, while many community members worked for J.R. Blackmore & Sons, many others worked independently. Thus, the court determined that the Bountiful community neither lived nor worked together and that it failed the first prong of the definition of "congregation."

Was the congregation a "religious organization"? To answer that, the court had to decide what the tax law meant by "religious organization." Again, it looked to the Hutterite colonies; in the Hutterite faith, the court said, multiple Hutterite colonies together made up the "the greater whole, the Hutterian Brethren Church." That Hutterian Brethren Church was the religious organization that the tax law demanded and each colony was a constituent part.

Was Blackmore's Bountiful community a constituent part of a religious organization? The court could think of five possible answers: (1) that it was part of Mormonism broadly, (2) that it was part of the LDS church, (3) that it was part of the FLDS church both before and after the 2002 schism, (4) that it had been part of the FLDS church before 2002 and had since become an independent group of Mormon fundamentalists, or (5) that it was an independent group of Mormon fundamentalists that had no affiliation with a religious organization.

Based on expert testimony, the court decided that "Mormonism" was best viewed as a religious tradition, not a religious organization. As such, even if the Bountiful community fit under the umbrella of Mormonism, that did not meet the second prong. The court also determined that the Bountiful community was not part of the LDS church and, in fact, had never claimed to be part of it.

The court did not accept the FLDS church as a religious organization. It believed that the excommunication of its leaders from the episcopal tradition of the LDS church severed it completely. Moreover, the court did not believe that the FLDS church was a reconstituted religious organization. Instead, it viewed the FLDS church as a "loose association of divergent groups."

As a factual matter, the court was almost certainly wrong in this particular conclusion. Its error did not matter with respect to Blackmore's petition, though: the court also determined that, even if the FLDS church *were* a religious organization under Canadian tax law, the Bountiful members did not self-identify as members of the FLDS church. Even those members who had self-identified as FLDS prior to 2002 stopped after the schism, and Blackmore himself tried to distance himself from the FLDS church. The Bountiful community, then, did not meet the second prong, either. Rather than making up

Polygamy and ... Taxes? • 147

part of a Hutterite-like religious organization, it was "an independent group of fundamentalist Mormons."

Could members of the Blackmore community own property? The court pointed out that the *tax law* did not forbid members of a religious community from owning property. Rather, it required that the community "in some tangible form" prohibit such ownership. The court read this prong strictly: the community prohibition had to be absolute. Even without looking to the Hutterite colonies as a model, the court held that the Bountiful community failed this prong and that this prong would be damning to Blackmore's case even if he had met the other prongs. Witnesses had provided evidence that members owned personal property, had bank accounts in their own names, and even had private lines of credit.

Based on these and other examples, the court found that there was no practical proscription on individual members owning property. Moreover, the court found no evidence of any express doctrinal prohibition. In many ways, the prohibition on individual ownership was central to the definition of a congregation under the Hutterite Rule, and the Bountiful community did not come close to meeting that prong.

Finally, the court decided that the Bountiful community did not "require" its members to devote their working lives to the activities of the congregation. While there was a general sense that members were supposed to work for and support the congregation, the court believed that a better reading of the statute would require them to actually work for the community on a daily, ongoing basis. Members of the Bountiful community, by contrast, were allowed—and in some cases encouraged—to obtain education and jobs outside of the community (and, of course, to contribute financially to the community).

Blackmore's Bountiful community failed all four prongs of the definition of a "congregation" for purposes of the Hutterite Rule. The court rejected his claim that his income belonged to the community and thus rejected any election that would allow (or require) members of the Bountiful community to pay taxes on their pro rata share of his income. Instead, Blackmore owed back taxes on about $1.8 million of income. On top of that, the court found that he had been grossly negligent in his failure to pay his taxes and upheld another nearly $150,000 in penalties that the taxing authority had imposed.[94]

By 2015, Blackmore owed the Canadian government more than $2 million. The Canadian Revenue Agency seized his personal assets in partial repayment of his tax obligations in 2015 and again in 2017.[95] His troubles with the Canadian government did not end with the seizure of his property, though. While Canadian law enforcement had historically chosen not to enforce its laws against

148 · TINKERING AROUND THE EDGES OF TAX AND RELIGION

polygamy, in 2017, the British Columbia Supreme Court found Blackmore guilty of polygamy.[96] The court sentenced him to six months under house arrest and twelve months of probation.

The Canadian Revenue Agency had left Blackmore two assets: the stock of Blackmore Farms Ltd. and Church of Jesus Christ (Original Doctrine) Inc. Those companies owned land and structures just outside the community center of Bountiful and in part supported Blackmore and the Bountiful community. While under house arrest, Blackmore put both companies, with a combined value of just over $800,000, up for sale to help pay his other creditors.[97]

* * *

Mormons' polygamy always set them apart from their neighbors. Western society was deeply uncomfortable with polygamy, a system of marriage the Supreme Court in the nineteenth century claimed "has always been odious among the northern and western nations of Europe."[98] Mormon nonconformity to marital norms often accompanied nonconformity to economic norms. And these two things together—polygamy and communitarianism—have often driven Mormons to the outskirts of society.

Still, moral judgments about polygamy should not play into questions of tax liability. After all, tax systems are designed to raise revenue in a neutral manner, not to enforce a particular morality. The Supreme Court has emphasized that the income tax is "a tax on net income, not a sanction against wrongdoing."[99]

The lived experience of polygamous Mormons belies this purported objectivity, though. In the first instance, the public's disapproval of Mormon polygamy pushed polygamist Mormons into situations where they faced different tax rules than their neighbors. And even where they were not pushed into the margins or into other countries, the IRS has applied the tax law differently to polygamists than it does to other similarly-situated taxpayers. Whether or not the tax law *expressly* makes moral judgments, as a practical matter, its implementation implicates public views on morality.

10

The Mormon Church's Lobbying

By the middle of the twentieth century, the Mormon Church had begun to feel comfortable with its relationship with the state. Having jettisoned polygamy, it embraced a new image as an all-American religion[1] and became a confident player on the national scene. That confidence meant, among other things, that the church was willing to lobby to protect its own tax privileges and to ensure that the state raised revenue in ways that it considered appropriate.

The church's participation in the political process was not new in the mid-twentieth century, of course. It had effectively functioned as the government in Nauvoo and in Deseret, and was willing to use its resources to protect its interests and privileges in the post—Civil War era. But by the 1950s, something had changed. The church was more confident—and more open—in its revenue-related lobbying, trying to shape government funding in a way that both protected the church's interests and protected the morals of the society in which the church operated.

Church Tax Exemptions

In 1950, Congress enacted a law requiring most charitable organizations to file annual information returns with the IRS. Because charitable organizations generally did not pay taxes, these returns did not look like the tax returns individual taxpayers filed; critically, they did not calculate a charitable organization's tax

150 · TINKERING AROUND THE EDGES OF TAX AND RELIGION

liability (because these charitable organizations had no tax liability). Rather, these information returns laid out the charitable organizations' income, expenses, disbursements, and other financial information. They served (and continue to serve) a dual purpose: providing information the IRS needs to ensure tax-exempt organizations comply with the law and giving members of the public information they need to donate wisely and hold tax-exempt organizations accountable.[2]

These disclosure rules did not apply to all charitable organizations, however. They explicitly excluded some charitable groups, including religious organizations and their affiliates, from the obligation to file a return. Within two decades, Congress had become uncomfortable with these exemptions from the filing rules. Twenty years' experience had taught Congress that it needed access to more information, quicker, from more tax-exempt organizations.

Galvanized by a series of scandals involving tax-exempt private foundations, Congress began to rethink the special benefits churches enjoyed.[3] In hearings before the House Ways and Means Committee, Professor Lawrence Stone of the UC Berkeley School of Law articulated Congress's concerns. Of all charities, churches needed these benefits least, he asserted—most donations to churches were relatively small and donors would likely make them even in the absence of deductibility. Moreover, churchgoers received "direct 'services'" in exchange for their donations, undercutting the justification for deductibility.

Even if churches retained their tax exemption, Professor Stone believed that equity between believers and non-believers demanded that churches file information returns, just like any other tax-exempt organization.[4] The House of Representatives agreed. Its version of the Tax Reform Act of 1969 eliminated the filing exception for churches. The House's bill surprised and galvanized churches, many of which did not want to file returns with the IRS. In the aftermath of this bill, churches—including the Mormon and Catholic churches—sent representatives to testify before Congress about the importance of maintaining the filing exception for religious organizations.[5]

One of those representatives was Dr. Ernest L. Wilkinson, the president of Mormon Church—owned Brigham Young University. Technically, Wilkinson did not testify on behalf of the church. Rather, he appeared on behalf of the American Association of Independent College and University Presidents, as well as on behalf of BYU. As a result, the bulk of his testimony had little to do with churches. Rather, he testified about the contributions private universities made to the country and requested an expansion of the beneficial treatment charitable gifts received for tax purposes.

The Mormon Church's Lobbying · 151

At the very end of his testimony, though, Wilkinson pivoted to issues of direct interest to churches and religiously affiliated universities. "We vigorously oppose," he testified, "the requirement of filing information returns" as provided in the House bill. (The "we" in this statement seems to have shifted from *members of the American Association of Independent College and University Presidents* to *BYU and the Mormon Church*.) The requirement would apply, he said, "not only to colleges and universities but to the churches that support many of these institutions." According to Wilkinson, any tax filing requirements would "prove extremely burdensome and costly to the universities and churches with no offsetting revenue to the government because colleges and churches are tax exempt."[6]

The lobbying from churches, including the Mormon Church, proved largely successful. While the House of Representatives would have broadened the filing requirements to include religious organizations, the Senate version of the bill removed the new filing requirement for churches. But the Senate did not grant churches a complete win: while it did not require churches to start filing information returns, it narrowed the pre-existing exemption. Rather than providing a broad exemption from filing for religious organizations, the Senate bill exempted churches, conventions of churches, and churches' "integrated auxiliaries."[7]

This exception to the filing requirements for churches, church conventions, and churches' integrated auxiliaries continues today, more than five decades since its enactment.[8] The language of the exemption appears to be a puzzle, though. *Churches* and *conventions of churches* have common enough meanings. But the phrase *integrated auxiliaries* "had no legal history, [and] no established meaning, either in civil or ecclesiastical law."

Where did the concept of *integrated auxiliaries* come from? It can trace its roots directly to the Mormon Church's organizational structure and Utah Senator Wallace Bennett. While Senator Bennett was a practicing member of the Mormon Church, he felt that his duties as a senator prevented him from going to the church for advice on legislation. Still, notwithstanding his political independence from the church, Senator Bennett worried that the narrowed filing exemption the Senate was considering would not encompass the church's Relief Society, primary, Young Men's and Young Women's Mutual Improvement Associations, or the Deseret Sunday School.[9] He wanted to ensure that these organizations, formally known as "Auxiliary Organizations" in the church, would not need to file information returns.

While the Senate accepted Senator Bennett's amendment, it decided not to adopt his (and, by extension, the Mormon Church's) precise language. Rather, the drafters appended the word "integrated" to "auxiliaries" as a signal that mere relation to a church would be insufficient to qualify for the filing exception. To qualify, an "integrated auxiliary" would need a "substantial connection with the parent church."[10]

Though it had been more than a century since the Mormon Church had explicitly acted in a governmental capacity, it was able, through lobbying and in conjunction with other religions, to preserve a tax privilege it enjoyed. But it had access to more than testimony to protect itself: it had members of the church who were also members of Congress; in 1969, two senators and three representatives were Mormon.[11] Through this indirect access to power, not only did the church protect its exemption from filing, but it actually saw its organizational structure enshrined in the tax law in a way other religions did not. While other churches also have "religious school, youth group, and men's and women's clubs,"[12] the codified exemption from information return filing can trace its language directly to the auxiliaries of Mormonism.[13]

Just two years after the tax reform, Senator Bennett's codification of church auxiliaries in the tax law lost a significant portion of its relevance. In 1971, the Mormon Church consolidated and restructured, greatly reducing the various auxiliaries' independence and autonomy and bringing them under the auspices of the centralized church.[14] And fifty years after the Senate codified Mormon terminology in the tax law, the church severed that connection entirely. In October 2019, the church announced its plans to jettison the term "auxiliaries," substituting the word "organization."[15] But while the church no longer has autonomous auxiliaries, the echo of Mormon auxiliaries lives on in a section of the tax code designed, in small part, to protect the church's interests.

Betting on Revenue

Not all governmental revenue comes from taxation. Some municipal governments raise a substantial portion of their revenue through fees and fines.[16] And many governments supplement their revenue by borrowing, especially to fund infrastructure costs.[17] While these fees, fines, and borrowed money differ from taxes in important ways, they ultimately substitute for taxes and provide governments with alternative sources of revenue.

In the 1980s, another important source of governmental revenue became popular: state lotteries. While lotteries raise money for the government, they, like fees, fines, and borrowings, are not precisely taxes. But because only a portion of the cost of each lottery ticket ends up being paid out to lottery winners, the government can use lotteries to raise additional revenue. In Georgia, for

The Mormon Church's Lobbying • 153

example, the state keeps thirty-five cents of every dollar people spend on lottery tickets. At least a portion of that revenue represents something other than ordinary profits on lotteries—in a public market for lotteries, lottery providers probably would not be able to earn a 35 percent profit. So even if we want to treat governments' non-tax revenue differently from its tax revenue, these excess profits enjoyed by states on their lottery revenue probably represent an implicit excise tax, collected on a single product.[18]

The use of lotteries to raise revenue in the United States dates back to colonial times when governments used lotteries extensively to finance various public projects. Explicit taxes were deeply unpopular and, until the country established a national banking system, debt financing was difficult to come by. While lotteries faced some objections—notably, New England Congregationalists and Pennsylvania Quakers opposed them—the opposition was far from universal. In fact, while colonial governments used lotteries primarily to fund public projects, a number of religious organizations also benefited from lottery proceeds. In general, colonial-era Americans viewed lotteries less as gambling and more as voluntary taxes or charitable contributions made for public purposes.[19]

Lotteries remained a popular way to raise revenue as the United States emerged into the nineteenth century and needed revenue to construct cities, roads, and canals. The proceeds of nineteenth-century lotteries continued to primarily benefit state and local governments, though religious and other nongovernmental organizations would also occasionally raise money through lotteries. The details of lotteries began to change, though, as states contracted with private firms to administer their lotteries. These specialized firms began selling tickets and holding drawings. Along with privatized lotteries came fraud, though. And with this fraud came increased opposition to lotteries. Social activists began campaigning for the abolition of lotteries. In 1833, Pennsylvania, New York, and Massachusetts banned lotteries. By 1863, all but three states had implemented similar bans.[20] And by the time the calendar flipped from the nineteenth to the twentieth century, every state in the United States banned lotteries, the result of both their controversial nature and states' scrutiny of corruption.[21]

It took more than six decades for the first state to reintroduce the lottery as a source of revenue. In 1964, New Hampshire implemented the first legal state lottery of the twentieth century. Other states joined in, building on New Hampshire's success. During the 1980s, state lotteries grew tenfold, becoming the largest form of commercial gambling in the United States. By the end of the 1980s, two out of every three states sponsored a lottery.[22] In 2019, Mississippi became the forty-fifth state to sponsor a lottery.[23] As of 2021, only Alabama, Alaska, Hawaii, Nevada, and Utah did not have a state lottery.[24]

154 · TINKERING AROUND THE EDGES OF TAX AND RELIGION

The story of lotteries' emergence in the twentieth and twenty-first centuries is a story of state finance. New Hampshire turned to a legalized lottery precisely because it needed a new source of revenue. With an almost constitutional aversion to income taxation,[25] New Hampshire adopted a state lottery to help fund the state government.[26] Other states, seeing New Hampshire's success, followed suit, largely out of a desire to exploit a new source of revenue to supplement state tax revenues.[27] State revenue comes by virtue of the state paying winners less than the full amount of money people spend to purchase lottery tickets. The difference between lottery revenues and payouts can be substantial—in 1985, as the growth in lotteries started to explode, states raised about $30 per person from their lotteries, money they then used to support other state activities.[28] In 2017, states raised more than $26 billion from their lotteries.[29] That same year, state governments raised about $1.3 trillion of total revenue.[30]

Though lotteries only accounted for about 2 percent of state revenues, that 2 percent is important. Legislators desperate for revenue consider lotteries an easier sell to their political constituents than increased taxes. After all, lottery revenue is voluntary—anybody can avoid paying simply by not purchasing a lottery ticket. People *do* buy lottery tickets, though. They consider the lottery fun, making them more likely and more willing to participate in the funding of government.[31]

In the early-to-mid-1980s, Utah was in a perfect position to embrace a lottery. It faced a number of economic crises and natural disasters that forced it to increase its tax rates. Between 1983 and 1987, for example, the Utah legislature raised its sales tax rate from 4 percent to 5.09 percent.[32]

Meanwhile, in response to California's property tax revolt and Proposition 13, which limited the ability of California to increase property taxes, Utah's legislature also worked to roll back property tax rates. In 1984, however, the state supreme court blocked these reductions, finding that the legislature's move—returning assessed property values back to their 1978 levels—was impermissible. As a result, the state adopted a procedure of reassessing property values on a regular basis instead.[33] The regular reassessments led to surprising and unpopular increases in Utahns' property taxes.[34]

From this milieu of increasing and uncertain taxes, Utah taxpayers could see other states enacting lotteries. Utahns wanted to join and began pushing for a state lottery as well. But even if it wanted to, the state legislature could not single-handedly permit a state lottery. The Utah Constitution prohibits the state legislature from authorizing "any game of chance, lottery or gift enterprise under any pretense or for any purpose."[35] To amend the state constitution, and

The Mormon Church's Lobbying • 155

thus to permit a lottery, requires a two-thirds vote in both legislative houses, and then approval by a majority of voters in the next general election.[36]

In 1986, Arlo James, a state representative, began the amendment process, gathering signatures to put the question of a state lottery to a voting initiative. James pointed out that in a mere five years, New York's lottery had put the state's finances on sound footing. In fact, every one of the twenty-two states with a lottery was financially stable. James believed that a lottery could raise $49 million for the state; without a lottery, the state would need to raise property taxes, increase the sales tax, limit the number of dependent deductions a family could take, or even cut either kindergarten or twelfth grade in the state.

If Utah did not move quickly, James feared, it would lose out on potential lottery revenue to neighboring states that were also considering their own lotteries.[37] His fear was well-founded: months later, voters in neighboring Idaho approved a state lottery, with 60 percent of voters in favor.[38] The success of Idaho's lottery demonstrated Utahns' appetite for a lottery. In the first six months of the Idaho lottery's existence, the store that sold the most lottery tickets was located in a small town a mile from the Utah border. A clerk at the store estimated that 95 percent of its sales went to Utahns crossing the border. (In fact, the store made and sold baseball caps with the words, "La Tienda, Franklin, Idaho, Home of the Utah Lottery.")[39]

In all, a lottery in Utah would have been popular and it would have provided the legislature with a ready source of revenue. (Rep. James paraphrased Thomas Jefferson, claiming that the "lottery is the only fair form of taxation."[40]) And yet the state has declined to authorize a state lottery.

Why?

At least a portion of the answer lies in the political power of the Mormon Church. The Mormon Church vehemently opposed the creation of a state lottery in Utah in the 1980s.

That opposition was not inevitable. Like most religions in the United States, the Mormon Church had not always opposed lotteries. Its members, in fact, had used (and recommended the use of) lotteries on multiple occasions during the nineteenth century. In New Orleans, for example, a backroom lottery helped fund Mormon emigrants traveling to Utah. Between 1848 and 1855, the church appointed agents in New Orleans. The agents led the local congregation of church members and helped emigrants navigate the city and continue through to Utah. On March 2, 1849, Lucius Scovil, the church's first New Orleans agent, was in a tight spot. He had failed to win converts and his money had almost run out. Walking through the streets, he heard "an audible voice" that told him to go

156 · TINKERING AROUND THE EDGES OF TAX AND RELIGION

to Caliboose Square. There, the voice told him, he would find a bookstore run by a Frenchman and he would buy a lottery ticket with the number 9998. Scovil obeyed the voice and bought the ticket (which was for the Havana lottery, since Louisiana did not permit lotteries). The proprietor sold ticket 9998 to Scovil for $2.50. Ten days later he learned that he had won $250. In spite of the fact that "buying a lottery ticket was alien to his natural feelings," Scovil recorded that he "felt truly thankful to God for what had happened."[41]

Two decades later, an F.A. Mitchell wrote to church president Brigham Young. While in school, Mitchell said, he had listened to several church leaders talk about Young's indebtedness resulting from the Union-Pacific Railroad grading project.[42] Mitchell proposed a solution to Young which he believed "would meet with a hearty response from the entire people." He wanted the church to sell 50,000 lottery tickets for $5 each. Winners would collectively receive 250 Utah Central Railroad bonds.[43] The prize would come at little upfront cost to Young and the church, given that the LDS Church owned the Utah Central Railroad.[44]

Young did not take Mitchell up on his suggestion, and the institutional church never seems to have embraced lotteries in its own financial plans. But the willingness of members to buy lottery tickets—with a divine mandate no less—and to recommend lotteries to the church president suggests that the Mormon Church did not actively oppose lotteries in the nineteenth century.

By the 1980s, however, the Mormon Church had definitively staked its opposition to lotteries. While Utah was no longer the theocratic territory it had been in the mid-nineteenth century, the Mormon Church still has the ability, when it chooses, to flex significant political muscle in the state. It has an effective lobbying arm in Salt Lake and its lobbyists "clearly get results on those occasions when they choose to take a stance." Beyond formal lobbying, Mormons represent a significant percentage of Utah's population and the church can often count on its members to push their legislators to enact specific policies.[45] In its opposition to the lottery, the church used both its lobbyists and its members.

The Mormon Church is not, of course, an unstoppable political juggernaut. In 1987, Dallin Oaks, a member of the church's governing Quorum of the Twelve, spoke against lotteries to a group of students at the LDS Church—owned Ricks College in Idaho. He claimed that lotteries were "sugar-coated with the phony sweetness of a good cause" but ultimately corrupted those who played, undermining "the virtues of work, industry, thrift and service to others."[46] Some Boise-area church leaders encouraged members to donate to an antilottery group named Consider. A church spokesperson endorsed the idea, explaining that, while the Mormon Church didn't usually make official political statements, "our stance on gambling and the lottery have been long-standing."[47] In spite of

The Mormon Church's Lobbying · 157

the church's efforts, and the fact that Mormons made up about 20 percent of Idaho's population,[48] Idaho legalized a state lottery.[49] The winning bloc included Mormons who ignored their church's opposition to state lotteries.[50]

Unlike Idaho, proponents of a lottery in Utah could not overcome the church's opposition. In 1992, with several proposals for legalized gambling—including a lottery—on the legislative docket, the church again came out against gambling. In a statement it mailed to each Utah legislator, the church argued that gambling would threaten "the cultivation and maintenance of strong family and community values."[51] The church not only opposed a state lottery; it went so far as to argue against the question being placed on the ballot. Polling indicated more than three-fourths of practicing Mormons believed that the question of a Utah lottery should be placed on the ballot and that more than half of Utah voters would vote in favor. The church believed, however, that gambling fell outside the scope of things that the public should vote on.[52] Unlike Idaho, the Mormon Church got its way in Utah. In spite of the broad support a state lottery enjoyed, the question of whether to implement a lottery never made it on the general election ballot.[53]

Proponents of a lottery in Utah looked longingly at their neighbors to the north. The editorial board of the University of Utah's student newspaper pointed out that, of the forty million lottery tickets sold in Idaho, 7 percent had been purchased by Utahns. By declining to create a lottery, Utah left a "substantial source" of potential revenue on the table. And did it need that income? The student newspaper believed that it did: "One needs to look no further than an overcrowded classroom with an underpaid teacher to know it does. One needs only to listen to legislators whine about how they don't have enough money to increase funding of education without raising taxes to know that more money is needed."[54]

The Mormon Church considered the potential benefits of additional state revenue subordinate to the harm of raising it through legalized, government-sponsored gambling. In a 1986 article in the church's official magazine, church hierarch William D. Oswald expressly addressed the question of whether it was "now appropriate for government to finance public needs through lotteries, when for most of our history gambling was punished as a vice." (In fact, as discussed previously, the United States had viewed lotteries as a legitimate source of revenue for much of its history.) He concluded that, because lotteries represented a cost to society, to the state, and to individuals, and because prophets opposed gambling, lotteries were an inappropriate way to fund the government. It was, in his opinion, "morally wrong for a state or a nation to exploit the weaknesses of its citizens through sponsorship of lotteries." Even if

158 • TINKERING AROUND THE EDGES OF TAX AND RELIGION

lotteries provided an easy source of revenue for cash-starved states, their moral failings trumped the additional revenue.[55]

Ultimately, it is probably impossible to know whether the Mormon Church's opposition to lotteries is the principal reason that Utah stands in the infinitesimal minority of states that have still not implemented a state lottery. Members—as voters and as legislators—do not always follow church directives. They are more likely to go along, though, where church leaders provide a unified front and where the church expends its own political capital in pushing an idea.[56] Whether or not a Utah lottery would have provided the state with needed revenue, church leaders expended their political capital and sent a unified message that the moral question was more important than the revenue one.

* * *

The Mormon Church's view that the state should not raise revenue from immoral sources goes beyond the question of lotteries. The church believes that the state has a moral imperative not to profit from immoral policies. For instance, many proponents of legalized recreational marijuana have argued for its legalization based, at least partly, on the potential revenue the state would gain from taxing marijuana sales.[57]

Potential revenue notwithstanding, the Mormon Church came out against recreational marijuana legalization. In a letter to church members in Arizona, Nevada, and California, church leaders asserted that the accessibility of marijuana in the home posed a distinct "danger to children,"[58] vaguely echoing their arguments against the community-destroying potential of a lottery. In neither case did the church directly address the question of increased state revenue. In both cases, though, the church demonstrated its willingness to expend political capital to oppose legalizing activities it considers immoral, irrespective of their ability to raise governmental revenue.[59]

11

Volunteer Missionaries and Paid Clergy

Mormonism emerged in an evangelical world. At the time of its birth, Methodists had been proselyting throughout the young country for decades. Baptists, Presbyterians, and Campbellites had followed in the Methodist footsteps, each sending their own missionaries to win converts. In 1830, almost immediately after Joseph Smith formally organized his Church of Christ, it, too, embraced missionary work.[1] Within three months of the church's formal organization, Joseph called his younger brother, Samuel Harrison Smith, on a mission to the town of Livonia, New York, to preach the new religion and, if possible, to sell copies of the Book of Mormon.[2]

While Samuel was the first missionary of the new church, he was far from the last. Before long, the percentage of Mormons engaged in missionary work had begun to outpace other evangelizing churches.[3] The young church did not outgrow its missionary zeal as it aged and matured. By the early 1980s, one in four or five Christian missionaries proselyted Mormonism.[4] In 2021, 54,539 members of the Church of Jesus Christ of Latter-day Saints served a full-time proselyting mission, and another 36,639 participated in service missions.[5]

As the church evolved, so did its methods of proselyting. In the earliest days, revelation called missionaries to leave for their mission field without "purse or scrip, neither two coats."[6] The church derived this model, which relied on strangers to provide room and board for the itinerant missionaries, from the New Testament, where Jesus appointed seventy to preach two by two, carrying "neither purse, nor scrip, nor shoes."[7] Even church hierarchs followed the pattern

160 · TINKERING AROUND THE EDGES OF TAX AND RELIGION

laid out in Mormon and Christian scripture. When Brigham Young left Nauvoo for a European mission in 1837, he and the other members of the Quorum of the Twelve left their homes penniless. They relied on God and the goodwill of the people they encountered in their travels. When they reached New York and found funds to buy tickets to cross the Atlantic, they considered their financial success miraculous.

Once in Europe, Young borrowed funds to print hymnals, Books of Mormon, tracts, and the *Millennial Star*, a church newspaper. Ultimately, with the profit from those endeavors, he paid off his debt and paid for his necessities in Europe. He believed his experience—traveling without funds and relying on grace to live and proselyte—to be normative.[8]

So, for instance, in 1846, Oliver Huntington recorded in his diary that, "[a]ll being well and right, we started without purse or scrip to preach the gospel." As a practical matter, traveling without any financial safety net often proved burdensome. Huntington first set his sights on Colne, where there was a member of the church. When he called on Brother Ridings, though, Ridings's wife answered the door. She "looked very illnaturedly, replied very shortly to us when we made ourselves known and stood there without asking us to come in." With that reception, Huntington and his companions decided not to request room and board but instead traveled another seven miles to see Mary Smith, who worked as a servant to a wealthy landowner. Smith or her employer let them spend the night there.[9]

While Huntington proved fortunate enough to find lodging, not all missionaries enjoyed that same luck. In 1852, James Farmer, a Mormon missionary in England, wrote that after taking tea and preaching, he asked the people he had preached to whether "any one could find us a bed as we were preaching without purse or scrip or if they would give us some money to get one." Nobody obliged, forcing Farmer to find a cheap public house for the night.[10] To avoid spending the night in cheap shelter or worse, missionaries often turned to other members to help them, a practice Young discouraged.

In spite of Young's preference for missionaries traveling without a safety net, by the 1860s, missionaries had begun to feel that they could take money with them. By 1890, the majority of Mormon missionaries in England declined to follow Young's example of teaching without purse or scrip. Rather, they drew on their personal resources for their support.[11] The need for missionaries to have money intensified in the twentieth century. By then, missionaries—especially missionaries in urban areas—had to have resources to pay for room and board. Even when carrying money became necessary, though, urban missionaries would sometimes try to experience the miracles of traveling without purse or scrip as they went "country tracting," leaving their money behind. In 1904, for

Volunteer Missionaries and Paid Clergy · 161

instance, James Duffin wrote in his diary that he had become "converted to traveling without purse or scrip."[12] Eight years later, missionary Claude Hawley recorded that he was visiting with two Elders (missionaries) who were "walking accros the continent doing mission work, traveling without purse or scrip."[13]

As the church moved further into the twentieth century, missionaries and the church almost entirely abandoned the idea of leaving for missionary service without purse or scrip, the practice sidelined to the exigencies of the modern world. During the Great Depression, the church published a serial story in *The Improvement Era*, an official church magazine, about mission work. In the introduction, we meet Louise Stone, "a modern Mormon girl with a fiance on a mission." Louise is worried because financial exigencies are set to force her fiancé to leave his mission early. His father, Louise explains to her uncle (who is also her bishop), got a pay cut. Where the family was sending him $30 each month before, they can now only afford $15.

Louise asks her uncle whether the ward can help make up the rest. If not, she asks, can her uncle—the owner of a bank—help personally? He recuses; the ward, he explains, is stretched too thin to help anybody else. And he cannot help personally, though he does not explain why not. Louise must come up with the rest of the money herself (something she does, in part, by foregoing her $5 monthly expenditure on silk stockings).[14] By the 1930s, then, the idea of having sufficient money to pay for one's mission had become mainstream enough to show up in church-published fiction.

And not only fiction. In a 1943 general conference address, apostle George Richards told the story of a 73-year-old member. Every winter over the previous eight years, Richards said, this man had spent about six months serving various missions. He planned on serving a ninth, provided he could "earn enough money for his keep in the mission" in the meantime.[15]

Still, there was not a clean break between traveling without purse and scrip and funding one's own mission. The idea of "country tracting" lasted until the beginning of the 1950s, with some mission presidents encouraging their missionaries to spend a portion of their proselyting time without funds. But by the early 1950s, between changes in mission leadership and changes in technology (particularly the increased availability of cars), the financing structure of Mormon missions changed. Rather than relying on strangers and proselytes for room and board while in rural areas, missionaries fully funded their own missions, bringing with them the money they needed.[16]

The ethic of saving money to fund one's own mission had become firmly ensconced in Mormon culture by the 1960s. For instance, in the February 1962

162 · TINKERING AROUND THE EDGES OF TAX AND RELIGION

volume of *The Improvement Era*, Bookcraft advertised a "3-section savings bank." Illustrations on each section would help children "save for mission, tithing, and own needs."[17] By the end of the decade, a future missionary could have upgraded from a cardboard bank to an actual bank—First Security Bank advertised accounts that would "assist you in accumulating the $2400 to $3000 generally needed for mission financing." It promised both the maximum interest—5 percent paid quarterly on accounts with at least $500—and FDIC insurance to help ensure that missionaries could, with the help of their parents, pay for their own missions.[18]

Soon, saving money for mission had become part of the financial training of Mormon children. In the church's semiannual general conference, future church president Gordon Hinckley encouraged boys (though not girls) to obey the church's commandments, deepen their gospel knowledge, learn a foreign language, and save money for their mission. Hinckley emphasized the importance of saving money, encouraging boys to "[s]ave it in a secure way so that it will be available when you need it."[19]

Four years later, Hinckley repeated his advice to "young boys": they should attend seminary, read the Book of Mormon, and "save money now for a future mission." That money, he counseled, should be deposited somewhere safe, not speculative. And that money could be increased by forgoing expensive consumption: Hinckley explained that he had heard of "costly youth excursions to exotic places." Instead of spending money on travel, he suggested, why not stay close to home and "put the money in your future missionary accounts?" Someday, he predicted, such savers would be grateful for their thrift and foresight.[20]

By the end of the 1980s, the institutional church played a very limited financial role in a missionary's service. The church paid for transportation to and from a missionary's mission. Otherwise, the missionary and the missionary's parents were responsible for funding a mission.[21] And what if the missionary and their parents lacked the resources to pay for a mission? In that case, the missionary could turn to other relatives or friends to help pay. Ultimately, if an individual still could not meet the cost of their mission, then, notwithstanding Louise's uncle's reticence, a missionary could turn to their local congregation to help pay for mission expenses.[22]

Government Subsidies for Mormon Missions

During the same period that the church's missionary finances were definitively shifting from eschewing to embracing purse and scrip, the United States adopted its federal income tax. In 1917, four years after its initial enactment, Congress

Volunteer Missionaries and Paid Clergy • 163

raised the tax rates substantially to help pay for World War I. Where five years earlier there had been no income tax, suddenly wealthy individuals faced a top marginal rate of 54 percent.[23] Charities worried that if taxes cut deeply into people's discretionary income, taxpayers would reduce their charitable giving. Without those private donations, the government would have to step in to either provide services charities could no longer provide or fund charities itself.[24]

Senator Henry Hollis amplified the charities' concerns. Speaking in favor of a limited charitable deduction, he asserted that people donated to charity out of their surplus. "After they have done everything else they want to do," he explained, "after they have educated their children and traveled and spent their money on everything they really want or think they want, then, if they have something left over, they will contribute it to a college or to the Red Cross or for some scientific purpose." With higher taxes, they would be tempted, he believed, to tighten their belts by reducing their charitable donations, unless the government reduced the cost of donating to charity through a charitable deduction.[25]

The charitable deduction that Congress enacted successfully reduced the cost of charitable donations for qualifying taxpayers. A taxpayer who has a deduction subtracts the amount of the deduction from their income. By reducing the amount of income they report, taxpayers can use deductions to reduce their ultimate tax bill. In 1917, it would look like this: a taxpayer in the 52 percent tax bracket could donate $100 to her church (a tax-exempt organization capable of receiving deductible donations). The taxpayer would then take a $100 deduction for that donation, reducing her income tax by $52. As a result, her $100 donation only cost her $48 in after-tax dollars. (Though her donation only cost her $48, her church received $100. Where did the other $52 come from? The government, which forwent collecting that revenue.)

In its initial iteration, the charitable deduction was available for "[c]ontributions or gifts actually made within the year to corporations or associations organized and operated exclusively for" qualifying charitable purposes.[26] Within a handful of years, the statutory language had expanded to grant deductibility to contributions made to "or for the use of" qualifying tax-exempt organizations.[27] (This change in wording will become relevant to the Mormon experience in the 1970s and 1980s.)

This strange economics of self, family and friend, and congregation-funded volunteer missionary work forced Mormon missionaries and their families into dialogue with US tax law. Specifically, it raised questions of whether missionaries had to pay taxes on support they received and whether their families and friends could deduct the amounts they paid to support missionaries.

164 · TINKERING AROUND THE EDGES OF TAX AND RELIGION

In 1962, the IRS provided some answers to these questions. While the IRS guidance did not explicitly refer to Mormon missionaries, the description of missionary finances it lays out lines up well with Mormon mission finance at the time. If the IRS guidance was not directed solely at Mormon missionaries, at the very least it provided parents of missionaries with a tax framework they could use.

In its guidance, the IRS described relevant mission finances in reasonable detail:

> In the instant case, the work of the local congregation in the field of missions is carried on by missionaries who are specially called from the congregation to devote their full time to missionary service for a period of specified duration and who are ordained for this purpose. The congregation has a number of missionaries presently serving missions in various parts of the world on a voluntary, noncompensated basis. Some of these missionaries are supported in whole or in part by their parents, some pay their expenses from their personal savings, and some have their traveling and living expenses entirely or partially reimbursed or paid from a church fund maintained for that purpose.
>
> The local congregation, through the contributions of its members, maintains the fund and members are encouraged to make personal contributions to the fund. All contributions to the fund are expended in pursuance of the purposes of the fund and no part thereof is earmarked for any individual.
>
> From this fund, missionaries are reimbursed for certain qualified living and traveling expenses incurred in the service of the church where such expenses are not covered by amounts received by the missionaries directly from their parents, from relatives or friends, or from their own savings. In order to justify reimbursement for his expenses, each missionary is required to submit a monthly report listing his receipts and expenses and in no case is the fund to supply amounts greater than the reports can validate.[28]

Based on this hypothetical outline of mission finances, the IRS answered a number of questions relevant to missionaries and their families. First, it looked at whether missionaries had to pay taxes on the money they received from the congregational missionary fund. The IRS noted that the definition of "gross income" for tax purposes is tremendously broad, encompassing all income from any source. However, the IRS did not believe that payments to missionaries fit within the expansive definition. The IRS noted that missionaries were motivated by religious conviction and a desire to serve. As a result, it characterized the payments as advances made to the missionary on behalf of, and at the request of, the missionary's church. These advances did not, in the IRS's opinion, constitute income to the volunteer missionary.[29]

Volunteer Missionaries and Paid Clergy • 165

This conclusion stands in stark contrast to the tax treatment of people the IRS characterized as "employee-missionaries." Like volunteer missionaries, employee-missionaries do not receive a salary, though they are guaranteed a minimum level of support. Unlike volunteer missionaries, employee-missionaries have to pay taxes on that support, even when it comes from voluntary donations by individuals and groups, designated for the support of a particular missionary.[30] The IRS never explains how to differentiate an employee-missionary from a volunteer missionary, notwithstanding the radically different tax consequences for each.

Second, the IRS looked at whether parents could take a charitable deduction for donations they made to a missionary fund established by their local congregation. The answer, the IRS explained, depended on the level of control the congregation exercised over the donated funds. If a donation were earmarked to support a particular missionary, the tax law would characterize the donation as a gift to that missionary and thus as not deductible. On the other hand, if the congregation had full control over the disposition of the fund, the parent could take a deduction, even if the money ultimately went to support their child.[31]

While the IRS did not explicitly address the question of whether a parent could deduct amounts they sent directly to their missionary-child, its ruling strongly implied that they could not. If the tax law treated a restricted donation made through a charitable fund as a nondeductible gift, it should presumably also treat a direct payment to a particular missionary as a nondeductible gift.[32]

While the first part of the IRS's ruling was beneficial to Mormon missionaries, the second part was not. In the 1960s, most Mormon missionary support went directly from parents to their missionary children, and that support was not deductible by parents. Without a deduction, parents bore the full (after-tax) cost of their children's missionary service.

IRS revenue rulings are not statutory tax law though; while they have some precedential value, that value largely lies in how persuasive they are. A taxpayer who chooses not to follow a revenue ruling does not face an underpayment penalty as long as there is a "realistic possibility" that a court would agree with their tax conclusion.[33] So, in the early 1980s, a number of Mormon parents chose to challenge the IRS's revenue ruling and deduct payments they sent directly to their missionary children.

The IRS disallowed these deductions, reasserting its position that direct payments made to missionaries were not deductible. Some of the parents sued, and in 1984, one of these families, the Whites, prevailed in the Tenth Circuit Court of Appeals. The Tenth Circuit determined that, at the very least, parents' payment of their missionary-child's expenses was "for the use of" the church.

166 · TINKERING AROUND THE EDGES OF TAX AND RELIGION

(Remember, the Internal Revenue Code allows deductions of contributions *to* or *for the use of* qualifying exempt organizations.[34]) Thus, according to the Tenth Circuit, the IRS's revenue ruling was wrong. Taxpayers could deduct money they sent directly to Mormon missionaries.

Within months of the Tenth Circuit's decision, the *Ensign*—the official magazine of the Mormon Church—informed church members about the ruling. The Tenth Circuit, it explained, had determined that missionaries' travel and living expenses were deductible, thus overruling the IRS's long-standing position. It suggested that affected church members should consult their personal tax adviser in filing tax returns for 1983, as well as deciding whether to file amended returns for previous years.[35]

The article piqued Bart Davis's attention. Bart was a young attorney with two younger brothers who had recently finished their missions. He mentioned the article to his parents, who mentioned it to their accountant. The accountant thought that the decision provided justification for the deduction, so he filed an amended return on their behalf, claiming a charitable deduction for the Davises' support of their two missionary sons.

The IRS rejected their refund request.

How could the IRS reject the Davises' refund request if the Tenth Circuit had just ruled that missionary expenses were deductible? Because the Davises lived in Idaho, which falls under the jurisdiction of the Ninth Circuit. And, while it seems strange, a Court of Appeals' interpretation of the tax law only applies within its jurisdiction. Another Court of Appeals may interpret the same provision of tax law differently. The IRS has to follow the court's holding in the circuit in which a taxpayer lives, but it can disregard judicial decisions from other circuits.

The Davises were unhappy with the IRS's decision and, at the urging of another attorney at Bart's law firm, decided to sue. Shortly after Bart filed the suit, he received a phone call from Wilford W. Kirton, the Mormon Church's general counsel. Kirton explained that the church had been interested in this question even before the Tenth Circuit issued its opinion in *White* and had been trying to establish a test case. There were two cases pending in the Ninth Circuit, he said, the Davises' and one other. Would the Davises be willing to let the church audit their case? And, if the church's attorneys thought the other case would be cleaner, would the Davises be willing to dismiss their case?

Bart checked with his parents, who agreed to let the church look at their case. Shortly after Bart relayed that information to Kirton, he received another call. Kirton told him the church wanted to move forward with the Davises' case. In addition, Kirton offered to represent the Davises *pro bono*.[36]

Volunteer Missionaries and Paid Clergy • 167

The Davises accepted, and Kirton proceeded to lose, first at the district court and then at the Ninth Circuit, both of which agreed with the IRS that direct payments made to volunteer missionaries were not deductible.[37] (Kirton also represented the Brinley family in Texas. The Fifth Circuit said it lacked sufficient information to decide whether the Brinleys made deductible payments to their missionary son, but agreed with the Tenth Circuit that, at least under some circumstances, parents could deduct amounts that they sent directly to their missionary children.[38])

The Davises appealed their case to the Supreme Court. The Supreme Court, which gets to decide whether it will hear any given case, is notoriously reluctant to adjudicate questions of tax.[39] One way to grab the Court's attention, though, is through a circuit split. Where two Courts of Appeals have come to opposite conclusions about the same question of law, the Supreme Court is substantially more likely to hear an appeal in the case.[40]

When it came to the deductibility of missionary funding, the Courts of Appeals were diametrically opposed. If the Supreme Court did not step in, parents of Mormon missionaries living in Louisiana, Mississippi, Texas, Colorado, Kansas, New Mexico, Oklahoma, Utah, and Wyoming would be able to deduct part of the amount they sent to their missionary children. Parents living in Alaska, Arizona, California, Hawaii, Idaho, Montana, Nevada, Oregon, and Washington, by contrast, would not be able to take charitable deductions for money they sent to support their missionary children. As for parents living in the other thirty-two states and the District of Columbia? As of the late 1980s, the IRS continued to disallow deductions for payments to missionary children, but the Courts of Appeals for those circuits had not yet ruled on the question.[41]

In light of the circuit split and the uncertainty it engendered, the Supreme Court agreed to hear the Davises' appeal.[42] The court held oral arguments on March 26, 1990. Rex E. Lee argued on the Davises' behalf.[43] Lee, a practicing Mormon, had been the founding dean of BYU's law school. He served as Solicitor General under President Ronald Reagan and, at the time he argued the case, had just been appointed president of Brigham Young University.[44]

Before addressing the Supreme Court's decision, handed down about two months after Lee argued in front of the court, it is worth noticing how far, in 1990, the church had come from its origins. In its earliest days, members paid the taxes that were demanded of them. Members sometimes tried to fit into exceptions from taxation (for instance, as missionaries), but the church itself lacked the sophistication or connections to challenge the taxes as applied.

By the 1980s, the church's general counsel was willing and able to take church members' cases, *pro bono*, and, when those cases went in front of the Supreme

168 · TINKERING AROUND THE EDGES OF TAX AND RELIGION

Court, could tap one of the most elite attorneys in the country to argue the case. It is further worth keeping in mind that, in spite of the church-sponsored representation, the church had little at stake institutionally. Whether or not parents could deduct support for their missionary children, the church faced no potential tax liability. At most, the lack of deductibility would marginally reduce the number of missionaries, to the extent that certain families could not afford to send their children on missions without the subsidy of tax deductibility, or it would marginally increase the cost to other members, who would have to step in to support those missionaries who could not otherwise go. And yet the church interposed itself into these judicial proceedings and engaged prestigious legal counsel and sophisticated legal arguments to expand that federal subsidy.

At oral argument, Lee conceded that the Davises would not have contributed the money they deducted had their sons not been missionaries (though he also pointed out that they had made other financial contributions to missionary work that had not gone to their sons). He emphasized, though, that the important motive was the Davises' motive to "support the church's efforts" because that motive demonstrated that their contributions were "for the use of the church."[45] In essence, because the Davises had not made a transfer *to* the church, Lee's argument rested on the language of Congress's 1920s expansion of the charitable deduction.

The Justices proved skeptical of Lee's description of motivation, pushing him on the idea that even if parents donated with or without children on missions, they donated more when their children were on missions. If that were the case, was not the primary motivation to support their children, not the church?

Lee responded that this idea of familial support for missionaries predated the federal income tax by more than a century. He described

> 160 years' worth of history in which the Mormon church prefers that its missionary work be a total family effort, including not only the family support, but also including specifically the direct payment.
>
> And if I may elaborate on that just a bit, these are reasons that go twice as deep as the history of the income tax laws themselves, and they are borne out by the church's amicus brief and by the affidavit of Elder Robert Backman, who at the time was the executive director of the missionary work.
>
> Over its 160-year history the church has found that missionary work has always been family centered, from the very beginning, with one or more members devoting full uncompensated time and effort, usually for a period of two years, while other family members have stayed at home but have participated through their prayers, their letters and most significantly, from the very beginning, their financial support.[46]

While Lee asserted (wrongly, as we have seen) that the church had an unbroken history of familial financial support for missionaries, he acknowledged that allowing an unlimited deduction to parents could allow them to transform personal expenses into charitable deductions. If, for instance, parents contributed $5,000 per month to their missionary children, who needed $500 to support themselves, the parents could transform $4,500 from a nondeductible gift to a deductible charitable contribution.

The church, Lee assured the Justices, did not want parents sending extra money to their missionary children. To the extent missionaries had money beyond their frugal needs, he explained, "then they have time to spend on things like movies, plays and so forth, and their missionary work decreases." Any responsible missionary would decline to accept money in excess of their basic needs. Moreover, to ensure that missionary parents did not transform nondeductible expenses into charitable donations, Lee acknowledged that the IRS could impose a ceiling on deductibility of whatever amount the church laid out as mission costs.[47]

Lee's analysis and assurances ultimately did not convince the Justices, who voted unanimously to uphold the Ninth Circuit's decision. While the court acknowledged that "for the use of" *could* support multiple interpretations, including both the IRS's and the Davises', it looked to the reason Congress had added those four words to the tax law. In congressional hearings on the 1921 tax bill, representatives of charitable interests testified that a number of communities had established community chests, charitable foundations, or charitable trusts. Individuals could donate money to a trustee who would invest it and eventually turn it over to a committee that would distribute the funds for charitable purposes. Because a trustee held legal title to the donations, donors and charitable organizations worried that donors would not get a charitable deduction because the donation was *to* the trustee, not the charitable organization.

The "for the use of" language, the court decided, was meant to capture this type of trustee intermediary. Moreover, almost immediately after Congress passed the updated statute, the Bureau of Internal Revenue officially stated that *for the use of* meant something similar to *in trust for*. It did not, by contrast, contemplate a donation to a non-charitable individual who would not ultimately turn the money over to a qualifying charitable organization. Because the Davises had not argued that they sent money to their sons to hold in trust for the church, the Supreme Court ruled that their (and, in consequence, any Mormon parent's) transfers to their missionary children did not qualify for a charitable deduction.[48] Mormon parents who supported missionary children had to bear the full after-tax cost of that support.

170 • TINKERING AROUND THE EDGES OF TAX AND RELIGION

Or, rather, they had to bear the full cost of that support for the next six months. Because six months later, the church changed how it asked missionaries to fund their missions. Effective January 1, 1991, the church announced that missionaries would no longer be responsible for paying the actual costs of missions. Instead, every missionary (and/or their family and friends) would be responsible for contributing a set amount of money to a church missionary fund monthly for the duration of their mission. Initially, the amount was set at $350 a month. (The church has increased this amount twice: in 2003 it increased to $400 and in 2020, to $500.[49])

Did the church change its funding model solely to provide tax benefits to its members in light of the Supreme Court's *Davis* decision? It is not clear that it did. When it announced the change, the church explained that its prior funding model put a disproportionate burden on some missionaries and their families. The actual cost of missions ranged from $100 a month to $750. And because missionaries did not pick where they went, they did not have a savings target (unless they assumed that they would bear the highest cost). By equalizing the amount missionaries paid, the church made the cost of missions more equitable among its members.

But although there were non-tax reasons for the church to change its funding model for missionary service, it is hard to ignore the Supreme Court's decision, given the timing and the substance of the change. Under its new funding model, parents and missionaries paid into a ward missionary account. The central church would pull money out of each ward missionary account based on the number of missionaries serving from a ward and it would send money to each separate mission. There, the mission president would allocate the money among missionaries.[50]

The change put the church's mission program squarely within the contours of the IRS's 1962 ruling. It established a congregational fund to which members—including missionaries and their families—could contribute, but contributors had no control over the disbursement of the fund. Contributions were not earmarked to any specific missionary; the church could allocate them however it chose. Within that structure, donations to the mission fund qualified as tax-deductible.

Ultimately, the question of the deductibility of missionary donations did not affect the church directly. It is possible that a higher after-tax cost of missions would have marginally reduced the number of missionaries, as potential missionaries got priced out of missionary service. But its impact likely would have been minimal—the church expressly encouraged other members to contribute where an individual missionary and their family could not afford the cost.[51]

Volunteer Missionaries and Paid Clergy · 171

In spite of having no direct consequence, though, the church decided to interpose itself to try to ensure the optimal tax consequences for its members, first by providing attorneys as members litigated the issue and then by changing the funding structure so that it conformed with IRS guidance. By the 1980s and 1990s, the church had become a sophisticated user of the US legal and tax systems.

Foreign Currencies and Mission Funding

A globe-spanning church needs to be a sophisticated user not only of the US legal and tax systems but of legal and tax regimes worldwide. With more than half of its membership outside of the United States,[52] Mormon parents throughout the world must figure out the local tax treatment of their mission payments. The church's sophistication in the United States does not automatically mean it has a sophisticated understanding of the non-US tax regimes that apply to these parents. Because the church has standardized its payment model worldwide, though, it does not take local tax regimes into account, which can lead to issues for parents of missionaries outside of the United States. (At the same time, though, as in the United States, the church is willing to litigate outcomes that are bad for its members.)

For instance, until 2015, New Zealand's Commissioner of Inland Revenue allowed a tax credit to taxpayers who donated to the missionary fund. In 2015, however, the Commissioner changed his mind and began disallowing those credits. The church and a Mr. Coward, the father of a Mormon missionary, challenged this change. As in the United States, non-US missionaries paid a set monthly amount to the church's missionary fund, irrespective of the actual costs of their mission. When Coward's daughter served her mission, the standard cost for missionaries from New Zealand was NZ$475 per month. The court acknowledged that the NZ$5,700 that Coward paid did not go directly to support his daughter. Moreover, the amount he paid bore no relationship to the costs of her mission. Still, to qualify for the credit, the court held, the payments had to be charitable gifts for tax purposes.

The church and Coward argued that the payments counted as gifts. They were, after all, given gratuitously, and parents did not receive any consideration in return. The Commissioner disagreed with the church's framing. He argued that there was, in fact, consideration—Coward and other parents of missionaries paid into the fund and, in return, the church paid the living expenses of their children while their children served as missionaries.

172 · TINKERING AROUND THE EDGES OF TAX AND RELIGION

In determining whether mission payments qualified as gifts, and thus qualified for a tax credit, the New Zealand High Court looked at each potential payor separately. Payments by missionaries themselves, the court held, did not qualify as gifts for tax purposes. The benefits a missionary received, including travel, accommodation, food, and personal expenses, were more than nominal. Similarly, while parents and grandparents did not personally enjoy the travel, accommodation, and other benefits the church provided to its missionaries, seeing their "child, who while no longer a child is still engaged in life education, being able to travel, live overseas, and experience being a missionary abroad" provided a real benefit to them. Payments by parents and grandparents therefore did not qualify for the tax credit.

By contrast, other relatives and ward members did not have the type of relationship with a missionary that created these indirect benefits. While the court acknowledged that friends and other families might be "dismayed" if, after they raised funds for a missionary, that missionary decided not to go, they would have no legal standing to get their money back. As a result, the New Zealand court held that payments by people other than the missionaries themselves, their parents, or their grandparents were gifts and therefore qualified for the tax credit.[53]

The court's disallowance of tax credits for parents and grandparents of missionaries proved a temporary setback. The Mormon Church reacted to the High Court's determination with disappointment and announced that it would appeal the decision to the New Zealand Court of Appeal.[54] The Court of Appeal agreed with the High Court that payments by friends and non-parent or-grandparent family qualified for the charitable tax credit. But it disagreed about payments by missionaries themselves, their parents, and their grandparents. In New Zealand, it explained, there were no Ward Missionary Funds. Rather, all missionary payments went to the Church of Jesus Christ of Latter-Day Saints Trust Board, which intermingled donations on behalf of missionaries with all other donations. Moreover, the church in New Zealand was not self-sufficient—the Salt Lake-based church had to pay for any shortfalls the New Zealand church experienced.

More importantly, though, the benefits of missionary service—both to the missionary and to their parents and grandparents—were immaterial. Yes, they enjoyed "spiritual and moral satisfaction," but the Court of Appeal believed that any type of charitable donor received the same warm glow. The tax law—which expressly provided for the charitable credit—did not consider satisfaction from doing good to be a material benefit that would disqualify a donor from receiving a tax credit. Further, even if the warm glow represented a material benefit, the connection between payments to a central church fund and payments to support missionaries was too attenuated to have legal significance. There was no legal connection between these two payments.[55] While New Zealand's tax law was not identical to that of the United States, the structure the Mormon Church put into place in 1991 provided a basis for the church to judicially challenge the disallowance of the New Zealand tax credit.

A Professional Clergy

Mormonism sees its ecclesial structure as an exception to a world of paid clergy. Apostle M. Russell Ballard explained that the "Lord in His infinite wisdom has designed His Church to operate with a lay ministry."[56] And, at the local level, the church is largely run by unpaid lay clergy.[57] But the church pays its top leadership; a leaked memo from 2014 announced that the church was raising its "base living allowance" for general authorities from $116,400 per year to $120,000.[58]

There is very little interesting about Mormon general authority pay from a tax perspective. The leaked paystub makes clear that the church treats the living allowance it pays general authorities as employee compensation, withholding federal and state income taxes in the same manner any other religious employer would. The paychecks do illustrate two interesting tax details, however. The first is that, while the church withholds state and federal income taxes, it does not withhold payroll taxes.[59] For employees, the employer is responsible for half of the taxes and the employee is responsible for the other half (currently 7.65 percent each). Congress decided that for payroll tax purposes it would treat ministers and other clergy as self-employed, freeing their religious employers from their half of payroll taxes.[60]

Self-employment merely shifts the payroll tax liability, however. Instead of an employer paying half, a self-employed individual owes the whole 15.3 percent payroll tax out of their own pocket. But Congress created a second special rule for clergy: Clergy can elect to be excluded from the Social Security system altogether.[61] If they opt out, not only does the church-employer not have to pay its share of payroll taxes, but the clergy member also does not have to pay self-employment taxes. Opting out does come with a downside, though: clergy that opt out of paying into the Social Security program will not receive any Social Security or Medicare benefits on the wages they earned in the church's employ.[62]

There is no way to know whether general authorities elect out of the Social Security program. Such election, filed with the IRS, is not public. Moreover, the form used to opt out does not need to be supplied to the employer church; it is ultimately an individual decision by each general authority. The Mormon

174 · TINKERING AROUND THE EDGES OF TAX AND RELIGION

Church, though, has decided to avail itself of the exemption for payroll taxes on its clergy employees.

The second interesting tax detail illustrated by the leaked paycheck is an earnings line that reads "Parsonage."[63] This line provides some insight into how the tax law has influenced the way the Mormon Church structures the compensation of its top officials. In addition to the special tax treatment clergy receive with respect to Social Security, the federal income tax has a special rule for church-provided housing and housing allowances.[64] Generally, any compensation an employer provides its employees is taxable, whether paid in cash or in kind (as, for instance, employer-provided housing). In the 1920s, though, Congress decided that, unlike most employees, "ministers of the gospel" could exclude the value of church-provided housing from their gross income.

Over the next three decades, the tax law tried to establish the scope of this exemption. The Bureau of Internal Revenue said it only applied where the church provided in-kind housing to its minister. A handful of courts disagreed, ruling that housing allowances paid to clergy also qualified for the exclusion. In 1954, at the request of religious organizations that believed the provision discriminated against smaller churches that could not afford to provide physical housing for their clergy, Congress formally enlarged the parsonage exemption, legislatively reversing the Bureau's interpretation of the law.[65] Today, "ministers of the gospel" (which the IRS reads expansively to include both Christian and non-Christian clergy) can exclude from gross income either church-provided housing or a housing stipend, as long as that stipend does not exceed the fair rental value of the clergy member's home.[66]

Returning to the leaked paystub: Henry Eyring earned $3,096.15 for the pay period between July 22 and August 4, 2000. But the church labeled $826.92 of the amount it paid "Parsonage." The church's designation is a critical part of this rental exclusion: Treasury Department regulations provide that cash ministerial housing allowances can only be excluded where the employer-church designates a portion of the pay as a parsonage allowance.[67]

This exclusion is not tremendously complicated and does not require a high level of sophistication on the part of the employing church. In fact, Congress added the cash exclusion precisely to benefit less wealthy and less sophisticated religions. Nonetheless, it does require affirmative action by a religious organization, affirmative action that the Mormon Church is both willing and able to take. Because Eyring met the IRS's definition of a *minister of the gospel* and because the church was willing to designate a portion of his pay as a parsonage allowance, he—and, presumably, other salaried general authorities—could treat a portion of his salary as a tax-free housing allowance.

Mission Presidents: Volunteers or Clergy?

Mormon prophets and apostles are not the only members the church compensates for their religious service. The questions around the payment of general authorities are interesting, but not complicated: they have the same tax benefits any other paid clergy receive. By contrast, the economics and tax questions surrounding Mormon mission presidents raise interesting questions. The church treats mission presidents as volunteers who pay their own way; in some ways, though, the financial arrangements mission presidents face belie that idea. Before reaching questions of the taxation of mission presidents, though, it is worth taking a brief detour into what a mission president is.

Unmarried Mormon men can serve as missionaries after they turn eighteen, and women can at nineteen. The standard male mission term is about two years, while the female mission term runs for eighteen months. The church assigns missionaries to "missions," which are geographic regions in which they spend their mission years. Each of these missions is overseen by a president—an adult man who is called by church leadership to spend three years overseeing the missionaries in a particular mission. Mormon mission presidents come, the church explains, from multiple walks of life, professions, and even geographic areas. When called, they put their careers or retirement on hold for their three-year term.[68]

Mission presidents do not have to fully self-fund their service. To make their three years away from work and from home more financially manageable, the church provides mission presidents with a number of financial benefits. Among other things, it provides them with housing, transportation, and insurance. It also reimburses mission presidents for various living expenses, including obvious expenses like food, clothing, household supplies, and medical treatment, and less obvious living expenses like Christmas, birthday, and anniversary gifts. In addition, the church reimburses mission presidents for the cost of school and for some extracurricular expenses for dependent children. It also reimburses them for their children's mission expenses and for a portion of their children's college tuition (to the extent it does not exceed BYU's famously low tuition).

Serving as a mission president does not provide mission presidents with a blank check, though. In addition to listing expenses it will reimburse, the church also provides mission presidents with examples of expenses it will not cover. These unreimbursed expenses range from paying off a mission president's personal debt to paying for personal investment management to reimbursement for the theft or loss of personal property while serving as a mission president.[69]

176 · TINKERING AROUND THE EDGES OF TAX AND RELIGION

So how should mission presidents treat payments they receive from the Mormon Church? The question seems to have come up for the first time in the 1940s. In 1943, Gustave Iverson, the president of the church's Eastern States Mission, wrote the church asking whether his "monthly family expense allowance" was subject to income taxation.

The church's response to Iverson's query began with a very lawyerly disclaimer: "We do not assume, of course, to advise a taxpayer as to his tax liability, since this is a personal responsibility with him." With that said, the First Presidency explained that they viewed the monthly payment not as salary, but as an advance on "personal expenses incurred while you are devoting your entire time as a missionary." As a result, they said, the family allowance paid to mission presidents was not compensation for services and was not taxable, a conclusion also arrived at by the state of Utah.

Still, while the church did not believe its payments to Iverson were taxable, it withheld 5 percent of Iverson's stipend for the Victory Tax.[70] The Victory Tax, enacted in 1942, brought the income tax, previously imposed solely on the wealthy, to a much wider swath of the American public. To the extent an American's gross income exceeded $624, they owed a 5 percent tax. In the course of one year, this new tax quadrupled the number of individuals subject to the income tax.[71]

With this new tax regime, one that not only applied to more taxpayers but also eliminated most deductions, the church had to figure out whether the Victory Tax applied to its payments to mission presidents. Unsure of the proper result, they decided to exercise caution and withheld the necessary amount. Still, they told Iverson that they did not believe that withholding the tax represented a concession that his stipend was subject to the Victory Tax and they hoped the question would be resolved before payment came due.[72]

Three months later, the First Presidency sent another letter to Iverson, this one accompanied by a check for $29.60. Church counsel had advised them that the Victory Tax did not apply to the allowances made to mission presidents. The enclosed check represented the amount that the church had withheld from the allowance for the first quarter of the year.[73]

The Victory Tax question proved a temporary hiccup in the church's tax compliance. Two years after its introduction, Congress repealed the Victory Tax.[74] The repeal did not eliminate the question of mission president tax liability, though: it was accompanied by a new income tax that essentially enshrined income taxation as a general public duty, not one limited to the wealthy.[75]

Even through the expansion of income taxation, the church has maintained its position that mission president stipends represent reimbursement, not

Volunteer Missionaries and Paid Clergy • 177

payment. As a result, the church tells its mission presidents that they do not need to treat funds they receive from the church as income or pay taxes on them. In its handbook for mission presidents, the church explains to mission presidents that

> [b]ecause you are engaged in volunteer religious service, no employer-employee relationship exists between you and the Church. As a result, any funds reimbursed to you from the Church are not considered income for tax purposes; they are not reported to the government, and taxes are not withheld with regard to these funds.[76]

(As a matter of positive US law, this explanation does not entirely make sense. An employer-employee relationship is not a critical hallmark of the definition of gross income. Gross income is a broad concept, capturing most accretions to wealth, unless explicitly exempted by statute.)

The church is forceful in its assertion that mission president stipends do not represent income to mission presidents. In its handbook for mission presidents, it affirmatively advises them to treat the stipend payments as non-taxable reimbursements. Mission presidents, it says, should not tell people that the church pays them for their services as mission president. They should not list amounts the church pays them on their tax returns. And they should not share information about amounts they receive with their tax or financial advisors. (The church explains that "most tax advisers are not aware of this information" and thus that their advice about how to treat the mission president stipends may be incorrect.)

It is worth keeping in mind that this advice does not represent an underlying opposition to tax compliance by the church. The church has a program to provide aid to members in financial difficulty. Sometimes that aid involves direct payment to landlords, health care providers, and others. Prior to 1990, when the church made payments on behalf of its destitute members, it sent not only the payment but an IRS Form 1099. (A Form 1099 provides information to payees and to the IRS about certain non-salary payments made.) In 1990, the IRS informed the church that it was no longer obligated to send form 1099s for payments made on behalf of church welfare recipients; until then, though, the church complied with its tax obligations (and even after, it continued to send 1099s in other circumstances).[77]

To the extent mission presidents have questions about their tax obligations with respect to their service, the church has a Tax Division. Unlike general tax advisors, the handbook explains, the Church Tax Division has access to tax rulings and other research that justify the characterization of mission president

178 · TINKERING AROUND THE EDGES OF TAX AND RELIGION

stipends as non-taxable.[78] The church has not made public its legal research or the rulings it relies on, so it is impossible to evaluate the soundness of its legal position. To comply with the church's instructions, though, mission presidents have to rely on the church's sophistication when it comes to income taxation.

* * *

Mormon missionaries are not motivated by money. In fact, they spend money to serve their missions. But while money is not a motivating factor, missions—even self-funded volunteer missions—are intricately wrapped up in questions of finance. And those questions of finance implicate the tax law.

The Mormon Church has been responsive to the finances of its member-missionaries and their families, initially supporting their bid to make mission payments deductible and, when that failed, changing the funding structure to something more favorable to members, both from a financial and a tax perspective. It has also been responsive to the tax needs of other members—for instance, it has set up a system that allows members to contribute appreciated property so that donors can take advantage of the extra tax benefits that come with donating appreciated property.[79]

The church is similarly attuned to the tax situation of its leaders and its mission presidents. While it has not actively lobbied for any particular tax treatment of its clergy or its mission presidents, it has structured its compensation for both in a way that provides them with the maximum tax benefits it can provide. The church has recognized the inextricable connection between taxes and the financial life of its members, even as those members serve the church.

12

Tax Exemption as a Lever for Change

The Mormon Church puts a high value on its tax-exempt status. That value is long-standing, going back at least as far as early twentieth-century New York, when it debated how to deal with property tax on the chapel it built in Brooklyn. This emphasis has continued through the present. The church's policy handbook tasks local church leaders with ensuring that their church activities do not "jeopardize the Church's tax-exempt status."[1] To ensure that local lay leaders and congregations do not jeopardize the church's tax exemption, the church instructs local leaders that they cannot use church buildings for political, business, or investment purposes. If one congregation "misuses the Church's tax-exempt status," the handbook warns, it could affect other church units as well.[2]

The Mormon Church is not only protective of its exemption internally; it has spent political capital, time, and money to ensure that the law continues to provide the benefits it has enjoyed over the last century or more. While the church has been successful at preserving its exemption, though, the obvious value it places on its tax-exempt status also has a cost: critics of church policies also understand its subjective value and have used that value to pressure the church to change policies to which they object.

Protecting an Uncapped Charitable Deduction

In many ways, the ability to receive tax-deductible donations is the most important benefit tax-exempt organizations enjoy. Deductibility reduces donors'

180 · TINKERING AROUND THE EDGES OF TAX AND RELIGION

after-tax cost of donations. Imagine a member of the Mormon Church in the top tax bracket. She donates $10,000 to the church. If she can deduct that $10,000 donation, her donation will cost her less than $10,000 in after-tax income. How much will it cost her? As of this writing, the top tax bracket in the United States is 37 percent. A $10,000 deduction will reduce her final tax bill by $3,700. After taxes, then, her $10,000 donation costs her $6,300. (Where does the other $3,700 come from? The government chips it in by forgoing $3,700 that, absent a deduction, it would have collected.)

As a practical matter, this donation for charitable giving is available to a tiny swathe of Americans. The charitable deduction is an itemized deduction, and taxpayers must choose between taking their itemized deductions and a standard deduction. Only if they choose to itemize can taxpayers deduct their charitable contributions. Historically, far fewer than half of taxpayers have itemized.[3] (In recent years, that number has declined precipitously—in 2019, only about 11 percent of taxpayers itemized their deductions.[4]) But even though the vast majority of Americans cannot deduct their charitable donations, the idea that charitable gifts are deductible is so salient, and the fact that many people cannot deduct their charitable gifts is so obscure, that deductibility may encourage their generosity anyway.[5]

In spite of the low percentage of taxpayers who itemize, charitable deductions are very expensive to the government. The Treasury Department estimated that in 2021 alone, the deduction for charitable contributions reduced federal revenue by almost $57 billion.[6] In light of their cost and their regressivity (that is, itemized deductions provide more benefit to high- than low-income taxpayers), in 2009 President Barack Obama proposed capping itemized deductions for taxpayers earning in excess of $250,000 annually. These high-income taxpayers would face a 28 percent rate ceiling on their itemized deductions.[7] To return to the example from the first paragraph of this section: if Congress had adopted President Obama's proposal, the 28 percent cap would have limited the high-income taxpayer's deduction to $2,800. Instead of an after-tax cost of $6,300, the tithe payer would face an after-tax cost of $7,200.

The Obama administration estimated that the cap on itemized deductions would raise an additional $318 billion for the government over ten years. It wanted to earmark that additional revenue to a reserve fund meant to modernize the country's health care system.[8] But the goal was not merely to raise revenue. The Obama administration wanted to rebalance the tax law so that it was more equitable.

Charitable organizations responded to the Obama proposal almost immediately. They feared that increasing the after-tax cost of donating would reduce the amounts given to charity. Researchers at Indiana University estimated that the proposal could reduce the wealthiest Americans' charitable giving by several billion dollars.[9]

Would this cap have affected tithes paid to the Mormon Church? It depends on what economists call the "elasticities" of Mormon tithes and offerings. Specifically, it depends on whether Mormons who donate to their church are sensitive to the after-tax cost of giving. To the extent they are, capping the deductibility of charitable giving would reduce the amount the wealthiest Mormons donated. Generally, economists have found that charitable giving *does* respond to the price of giving. It is possible that religious giving is less responsive than non-religious giving, but even religiously obligatory giving likely has some sensitivity to after-tax costs.

Whatever the elasticities of Mormon tithing, the church values the full deductibility of charitable donations. In 2011, the Senate Committee on Finance held hearings on tax incentives for charitable giving. Senator Orrin Hatch, both a senator from Utah and a member of the Church of Jesus Christ of Latter-day Saints, gave opening remarks at the hearing. In his remarks, he emphasized the importance of charitable deductions to religion, explaining that the tax treatment of charitable giving was important to him, to "the people of Utah, and to millions of Americans who give every year to their churches and their communities." He worried that the charitable deduction was under "quiet assault." Deliberately or not, he reiterated Senator Hollis's justification for a charitable deduction from nearly a century earlier: as more people were turning to charities for help, he said, Congress should not interrupt charitable giving, the lifeblood of charities.[10]

Among the several witnesses who testified before the Committee was Dallin Oaks, at the time a member of the Mormon Church's Quorum of the Twelve Apostles. Oaks's testimony underscored the importance of charitable deductions to the Mormon Church: he testified that charitable deductions were "vital" to the charitable sector.

While he spoke to the importance of the charitable deduction to the nonprofit sector as a whole, he emphasized the importance of religion in the American character. He quoted John Adams's statement that the Constitution was made only for a "moral and religious People. It is wholly inadequate to the government of any other."[11] The country, Oaks explained, was united and held together not just by law, but by norms. A significant portion of Americans learn and internalize those norms through religious instruction. To preserve the vitality of this religiosity that is so critical to the country's foundation, and to preserve "pluralism and freedom in our Nation," Oaks urged that Congress make no changes to the charitable deduction.[12]

182 • TINKERING AROUND THE EDGES OF TAX AND RELIGION

Later, in response to a question from Senator Hatch, Oaks elaborated on why the charitable deduction was so important to him and to the church. Irrespective of the elasticity of Mormon tithes and offerings, Oaks described the charitable deduction as expressive. After all, Oaks acknowledged, some portion of charitable donors cannot take a deduction for their charitable donations. And even more donate their time, in addition to or in place of money and property. (Irrespective of whether a taxpayer itemizes, there is no charitable deduction for the donation of services.[13]) If Congress substantively changed the charitable deduction, Oaks argued, that would "be understood as a teaching message by the Government of the United States to its citizens generally that the private sector and charitable works are less important in our picture, and that the government is assuming this function. It is that message that I speak against."[14]

In Oaks's telling, the charitable deduction is not just about revenue and elasticities, as important as those revenues and elasticities are. The charitable deduction also sends a message to the public about what the government values; in some ways, the charitable deduction legitimizes the efforts of the charitable sector. While the charitable deduction does not constitutionally endorse religion, at the very least it tells Americans that religion—in Oaks's telling, the very foundation of our society—is something important, something they should give to, volunteer with, and attend. The Mormon Church used its connections and expended the time of its leaders to ensure that the government not only continued to subsidize charitable donations but that the government stayed on message about the important place of the charitable sector.

Bob Jones and Tax as Leverage

Over the years, critics of the Mormon Church have tried to use the high value the church places on its tax exemption to pressure it into changing certain policies and practices. Underlying this pressure is the Supreme Court's *Bob Jones* decision. Ultimately, this activist pressure misunderstands the legal context in which the IRS uses *Bob Jones* but, even though the pressure lacks legal weight, it provides a public challenge to the church's claim to legitimacy-via-exemption, essentially a mirror image of Oaks's vision of the expressive content of the charitable deduction.

The use of tax exemption as a policy pressure point is a relatively recent innovation. Prior to 1970, it would have been largely unthinkable. But in 1970, a federal district court in Mississippi told the IRS to stop granting tax exemptions to private grade schools that discriminated against Black students.

The origins of the Court's order are rooted in the Supreme Court's *Brown v. Board of Education* decision sixteen years earlier. In *Brown*, the Supreme Court declared that racially segregating public schools violated the Equal Protection Clause of the Fourteenth Amendment.[15] A year later, the Supreme Court ordered district courts to oversee the transition from segregated to desegregated public schools "with all deliberate speed."[16] Thirteen years later, some school districts were still dragging their feet, maintaining a system of formally desegregated, but in practice racially segregated, schools. The Supreme Court found this unacceptable and held that school boards had an affirmative obligation to not only allow for desegregation but to actually proactively implement it.[17]

As schools started to comply with the Supreme Court's order, a wave of white parents, especially in the South, withdrew their children from the newly desegregated public schools and enrolled them instead in white-only private schools. Because private schools are not state actors, the Fourteenth Amendment did not apply to them. If enough white parents enrolled their children in these private "segregation academies," they would effectively resegregate the public schools. In the wake of the Supreme Court's implementing an affirmative duty on schools to desegregate, private school enrollments in the South exploded, from about 25,000 students in 1966 to 535,000 in 1972. While not every private school in the South was a segregation academy, even in private schools that did not exclude students of color, the student bodies were predominantly white, and the massive increase in private school enrollment was driven largely by white parents who did not want their children to attend school with Black children.[18]

The federal government tried to counter this resegregation. The year after Congress passed the Civil Rights Act of 1964, the IRS stopped processing tax exemption applications from segregated private schools. But in 1967, the IRS unfroze the applications. It believed that it lacked authority to deny tax exemptions to private schools on the basis of racial discrimination.[19]

Three years later, a group of Black parents and students in Mississippi sued the IRS. They argued that state support of segregated schools through exemption and through the ability to receive deductible donations violated the Constitution. The district court agreed and ordered the IRS to temporarily stop granting tax exemptions to any private school in Mississippi unless the IRS affirmatively determined that the school did not discriminate on the basis of race. The Court declined, however, to order the IRS to revoke the exemptions of discriminatory private schools that had already received an exemption.[20]

The IRS not only complied with the Court's ruling, it went even further. The IRS announced that it would no longer approve tax exemption applications from private schools that discriminated, not just in Mississippi, but throughout the United States. Moreover, it would revoke the exemptions of racially discriminatory private schools that had already successfully applied.[21] The IRS explained

184 · TINKERING AROUND THE EDGES OF TAX AND RELIGION

that racial discrimination in education violated a decades-long federal policy. Under the law of charitable trusts, it said, an organization whose purpose violated public policy did not qualify as charitable. Under this analysis, racially discriminatory schools were not charitable and could not qualify for federal income tax exemption.[22]

As the IRS adopted and broadened the Mississippi court's order, it sent a letter to schools, including Bob Jones University, warning that if they discriminated on the basis of race, the IRS would revoke their exemptions. While Bob Jones University did not formally affiliate with any particular Christian denomination, it was a religious school that required its professors to be professing Christians and to teach according to the Bible.

The university's board of directors believed that the Bible forbade interracial dating and marriage. Because of these beliefs, the school did not admit nonwhite students until 1971. Beginning in 1971, it began to admit Black students, but only if they were married and their spouses were also Black. In 1975, after the Supreme Court held that discriminatory admissions policies violated US civil rights laws even for private schools,[23] Bob Jones University began to allow unmarried nonwhite students to apply but continued to forbid interracial dating or marriage among its students under penalty of expulsion. The IRS was not impressed. In 1975, the IRS informed Bob Jones University that it planned to revoke the school's exemption retroactively to December 1, 1970, the day after the IRS had informed the university of its new policy.

Bob Jones University challenged the IRS's revocation of its tax-exempt status.[24] Among other things, the university argued that the Free Exercise Clause of the First Amendment meant that, even if the IRS could generally revoke the tax exemption of racially discriminatory schools, it could not revoke Bob Jones University's exemption. With the school's discrimination grounded in sincere religious belief, revoking its exemption for exercising that belief was unconstitutional.

The Supreme Court agreed that the Free Exercise Clause protected practice grounded in religious belief. But, it said, that protection was not absolute. The government could burden religious practice where that burden was critical to the government's accomplishing a compelling government interest. The Supreme Court said that stamping out racial discrimination in private schools was such a compelling government interest (the Court used phrases like *established public policy* and *fundamental public policy* to describe these nondiscrimination norms) that it trumped religiously motivated behavior. Notwithstanding the university's belief that the Bible required discrimination against Black students, doing so violated a fundamental public policy, which meant the school was ineligible for tax exemption.[25]

The Supreme Court's 8–1 decision came as a shock to the Christian Right. Various Evangelical publications characterized the decision as the death of religious freedom and a violation of the Religion Clauses of the First Amendment. Bob Jones University published a pamphlet calling the decision a "bomb" dropped on the university, the shockwaves of which would eventually reach not only religiously affiliated schools but churches themselves.[26]

In retrospect, this reaction to the Supreme Court's *Bob Jones University* decision has proven unfounded. While the Supreme Court upheld the IRS's determination that violation of fundamental public policy was incompatible with tax exemption, both the IRS and the courts have largely cabined their application of the fundamental public policy rule to racially discriminatory private schools.[27] But the decision marked a sea change in the way people engaged with churches and other tax-exempt charities they believed were acting poorly.

Equal Rights and Tax Exemptions

The success of Black Mississippi parents in the Court and with the IRS provided a new toolbox for activists who wanted to pressure tax-exempt organizations to change. With the introduction of fundamental public policy as a criterion of tax exemption, activists could use taxes to try to effect change in churches. As early as 1972, the Feminist Party filed a complaint with the IRS challenging the tax exemption of the Catholic Church and its affiliates over their opposition to abortion. In this pre-*Bob Jones* era, the complaint did not allege that the Catholic Church should lose its exemption because it violated public policy. Rather, the Feminist Party claimed, in asking its parishioners to send anti-abortion petitions to their legislators and in otherwise speaking against abortion the Church had engaged in impermissible lobbying and violated the conditions of tax exemption.[28]

This challenge was always a quixotic one, whether or not the Feminist Party understood that. The tax code did not prohibit tax-exempt organizations from lobbying—rather, it provided that "no substantial part" of a tax-exempt organization's actions could consist of lobbying.[29] And while the courts have not provided a bright-line definition of what constitutes "no substantial part," general consensus holds that it relates to the proportion of a tax-exempt organization's overall activities made up by lobbying.[30] The Catholic Church encouraging its members to lobby against legalized abortion almost certainly does not rise to the level of *substantial* and almost certainly does not violate the prohibition.

This conclusion is bolstered by the fact that the Catholic Church did not lose its tax exemption. However, the Church's continued exemption did not prove fatal to feminist activists. They cared less about the actual revocation of the Church's exemption (though, presumably, they would not object if that

186 · TINKERING AROUND THE EDGES OF TAX AND RELIGION

happened) and more about the rhetorical power of assailing the Church's political actions as being illegitimate and illegal. With their goal a rhetorical, rather than legal, one, the continued exemption of the Catholic Church did not dissuade activists from accusing churches of improper political actions and rhetorically attacking their tax exemption.

By the end of the 1970s, feminist activists had taken notice of the Mormon Church. In the 1970s, though, the Mormon Church was not a large player in abortion politics. Instead, feminists attacked the Mormon Church's tax exemption because of its stance on the Equal Rights Amendment. Originally drafted in 1923, the ERA provided that "[e]quality of rights under the law shall not be denied or abridged by the United States or by any State on account of sex."[31] Almost fifty years after it was introduced, Congress passed the ERA and sent it to the states for ratification. The amendment quickly racked up approval in a number of states but, as opposition mounted and organized, the support petered out, leaving the ERA three states short of ratification.[32]

At first, the Mormon Church did not join with this opposition. Spencer Kimball, the church's president, declined to comment on the ERA and, while Utah did not ratify it, legislative sponsors in the state included Mormons.[33] But the church's indifference to the ERA began to shift in 1974, when its Special Affairs Committee (a committee made up of four of the church's twelve Apostles that reviews "potentially questionable" legislation[34]) began to formulate a strategy for defeating the ERA.[35]

The shift became explicit and public in an editorial in the *Church News* published at the beginning of 1975. The editorial claimed that the ERA was not only imperfect but potentially dangerous. The country had already enacted laws to protect women, it explained; to the extent women were treated worse, that treatment demonstrated a lack of enforcement, not a lack of law. And no law—including a constitutional amendment—would change the fact that "men and women are different, made so by a Divine Creator."[36]

President Kimball subsequently condemned the ERA as a "threat to morality and traditional family life." Mormon groups began to oppose the ERA in a number of state legislatures.[37] After defeating the ERA in Utah, the Mormon Church turned its focus to Nevada. While Mormons only made up about 10 percent of the state's population, they often represented 30 percent of the voters in any given election. They used their outsized political influence both to ensure that the state senate did not ratify the amendment and to defeat a referendum, thus preventing at least one additional state from ratifying the ERA.[38]

The Mormon Church's entrance into the ERA fray coincided with feminist activists' expansion of their rhetorical invocation of tax exemption. A

1975 women's awareness conference at the University of Utah featured Gloria Steinem, editor of *Ms. Magazine*. Prior to the conference, she spoke with reporters, who asked her what she thought of the Mormon Church's opposition to the ERA. She responded that the church had the right to believe and say anything it wanted about women's roles and that, in fact, she would defend the church's right to do so. At the same time, she believed that defending the separation between church and state was critical and, if a religious organization (she meticulously avoided mentioning the Mormon Church) wanted to use its resources to lobby against the ERA, proponents of the ERA could challenge that organization's tax-exempt status. (In the same press conference, Dr. Warren Ferrell, author of *The Liberated Man*, asserted that patriarchal churches should be sued "for giving their members sexual hangups," a cause of action that, even without the First Amendment, is not a thing.)[39]

At the direction of their church leaders, Mormon women attended a number of state International Women's Year conferences, at least in part to temper enthusiasm for the ERA. Their participation surprised feminist leaders, who were not happy with the Mormon women's goals. At the 1977 National Women's Political Caucus in San Jose, Liz Carpenter, co-chair of ERAmerica, expressed her frustration with the church's active opposition to the ERA. The United States, she explained, should not follow the lead of Salt Lake, where "church leaders historically overmarried," or Rome, where "the head of the church never marries," in determining what constitutes the American family. Still, she did not entirely follow either the Feminist Party or Steinem; rather than demanding the revocation of the Mormon Church's exemption, she argued that the tax-exempt church owed the public a duty of transparency. In her telling, thanks to the tax-exempt status of the church, the public had the right to know whether it was using Mormon missionaries to preach an anti-ERA message.[40]

By the end of the decade, the campaign against the Mormon Church's tax exemption had shifted into high gear. The steering committee of the New Mexico Women's Political Caucus, for instance, took up Steinem's call and passed a resolution calling for the IRS to audit the Mormon Church and other tax-exempt entities that actively opposed the ERA. Similar to Steinem's assertions in Salt Lake, the New Mexico Women's Political Caucus asserted that the church's political actions violated the sacrosanct separation of church and state.[41]

The rhetorical appeal of demanding that the IRS revoke the church's tax exemption for inappropriate political actions extended beyond organizations and elite movement leaders. On the fiftieth anniversary of the enshrinement of women's suffrage in the 19th Amendment, members of a local National Organization of Women chapter protested outside of a Mormon meetinghouse

188 · TINKERING AROUND THE EDGES OF TAX AND RELIGION

in Maryland. Nestled among signs reading "Patriarchy is malarky," and "Strengthen families with the ERA," one protestor held a sign reading, "The Mormon Church should pay taxes or get out of politics." Elaine Raksis, the co-coordinator of the demonstration, told reporters that demonstrators objected to the church's "improper" activity against the ERA. She claimed that the church was acting more like a political party than a tax-exempt organization. Still, she understood the limits of her protest—she wasn't trying to change the Mormon Church's position, just reduce its political effectiveness (in part by invalidating the implicit approval it received as a result of its tax-exempt status).[42]

While the IRS was always unlikely to revoke the Mormon Church's tax exemption, the repeated assertions that the church *should* lose its exemption bled into public, and even legislative, discourse. In 1980, University of Utah political scientist and member of the Mormon Church J.D. Williams told a reporter that he believed the church's actions on the ERA fell on the wrong side of the rules governing tax-exempt organizations. He further believed that the church's political activities violated church-state separation and placed its tax exemption in "increasing jeopardy."[43] Then, when the church excommunicated Sonia Johnson, the founder of Mormons for ERA, other members also began to ask whether the vehemence of the church's opposition to the ERA violated the terms of its tax exemption.[44]

These concerns even arose in Senate hearings about the ERA. Orrin Hatch, Senator from Utah and practicing Mormon, asked Massachusetts Senator Paul Tsongas whether the ERA would allow the Catholic Church (which denied priesthood to women), the Mormon Church (which also denied priesthood to women), or Orthodox Jewish synagogues (which sometimes separated men and women) to qualify for tax exemption. Sen. Tsongas responded that he foresaw some conflict between the ERA and religious liberty, conflict that would have to be resolved by the courts. Sen. Hatch responded that, in light of the Supreme Court's then-recent decision in *Bob Jones*, the ERA would effectively allow the government to impose its beliefs on Mormons, Catholics, and Jews, unless those (and presumably other) religions were willing to give up their tax exemptions.

Ultimately, and unsurprisingly, the IRS did not revoke the Mormon Church's tax exemption as a result of its lobbying against the ERA. In fact, there is no evidence that it even considered the possibility. However, the rhetorical idea that tax exemption could function as a lever to encourage changes in church policy had, by the early 1980s, become mainstream. And with the Supreme Court's *Bob Jones* decision, it became clear that religious belief would, alone, be insufficient to prevent such revocation.

Racism and Tax Exemption

In an 1852 speech to the Utah territorial legislature, Mormon president Brigham Young announced that men and women of African descent could neither hold the priesthood nor participate in temple worship. He framed this exclusion as the result of Cain's biblical murder of Abel. Young's move was not particularly unique—the "cursing of Ham and the cursing of Cain were the two favorite explanations offered for the origin of the black races."[45] Young brought a uniquely Mormon twist to this story, though: Cain's murder of Abel had affected not only Abel but also all of the descendants Abel would have had if he had lived. Abel's death meant that these prospective descendants were not "liturgically welded to one another through the temple priesthood." According to Young, Black people would not have access to the priesthood or temple until after every spirit that would have descended from Abel had access to priesthood and temple. This premise led Young to preach that in this life, Black men would not hold "one jot nor tittle of priesthood."[46] The race-based restriction on priesthood and temple access that Young introduced in 1852 continued for more than 130 years, until church president Spencer Kimball removed the restrictions in 1978.

During the last half of the nineteenth century, American culture maintained a deep antagonism toward Mormonism. That antagonism was grounded largely in distrust of Mormon polygamy, not in the church's racist treatment of Black members. The distrust began to largely dissipate once the church abandoned polygamy and worked to transform its image from a radical group of dissenters to a respectable American polity. By the early twentieth century, the church had largely succeeded in this transformation and the United States began to view Mormons as model Americans. That view peaked in the 1950s.[47]

But in the 1950s the United States began to reckon with the harms its institutionalized racism had perpetrated on people of color. In 1954, the Supreme Court held that the doctrine of "separate but equal" that had earlier permitted school segregation violated the constitutional guarantee of equal protection under the law.[48] A decade later, Congress enacted the Civil Rights Act of 1964 which prohibited discrimination on the basis of race in, among other things, education and employment.[49] The church's race-based priesthood and temple restrictions began to prove untenable, doing damage both to the reputation and the work of the church.

For instance, in the early 1960s when the Mormon Church refused to endorse pending civil rights legislation, civil rights leaders considered demonstrating at the church's semiannual General Conference. As the church continued to

190 · TINKERING AROUND THE EDGES OF TAX AND RELIGION

avoid supporting specific legislative proposals, the Utah chapters of the NAACP introduced a resolution asking foreign governments to refuse to grant visas to Mormon missionaries "for promulgating a doctrine of black inferiority."

While the demonstrations failed to materialize, by the end of the 1960s, civil rights protests against the church began to coalesce around BYU. Protests and boycotts focused on the church-owned school's athletics. Stanford cut all ties with BYU.[50] Then in 1969, fourteen Black members of the University of Wyoming's football team planned to wear black armbands in a game against BYU as a protest against the Mormon Church's discriminatory policies.[51] The night before the game, the fourteen Black players were kicked off the team.

Unsurprisingly, the students' expulsion failed to lower the temperature on BYU protests. A week after the University of Wyoming kicked the Black players off the team, San Jose State's players wore armbands in their game against BYU as a show of support for the Wyoming players.[52] Students at other Western Athletic Conference schools demanded that their schools not play against BYU (and, in some cases, against Wyoming until it reinstated the protesting Black players).[53] The New Mexico Civil Liberties Union went as far as asking the University of New Mexico to withdraw from what it characterized as the racist and repressive Western Athletic Conference.[54]

In addition to the direct activist pressure the church faced, it also faced structural impediments with maintaining its race-based exclusion. The church was expanding, notably in Brazil, where a significant portion of the population descended from African ancestors, and in Nigeria. In both countries, maintaining race-based limitations on church participation would have impeded the church's continuing growth.[55]

This very public disenchantment with the church's treatment of Black people would, by itself, have been enough to pressure the church to rethink its policies. But the Supreme Court's *Bob Jones* decision in many ways would have given antiracist activists the tools they needed, had it appeared earlier. The Supreme Court explicitly blessed the IRS's policy that tax-exempt organizations could not enact racially-exclusive policies and keep their exemptions. Moreover, the Supreme Court found that religious belief did not trump a tax-exempt organization's duty to not discriminate. *Bob Jones* was not a perfect match; a religiously-affiliated school is different from an actual church, and the Supreme Court's decision only addressed religiously-affiliated schools. Still, when the Supreme Court issued its decision, nobody knew that the IRS would use the fundamental public policy rule almost exclusively to disqualify racially discriminatory private schools.

Did the risk of losing its tax exemption influence the church's abandonment of its priesthood and temple ban? It is possible, but unlikely. A small handful of

Tax Exemption as a Lever for Change · 191

accounts exist that assert that the church did consider its tax-exempt status when reassessing its exclusionary policy. Shortly after the policy change, for instance, church historian Leonard Arrington posited that the "Lord might have permitted the announcement at this particular moment" because a number of states refused to exempt church property from tax. He pointed in particular to Wisconsin.[56]

Arrington was right that in the early 1970s, a Wisconsin court held that granting property tax exemptions to racially discriminatory fraternal and benevolent societies violated the Constitution. After that decision, the Wisconsin Department of Revenue began investigating almost 10,000 tax-exempt organizations' by-laws. It eventually selected thirty organizations to investigate in more depth and ultimately decided that several Masonic lodges had membership practices that effectively allowed them to discriminate against potential Black members. The lodges sued, asking a court to stop the Department of Revenue's investigation. In November 1977, the trial court refused, and on June 30, 1978 (about three weeks after the church changed its policy), the state supreme court upheld its refusal, allowing the Department of Revenue to continue looking into racially discriminatory policies at a handful of Masonic lodges.[57]

There is no evidence that Wisconsin ever investigated, or threatened, the Mormon Church's property tax exemption. Similarly, legal databases have no record of the Mormon Church challenging any other state's denial of a property tax exemption based on its racially exclusionary policies (or, for that matter, anything else).

Arrington's assertion illustrates the main problems with most claims that the church changed its policy because of the potential loss of tax exemption: these claims appeared after the fact, without any evidence that the Mormon Church was at risk of losing its tax exemption, and without any evidence that church leaders considered the church's tax exemption in deciding to do away with the racial temple and priesthood ban. These same problems showed up in coverage of the ten-year anniversary of the church removing these restrictions, where a newspaper article quoted a former member's assertion that the change happened because the church did not want to lose its federal tax exemption.[58] Three decades after that, a sociologist and academic posited again that the church may have rethought its racially exclusionary policies for fear of losing its tax exemption.[59]

These retrospective accounts would make sense in light of the *Bob Jones* decision. After all, the Supreme Court held explicitly that racial discrimination violated fundamental public policy and that religious belief and practice did not excuse that violation for tax exemption purposes. While the church's policies were not directly addressed by the Court, they were at least analogous.

192 · TINKERING AROUND THE EDGES OF TAX AND RELIGION

But the Mormon Church changed its policy five years before the Supreme Court made clear that religious belief did not overcome the nondiscrimination rules implicit in federal tax exemption. There is some evidence that church leaders worried about the church's tax exemption, but there is no contemporaneous evidence that church leaders considered questions of tax exemption in making that decision. It thus appears unlikely that the risk of losing its tax exemption—a risk that was at best deeply attenuated and anachronistic in 1978—played any significant part in the church's reversal of its policy, especially when there were so many other existing pressure points on the church.[60]

Still, even if the risk of losing its tax exemption did not play a role in the Mormon Church revoking its priesthood and temple restrictions, the collective retrospective assumption that it did says something about public perception of the value the Mormon Church placed on its tax exemption and how it would respond to the risk of losing that exemption. And that perception played out yet again in the 2000s, as the Mormon Church attempted to flex its political muscles to oppose the legalization of same-sex marriage.

The Fight Against Same-Sex Marriage

In 1990, three same-sex couples applied for marriage licenses in Hawai'i. The state denied their applications and they sued. The trial court ruled against the couples, who went on to appeal their loss. Ultimately, their case ended up in front of Hawai'i's Supreme Court, which ruled that the state constitution did not include a fundamental right to same-sex marriage. At the same time, though, the Court recognized that sex was a "suspect category" for constitutional purposes. As such, if the state wanted to limit marriage to opposite-sex couples, it had to demonstrate that refusing to recognize same-sex marriage furthered "compelling state interests" in the narrowest manner possible.[61]

While the Court did not require Hawai'i to recognize same-sex marriages, it started a political and judicial conversation in the state about the future of same-sex marriage. In the meantime, other states began to debate what they would do if Hawai'i decided to recognize same-sex marriage. The Mormon Church, together with the Catholic Church, stepped into this conversation, opposing any legal recognition of same-sex marriage. The Mormon Church committed $500,000 in Hawai'i—and then Alaska—to the anti-same-sex marriage cause. In addition to monetary donations, the church mobilized its members. In 1998, both Hawaiian and Alaskan voters overwhelmingly voted to amend their respective state constitutions to limit marriage to opposite-sex couples.[62]

The Mormon Church next turned its attention to California. It put its weight behind Proposition 22, a ballot initiative that banned the state from recognizing same-sex marriages. The initiative literally had Mormon fingerprints on it—California Senator Pete Knight asked Lynn Wardle, a BYU law professor and member of the Mormon Church, to review the language of the initiative before he filed it. Wardle in turn passed it on to a handful of other people, including two members of his church's Quorum of the Seventy.[63]

Proponents of Proposition 22 raised almost $5 million in 1999 alone. While that $5 million came from about 15,000 donors, a significant portion came from California's Catholic dioceses and the Mormon Church.[64] Church president Gordon Hinckley praised those members who donated to support Proposition 22 in the church's 1999 General Conference. Their efforts, he said, contributed to a "cause that in some quarters may not be politically correct but which nevertheless lies at the heart of the Lord's eternal plan for His children, just as those of many other churches are doing." While he made no direct mention of the church's tax-exempt status, he did emphasize both the individual contributions from members and the fact that they participated in a coalition that included other faith groups as well.[65] In the end, with $8 million behind it, California voters passed Proposition 22 and prevented the state from recognizing same-sex marriage.[66]

The Mormon Church's initial foray into these late-twentieth-century same-sex marriage fights elicited minimal public comment. In one of the rare responses to the church's political activism around Proposition 22, San Francisco Supervisor Mark Leno argued that the Mormon Church was "aggressively" using its resources to oppose same-sex marriage, in spite of the fact that those resources came from tax-deductible contributions. "You and I subsidize those resources," he said, and yet the church used those subsidized resources to wage a "political battle."[67]

Leno and other San Francisco supervisors requested that the IRS investigate the church's participation in the Proposition 22 campaign. While the Supreme Court had endorsed the idea that religious belief did not vitiate the fundamental public policy rule more than fifteen years earlier, that was not the approach that the supervisors took. Rather, they followed the pattern of ERA proponents from two decades earlier, arguing that the church's lobbying efforts had risen to impermissibly substantial levels.[68]

As with complaints filed against the Mormon Church about its ERA activism, nothing substantive came of these complaints. But they set the template for eight years later, when the church again entered the same-sex marriage fray in California, using its institutional power to push for the passage of California's Proposition 8, which would again prevent the state from recognizing same-sex marriage.

194 • TINKERING AROUND THE EDGES OF TAX AND RELIGION

And why did California voters again confront the question of banning same-sex marriage? Because eight years after the passage of Proposition 22, the Supreme Court of California struck down the state's ban on same-sex marriage. The state's interest in preserving marriage exclusively for opposite-sex couples, the Court held, did not constitute a sufficiently compelling state interest under California's constitution. Proposition 22 could not stand.[69]

This decision was not entirely unexpected. In anticipation of the Court striking down Proposition 22, a group of conservative public policy organizations and religions, including the Mormon Church, joined together to prepare a ballot initiative that would re-entrench the prohibition on same-sex marriage. After the Court's decision, they gathered nearly two million signatures to put Proposition 8 on the November 2008 ballot. Unlike Proposition 22's statutory prohibition on same-sex marriage, Proposition 8 would amend California's constitution, committing the state to only recognizing marriages between a man and a woman.[70]

The Mormon Church not only helped lay the groundwork for Proposition 8, but it also worked to improve the Proposition's ground game. In June 2008, the church's First Presidency sent a letter to be read in all California congregations. The First Presidency explained that the church, as part of its coalition with other religious and secular organizations, intended to work toward Proposition 8's passage. The letter encouraged members to "do all you can to support" the constitutional amendment by donating both time and resources to the effort. Moreover, the letter said, local leaders would tell members how they could help campaign on behalf of the Proposition.[71]

Mormons in and out of California responded. The church itself provided a little less than $200,000 in monetary and non-monetary contributions to the Proposition 8 efforts. (Much of its non-monetary contributions involved time spent by church employees on the effort.)[72] Mormons themselves, however, donated considerably more. Opponents of Proposition 8 estimated that Mormons contributed more than $20 million to support the constitutional amendment. Because campaign donation disclosures do not have a box for donors' religious affiliation, that number cannot be confirmed. But its scope illustrates the popular perception that Mormons and their church were a driving force behind the ultimately successful attempt to constitutionalize the state's ban on same-sex marriage.

This time, the public noticed. Proponents of same-sex marriage demonstrated outside of Mormon temples, boycotted Utah businesses, and otherwise expressed their displeasure with the church's participation in the campaign.[73] On top of that, they turned their gaze to the church's tax exemption. In the aftermath of Proposition 8's passage, supporters of same-sex marriage complained "that

Tax Exemption as a Lever for Change   •   195

churches that supported the ballot measure violated their tax-exempt status." One protestor explained that she believed the Mormon Church had gone too far; in her view, tax-exempt churches "clearly are not supposed to be involved in political activities." The idea that the Mormon Church had violated the terms of tax exemption became so common that the "No on 8" executive committee asked attorneys to look into the question, even though tax experts widely (and accurately) agreed that the chances of successfully arguing that the Mormon Church, or any other, had violated their tax exemption was basically zero.[74]

While previous questions about whether the Mormon Church's political activity violated the terms of its tax exemption largely stayed in the activist realm, after Proposition 8, it transcended that world. Academics began looking at the question. Tax professor Brian Galle, for instance, took a technical look at the church's participation. While he acknowledged that under the law as it existed at the time, the church had probably not violated the terms of its tax exemption, he proposed an alternate approach that would assign more value to the use of church assets, including mailing lists, thus making it more likely that the church had expended more than an insubstantial part of its assets lobbying.[75] Non-tax law professor Jonathan Turley, by contrast, predicted (incorrectly, as it turns out) that within a decade, the fundamental public policy rule would put the tax exemptions of churches opposed to same-sex marriage at risk.[76]

In the wake of its Proposition 8 activism, the rhetorical assault on the Mormon Church's tax exemption has demonstrated staying power. A decade and a half after the passage of Proposition 8, MormonTips.com, an organization set up by activist Fred Karger, solicits the public for information to help in what it describes as "the biggest, loudest and most comprehensive challenge to a Church's tax-exempt status in history." It argues that the Mormon Church's participation in politics is a blatant violation of its tax-exempt status.[77] In 2018, Karger even filed a complaint with the IRS about the Mormon Church-owned Polynesian Cultural Center, though only a small portion of the complaint dealt with the church's lobbying against LGBTQ rights.[78]

Karger acknowledged that his campaign was unlikely to succeed in convincing the IRS to revoke the Mormon Church's tax exemption. Rather, he explained, his goal was to get under the church's skin and force change.[79] And, while the various campaigns against the church's tax exemption have not succeeded in forcing the church to change its policy on same-sex marriage, they have certainly gotten under the church's skin. Less than a month after the Proposition 8 vote, the church-owned *Deseret News* complained that, although the church had only directly contributed a small fraction of the money used to support Proposition 8, opponents of the Proposition demonized the church and demanded the revocation of its tax exemption. Why, the author asked, were they going after

196 · TINKERING AROUND THE EDGES OF TAX AND RELIGION

the Mormons and not the Catholics, who had contributed significantly more money?[80] (It is worth noting that, contrary to the *Deseret News* writer's impression, activists did, in fact, also challenge the Catholic Church's tax-exempt status in the wake of Proposition 8.[81])

The church itself also responded to calls for the loss of its tax-exempt status. In an essay posted to its website, the church wrote about how it believed legalized same-sex marriage would affect religious freedom. It argued broadly that the constitutionally protected free exercise of religion was coming under increased pressure as "proponents [of same-sex marriage] advocate that tax exemptions and benefits should be withdrawn from any religious organization that does not accept such marriages."[82] Elsewhere on its website, the church asserts that "calls that tax exemptions and benefits be withdrawn from any religious organization that does not accept same-sex marriages" represent one significant challenge facing religious freedom in the United States.[83]

The Mormon Church's concern about preserving its tax-exempt status goes beyond mere rhetoric and essays, though. In 2022, the church expressed public support for the Respect for Marriage Act.[84] The Respect for Marriage Act requires states to recognize marriages performed in another state irrespective of the "sex, race, ethnicity, or national origin" of the married couple. It also provides an explicit recognition that religious institutions, unlike states, do not have to recognize marriages and face no legal liability for refusing to recognize marriages they oppose.[85]

Months after the bill's passage, Dallin Oaks of the Mormon First Presidency expressed concern that church members might misunderstand the church's reasoning in supporting the new law. He explained that the church's aim was not protecting same-sex marriage rights—those, he said, had already been ensured by the Supreme Court's *Obergefell* decision, rendering the bill's protection for marriage rights unnecessary.[86] The church saw an opportunity, though, to codify "the necessary protections for religious freedom" in federal law. Among those necessary protections? The Respect for Marriage Act protected the "tax-exempt status of religious organizations."[87]

As we have seen, the church's tax exemption was at no risk. But again, as with the church's Brooklyn building about a century earlier, the church proved willing to disregard some of its policy preferences to preserve its exemption. Unlike Brooklyn, though, with the Respect for Marriage Act, the church was not just looking at a corporate organizational change; rather, it supported legislation that facially went against its religious policies in the interest of ensuring it kept its tax-exempt status.

Tax Exemption as a Lever for Change • 197

* * *

In the contemporary United States, it is almost unthinkable to tax churches. They have enjoyed exemption from almost any form of taxation since the country's earliest days. Churches—including the Mormon Church—have come to rely on that exemption, both for the financial benefits it provides and its apparent governmental stamp of approval.

The Mormon Church has demonstrated the importance it places on its exemption from generally applicable tax rules. And as its sophistication and public legitimacy have increased, it has used that legitimacy and sophistication to protect its privileged place in the tax system. But the value it places on its exemption cuts two ways; over the last four decades, activists have discovered that they can use the value the church places on its exemption to push for change, particularly in the area of civil rights. And these four decades of activism seem to have reached the Mormon Church: on part of its website intended to answer questions related to religious freedom, it lists "[p]rominent voices" that want to "deny churches tax-exempt status" as one of those threats.[88]

The twenty-first-century Mormon Church's sophistication means that its actions almost certainly do not violate the terms of its tax-exempt status. But violating the law and violating public perception of the law are two different things. While activists may not overcome the church's generally careful attention to legal details,[89] their rhetorical attacks on its exemption function quite effectively as an attack on the church's legitimacy and its relationship to the state.

Today, there is no question of the Mormon Church's ability to coexist with the state and to comply with tax law. But its ability to comply with the law as perceived by the lay public is less clear. Going forward, these questions of public perception, as opposed to technical compliance, are likely to weigh more heavily and occupy a more central role in the Mormon Church's relationship to the society in which it operates.

Conclusion

Since its first days, Mormonism has had an intimate relationship with the state. On April 6, 1830, Joseph Smith formally founded the Church of Christ, "it being regularly organized and established agreeable to the laws of our country."[1] Records, if any, of the incorporation of the church no longer exist, so it is unclear whether Smith actually incorporated the fledgling church. But it is clear that, whether or not he was successful, he attempted to create a church organization recognized by the laws of New York, a move that both recognized the authority of the state and the importance of how the church related to the state.[2]

Over time, the Mormon Church became more adept at interacting with the state, successfully navigating its strictures while preserving the rights and practices that the church preferred. The church's interaction with various tax systems illustrates both this interaction and the church's growth in understanding the governmental systems that surrounded it. While taxes were not the proximate cause of the emergence of Mormonism, they played a role in its prologue, setting the stage for both the Smith family's history of religious dissent and for the Great Awakening that inspired young Joseph Smith to look for the true church.

Similarly, while taxes were not the proximate cause of Smith's death and the closing of the first chapter of Mormonism, they played a role there, too. In Chapter 3, we saw Walter Bagby, the Carthage, Illinois, tax collector,[3] demand that Smith pay taxes on land in Nauvoo. Smith paid the county and state taxes but refused to pay Commerce city and town taxes.[4] The city of Commerce, he

200 · *Conclusion*

explained, no longer existed, having been "included in the city plot of Nauvoo." Smith believed that "enemies" of the Mormons had kept Nauvoo property on the "Tax lists" as a way of taking their money.[5]

A year and a half later, a Mr. Hamilton from Carthage purchased one of Smith's Nauvoo lots in a tax sale. On September 5, 1843, he met Smith to claim his property. Smith believed, however, that he had paid all necessary taxes on the lot, making the tax sale—and thus Hamilton's claim of ownership—illegitimate.[6]

A month later, Bagby approached Smith, who was speaking with Jacob Backenstos and William Clayton. Smith accused Bagby of wrongly seizing his property. Bagby retorted that Smith was a liar. In a subsequent sermon, Smith narrated the experience, telling his followers that Bagby had "exercised more despotic power" over the Mormons in Nauvoo "than any despot of the Eastern country." Bagby "gave me some abusive language took up a stone to throw at me I siezed him by the throat to choke him off."[7] Smith ended up facing charges for assault and battery and paying a fine as a result of his attack.[8]

There is more to the story, though: this process, which ended up with Smith paying a fine, proved unsatisfactory to Bagby, and to other Illinoisans in the region. On August 18, 1843, a group of residents, including Bagby, met at the Carthage courthouse to revive the Anti-Mormon Party.[9] The Party immediately issued a report listing its grievances against Smith and the Mormons. This report placed Smith's assault of Bagby toward the beginning of the grievances. Smith, the report explained, "has been heard to threaten—nay, he *has* committed violence upon the person of an officer, because that officer dared honestly do his duty according to the law."

The report concluded by resolving that Mormon lawlessness had to be constrained, peaceably if possible "but forcibly if we must." Ultimately, the members of the Anti-Mormon Party demanded that Joseph Smith be arrested and delivered to Missouri authorities. Moreover, they volunteered to enforce any arrest order against Smith.[10] These demands for Smith's arrest—and willingness to resort to violence if necessary—presaged his extra-legal murder the following year.

To the surprise of many, Joseph Smith's murder and the Mormons' expulsion from Nauvoo did not end Mormonism. Similarly, Smith's violent confrontation with the Carthage tax collector did not end Mormonism's interaction with the tax system. While taxes have rarely been central to the journey of Mormonism, they have been a constant (and growing) part of that journey nonetheless.

The growing interaction between Mormonism and taxes makes sense. Over the nearly two centuries of Mormonism's existence, the government—and the taxes that fund it—have expanded enormously. In the United States, the New

Deal marked a significant shift in the federal government's presence in American life. Public spending as a percentage of the United States' gross national product almost quintupled between 1900 and the early 1990s.[11] This growth in government spending was fueled by an increase in the amount and sophistication of taxes, which rose from about 6 percent of gross domestic product at the beginning of the twentieth century to more than 25 percent by its end.[12]

This radical growth in the federal government meant that government has become omnipresent in a way it had not been in the earliest days of the country and the church. And it meant that, even for tax-exempt organizations, tax was always just around the corner. For its whole existence, the Mormon Church has operated in the shadow of various tax systems.

As we have seen throughout this book, the tax law could and did influence—and even change—the choices made by the Mormon Church. The relationship between Mormonism and taxes is not a one-way street though. Even in its earliest days, Mormonism helped shape taxes and, through Mormon legislators and Mormon lobbying, Mormonism has been inscribed into the statutory language of the federal income tax even today.

In many ways, then, the relationship between taxes and Mormonism illuminates more broadly the inevitable interaction between church and state. But it does not paint a perfect picture. Just as I was putting the finishing touches on this book, the Securities and Exchange Commission announced that it was imposing a $1 million fine on the church, along with a $4 million fine on Ensign Peak Advisors, the church's investment advisor. For about twenty-two years, Ensign Peak Advisors, at the bequest of the First Presidency and the Presiding Bishopric, had not complied with US securities law.

While a detailed analysis of securities law goes beyond the scope of this book, the abbreviated version of the violation goes like this: any institutional investment manager that exercises investment discretion over $100 million or more of securities has to file a quarterly report with the SEC.[13] When Ensign Peak Advisors informed church leaders of this obligation, they worried that public disclosure of the church's holdings would be harmful to the church. Instead, they directed Ensign Peak Advisors to form a limited liability company that could not be connected to the church to file the report. Years later, when they worried that the LLC could perhaps be tied to the church, they formed a new one. And a few years later, they formed about a dozen LLCs that collectively filed the necessary reports.

Up until this point, this securities story looks like the church engaging with another regulatory regime in a sophisticated manner, much like it does in the tax system. But here the story takes a twist. Because, while Ensign Peak Advisors

202 · *Conclusion*

formed various LLCs which filed the necessary forms, it never gave those LLCs investment discretion, keeping that power for itself. The LLCs existed purely to distance the church from the disclosure in the quarterly reports. But without investment discretion, the LLCs were the wrong party to file the reports—that obligation remained with Ensign Peak Advisors.[14] Thus, the church, perhaps overconfident in its sophistication, broke the law.

Since its beginnings as a small Restorationist church, dissenting from the majority Christianity of its day, the Mormon Church has become a much more sophisticated player, able to navigate a relationship with the state that generally allows the church room to act as it wishes. And nowhere is this sophistication better represented than its interactions with the tax system, as a tax writer, taxpayer, tax-exempt organization, and body of individuals, all of whom are subject to taxation. Is its facility in navigating law limited to the world of tax? Or was its failed attempt to negotiate the securities law an aberration, born of a desire to maintain in the world of securities regulation the privacy it enjoys in the world of tax? Only the future will tell.

Notes

Introduction

1. Thomas Jefferson to Nehemiah Dodge, Ephraim Robbins, & Stephen S. Nelson, January 1, 1802, https://www.loc.gov/loc/lcib/9806/danpre.html [https://perma.cc/794C-SKDT]. The perma.cc links in square brackets after internet citations are intended to prevent link rot. Even if the actual URL of a source changes, the perma.cc URL will provide a mirror. I was reminded of the importance of including perma.cc links as I put the finishing touches on this book. I originally decided not to create a perma.cc URL for sources from the Joseph Smith Papers. Sometime between 2021 when I first drafted chapters 2 and 3 and 2023 when everything came together, though, the Joseph Smith Papers changed some (though fortunately not all) of the URLs. I had to go through all of my citations to the Joseph Smith Papers and, if the link was broken, find again the underlying source. So that that does not happen to readers, then, I went through and created the links that you will find in the square brackets.

2. For instance, Trinity Lutheran Church wanted to participate in a program under which the Missouri Department of Natural Resources helped schools and daycares purchase rubber playground surfaces. Did that represent state aid to religion in violation of the Establishment Clause? A divided Supreme Court decided it did not. *Trinity Lutheran Church of Columbia, Inc. v. Comer*, 582 U.S. 449, 137 S. Ct. 2012, 198 L. Ed. 2d 551 (2017).

3. For example, the owners of Hobby Lobby argued that they should be exempt from the Affordable Care Act mandate that their employee insurance cover contraception, based on their religious beliefs that birth begins at conception. The Supreme Court agreed. *Burwell v. Hobby Lobby Stores, Inc.*, 573 U.S. 682, 134 S. Ct. 2751, 189 L. Ed. 2d 675 (2014).

204 · *Notes to Introduction*

4. According to a 2021 Pew Research Center poll, 55% of Americans strongly or moderately support the separation of church and state. On the other side, only 14% want the two integrated. "In U.S., Far More Support Than Oppose Separation of Church and State," *Pew Research Center*, October 28, 2021, https://www.pewresearch.org/religion/2021/10/28/in-u-s-far-more-support-than-oppose-separation-of-church-and-state/ [https://perma.cc/2HYY-262H].

5. Jack N. Rakove, *Beyond Belief, Beyond Conscience: The Radical Significance of the Free Exercise of Religion* (New York: Oxford University Press, 2020), 103–104.

6. John G. Turner, *Brigham Young: Pioneer Prophet* (Cambridge, MA: The Belknap Press of Harvard University Press, 2012), 142.

7. Christine A. Klein, "Treaties of Conquest: Property Rights, Indian Treaties, and the Treaty of Guadalupe Hidalgo," *New Mexico Law Review* 26, no. 2 (Spring 1996): 201–256; Brent M. Rogers, *Unpopular Sovereignty: Mormons and the Federal Management of Early Utah Territory* (Lincoln, NE: University of Nebraska Press, 2017), 34, 40–41.

8. Rakove, *Beyond Belief*, 83–84.

9. Anna Grzymała-Busse, *Sacred Foundations: The Religious and Medieval Roots of the European State* (Princeton, NJ: Princeton University Press, 2023), 5.

10. Edward A. Zelinsky, *Taxing the Church: Religion, Exemptions, Entanglement, and the Constitution* (New York: Oxford University Press, 2017), 113.

11. Samuel D. Brunson, *God and the IRS: Accommodating Religious Practice in United States Tax Law* (New York: Cambridge University Press, 2018), 34.

12. Edgar Kiser and Steven M. Karceski, "Political Economy of Taxation," *Annual Review of Political Science* 20 (2017): 75–92; Isaac William Martin and Monica Prasad, "Taxes and Fiscal Sociology," *Annual Review of Sociology* 40 (2014): 331–345.

13. Ajay K. Mehrotra, *Making the Modern American Fiscal State: Law, Politics, and the Rise of Progressive Taxation, 1877–1929* (New York: Cambridge University Press, 2013), 6.

14. D. Michael Quinn, *The Mormon Hierarchy: Wealth & Corporate Power* (Salt Lake City, UT: Signature Books, 2017), 124–128.

15. Leonard J. Arrington, *Great Basin Kingdom: AN Economic History of the Latter-day Saints, 1830–1900* (Chicago: University of Illinois Press, 2005), 59, 189.

16. Val D. Rust, *Radical Origins: Early Mormon Converts and their Colonial Ancestors* (Urbana: University of Illinois Press, 2004), 2–7.

17. Thomas F. O'Dea, *The Mormons* (Chicago: University of Chicago Press, 1957), 42–53.

18. Sarah Barringer Gordon, *The Mormon Question: Polygamy and Constitutional Conflict in Nineteenth Century America* (Chapel Hill, NC: University of North Carolina Press, 2002), 157, 206–207; Merle W. Wells, "The Idaho Anti-Mormon Test Oath, 1884–1892," *Pacific Historical Review* 24, no. 3 (1955): 235–252.

19. Public Religion Research Institute, *The 2020 Census of American Religion*, https://www.prri.org/wp-content/uploads/2021/07/PRRI-Jul-2021-Religion.pdf [https://perma.cc/9BBH-JX9P].

20. Lee Davidson, "Newest Congress Has Fewest Latter-day Saints in 32 Years. How Might That Impact the Church?" *Salt Lake Tribune*, January 10, 2021, https://www

.sltrib.com/news/politics/2021/01/10/new-congress-has-fewest/ [https://perma.cc/VWF8-YJAM].

21. "Professor Noah Feldman Examines Mormonism and Presidential Politics," *Harvard Law Today*, January 6, 2008, https://hls.harvard.edu/today/professor-noah-feldman-examines-mormonism-and-presidential-politics/ [https://perma.cc/GPF6-GW6V].

22. Jonathan Barrett, "Tax Determinism and the Cityscape: A Skeptical Approach," *Tax Law Review* 75, no. 2 (Spring 2022): 271–314.

23. In a casebook he has authored, my colleague writes, "Taxes are an important consideration in ever financial matter. However, the economic implications of a transaction are more important than the tax consequences." Jeffrey L. Kwall, *The Federal Income Taxation of Individuals: An Integrated Approach* (St. Paul, MN: Foundation Press, 2020), 9.

Part I. Frontier Religion, Frontier Taxation

1. Curtis D. Johnson, "The Protracted Meeting Myth: Awakenings, Revivals, and New York State Baptists, 1789–1850," *Journal of the Early Republic* 34, no. 3 (2014): 349–383.

2. Nathan B. Oman, "'Established Agreeable to the Laws of Our Country': Mormonism, Church Corporations, and the Long Legacy of America's First Disestablishment," *Journal of Law and Religion* 39, no. 2 (2021): 202–229.

3. Peter Harris, *Income Tax in Common Law Jurisdictions: From the Origins to 1820* (Cambridge: Cambridge University Press, 2006), 412.

4. Steven R. Weisman, *The Great Tax Wars: Lincoln to Wilson—The Fierce Battles over Money and Power That Transformed the Nation* (New York: Simon & Schuster, 2002), 14.

5. Ajay K. Mehrotra, "Render unto Caesar: Religious/Ethics, Expertise, and the Historical Underpinnings of the Modern American Tax System," *Loyola University Chicago Law Journal* 40, no. 2 (2009): 321–368.

6. Samuel D. Brunson, "God Is My Roommate? Tax Exemptions for Parsonages Yesterday, Today, and (if Constitutional) Tomorrow," *Indiana Law Journal* 96, no. 2 (2021): 521–570.

7. John R. Brooks and David Gamage, "Taxation and the Constitution, Reconsidered," *Tax Law Review* 76, no. 1 (2022): 75–157.

Chapter 1. Mormon Origins

1. Mark Lyman Staker, *Hearken, O Ye People: The Historical Setting of Joseph Smith's Ohio Revelations* (Salt Lake City: Greg Kofford Books, 2009), 135–136.

2. Kelly Olds, "Privatizing the Church: Disestablishment in Connecticut and Massachusetts," *Journal of Political Economy* 102, no. 2 (April 1994): 277–297 (278).

3. Toleration Act 1688 (1 Will & Mary c 18).

4. Thomas S. Kidd and Barry Hankins, *Baptists in America* (Oxford: Oxford UP, 2015): 22.

5. Joel H. Swift, "To Insure Domestic Tranquility: The Establishment Clause of the First Amendment," *Hofstra Law Review* 16, no. 2 (1988): 473–501.

206 · *Notes to Chapter 1*

6. Nina J. Crimm and Laurence H. Winer, *Politics, Taxes, and the Pulpit: Provocative First Amendment Conflicts* (New York: Oxford University Press, 2011): 74.

7. Kelly Olds, "Privatizing the Church: Disestablishment in Connecticut and Massachusetts," *Journal of Political Economy* 102, no. 2 (April 1994): 277–297.

8. John Witte Jr., "Tax Exemption of Church Property: Historical Anomaly or Valid Constitutional Practice?" *Southern California Law Review* 64, no. 2 (1991): 363–416.

9. Stephanie Hoffer, "Caesar as God's Banker: Using Germany's Church Tax as An Example of Non-Geographically Bounded Taxing Jurisdiction," *Washington University Global Studies Law Review* 9, no. 4 (2010): 595–637.

10. Carl H. Esbeck, "Dissent and Disestablishment: The Church-State Settlement In the Early American Republic," *Brigham Young University Law Review* 2004, no. 4 (2004): 1385–1592.

11. Kellen Funk, "Church Corporations and the Conflict of Laws in Antebellum America," *Journal of Law and Religion* 32, no. 2 (2017): 263–84.

12. Roger Finke and Laurence R. Iannaccone, "Supply-Side Explanations for Religious Change," *The ANNALS of the American Academy of Political and Social Science* 527, no. 1 (May 1, 1993): 29–30.

13. Shelby M. Balik, "Equal Right and Equal Privilege: Separating Church and State in Vermont," *Journal of Church and State* 50, no. 1 (2008): 42.

14. Frederick Augustus Wood, *History of Taxation in Vermont* (Columbia University, 1894), 104.

15. William Slade, *Vermont State Papers: Being a Collection of Records and Documents, Connected with the Assumption and Establishment of Government by the People of Vermont; Together with the Journal of the Council of Safety, the First Constitution, the Early Journals of the General Assembly, and the Laws from the Year 1779 to 1786, Inclusive. To Which Are Added the Proceedings of the First and Second Councils of Censors* (J. W. Copeland, printer, 1823)., 472.

16. Slade, *Vermont State Papers*, 473.

17. Marvin S. Hill, "Quest for Refuge: An Hypothesis as to the Social Origins and Nature of the Mormon Political Kingdom," *Journal of Mormon History* 2 (1975): 3–20.

18. Richard L. Bushman, *Joseph Smith and the Beginnings of Mormonism* (University of Illinois Press, 1984), 28.

19. Matthew Bowman, *The Mormon People: The Making of an American Faith* (Random House, 2012), 9.

20. Richard Lyman Bushman, *Joseph Smith: Rough Stone Rolling* (New York: Knopf, 2005), xiii.

21. Bushman, *Joseph Smith*, 28.

22. Joseph Smith-History 1:5–19.

23. Gregory A. Prince, "Joseph Smith's First Vision in Historical Context: How a Historical Narrative became Theological," *Journal of Mormon History* 41, no. 4 (2015): 74–95.

24. RoseAnn Benson, "Alexander Campbell: Another Restorationist," *Journal of Mormon History* 41, no. 4 (2015): 1–42.

Notes to Chapter 1 • 207

25. Prince, "Joseph Smith's First Vision," 76.

26. David Brion Davies and Steven Mintz, *The Boisterous Sea of Liberty: A Documentary History of America from Discovery Through the Civil War* (New York: Oxford University Press, 1998), 333.

27. John C. Chommie, *The Internal Revenue Service* (New York: Praeger, 1970), 8.

28. Peter Andreas, *Smuggler Nation: How Illicit Trade Made America* (New York: Oxford University Press, 2013), 17.

29. John Joseph Wallis, "American Government Finance in the Long Run: 1790 to 1990," *Journal of Economic Perspectives* 14, no. 1 (March 2000): 67.

30. Don Conger Sowers, *The Financial History of New York State from 1789 to 1912*, Columbia University Studies in History, Economics and Public Law, vol. LVII, no. 2 (New York: Longmans, Green and Company, 1914), 114.

31. Richard Sylla, John B. Legler, and John J. Wallis, "Banks and State Public Finance in the New Republic: The United States, 1790–1860," *The Journal of Economic History* 47, no. 2 (1987): 391–403.

32. Bushman, *Joseph Smith*, 19.

33. Bushman, *Joseph Smith*, 31–33.

34. William P. Van Ness and John Woodworth, *Laws of the State of New York Revised and Passed at the Thirty-Sixth Session of the Legislature* (Albany: H.C. Southwick & Co., 1813), 509.

35. Van Ness and Woodworth, *Laws of the State of New York*, 510.

36. Van Ness and Woodworth, *Laws of the State of New York*, 511.

37. Bushman, *Joseph Smith*, 47.

38. Economically, they almost certainly still bore the incidence of at least some of the property tax. The new owner would likely have increased their rent to account for at least some of the property taxes he bore on the land. But the Smith family would no longer be assessed nor would they directly pay the collector.

39. Van Ness and Woodworth, *Laws of the State of New York*, 271–72.

40. Van Ness and Woodworth, *Laws of the State of New York*, 272.

41. H. Michael Marquardt and Wesley P. Walters, *Inventing Mormonism* (Salt Lake City, UT: Signature Books, 1998), 3–4.

42. Bushman, *Joseph Smith*, 47–48.

43. Jennifer Reeder, *First: The Life and Faith of Emma Smith* (Salt Lake City: Deseret Book, 2021), 8–9; Emily C. Blackman, *A History of Susquehanna County, Pennsylvania* (Philadelphia: Claxton, Remsen & Haffelfinger, 1873), 96.

44. Alexander L. Baugh, "Parting the Veil: The Visions of Joseph Smith," *BYU Studies Quarterly* 38, no. 1 (1999): 23–69.

45. Nathaniel Hinckley Wadsworth, "Securing the Book of Mormon Copyright in 1829," in *Sustaining the Law: Joseph Smith's Legal Encounters*, eds. Gordon A. Madsen, Jeffrey N. Walker, and John W. Welch (Provo, UT: BYU Studies, 2014), 93.

46. David Keith Stott, "Legal Insights into the Organization of the Church in 1830," *BYU Studies* 49, no. 2 (2010): 121–48.

208 · *Notes to Chapter 1*

47. Van Ness and Woodworth, *Laws of the State of New York*, 519.

48. "Exemption From Taxation," *The (Palmyra) Reflector*, Jul. 7, 1830, https://nyshistoric newspapers.org/lccn/sn83032054/1830-07-07/ed-1/seq-5/.

49. *Prosser v. Secor*, 5 Barb. 607, 607 (N.Y. Gen. Term. 1849).

50. *Barhyte v. Shepherd*, 35 N.Y. 238, 238–39 (1866).

51. License for John Whitmer, June 9, 1830, https://www.josephsmithpapers.org/paper-summary/license-for-john-whitmer-9-june-1830/1.

52. License for Christian Whitmer, June 9, 1830, https://www.josephsmithpapers.org/paper-summary/license-for-christian-whitmer-9-june-1830/1.

53. License for Joseph Smith Sr., June 9, 1830, https://www.josephsmithpapers.org/paper-summary/license-for-joseph-smith-sr-9-june-1830/1.

54. H. Michael Marquardt, "Manchester as the Site of the Organization of the Church on April 6, 1830," *The John Whitmer Historical Association Journal* 33, no. 1 (2013): 141–53.

55. Van Ness and Woodworth, *Laws of the State of New York*, 271–72.

56. Leland H. Gentry and Todd M. Compton, *Fire and Sword: A History of the Latter-day Saints in Northern Missouri, 1836–39* (Salt Lake City, UT: Greg Kofford Books, 2011), 8–9.

57. Alexander L. Baugh, "Kirtland Camp, 1838: Bringing the Poor to Missouri," *Journal of the Book of Mormon and Other Restoration Scripture* 22, no. 1 (2013): 58–61.

58. Gentry and Compton, *Fire and Sword*, 462.

59. *The Statutes of Ohio and of the Northwest Territory Adopted or Enacted From 1788 to 1833 Inclusive Together With the Ordinance of 1787*, vol. II, ed. Salmon P. Chase (Cincinnati, OH: Corey & Fairbank, 1834), 1476.

60. R. Kent Fielding, "The Mormon Economy In Kirtland, Ohio," *Utah Historical Quarterly* 27, no. 4 (1959): 330–356; Larry T. Wimmer, "Kirtland Economy," in *Encyclopedia of Mormonism* (New York: Macmillan Publishing Company, 1992), 792.

61. *The Public Statutes of the State of Ohio From the Close of Chase's Statutes, February 1833, to the Present Time*, vol. I, ed. Maskell E. Curwen (Cincinnati, 1853), 326.

62. Curwen, *The Public Statutes of the State of Ohio*, 319.

63. Curwen, *The Public Statutes of the State of Ohio*, 320.

64. Bushman, *Joseph Smith*, 216.

65. David J. Howlett, *Kirtland Temple: The Biography of a Shared Mormon Sacred Space* (Urbana: University of Illinois Press, 2014), 17; Robert Winter, "Architecture on the Frontier: The Mormon Experiment," *Pacific Historical Review* 43, no. 1 (1974): 50–60.

66. Howlett, *Kirtland Temple*, 17.

67. Staker, *Hearken, O Ye People*, 436.

68. Richard O. Cowen, "What Is a Temple? Fulfillment of the Covenant Purposes," *Foundations of the Restoration Fulfillment of the Covenant Purposes*, eds. Craig James Ostler, Michael Hubbard MacKay, and Barbara Morgan Gardner (Provo, UT: Religious Studies Center, 2016), 273.

69. Chase, *The Statutes of Ohio*, 1477.

Notes to Chapter 1 · 209

70. Kim L. Loving, "Ownership of the Kirtland Temple: Legends, Lies, and Misunderstandings," *Journal of Mormon History* 30, no. 2 (2004): 1–80.

71. Matthew C. Godfrey, "The Role of Church Members in Financing Church Operations, 1834–1835," *Journal of Mormon History* 43, no. 3 (2017): 1–21.

72. Jeffrey N. Walker, "The Kirtland Safety Society and the Fraud of Grandison Newell: A Legal Examination," *BYU Studies Quarterly* 54, no. 3 (2015): 32–148.

73. U.S. Const. Art. 1 sec. 10.

74. Eric Helleiner, *The Making of National Money: Territorial Currencies in Historical Perspective* (Ithaca: Cornell University Press, 2003), 63.

75. Dale W. Adams, "Chartering the Kirtland Bank," *Brigham Young University Studies* 23, no. 4 (1983): 467–482.

76. In 1812 Ohio enacted a general incorporation statute for manufacturing corporations. Under that statute, rather than requiring legislative action, founders of a manufacturing company could incorporate by an informational certificate with the government. While this democratized and simplified the process of incorporation, Ohio repealed its general incorporation statute in 1824. General incorporation did not return to Ohio until 1846, long after Joseph Smith and his followers had left Ohio. Eric Hilt, "Corporation Law and the Shift Toward Open Access in the Antebellum United States," NBER Working Paper 21195 (2015), https://www.nber.org/system/files/working_papers/w21195/w21195.pdf [https://perma.cc/YSC9-A4LG].

77. Walker, "The Kirtland Safety Society," 45–47.

78. *Statutes of the State of Ohio* (Columbus, OH: Samuel Medary, State Printer, 1841), 916–917.

79. Maskell E. Curwen, *The Public Statutes at Large, of the State of Ohio* (Cincinnati: 1853), 257.

80. Stanley B. Kimball, "Sources on the History of the Mormons in Ohio: 1830–38," *Brigham Young University Studies* 11, no. 4 (1971): 524–40.

81. Rousseau, Peter L. "Jacksonian Monetary Policy, Specie Flows, and the Panic of 1837." *The Journal of Economic History* 62, no. 2 (2002): 457–88.

82. Jeffrey N. Walker "The Kirtland Safety Society and the Fraud of Grandison Newell: A Legal Examination," BYU Studies Quarterly 54, no. 3 (2015): 33–117.

83. Leland H. Gentry and Todd M. Compton, *Fire and Sword: A History of the Latter-day Saints in Northern Missouri, 1836–39* (Salt Lake City: Greg Kofford Books, 2011), 76–77.

84. W. Paul Reeve, *Religion of a Different Color: Race and the Mormon Struggle for Whiteness* (New York: Oxford University Press, 2015), 67.

85. *Revised Statutes of the State of Missouri,* 2nd ed. (St. Louis: Chambers, Knapp & Co., 1840), 529–530.

86. *Revised Statutes of the State of Missouri,* 549.

87. C. Mark Hamilton, *Nineteenth-Century Mormon Architecture & City Planning* (New York: Oxford University Press, 1995), 16, 55.

88. Baugh, "Company of Danites," 18–19.

89. Gentry and Compton, *Fire and Sword,* 469.

210 · Notes to Chapters 1 and 2

90. Clark V. Johnson, "The Missouri Redress Petitions: A Reappraisal of Mormon Persecutions in Missouri," *Brigham Young University Studies* 26, no. 2 (1986): 31–44.

91. Rogers, "To the 'Honest and Patriotic Sons of Liberty,'" 37–38.

92. Annette P. Hampshire, "Thomas Sharp and Anti-Mormon Sentiment in Illinois, 1842–1845," *Journal of the Illinois State Historical Society* 72, no. 2 (1979): 82–100.

93. "General Joseph Smith's Appeal to the Green Mountain Boys, December 1843," p. 5, The Joseph Smith Papers, accessed March 1, 2021, https://www.josephsmithpapers.org/paper-summary/general-joseph-smiths-appeal-to-the-green-mountain-boys-december-1843/5.

94. Letter from Elizabeth C. Stanton (Sept. 6, 1852), *The Proceedings of the Woman's Rights Convention, Held at Syracuse, September 8th, 9th & 10th, 1852*, 30 (Syracuse, J.E. Masters 1852).

95. Camille Walsh, *Racial Taxation: Schools, Segregation, and Taxpayer Citizenship, 1869–1973* (Chapel Hill: University of North Carolina Press, 2018), 6.

96. Brent M. Rogers, "'Armed men are coming from the state of Missouri': Federalism, Interstate Affairs, and Joseph Smith's Final Attempt to Secure Federal Intervention in Nauvoo," *Journal of the Illinois State Historical Society* 109, no. 2 (2016): 148–79.

Chapter 2. Funding a City

1. Benjamin E. Park, *Kingdom of Nauvoo: The Rise and Fall of a Religious Empire on the American Frontier* (New York: Liveright Publishing Corporation, 2020), 16–22.

2. Louis C. Zucker, "Joseph Smith as a Student of Hebrew," *Dialogue: A Journal of Mormon Thought* 3, no. 2 (1968): 41–55.

3. Spencer W. McBride, *Joseph Smith for President: The Prophet, the Assassins, and the Fight for American Religious Freedom* (New York: Oxford University Press, 2021), 46.

4. Richard E. Bennett and Rachel Cope, "'A City on a Hill'—Chartering the City of Nauvoo," *The John Whitmer Historical Association Journal* (2002): 17–40.

5. James L. Kimball, "A Wall to Defend Zion: The Nauvoo Charter," *Brigham Young University Studies* 15, no. 4 (1975): 491–98.

6. John C. Bennett, *A History of the Saints, or, An Exposé of Joe Smith and Mormonism* (Urbana: University of Illinois Press, 2000), 19, 26.

7. "Nauvoo City Officers," The Joseph Smith Papers, https://www.josephsmithpapers.org/back/nauvoo-city-officers-1841–1844 [https://perma.cc/M7EV-A7UH].

8. In addition to Young, Taylor, and Woodruff, the list of current and future apostles elected to the Nauvoo city council included Charles C. Rich, Amasa Lyman, Orson Pratt, George A. Smith, Heber C. Kimball, Lyman Wight, Willard Richards, and Orson Hyde.

9. "Nauvoo City Officers."

10. John E. Hallwas, "Mormon Nauvoo from a Non-Mormon Perspective," *Journal of Mormon History* 16 (1990): 53–69.

11. "Minute Book 2," pp. 89–92, The Joseph Smith Papers, accessed January 29, 2021, https://www.josephsmithpapers.org/paper-summary/minute-book-2/91 [https://perma.cc/LL72-QEJC].

Notes to Chapter 2 • 211

12. Mitchell K. Schaefer and Sherilyn Farnes, "'Myself . . . I Consecrate to the God of Heaven': Twenty Affidavits of Consecration in Nauvoo, June-July 1842," *Brigham Young University Studies* 50, no. 3 (2011): 101–32.

13. Thomas Carter, *Building Zion: The Material World of Mormon Settlement* (Minneapolis: University of Minnesota Press, 2015), 66. At the time, both consecration and tithing were relatively uncommon avenues for churches to raise revenue. Few religions in the United States adopted a consecration regime and tithing only began to find its footing in the broader American religious community after the Civil War. James Hudnut-Beumler, *In Pursuit of the Almighty's Dollar: A History of Money and American Protestantism* (Chapel Hill: University of North Carolina Press, 2007), 50–51.

14. "A Proclamation, To the Saints Scattered Abroad; Greeting," *Times and Seasons* 2, no. 6 (1841): 273.

15. John S. Dinger, "Joseph Smith and the Development of Habeas Corpus in Nauvoo, 1841–44," *Journal of Mormon History* 36, no. 3 (2010): 135–171.

16. An Act to Incorporate the City of Nauvoo § 8 (1840), https://www.cyberdrive illinois.com/departments/archives/online_exhibits/100_documents/1840-charter -city-nauvoo-more.html [https://perma.cc/B8RL-AXEW].

17. An Act to Incorporate the City of Springfield, Art, V § 1, *Laws of the State of Illinois, Passed By the Eleventh General Assembly* (Springfield: William Walters, 1840), 9, https:// archive.org/details/lawsofstateofill183940illi/page/n13/mode/2up.

18. An Act to Incorporate the City of Quincy, Art, V § 1, *Laws of the State of Illinois, Passed By the Eleventh General Assembly* (Springfield: William Walters, 1840), 116. https:// archive.org/details/lawsofstateofill183940illi/page/n13/mode/2up.

19. An Act to Incorporate the City of Chicago (Chicago: The Chicago Democrat, 1837), 10, https://archive.org/details/acttoincorporate00chic/page/n9/mode/2up.

20. An Act to Incorporate the City of Nauvoo, § 12.

21. An Act to Incorporate the City of Nauvoo, § 13.

22. An Act to Incorporate the City of Springfield, Art. V, § 21.

23. An Act to Incorporate the City of Springfield, Art. V, §§ 19–20.

24. Max H. Parkin, "Joseph Smith and the United Firm: The Growth and Decline of the Church's First Master Plan of Business and Finance, Ohio and Missouri, 1832–1834," *BYU Studies Quarterly* 46, no. 3 (2007): 5–62.

25. Samuel D. Brunson, "Taxing Utopia," *Seton Hall Law Review* 47, no. 1 (2016): 137–96.

26. Sharon Ann Murphy, "Financing Faith: Latter-day Saints and Banking in the 1830s and 1840s," in *Business and Religion: The Intersection of Faith and Finance*, ed. Matthew C. Godfrey and Michael Hubbard MacKay (Provo, UT: Religious Studies Center, 2019), 21–41.

27. Ajay K. Mehrotra, *Making the Modern American Fiscal State: Law, Politics, and the Rise of Progressive Taxation, 1877–1929* (New York: Cambridge University Press, 2013), 109. In fact, in the 1920s, one of the United States' foremost political economists described the state of economics as "still a youthful discipline in America." Economists, he explained, had not yet come to a consensus regarding "many of the problems which must guide

212 · Notes to Chapter 2

the legislator." Edwin R. A. Seligman, "The Problem in General," in *The Federal Income Tax*, ed. Robert Murray Haig (New York: Columbia University Press, 1921), vii–xii.

28. A "regressive" tax is one that collects a higher percentage of income from low-income individuals than from high-income individuals. Leonard E. Burman and Joel Slemrod, *Taxes in America: What Everyone Needs to Know* (New York: Oxford University Press, 2013), 264–265. A head tax is the quintessential example of a regressive tax. If the government collects $1,000 from each taxpayer, taxpayers earning $10,000 per year pay 10% of their income in taxes. Taxpayers earning $100,000, by contrast, only pay 1%.

29. Ronald W. Walker, "Cradling Mormonism: The Rise of the Gospel in Early Victorian England," *Brigham Young University Studies* 27, no. 1 (1987): 25–36.

30. Thomas L. Hungerford, "U.S. Federal Government Revenues: 1790 to the Present," CRS Reports (2006), https://www.everycrsreport.com/files/20060925_RL33665 _4a8c6781ce519caa3e6b82f95c269f73021c5fdf.pdf [https://perma.cc/H3YF-YYVT].

31. Douglas A. Irwin, *Clashing Over Commerce: A History of US Trade Policy* (Chicago: University of Chicago Press, 2017), 158, 176.

32. Letter from Brigham Young and Willard Richards, September 5, 1840, https:// www.josephsmithpapers.org/paper-summary/letter-from-brigham-young-and -willard-richards-5-september-1840/1 [https://perma.cc/N5AL-66RH].

33. Ibid. Young's and Richards's description of British taxes in many ways presages four Liverpudlians, more than a century later, who wrote, "I'll tax the street/(If you try to sit, sit)/I'll tax your seat/(If you get too cold, cold)/I'll tax the heat/(If you take a walk, walk)/I'll tax your feet." Beatles, "Taxman," *Revolver* (1966).

34. P. P. Pratt, "Emigration," *The Latter-day Saints' Millennial Star* 2, no. 10 (February 1842): 154.

35. Stephen Dowell, *A History of Taxation and Taxes in England: From the Earliest Times to the Present Day, vol. IV* (London: Longmans, Green, and Co., 1884), 8–12.

36. Norman McCord, *The Anti-Corn Law League, 1838–1846* (London: Routledge, 1958), 16.

37. *The Anti-Bread-tax almanack for the year . . . 1842 . . .: containing . . . a great amount of valuable statistical information.* Manchester: J. Gadsby, [1842]. *The Making of the Modern World* (accessed March 18, 2021).

38. "Nauvoo City Council Rough Minute Book, February–December 1841," pp. 36–38, The Joseph Smith Papers, accessed February 4, 2021, https://www.josephsmithpapers .org/paper-summary/nauvoo-city-council-rough-minute-book-february-december -1841/38 [https://perma.cc/F82Q-HVXU].

39. Lisi Krall, "Thomas Jefferson's Agrarian Vision and the Changing Nature of Property," *Journal of Economic Issues* 36, no. 1 (2002): 131–150.

40. Ron Durst and James Monke, "Effects of Federal Tax Policy on Agriculture," Food and Rural Economics Division, Economic Research Service, U.S. Department of Agriculture, Agricultural Economic Report No. 800, https://www.ers.usda.gov/ webdocs/publications/41302/19671_aer800_1_.pdf?v=0 [https://perma.cc/TD6Q -DMSZ].

Notes to Chapter 2 • 213

41. Charles M. Hardin, "The Politics of Agriculture in the United States," *Journal of Farm Economics* 32, no. 4 (1950): 571–583.

42. "Nauvoo City Council Rough Minute Book, February–December 1841," pp. 36–38, The Joseph Smith Papers, accessed February 4, 2021, https://www.josephsmith papers.org/paper-summary/nauvoo-city-council-rough-minute-book-february -december-1841/38 [https://perma.cc/K9GM-939K].

43. "Nauvoo City Council Rough Minute Book, February–December 1841," pp. 39–40, The Joseph Smith Papers, accessed February 4, 2021, https://www.josephsmith papers.org/paper-summary/nauvoo-city-council-rough-minute-book-february -december-1841/40 [https://perma.cc/FHA3-LBNU].

44. "Nauvoo City Council Minute Book, 1841–1845," p. 106, The Joseph Smith Papers, accessed December 21, 2023, https://www.josephsmithpapers.org/paper-summary/ nauvoo-city-council-minute-book-1841-1845/112 [https://perma.cc/P8SU-6JZ8].

45. "An Act Concerning the Public Revenue § 1 (Feb. 26, 1839)," in *A Compilation of All the General Laws Concerning Real Estate, and the Title Thereto, in the State of Illinois, Including All Such Laws As Relate to Descents, Limitations, Judgments, Executions, Partitions, Dower, Conveyances, and Revenue, From the Organization of the Territory Northwest of the Ohio, to the Present Time*, ed. N. H. Purple (Quincy: Published for the Compiler, 1849), 241.

46. *M'Culloch v. State*, 17 U.S. 316, 436, 4 L. Ed. 579 (1819).

47. "An Act Concerning the Public Revenue § 1 (Feb. 26, 1839)," in *A Compilation of All the General Laws Concerning Real Estate, and the Title Thereto, in the State of Illinois, Including All Such Laws As Relate to Descents, Limitations, Judgments, Executions, Partitions, Dower, Conveyances, and Revenue, From the Organization of the Territory Northwest of the Ohio, to the Present Time*, ed. N. H. Purple (Quincy: Published for the Compiler, 1849), 241.

48. Paul Finkelman, "Slavery, the 'More Perfect Union,' and the Prairie State," in *Illinois History: A Reader*, ed. Mark Hubbard (Champaign: University of Illinois Press, 2018), 57–85.

49. Jerome B. Meites, "The 1847 Illinois Constitutional Convention and Persons of Color," *Journal of the Illinois State Historical Society* 108, no. 3–4 (2015): 266–95.

50. Benjamin E. Park, *Kingdom of Nauvoo: The Rise and Fall of a Religious Empire on the American Frontier* (New York: Liveright Publishing Corporation, 2020), 141.

51. Newell G. Bringhurst, "Four American Prophets Confront Slavery: Joseph Smith, William Miller, Ellen G. White and Mary Baker Eddy," *The John Whitmer Historical Association Journal* 26 (2006): 120–141.

52. Newell G. Bringhurst, "The Mormons and Slavery: A Closer Look," *Pacific Historical Review* 50, no. 3 (1981): 329–338.

53. Park, *Kingdom of Nauvoo*, 141.

54. Kenneth W. Godfrey, "The Importance of the Temple in Understanding the Latter-day Saint Nauvoo Experience Then and Now," in *Collected Leonard J Arrington Mormon History Lectures*, ed. Leonard J. Arrington (Logan, UT: Utah State University Press, 2005), 119–53.

55. *Doctrine and Covenants*, 124:27–28.

214 · *Notes to Chapter 2*

56. Ronald K. Esplin, "The Significance of Nauvoo for Latter-day Saints," *Journal of Mormon History* 16 (1990): 71–86.

57. Godfrey, "The Importance of the Temple," 119–153.

58. Park, *Nauvoo*, 97.

59. Esplin, "The Significance of Nauvoo," 72.

60. "Petition from Temple Committee, 12 December 1843," p. [1], The Joseph Smith Papers, accessed February 26, 2021, https://www.josephsmithpapers.org/paper-summary/petition-from-temple-committee-12-december-1843/1 [https://perma.cc/PF69-AHFQ].

61. "Nauvoo City Council Rough Minute Book, November 1842–January 1844," p. 24, The Joseph Smith Papers, accessed February 26, 2021, https://www.josephsmith papers.org/paper-summary/nauvoo-city-council-rough-minute-book-november-1842-january-1844/24 [https://perma.cc/BX5W-W8FE].

62. "Nauvoo City Council Rough Minute Book, February–December 1841," pp. 39–40, The Joseph Smith Papers, accessed February 4, 2021, https://www.josephsmith papers.org/paper-summary/nauvoo-city-council-rough-minute-book-february-december-1841/40 [https://perma.cc/JC54-AJXZ].

63. Lynn Festa, "Person, Animal, Thing: The 1796 Dog Tax and the Right to Superfluous Things," *Eighteenth-Century Life* 33, no. 2 (2009): 1–44.

64. "Ordinances," *The Illinois Free Trader and LaSalle County Commercial Advertiser*, April 28, 1843, 3.

65. "The Rate of Taxation For the Year 1846, Is As Follows," *Richmond Palladium*, June 23, 1846, 3.

66. "Fiscal Statement of the Receipts and Expenditures of the City of Burlington, From the 8th Day of February, A.D. 1848, to April 9th, A.D. 1849," *Burlington Hawk-Eye*, May 10, 1849, 3.

67. "[Communicated.]," *Alexandria Gazette*, June 14, 1837, 3.

68. *Midgeville Southern Recorder*, February 28, 1843, 3.

69. "A Lover of Good Dogs," letter to the editor, *Sangamo Journal*, July 18, 1851, 2.

70. "Dogs," *Sangamo Journal*, January 29, 1853, 2.

71. "Sheep and Their Enemies. Fence," letter to the editor, *Chicago Prairie Farmer*, December 1, 1844, 2.

72. *New Market Richmond Enquirer*, February 25, 1843, 2.

73. "The State Legislature," *New Market Richmond Enquirer*, October 8, 1844, at 4. This use of taxation to reduce and ameliorate undesirable things is still with us, today in the form of sin taxes on things like alcohol, tobacco, and sugary drinks.

74. "Hydrophobia," *Williamsport Lycoming Gazette*, January 8, 1834.

75. "Mad Dogs," *Macomb Mdonough Independent*, April 29, 1853, 2.

76. Nauvoo City Council Rough Minute Book, February–December 1841," pp. 39–40, The Joseph Smith Papers, accessed February 5, 2021, https://www.josephsmith papers.org/paper-summary/nauvoo-city-council-rough-minute-book-february-december-1841/40 [https://perma.cc/4ZA5-9YQD].

Notes to Chapter 2 · 215

77. Tom Burns Haber, "Canine Terms Applied to Human Beings and Human Events: Part I," *American Speech*, no. 2 (1965): 83–101.

78. "Nauvoo City Council Rough Minute Book, February–December 1841," pp. 39–40, The Joseph Smith Papers, accessed February 5, 2021, https://www.josephsmith papers.org/paper-summary/nauvoo-city-council-rough-minute-book-february -december-1841/40 [https://perma.cc/7DE3-D9LH].

79. "Minutes, 29 March 1841," p. 15, The Joseph Smith Papers, accessed December 21, 2023, https://www.josephsmithpapers.org/paper-summary/minutes-29-march -1841/1 [https://perma.cc/TAC6-XFQV].

80. "Petition from Robert L. Campbell and Others, 13 January 1844," p. [1], The Joseph Smith Papers, accessed January 29, 2021, https://www.josephsmithpapers.org/ paper-summary/petition-from-robert-l-campbell-and-others-13-january-1844/1 [https://perma.cc/P4AN-RJ8P].

81. Alexander L. Baugh, "Joseph Smith's Dog, Old Major," *BYU Studies Quarterly* 56, no. 4 (2017): 53–67.

82. "Nauvoo City Council Rough Minute Book, November 1842–January 1844," p. 42, The Joseph Smith Papers, accessed February 5, 2021, https://www.josephsmith papers.org/paper-summary/nauvoo-city-council-rough-minute-book-november -1842-january-1844/44 [https://perma.cc/Q8Q7–59H4].

83. "Minutes, 8 March 1841," p. 11, The Joseph Smith Papers, accessed December 21, 2023, https://www.josephsmithpapers.org/paper-summary/minutes-8-march -1841/2 [https://perma.cc/5Q2U-KTT4].

84. "Nauvoo City Council Minute Book, 1841–1845," p. 16, The Joseph Smith Papers, accessed December 21, 2023, https://www.josephsmithpapers.org/paper-summary/ nauvoo-city-council-minute-book-1841-1845/22 [https://perma.cc/4EU6-TXGX].

85. "Minutes, 12 February 1842," p. 11, The Joseph Smith Papers, accessed February 8, 2021, https://www.josephsmithpapers.org/paper-summary/minutes-12-february -1842/2 [https://perma.cc/F9QA-S9RV]; "Resolution, 12 February 1842," p. [1], The Joseph Smith Papers, accessed February 8, 2021, https://www.josephsmithpapers .org/paper-summary/resolution-12-february-1842/1 [https://perma.cc/RN7C -VL7Q].

86. Parks, *Roads and Travel*, 8.

87. "Minutes, 8 October 1842," p. 42, The Joseph Smith Papers, accessed February 8, 2021, https://www.josephsmithpapers.org/paper-summary/minutes-8-october -1842/1 [https://perma.cc/P6F9-2PYL].

88. "Resolution, 30 January 1843-A," p. 148, The Joseph Smith Papers, accessed February 8, 2021, https://www.josephsmithpapers.org/paper-summary/resolution -30-january-1843-a/1 [https://perma.cc/T2B9-FEH8].

89. "Nauvoo City Council Rough Minute Book, November 1842–January 1844," pp. 4–5, The Joseph Smith Papers, accessed February 8, 2021, https://www.josephsmith papers.org/paper-summary/nauvoo-city-council-rough-minute-book-november -1842-january-1844/4 [https://perma.cc/UD26-EDD6].

216 · *Notes to Chapter 2*

90. "Petition from Thomas Grover and Others, 2 May 1842," p. [1], The Joseph Smith Papers, accessed February 9, 2021, https://www.josephsmithpapers.org/paper-summary/petition-from-thomas-grover-and-others-2-may-1842/1 [https://perma.cc/9ST8-3QZ8].

91. Roger N. Parks, *Roads and Travel in New England 1790–1840* (Sturbridge, Mass.: Old Sturbridge Village, 1967), 8.

92. "Minutes, 14 May 1842," p. 26, The Joseph Smith Papers, accessed February 9, 2021, https://www.josephsmithpapers.org/paper-summary/minutes-14-may-1842/2 [https://perma.cc/T62M-57PA].

93. *Armour & Co. v. City of Pittsburgh*, 363 Pa. 109, 113, 69 A.2d 405, 407 (1949).

94. "Petition from Stephen Wilkinson and Others, circa 14 May 1842," p. [1], The Joseph Smith Papers, accessed March 5, 2021, https://www.josephsmithpapers.org/paper-summary/petition-from-stephen-wilkinson-and-others-circa-14-may-1842/1 [https://perma.cc/44ES-TGLZ].

95. "Minutes, 14 May 1842," p. 26, The Joseph Smith Papers, accessed March 5, 2021, https://www.josephsmithpapers.org/paper-summary/minutes-14-may-1842/2 [https://perma.cc/CCF8-UMQ9]. At the same time, the city council also repealed laws regulating "Hawkers, Pedlers, & public Shows & Exhibitions," regulating auctions, and regulating "Taverns & Ordinaries." "Ordinance, 14 May 1842-B," p. [1], The Joseph Smith Papers, accessed March 5, 2021, https://www.josephsmithpapers.org/paper-summary/ordinance-14-may-1842-b/1 [https://perma.cc/S7FY-K4WH].

96. Joseph Smith, *History of the Church* 4:178.

97. Dennis Rowley, "Nauvoo: A River Town," *Brigham Young University Studies* 18, no. 2 (1978): 255–272.

98. *Times and Seasons* 2 (15 February 1841): 318.

99. "Report of Committee, circa 8 February 1841," p. [1], The Joseph Smith Papers, accessed February 18, 2021, https://www.josephsmithpapers.org/paper-summary/report-of-committee-circa-8-february-1841/1 [https://perma.cc/9AW9-JENV].

100. "Minutes, 8 February 1841," p. 3, The Joseph Smith Papers, accessed December 21, 2023, https://www.josephsmithpapers.org/paper-summary/minutes-8-february-1841/2 [https://perma.cc/L54R-RVHB].

101. Donald L. Enders, "A Dam for Nauvoo: An Attempt to Industrialize the City," *Brigham Young University Studies* 18, no. 2 (1978): 246–254.

102. "Minutes, 5 March 1844," p. 3, The Joseph Smith Papers, accessed February 9, 2021, https://www.josephsmithpapers.org/paper-summary/minutes-5-march-1844/1 [https://perma.cc/S2R9-YYCS].

103. "Discourse, 7 March 1844-A, as Reported by Willard Richards," p. [12], The Joseph Smith Papers, accessed February 9, 2021, https://www.josephsmithpapers.org/paper-summary/discourse-7-march-1844-a-as-reported-by-willard-richards/3 [https://perma.cc/PF87-XN66].

104. "Minutes, 9 March 1844," p. 8, The Joseph Smith Papers, accessed February 9, 2021, https://www.josephsmithpapers.org/paper-summary/minutes-9-march-1844/4 [https://perma.cc/K4WN-C4JZ].

Notes to Chapters 2 and 3 • 217

105. "Journal, December 1842–June 1844; Book 4, 1 March–22 June 1844," p. [28] n.52, The Joseph Smith Papers, accessed February 18, 2021, https://www.josephsmith papers.org/paper-summary/journal-december-1842-june-1844-book-4-1-march -22-june-1844/30 [https://perma.cc/K9BM-7ZGK].

Chapter 3. Collecting Taxes in Nauvoo

1. Catherine S. Menand, "The Things That Were Caesar's: Tax Collecting In Eighteenth-Century Boston," *Massachusetts Historical Review* 1 (1999): 49–77. Into the nineteenth century, the town sheriff generally also served as collector and assessor. The roles separated during the 1800s, with the separation making its way across the country from east to west; rural and western communities separated the roles later than eastern and urban areas. Richard Henry Carlson, "A Brief History of Property Tax," *Fair & Equitable* (Feb. 2005): 3–10, https://info.bcassessment.ca/about/Shared %20Documents/A%20Brief%20History%20of%20Property%20Tax%20-%20Article .pdf [https://perma.cc/2NNK-NMTC].

2. Chapter 5 will look at the federal government's attempt to collect income tax from Brigham Young. In the federal Civil War-era income tax, the role of assessor was separate and distinct from the role of collector; as we will see, Young perceived the assessor as anti-Mormon and hostile, while he saw the collector as, if not an ally, at least not an enemy.

3. "Nauvoo City Council Minute Book, 1841–1845," p. 106, The Joseph Smith Papers, accessed December 8, 2023, https://www.josephsmithpapers.org/paper-summary/ nauvoo-city-council-minute-book-1841-1845/112 [https://perma.cc/HX7P-L6U2].

4. "Motion from Hyrum Smith, 5 March 1842," p. [1], The Joseph Smith Papers, accessed February 18, 2021, https://www.josephsmithpapers.org/paper-summary/ motion-from-hyrum-smith-5-march-1842/1 [https://perma.cc/CY3B-BESB].

5. "Nauvoo City Council Minute Book, 1841–1845," p. 106–111, The Joseph Smith Papers, accessed December 8, 2023, https://www.josephsmithpapers.org/paper -summary/nauvoo-city-council-minute-book-1841-1845/112 [https://perma.cc/ SC7K-S47W].

6. "Nauvoo City Council Minute Book, 1841–1845," p. 129, The Joseph Smith Papers, accessed December 8, 2023, https://www.josephsmithpapers.org/paper-summary/ nauvoo-city-council-minute-book-1841-1845/135 [https://perma.cc/4VDV-T8UP].

7. "Ordinance, 31 October 1842," p. 117, The Joseph Smith Papers, accessed February 11, 2021, https://www.josephsmithpapers.org/paper-summary/ordinance-31-october -1842/12 [https://perma.cc/S3LJ-EYB8].

8. "Nauvoo City Council Rough Minute Book, February 1844–January 1845," p. 48, The Joseph Smith Papers, accessed February 11, 2021, https://www.josephsmith papers.org/paper-summary/nauvoo-city-council-rough-minute-book-february -1844-january-1845/50 [https://perma.cc/78PU-CV9Y].

9. "Nauvoo City Council Minute Book, 1841–1845," p. 146, The Joseph Smith Papers, accessed December 8, 2023, https://www.josephsmithpapers.org/paper-summary/ nauvoo-city-council-minute-book-1841-1845/152 [https://perma.cc/YL43-4ZHK].

218 • *Notes to Chapter 3*

10. "Petition from Lewis Robison, 11 June 1842," p. [1], The Joseph Smith Papers, accessed February 18, 2021, https://www.josephsmithpapers.org/paper-summary/petition-from-lewis-robison-11-june-1842/1 [https://perma.cc/WP7C-TY74].

11. "Letter, Horace Hotchkiss to Sidney Rigdon, 8 November 1842," p. [1], The Joseph Smith Papers, accessed March 18, 2021, https://www.josephsmithpapers.org/paper-summary/letter-horace-hotchkiss-to-sidney-rigdon-8-november-1842/1 [https://perma.cc/5GEN-WLT3].

12. "Minutes, 12 October 1844," Draft, p. 1, The Joseph Smith Papers, accessed December 8, 2023, https://www.josephsmithpapers.org/paper-summary/minutes-12-october-1844-draft/1 [https://perma.cc/B4RN-HVMD].

13. Thomas P. Slaughter, *The Whiskey Rebellion* (New York: Oxford University Press, 1986), 12–13.

14. "To Tax Payers," *Times and Seasons*, March 1, 1841, 2:334.

15. "Journal, December 1841–December 1842," p. 88, The Joseph Smith Papers, accessed November 2, 2022, https://www.josephsmithpapers.org/paper-summary/journal-december-1841-december-1842/19 [https://perma.cc/8Q9Q-RJSW].

16. "Introduction to State of Illinois v. JS for Assault and Battery," The Joseph Smith Papers, accessed November 2, 2022, https://www.josephsmithpapers.org/paper-summary/introduction-to-state-of-illinois-v-js-for-assault-and-battery/1 [https://perma.cc/B5EN-KH9L].

17. Robert Wicks and Fred R Foister, *Junius And Joseph: Presidential Politics and the Assassination of the First Mormon Prophet* (Logan: Utah State University Press, 2005), 49.

18. Gordon A. Madsen, Jeffrey N. Walker, and John W. Welch, *Sustaining the Law: Joseph Smith's Legal Encounters* (Provo, UT: BYU Studies, 2014), 502.

19. "Letter to Reuben McBride, 18 January 1844," p. [1], The Joseph Smith Papers, accessed February 12, 2021, https://www.josephsmithpapers.org/paper-summary/letter-to-reuben-mcbride-18-january-1844/1 [https://perma.cc/MC2X-RZZA].

20. "Letter to Joseph Coe, 18 January 1844," p. [1], The Joseph Smith Papers, accessed February 12, 2021, https://www.josephsmithpapers.org/paper-summary/letter-to-joseph-coe-18-january-1844/1 [https://perma.cc/XQ28-HJ7G].

21. "Letter from Reuben McBride, 28 February 1844," p. 2, The Joseph Smith Papers, accessed February 12, 2021, https://www.josephsmithpapers.org/paper-summary/letter-from-reuben-mcbride-28-february-1844/2 [https://perma.cc/69KT-W5HT].

22. "Nauvoo City Council Minute Book, 1841–1845," p. 106–111, The Joseph Smith Papers, accessed November 7, 2023, https://www.josephsmithpapers.org/paper-summary/nauvoo-city-council-minute-book-1841-1845/112 [https://perma.cc/9ZWV-3EJQ].

23. Illinois, *Public and General Statute Laws of the State of Illinois: Containing All the Laws Published in the Revised Statutes of 1833, Except Such as are Repealed, Together with All the Acts of a General and Public Nature, Passed by the Ninth General Assembly* (Chicago: S.F. Gale, 1939), 566.

24. "Nauvoo City Council Rough Minute Book, February 1844–January 1845," p. [4–5], The Joseph Smith Papers, accessed February 12, 2021, https://www.josephsmith

Notes to Chapter 3 · 219

papers.org/paper-summary/nauvoo-city-council-rough-minute-book-february
-1844-january-1845/60 [https://perma.cc/FEW5-86PM].

25. "Nauvoo City Scrip, 14 July 1842," p. 0, The Joseph Smith Papers, accessed November 8, 2023, https://www.josephsmithpapers.org/paper-summary/nauvoo-city
-scrip-14-july-1842/3 [https://perma.cc/Q6PJ-R3Q9].

26. Sharon Ann Murphy, "Financing Faith: Latter-day Saints and Banking in the 1830s and 1840s," in *Business and Religion: The Intersection of Faith and Finance* (Provo: Religious Studies Center, 2019), 33.

27. "Ordinance, 31 October 1842," p. 6, The Joseph Smith Papers, accessed December 21, 2023, https://www.josephsmithpapers.org/paper-summary/ordinance-31
-october-1842/6 [https://perma.cc/2NNZ-VMFF].

28. "Ordinance, 4 March 1843," p. 167, The Joseph Smith Papers, accessed February 11, 2021, https://www.josephsmithpapers.org/paper-summary/ordinance-4
-march-1843/1 [https://perma.cc/G9ND-J4NN].

29. "Nauvoo City Council Rough Minute Book, February 1844–January 1845," p. 7, The Joseph Smith Papers, accessed February 11, 2021, https://www.josephsmith
papers.org/paper-summary/nauvoo-city-council-rough-minute-book-february
-1844-january-1845/7 [https://perma.cc/KHY8-RX9Y].

30. "Petition from Davis McOlney and Others, 8 August 1844," p. [1], The Joseph Smith Papers, accessed February 17, 2021, https://www.josephsmithpapers.org/paper
-summary/petition-from-davis-mcolney-and-others-8-august-1844/1 [https://
perma.cc/GQS6-SLY6].

31. "Nauvoo City Council Rough Minute Book, February 1844–January 1845," pp. 42–45, The Joseph Smith Papers, accessed February 17, 2021, https://www.joseph
smithpapers.org/paper-summary/nauvoo-city-council-rough-minute-book-february
-1844-january-1845/44 [https://perma.cc/4U5P-GTAT].

32. "Bill, 10 August 1844-B," p. 1, The Joseph Smith Papers, accessed December 21, 2023, https://www.josephsmithpapers.org/paper-summary/bill-10-august-1844-b/1
[https://perma.cc/SW2L-34C4].

33. "Nauvoo City Council Rough Minute Book, February 1844–January 1845," p. 44–45, The Joseph Smith Papers, accessed February 18, 2021, https://www.josephsmith
papers.org/paper-summary/nauvoo-city-council-rough-minute-book-february
-1844-january-1845/47 [https://perma.cc/28YJ-D6BC].

34. "Minutes, 17–18 February 1842," pp. 14–15, The Joseph Smith Papers, accessed February 25, 2021, https://www.josephsmithpapers.org/paper-summary/minutes
-17-18-february-1842/2 [https://perma.cc/YMS7-Q2JD].

35. "Minutes, 15 April 1843," p. 14, The Joseph Smith Papers, accessed February 25, 2021, https://www.josephsmithpapers.org/paper-summary/minutes-15-april-1843/3
[https://perma.cc/BSS7-4JG5].

36. Clyde E. Buckingham, "Mormonism in Illinois," *Journal of the Illinois State Historical Society* 32, no. 2 (1939): 173–192.

37. *Port-Gibson Herald*, Jan. 12, 1843, at 3, https://chroniclingamerica.loc.gov/lccn/
sn87090149/1843-01-12/ed-1/seq-3/.

220 · Notes to Chapters 3 and 4

38. William Shepard, "'Marshalled and Disciplined for War': A Documentary Chronology of Conflict in Hancock County, Illinois 1839–1845," *The John Whitmer Historical Association Journal* 33, no. 2 (2013): 79–131.

39. *The Wasp*, March 15, 1843, at 2.

40. "New Paper in Nauvoo," *New York Daily Tribune*, June 5, 1844, at 1.

41. John Lee Allaman, "Policing in Mormon Nauvoo," *Illinois Historical Journal* 89, no. 2 (1996): 85–98.

42. "Deaf and Dumb," *New York Daily Tribune*, March 7, 1845, at 1.

43. "Petition from George A. Smith and Daniel H. Wells, circa 8 February 1845," p. [1], The Joseph Smith Papers, accessed March 11, 2021, https://www.josephsmith papers.org/paper-summary/petition-from-george-a-smith-and-daniel-h-wells -circa-8-february-1845/1 [https://perma.cc/UPQ8-JQ74].

44. "Nauvoo City Council Rough Minute Book, February–March 1845," p. [5], The Joseph Smith Papers, accessed March 11, 2021, https://www.josephsmithpapers.org/ paper-summary/nauvoo-city-council-rough-minute-book-february-march-1845/5 [https://perma.cc/V6PC-RPHB].

Chapter 4. The Mormons' Utah Home

1. Benjamin E. Park, *Kingdom of Nauvoo: The Rise and Fall of a Religious Empire on the American Frontier* (New York: Liveright Publishing Corporation, 2020), 247–248.

2. Jennifer Reeder, *First: The Life and Faith of Emma Smith* (Salt Lake City: Deseret Book, 2021), 162.

3. Park, *Kingdom of Nauvoo*, 257.

4. Jedediah S. Rogers, *The Council of Fifty: A Documentary History* (Salt Lake City: Signature Books, 2014), 116.

5. Lewis Clark Christian, "Mormon Foreknowledge of the West," *Brigham Young University Studies* 21, no. 4 (1981): 403–15.

6. Dale L. Morgan, *The State of Deseret* (Logan, UT: Utah State University Press, 1987), 9–11.

7. Morgan, *Deseret*, 14–15.

8. Salt Lake Stake papers, 1847–1849; Acts and orders, 1847–1848; Church History Library, accessed May 6, 2021, https://catalog.churchofjesuschrist.org/assets ?id=7e8f5617–73e6–4da8-a7c8–724a1eb57dc7&crate=0&index=0.

9. Specifically, the High Council authorized the "Captains of 100s" to build fences. In Nebraska, Brigham Young had organized the Mormon pioneers into companies with "captains of hundreds, captains of fifties, and captains of tens, with a president and two councilors at their head, under the direction of the Twelve Apostles." D&C 136:3.

10. Salt Lake Stake papers, 1847–1849; Minutes, 1848 April 1–June 11; Church History Library, accessed, May 6, 2021, https://catalog.churchofjesuschrist.org/ assets?id=1466268f-1029-4a7f-a71f-aea747b9fb73&crate=0&index=26.

11. Salt Lake Stake minutes Aug. 13, 1848, 1847–1848; 1848 April-August; Church History Library, accessed October 11, 2021, https://catalog.churchofjesuschrist.org/ assets/93f2d175-df92–44ec-a9ec-2e079fb7cfdf/0/17.

Notes to Chapters 4 and 5 · 221

12. Morgan, *Deseret*, 22–23.

13. In the Book of Mormon, "deseret" meant "honeybee" in an ancient lost language. Ether 2:3. Young named the Mormons' new home after bees to invoke the industriousness of bees and as an aspirational hope for his people's future. Bee Wilson, *The Hive: The Story of the Honeybee and Us* (New York: Thomas Dunne Books, 2004), 39.

14. Morgan, *Deseret*, 29–33.

15. Gustive O. Larson, "Federal Government Efforts to 'Americanize' Utah Before Admission to Statehood," *Brigham Young University Studies* 10, no. 2 (1970): 218–32.

16. Thomas G. Alexander, "Reed Smoot, the L.D.S. Church, and Progressive Legislation, 1903–1933," *Dialogue: A Journal of Mormon Thought* 7, no. 1 (1972): 47–56.

17. Morgan, *Deseret*, 52–53.

18. Morgan, *Deseret*, 59.

19. Deseret (State) papers, 1849–1851; Ordinances, 1850 December–1851 February; Church History Library, accessed May 5, 2021, https://catalog.churchofjesuschrist .org/assets?id=682f081b-6712-4b32-a783-0328e86ae4b5&crate=0&index=104.

20. Ibid.

21. Ronald W. Walker, "The Affair of the 'Runaways': Utah's First Encounter with the Federal Officers: Part 1," *Journal of Mormon History* 39, no. 4 (2013): 1–43.

22. Morgan, *Deseret*, 110–111.

23. Edwin Brown Firmage and Richard Collin Mangrum, *Zion in the Courts: A Legal History of the Church of Jesus Christ of Latter-day Saints, 1830–1900* (Urbana: University of Illinois Press, 2001), 263.

24. Nathan B. Oman, "Preaching to the Court House and Judging in the Temple," *Brigham Young University Law Review* 2009, no. 1 (2009): 157–224.

25. Firmage and Mangrum, *Zion*, 277.

26. Raymond T. Swenson, "Resolution of Civil Disputes by Mormon Ecclesiastical Courts," *Utah Law Review* 1978, no. 2 (1978): 573–596.

27. Firmage and Mangrum, *Zion*, 267.

28. George F. Gibbs, et al., *Journal of Discourses by President John Taylor and Other Members of the Quorum of the Twelve Apostles* (Liverpool: William Budge, 1880), 104.

29. Firmage and Mangrum, *Zion*, 264.

30. Presiding Bishopric bishops meeting minutes, 1851–1884; Minutes, 1862–1879; Church History Library, https://catalog.churchofjesuschrist.org/assets/e9b0c4cc -2d99-497a-b4ce-f5afe97ea098/0/0?lang=eng (accessed August 20, 2024), 238.

Chapter 5. Brigham Young and Federal Taxation

1. Presiding Bishopric bishops meeting minutes, 1851–1884; Minutes, 1862–1879; Church History Library, accessed August 30, 2021, https://catalog.churchofjesuschrist .org/assets/e9b0c4cc-2d99-497a-b4ce-f5afe97ea098/0/0, 238.

2. Leonard J. Arrington, *Brigham Young: American Moses* (New York: Vintage Books, 2012), iv.

3. Arrington, *Brigham Young*, 167.

222 • *Notes to Chapter 5*

4. Richard S. Van Wagoner, *The Complete Discourses of Brigham Young, Vol. 1* (Salt Lake City, UT: The Smith-Pettite Foundation, 2009), 146.

5. Amanda Hendrix-Komoto, *Imperial Zions: Religion, Race, and Family in the American West and Pacific* (Lincoln, NE: University of Nebraska Press, 2022), 79.

6. Hendrix-Komoto, *Imperial Zions*, 267.

7. Hendrix-Komoto, *Imperial Zions*, 321.

8. Hendrix-Komoto, *Imperial Zions*, 1393.

9. Russell W. Belk, "Battling Worldliness in the New Zion: Mercantilism Versus Homespun in Nineteenth-Century Utah," *Journal of Macromarketing* 14, no. 1 (1994): 9–22.

10. Leonard J. Arrington, "Banking Enterprises in Utah, 1847–1880," *The Business History Review* 29, no. 4 (1955): 312–334.

11. Van Wagoner, *Complete Discourses*, 1737–1738.

12. Van Wagoner, *Complete Discourses*, 1739.

13. Peter L. Rousseau, "Jacksonian Monetary Policy, Specie Flows, and the Panic of 1837," *The Journal of Economic History* 62, no. 2 (2002): 457–488.

14. Morton J. Horowitz, *The Transformation of American Law, 1870–1960 : The Crisis of Legal Orthodoxy* (New York: Oxford University Press, 1992), 21.

15. G. Alan Tarr, "Models and Fashions in State Constitutionalism," *Wisconsin Law Review* 1998, no. 3 (1998): 729–746.

16. E. Estabrook, *The Revised Statutes of the Territory of Nebraska* (Omaha: E.B. Taylor, 1866), 311–312.

17. Even today, the ratio of assessed value to true value of property varies by assessor. Eugene C. Lee, "State Equalization of Local Assessments," *National Tax Journal* 6, no. 2 (1953): 176–187.

18. Van Wagoner, *Complete Discourses*, 1738.

19. Van Wagoner, *Complete Discourses*, 1739.

20. Van Wagoner, *Complete Discourses*, 410.

21. Van Wagoner, *Complete Discourses*, 1724.

22. Van Wagoner, *Complete Discourses*, 2887.

23. Van Wagoner, *Complete Discourses*, 1734.

24. Max Perry Mueller, *Race and the Making of the Mormon People* (Chapel Hill: University of North Carolina Press, 2017), 174.

25. Mueller, *Race and the Making of the Mormon People*, 3151.

26. Mueller, *Race and the Making of the Mormon People*, 748.

27. Van Wagoner, *Complete Discourses*, 2389.

28. Van Wagoner, *Complete Discourses*, 2410.

29. Van Wagoner, *Complete Discourses*, 1924.

30. Samuel D. Brunson, "'To Omit Paying Tithing': Brigham Young and the First Federal Income Tax," in *Business and Religion: The Intersection of Faith and Finance*, ed. Matthew C. Godfrey and Michael Hubbard MacKay (Provo, UT: Religious Studies Center, 2019), 255–288.

31. Van Wagoner, *Complete Discourses*, 1937.

Notes to Chapter 5 • 223

32. Brunson, "To Omit Paying Tithing," 261–262.

33. For a far more in-depth look at this year and a half battle between Brigham Young and the federal government, as well as context concerning the at-the-time new federal income tax, *see* Samuel D. Brunson, "Mormon Profit: Brigham Young, Tithing, and the Bureau of Internal Revenue," *Brigham Young University Law Review* 2019, no. 1 (2019): 41–105.

34. Brunson, "Mormon Profit," 64.

35. Robert J. Chandler, "An Uncertain Influence: The Role of the Federal Government in California, 1846–1880," *in Politics Government, and Law in Pioneer California*, eds. John F. Burns, Richard J. Orsi, and Marlene Smith-Baranzini (Berkeley, CA: University of California Press, 2003), 224–271; Harold M. Hyman, "Portrait of Patronage: 'Political History of Employees in the Treasure Department,' 1869," *Journal of Southern History* 22, no. 1 (1956): 91–96.

36. Brunson, "Mormon Profit," 64.

37. Comm. on the Territories, "Execution of the Laws in Utah," Testimony of John P. Taggart, H.R. Rep. no. 41–21, pt. 2 (1870).

38. Letter from Brigham Young, President, The Church of Jesus Christ of Latter-day Saints, to Columbus Delano, Internal Revenue Comm'r (Mar. 18, 1870) (on file with the Church History Library, The Church of Jesus Christ of Latter-day Saints, Salt Lake City, Utah).

39. Brunson, "Mormon Profit," 68.

40. Letter (unsent) from O.J. Hollister, Collector of Internal Revenue for the Territory of Utah, to Columbus Delano, Internal Revenue Comm'r (Mar. 1, 1870) (on file with the Church History Library, The Church of Jesus Christ of Latter-day Saints, Salt Lake City, Utah).

41. Brunson, "Mormon Profit," 71.

42. Brunson, "Mormon Profit," 71.

43. It is hard to calculate precisely what $60,000 in 1869 would be worth in 2021 dollars. The Minneapolis Federal Reserve has spliced a number of measures of inflation to create a year-by-year index going back to 1800. Using that index, the 2021 value of $60,000 in 1869 is calculated as 60,000 × (815.5 ÷ 40). "Consumer Price Index, 1800–," https://www.minneapolisfed.org/about-us/monetary-policy/inflation-calculator/consumer-price-index-1800- [https://perma.cc/KTR2-JX2Q].

44. David J. Herzig and Samuel D. Brunson, "Let Prophets Be (Non) Profits," *Wake Forest Law Review* 52, vol. 5 (2017): 1111–1161.

45. George S. Boutwell, *A Manual of the Direct and Excise Tax System of the United States; Including the Forms and Regulations Established by the Commissioner of Internal Revenue, the Decisions and Rulings of the Commissioner, Together With Extracts From the Correspondence of the Office* (Boston: Little, Brown & Company, 1863), 274.

46. George S. Boutwell, "Returns of Incomes of Shaker and Other Like Communities—Basis of Taxation—New Rule Governing $1000 Exemption," *Internal Revenue Record and Customs Journal* 10, no. 6 (August 7, 1869): 39–40.

47. Brunson, "Mormon Profit," 74–75.

224 · *Notes to Chapter 5*

48. Letter from J.W. Douglass, Comm'r of Internal Revenue, to John P. Taggart, Internal Revenue Assessor for the Territory of Utah (July 26, 1870) (on file with the Church History Library, The Church of Jesus Christ of Latter-day Saints, Salt Lake City, Utah).

49. Bryan T. Camp, "Theory and Practice in Tax Administration," *Virginia Tax Review* 29, no. 2 (2009): 227–275.

50. Aaron About, "What Shall Be Done with the Mormons?" *Chicago Tribune*, February 15, 1870, 2.

51. Revenue Act of 1862, ch. 119, § 24, 12 Stat. 442.

52. Letter from Daniel H. Wells, Second Counselor to the First Presidency, The Church of Jesus Christ of Latter-day Saints, to Brigham Young, President, The Church of Jesus Christ of Latter-day Saints (Jan. 1, 1871 [misdated as 1870]) (on file with the Church History Library, The Church of Jesus Christ of Latter-day Saints, Salt Lake City, Utah).

53. Brunson, "Mormon Profit," 78–79.

54. Form 47, 23 Feb. 1870 (Box 49, Folder 31, Brigham Young Office Files: 1869–1870 Mar., Church History Library, The Church of Jesus Christ of Latter-day Saints, Salt Lake City, Utah).

55. Letter from Brigham Young (per Daniel H. Wells), President, The Church of Jesus Christ of Latter-day Saints, to W.H. Hooper, Representative of the Territory of Utah, Mar. 15, 1870 (on file with the Church History Library, The Church of Jesus Christ of Latter-day Saints, Salt Lake City, Utah).

56. Letter from O.J. Hollister, Collector of Internal Revenue for the Territory of Utah, to Brigham Young, President, The Church of Jesus Christ of Latter-day Saints, Mar. 2, 1870 (on file with the Church History Library, The Church of Jesus Christ of Latter-day Saints, Salt Lake City, Utah).

57. Letter from O.J. Hollister to Brigham Young, Mar. 2, 1870.

58. Letter from O.J. Hollister, Collector of Internal Revenue for the Territory of Utah, to Columbus Delano, Internal Revenue Comm'r, Mar. 7, 1870 (on file with the Church History Library, The Church of Jesus Christ of Latter-day Saints, Salt Lake City, Utah).

59. Letter from O.J. Hollister to Columbus Delano, Mar. 7, 1870.

60. 12 Stat. 501 (1855–1863).

61. Letter from O.J. Hollister to Columbus Delano, Mar. 7, 1870.

62. Letter from Daniel H. Wells, Second Counselor to the First Presidency, The Church of Jesus Christ of Latter-day Saints, to W.H. Hooper, Representative for the Territory of Utah, Jan. 2, 1871 (on file with the Church History Library, The Church of Jesus Christ of Latter-day Saints, Salt Lake City, Utah).

63. Leonard J. Arrington, *Great Basin Kingdom* (Cambridge: Harvard University Press, 1958), 139.

64. Letter from T.W. Ellerbeck, Clerk to Brigham Young, to W.H. Hooper, Representative for the Territory of Utah, Dec. 17, 1870 (on file with the Church History Library, The Church of Jesus Christ of Latter-day Saints, Salt Lake City, Utah).

65. Treas. Reg. § 1.61–1(a) (as republished in 1960).

Notes to Chapter 5 • 225

66. Conversation between the former assistant Assessor of 8th Division District of Utah and Brigham Young, President, The Church of Jesus Christ of Latter-day Saints, on the subject of the Government taxing the Tithing or donations paid by the people called Latter day Saints, Dec. 31, 1870) (Box 49, Folder 32, Brigham Young office files: 1870 July–1871, Church History Library, The Church of Jesus Christ of Latter-day Saints, Salt Lake City, Utah).

67. While sometimes true, this argument was probably not accurate in most circumstances. With a $1,000 exemption amount, the vast majority of Americans did not pay the Civil War income tax. While it is hard to compare Civil War-era incomes with modern income, Congress specifically created the exemption amount to ensure that only the wealthy would pay income tax. Sheldon D. Pollack, "The First National Income Tax, 1861–1872," *The Tax Lawyer* 67, no. 2 (2014): 311–330. 320

68. Letter from Brigham Young to Columbus Delano, Mar. 18, 1870 (on file with the Church History Library, The Church of Jesus Christ of Latter-day Saints, Salt Lake City, Utah).

69. Revenue Act of 1870, ch. 255, § 8, 16 Stat. 258.

70. Letter from J.W. Douglass, Internal Revenue Comm'r, to John P. Taggart, July 29, 1870 (on file with the Church History Library, The Church of Jesus Christ of Latter-day Saints, Salt Lake City, Utah).

71. Letter from Brigham Young to Columbus Delano, Sept. 29, 1870 (on file with the Church History Library, The Church of Jesus Christ of Latter-day Saints, Salt Lake City, Utah).

72. Letter from O.J. Hollister, Collector of Internal Revenue for the Territory of Utah, to Brigham Young, President, The Church of Jesus Christ of Latter-day Saints, Sept. 26, 1870 (on file with the Church History Library, The Church of Jesus Christ of Latter-day Saints).

73. Letter from O.J. Hollister, Collector of Internal Revenue for the Territory of Utah to Brigham Young, President, The Church of Jesus Christ of Latter-day Saints, Oct. 7, 1870 (on file with the Church History Library, The Church of Jesus Christ of Latter-day Saints).

74. Letter from O.J. Hollister, Collector of Internal Revenue for the Territory of Utah, to Brigham Young, President, The Church of Jesus Christ of Latter-day Saints, Sept. 26, 1870 (on file with the Church History Library, The Church of Jesus Christ of Latter-day Saints).

75. Letter from Daniel H. Wells, Second Counselor to the First Presidency, The Church of Jesus Christ of Latter-day Saints, to W.H. Hooper, Representative for the Territory of Utah, Dec. 8, 1870 (on file with the Church History Library, The Church of Jesus Christ of Latter-day Saints, Salt Lake City, Utah).

76. Letter from Brigham Young to W.H. Hooper, May 26, 1870 (on file with the Church History Library, The Church of Jesus Christ of Latter-day Saints).

77. Joe Thorndike, "An Army of Officials: The Civil War Bureau of Internal Revenue," *Tax Notes* 93, no. 13 (Dec. 24, 2001): 1739–1760.

78. Brunson, "Mormon Profit," 94.

226 · *Notes to Chapter 5*

79. Letter from Brigham Young, President, The Church of Jesus Christ of Latter-day Saints, to Daniel H. Wells, Second Counselor to the First Presidency, The Church of Jesus Christ of Latter-day Saints, Dec. 30, 1870 (on file with the Church History Library, The Church of Jesus Christ of Latter-day Saints, Salt Lake City, Utah).

80. Letter from Daniel H. Wells, Second Counselor to the First Presidency, The Church of Jesus Christ of Latter-day Saints, to Brigham Young, President, The Church of Jesus Christ of Latter-day Saints, Jan. 1, 1871 (misdated as 1870; on file with the Church History Library, The Church of Jesus Christ of Latter-day Saints, Salt Lake City, Utah).

81. "Brigham Young's Income Tax: The Income from Mormon Church Property Decided to Be Taxable—Brigham Young's Points Overruled," *New York Times*, December 3, 1870, 1.

82. Letter from Brigham Young, President, The Church of Jesus Christ of Latter-day Saints, to Daniel H. Wells, Second Counselor to the First Presidency, The Church of Jesus Christ of Latter-day Saints, Dec. 14, 1870 (on file with the Church History Library, The Church of Jesus Christ of Latter-day Saints, Salt Lake City, Utah).

83. Letter from Brigham Young (per Daniel H. Wells) to W.H. Hooper, Mar. 15, 1870 (on file with the Church History Library, The Church of Jesus Christ of Latter-day Saints, Salt Lake City, Utah).

84. Letter from unknown sender [probably Brigham Young, President of The Church of Jesus Christ of Latter-day Saints], to Daniel H. Wells, Second Counselor to the First Presidency, The Church of Jesus Christ of Latter-day Saints, Jan. 3, 1871 (on file with the Church History Library, The Church of Jesus Christ of Latter-day Saints, Salt Lake City, Utah).

85. Arrington, *Great Basin Kingdom*, 353.

86. D&C 119:4. In 1844, the church canonized the revelation as section 107 of the Doctrine and Covenants. "Doctrine and Covenants, 1844," p. 430, The Joseph Smith Papers, accessed September 21, 2021, https://www.josephsmithpapers.org/paper-summary/doctrine-and-covenants-1844/432.

87. Letter from Brigham Young, President, The Church of Jesus Christ of Latter-day Saints, to Daniel H. Wells, Second Counselor to the First Presidency, The Church of Jesus Christ of Latter-day Saints, Jan. 4, 1871 (on file with the Church History Library, The Church of Jesus Christ of Latter-day Saints, Salt Lake City, Utah).

88. Letter from Brigham Young, President, The Church of Jesus Christ of Latter-day Saints, to the Bishops throughout the territory, Jan. 4, 1871 (on file with the Church History Library, The Church of Jesus Christ of Latter-day Saints, Salt Lake City, Utah).

89. "Home and Foreign Gossip," *Harper's Weekly*, Jan. 14, 1871, 35.

90. Brunson, "Mormon Profit," 102.

91. Brunson, "Mormon Profit," 99–100.

92. Letter from Alfred Pleasonton, Comm'r of Internal Revenue, to John P. Taggart, Assessor of Internal Revenue for the Territory of Utah, Jan. 13, 1871 (on file with the Church History Library, The Church of Jesus Christ of Latter-day Saints, Salt Lake City, Utah).

Notes to Chapters 5 and 6 · 227

93. Letter from Brigham Young, President, The Church of Jesus Christ of Latter-day Saints, to John McCarthy, Jan. 23, 1871 (on file with the Church History Library, The Church of Jesus Christ of Latter-day Saints, Salt Lake City, Utah).

94. Letter from Brigham Young, President, The Church of Jesus Christ of Latter-day Saints, to Edwin Taggart, Mar. 23, 1871 (on file with the Church History Library, The Church of Jesus Christ of Latter-day Saints, Salt Lake City, Utah).

95. Ajay K. Mehrotra, "From Contested Concept to Cornerstone of Administrative Practice: Social Learning and the Early History of U.S. Tax Withholding," *Columbia Journal of Tax Law* 7, no. 1 (2016): 144–168.

96. *Reynolds v. United States*, 98 U.S. 145, 161, 25 L. Ed. 244 (1878).

97. Sarah Barringer Gordon, *The Mormon Question: Polygamy and Constitutional Conflict in Nineteenth Century America* (Chapel Hill, NC: University of North Carolina Press, 2002), 220, 235.

98. Maura Strassberg, "The Crime of Polygamy," *Temple Political & Civil Rights Law Review* 12, no. 2 (2002): 353–431.

99. Wilford Woodruff, "Official Declaration," *The Latter-day Saints Millennial Star* 52, no. 41 (Oct. 13, 1890): 648.

100. *Proceedings Before the Committee on Privileges and Elections of the United States Senate in the Matter of the Protests Against the Right of Hon. Reed Smoot, a Senator from the State of Utah, to Hold His Seat*, vol. 1 (Washington: Government Printing Office, 1906), 331.

101. The Corporate Tax Act of 1909 imposed a one-percent excise tax on corporate net income in excess of $5,000. However, the Act exempted "any corporation or association organized and operated exclusively for religious . . . purposes." Revenue Act of 1909, ch. 6 § 38, 36 Stat. 11, 113.

Chapter 6. Enlarging Mormonism's Borders

1. Leonard J. Arrington, "The Mormon Cotton Mission in Southern Utah," *Pacific Historical Review* 25, no. 3 (1956): 221–238.

2. Herbert E. Gregory, "Population of Southern Utah," *Economic Geography* 21, no. 1 (1945): 29–57; D.W. Meinig, "The Mormon Culture Region: Strategies and Patterns in the Geography of the American West, 1847–1964," *Annals of the Association of American Geographers* 55, no. 2 (1965): 191–220.

3. Milton R. Hunter, "The Mormons and the Colorado River," *The American Historical Review* 44, no. 3 (1939): 549–555.

4. James W. Hulse, *The Silver State: Nevada's Heritage Reinterpreted* (Reno, NV: University of Nevada Press, 1991), 95–96.

5. Russell R. Elliott, *History of Nevada*, 2nd ed. (Lincoln, NE: University of Nebraska Press, 1987), 89.

6. James E. Hill, Jr., "Nevada South of 37° North: An Unprecedented Political Blunder," *Yearbook of the Association of Pacific Coast Geographers* 35 (1973): 61–74.

7. W. Paul Reeve, *Making Space on the Western Frontier: Mormons, Miners, and Southern Paiutes* (Chicago: University of Illinois Press, 2006), 88–89.

228 · Notes to Chapter 6

8. Thomas P. Slaughter, *The Whiskey Rebellion: Frontier Epilogue to the American Revolution* (New York: Oxford University Press, 1986), 11–12.

9. *The Bossier Banner*, April 12, 1873, 2.

10. "A Little Excitement," *Idaho Semi-Weekly World*, February 14, 1882, 3.

11. "Will Resort to Force," *Fort Worth Daily Gazette*, May 26, 1888, 6.

12. "Blue Blood Boiling," *The Evening Bulletin*, July 2, 1895, 1.

13. James W. Hulse, *The Nevada Adventure: A History* (Reno, NV: University of Nevada Press, 1965), 148.

14. Warren Foote, *Autobiography of Warren Foote*, https://wchsutah.org/people/warren-foote-journal1-2.pdf#page=145 [https://perma.cc/LN6N-5EM8].

15. Brigham Young office files, 1832–1878 (bulk 1844–1877); General Correspondence, Incoming, 1840–1877; General Letters, 1840–1877; T-Y, 1871; Joseph W. Young letter, Feb. 24, 1871; Church History Library, accessed September 27, 2021, https://catalog.churchofjesuschrist.org/assets/e37dd58d-4831-4e57-9c2c-6e1d5a809949/0/1.

16. Joseph Ellison, "The Currency Question on the Pacific Coast During the Civil War," *The Mississippi Valley Historical Review* 16, no. 1 (1929), 50–66.

17. *Rhodes v. O'Farrell*, 2 Nev. 60, 64 (1866).

18. An Act in Regard to Currency, *Statutes of the State of Nevada Passed at the Second Session of the Legislature, 1866* (Carson City, NV: John Church, State Printer, 1866), 190.

19. *Lane Cty. v. State of Oregon*, 74 U.S. 71, 81, 19 L. Ed. 101 (1868).

20. An Act to Establish the Financial Transactions of the State Upon a Coin Basis, *The Complied Laws of the State of Nevada Embracing Statutes of 1861 to 1873, Inclusive*, vol. 1 (Carson City, NV: Charles A.V. Putnam, State Printer, 1873), 12.

21. Hulse, *Silver State*, 97.

22. Joseph Young letter, February 24, 1871.

23. Larry D. Ball, "Frontier Sheriffs at Work," *Journal of Arizona History* 27, no. 3 (1986): 283–296.

24. "Arizona," *The Daily State Register*, Mar. 5, 1871, 2.

25. Pearson Starr Corbett, "Settling the Muddy River Valley," *Nevada Historical Society Quarterly* 18, no. 3 (1975): 142–151.

26. Audrey M. Godfrey, "Colonizing the Muddy River Valley: A New Perspective," *Journal of Mormon History* 22, no. 2 (1996): 120–142.

27. Reeve, *Making Space*, 90.

28. Reeve, *Making Space*, 192 n.21.

29. Amanda Hendrix-Komoto, *Imperial Zions: Religion, Race, and Family in the American West and the Pacific* (Lincoln: University of Nebraska Press, 2022), 123–124.

30. "Missionary Intelligence," *The Latter-day Saints Millennial Star*, March 12, 1877, 171; D. Michael Quinn, "They Served: The Richards Legacy in the Church," *Ensign*, January 1980, https://www.churchofjesuschrist.org/study/ensign/1980/01/they-served-the-richards-legacy-in-the-church?lang=eng [https://perma.cc/B8FT-TSHZ].

31. Jennifer M.L. Chock, "One Hundred Years of Illegitimacy: International Legal Analysis of the Illegal Overthrow of the Hawaiian Monarchy, Hawai'i's Annexation, and Possible Reparations," *University of Hawai'i Law Review* 17, no. 2 (1995): 463–512.

Notes to Chapters 6 and 7 · 229

32. "Local and Other Matters," *Deseret News*, November 28, 1877, 3.

33. The Civil Code of the Hawaiian Islands, § 480 (1859).

34. The Civil Code of the Hawaiian Islands, § 486.

35. The Civil Code of the Hawaiian Islands, § 487. Just like other road taxes, men could substitute labor for money. In this case, six eight-hour days would meet an individual's road tax obligation. Ibid., § 488.

36. The Civil Code of the Hawaiian Islands, §§ 481–484.

37. The Civil Code of the Hawaiian Islands, § 513.

38. *Kupau v. Richards*, 6 Haw. 245 (1879).

39. Terry D. Webb, "Highly Structured Tourist Art: Form and Meaning of the Polynesian Cultural Center," *The Contemporary Pacific* 6, no. 1 (1994): 59–86.

40. Pamela G. Hollie, "Cultural Center in Hawaii Fights I.R.S. Tax Ruling," *New York Times*, March 26, 1981, A16.

41. BYU-Hawai'i Quick Facts 2019–2020, https://about.byuh.edu/00000177-1ce4 -d89c-af77-7df626210000/20-11-09-quickfactsupdate-pdf [https://perma.cc/ V6KD-LLR3].

42. Hollie, "Cultural Center," A16.

43. https://www.polynesia.com/packages [https://perma.cc/4HC3-H52R].

44. Polynesian Cultural Center Form 990, 2019.

45. Hollie, "Cultural Center," A16.

46. Webb, "Highly Structured," 83.

47. The Holy Land Experience Ministries Form 990, 2019; Daniel Silliman, "The Holy Land Experience Never Made It to the Financial Promised Land," *Christianity Today*, August 10, 2021, https://www.christianitytoday.com/news/2021/august/holy-land -experience-closes-sells-tbn-adventist-rosenthal.html [https://perma.cc/SR9P-LYZ7].

48. Caroline Winter, Katherine Burton, Nick Tamasi, and Anita Kumar, "The Money Behind the Mormon Message," *Salt Lake Tribune*, October 5, 2012, https://archive.sltrib .com/article.php?id=54478720&itype=cmsid [https://perma.cc/TAH9-SL6U].

49. "Polynesian Center Loses Tax Court Fight," *Deseret News*, August 6, 1992, https:// www.deseret.com/1992/8/6/18998267/polynesian-center-loses-tax-court-fight [https://perma.cc/DX3A-RTVT].

50. Kathleen Gallagher, "Hawaii's Polynesian Cultural Center Files Tax Appeal for $2.3M," *Pacific Business News*, July 6, 2016, https://www.bizjournals.com/pacific/ news/2016/07/06/hawaiis-polynesian-cultural-center-files-tax.html [https://perma .cc/QJV2-C9WS?type=image]; Department of Taxation, State of Hawaii, Annual Report 2018–2019 at 74, https://files.hawaii.gov/tax/stats/stats/annual/19annrpt .pdf [https://perma.cc/BSE6-3ASJ].

Chapter 7. A Corporate Church in Brooklyn

1. "Mormons Dedicate First Church Here," *The Sun*, Feb. 17, 1919, 14.

2. Urban Institute, "Soda Taxes," https://www.urban.org/policy-centers/cross-center -initiatives/state-and-local-finance-initiative/state-and-local-backgrounders/soda -taxes [https://perma.cc/XM58-WHVW].

230 • *Notes to Chapter 7*

3. Richard A. Westin, "When One-Eyed Accountants are Kings: A Primer on Microeconomics, Income Taxes, and the Shibboleth of Efficiency," *Minnesota Law Review* 69, no. 5 (1985): 1097–1110.

4. The one way to avoid a head tax, of course, is to die.

5. A thorough and fulsome look at the corporate history of the Mormon Church is beyond the scope of this book. In short, though, since its formation in 1830, the church tried to take advantage of corporate structures that became increasingly available to churches in the United States in the nineteenth century. By the beginning of the twentieth century, it had come to prefer a corporation sole to own and manage property, though, as we will see in this chapter, where a Utah corporation sole did not serve its purposes, it would sometimes fracture its corporate identity to use a different legal form. For a more in-depth look at the extensive history of the Mormon Church and corporate formation, *see* Nathan B. Oman, "'Established Agreeable to the Laws of Our Country': Mormonism, Church Corporations, and the Long Legacy of America's First Disestablishment," *Journal of Law and Religion* 36, no. 2 (2021): 202–229.

6. These amounts were not insignificant. A Bureau of Labor Statistics CPI calculator estimates that $800-$900 in January 1917 would have the same buying power as roughly $20,500-$23,000 in January 2023. CPI Inflation Calculator, https://data.bls.gov/cgi-bin/cpicalc.pl.

7. Walter P. Monson to Joseph F. Smith, January 5, 1917, Church History Library.

8. *The Consolidated Laws of the State of New York*, vol. 5 (Albany, J.B. Lyon Printers, 1909), 4023.

9. *The Consolidated Laws of the State of New York*, vol. 5, 4025.

10. Walter P. Monson to Joseph F. Smith, January 5, 1917, Church History Library.

11. Walter P. Monson to Joseph F. Smith, January 9, 1917, Church History Library.

12. George F. Gibbs to Walter P. Monson, January 12, 1917, Church History Library.

13. Franklin S. Richards to First Presidency, January 22, 1917, Church History Library.

14. Joseph F. Smith, Anthon H. Lund, and Charles W. Penrose to Walter P. Monson, August 30, 1917, Church History Library.

15. Stephen M. Bainbridge and Aaron H. Cole, "The Bishop's Alter Ego: Enterprise Liability and the Catholic Priest Sex Abuse Scandal," *Journal of Catholic Legal Studies* 46, no. 1 (2007): 65–106.

16. Franklin S. Richards to First Presidency, January 22, 1917, Church History Library.

17. *Blakeslee v. Hall*, 94 Cal. 159, 160–161, 29 P. 623, 624 (1892).

18. Carl Zollmann, "Classes of American Religious Corporations," *Michigan Law Review* 13, no. 7 (1915): 566–83.

19. *The Consolidated Laws of the State of New York* vol IV, ed. Frederick E. Wadhams (New York: The American Law Book Company, 1909), 3747–3748.

20. Philip Hamburger, "Illiberal Liberalism: Liberal Theology, Anti-Catholicism, & Church Property," *Journal of Contemporary Legal Issues* 12, no. 2 (2002): 693–726.

21. "Mormon Church Not Exempt from Taxes," *Brooklyn Daily Eagle*, July 3, 1917, 18.

22. Walter P. Monson to Joseph F. Smith, July 7, 1917, Church History Library.

Notes to Chapter 7 · 231

23. "Threat to Dynamite New Mormon Temple," *The Sun*, August 6, 1916, 4.

24. Walter P. Monson to Joseph F. Smith, January 9, 1917, Church History Library.

25. Franklin S. Richards to First Presidency, July 13, 1917, Church History Library.

26. Joseph F. Smith, Anthon E. Lund, and Charles W. Penrose to Walter P. Monson, July 14, 1917, Church History Library.

27. *The Consolidated Laws of the State of New York*, vol. 5 (Albany, J.B. Lyon Printers, 1909), 4025.

28. *People ex rel. Corp. of the Presiding Bishop of the Church of Jesus Christ of Latter Day Saints v. Purdy*, 184 A.D. 915, 915, 170 N.Y.S. 1104 (App. Div. 1918).

29. Stuart M. Kohn to Walter P. Monson, July 19, 1917, Church History Library.

30. Walter P. Monson to Joseph F. Smith, July 20, 1917, Church History Library.

31. Walter P. Monson to Joseph F. Smith, August 10, 1917, Church History Library.

32. George F. Gibbs to Walter P. Monson, August 14, 1917, Church History Library.

33. Stuart M. Kohn to George F. Gibbs, August 21, 1917, Church History Library.

34. George F. Gibbs to Stuart M. Kohn, August 25, 1917, Church History Library.

35. Joseph F. Smith, Anthon H. Lund, and Charles W. Penrose to Walter P. Monson, August 30, 1917, Church History Library.

36. *Trotta v. Ollivier*, 933 N.Y.S.2d 66, 69 (2011).

37. *Bambauer v. Schleider*, 176 A.D. 562, 564, 163 N.Y.S. 186, 188 (App. Div. 1917).

38. Walter P. Monson to Joseph F. Smith and counsellors, Sept. 8, 1917, Church History Library.

39. Stephen Diamond, "Efficiency and Benevolence: Philanthropic Tax Exemptions in 19th-Century America," in *Property-Tax Exemption for Charities* (Washington, D.C.: The Urban Institute Press, 2002), 118.

40. Walter P. Monson to Joseph F. Smith and counselors, Sept. 8, 1917, Church History Library.

41. Franklin S. Richards to First Presidency, Sept. 21, 1917, Church History Library.

42. Minutes of the Meeting Held for the Purpose of Organizing the Eastern States Mission Corporation, September 24, 1917, Eastern States Mission corporation records, 1918–1964, Church History Library, Salt Lake City.

43. Walter P. Monson to Joseph Fielding Smith, Sept. 25, 1917, Church History Library.

44. Minutes of the Meeting Held for the Purpose of Organizing the Eastern States Mission Corporation, September 24, 1917, Eastern States Mission corporation records, 1918–1964, Church History Library, Salt Lake City. A year later, the new corporation seems to have forgotten the trustees' terms; instead, Smith was nominated for the open office and elected unanimously. Minutes of the Meeting of the Members of the Eastern States Mission of the Church of Jesus Christ of Latter Day Saints for the Purpose of Electing a Trustee for the Term of Three Years, October 15, 1918, Eastern States Mission corporation records, 1918–1964, Church History Library, Salt Lake City.

45. Walter P. Monson to Joseph Fielding Smith, Sept. 25, 1917, Church History Library.

232 · Notes to Chapter 7 and Part II

46. By-Laws of Eastern States Mission of the Church of Jesus Christ of Latter Day Saints, Eastern States Mission corporation records, 1918–1964, Church History Library, Salt Lake City.

47. *People ex rel. Corp. of the Presiding Bishop of the Church of Jesus Christ of Latter Day Saints v. Purdy*, 184 A.D. 915, 915, 170 N.Y.S. 1104 (App. Div. 1918).

48. *Williams Institutional Colored Methodist Episcopal Church v. City of New York*, 275 A.D. 311, 89 N.Y.S.2d 300 (App. Div. 1949), aff'd, 300 N.Y. 716, 92 N.E.2d 58 (1950).

49. *Williams Institutional Colored Methodist Episcopal Church v. City of New York*, 300 N.Y. 716, 92 N.E.2d 58 (1950).

50. Val G. Hemming, "Ricks College: The Struggle for Permanency and Place, 1954–60," *Journal of Mormon History* 26, no. 2 (2000): 51–109.

51. Delbert G. Taylor to First Presidency, undated, Eastern States Mission. Eastern States Mission corporation records, 1918–1964, Church History Library, Salt Lake City.

52. Minutes of the Meeting Held by the Trustees of the Eastern States Mission, April 23, 1955. Eastern States Mission corporation records, 1918–1964, Church History Library, Salt Lake City.

53. John B. Lawless to Gerald G. Smith, November 11, 1959, Eastern States Mission corporation records, 1918–1964, Church History Library, Salt Lake City.

54. Gerald G. Smith to John B. Lawless, November 23, 1959, Eastern States Mission corporation records, 1918–1964, Church History Library, Salt Lake City.

55. John B. Lawless to Gerald G. Smith, December 5, 1959, Eastern States Mission corporation records, 1918–1964, Church History Library, Salt Lake City.

56. Gerald G. Smith to First Presidency, December 19, 1959, Eastern States Mission corporation records, 1918–1964, Church History Library, Salt Lake City.

57. Vernon Snyder to Gerald Smith, January 4, 1960, Eastern States Mission corporation records, 1918–1964, Church History Library, Salt Lake City.

58. Oman, "Established Agreeable," 228.

59. The date of the dissolution is unclear. While the Church likely filed a notice with the state that it was dissolving the Eastern States Mission, the corporate records housed in the Church History Library do not contain any such notice.

60. "Building of the Day: 269 Gates Avenue," *Brownstoner*, November 5, 2020, https://www.brownstoner.com/architecture/building-of-the-175/ [https://perma.cc/TD5B-AC6N].

Part II. Tinkering around the Edges of Tax and Religion

1. Deborah H. Schenk, "The Income Tax at 100," *Tax Law Review* 66, no. 4 (2013): 357–378.

2. Ajay K. Mehrotra, "Render unto Caesar: Religious/Ethics, Expertise, and the Historical Underpinnings of the Modern American Tax System," *Loyola University Chicago Law Journal* 40, no. 2 (2009): 321–368.

Notes to Part II and Chapter 8 • 233

3. Daniel Shaviro, *Federalism in Taxation: The Case for Greater Uniformity* (Washington, DC: The AEI Press, 1993), 3–4.

4. Aniel R. Feenberg and Harvey S. Rosen, "State Personal Income and Sales Taxes, 1977–1983," in *Studies in State and Local Public Finance*, ed. Harvey S. Rosen (Chicago: University of Chicago Press, 1986), 139.

5. J. Richard Aronson and John L. Hilley, *Financing State and Local Governments*, 4th ed. (Washington, DC: The Brookings Institution, 1986), 88.

6. Allison Christians, "Networks, Norms, and National Tax Policy," *Washington University Global Studies Law Review* 9, no. 1 (2010): 1–37.

Chapter 8. Mormon Protest Against Taxation

1. Charles Adams, *Those Dirty Rotten Taxes: The Tax Revolts That Built America* (New York: The Free Press, 1998), 44–45.

2. Adams, *Those Dirty Rotten Taxes*, x.

3. Marjorie E. Kornhauser, "Legitimacy and the Right of Revolution: The Role of Tax Protests and Anti-Tax Rhetoric in America," *Buffalo Law Review* 50, no. 3 (2002): 819–930.

4. Beverly Beeton, "Women Suffrage in Territorial Utah," in *Battle for the Ballot: Essays on Woman Suffrage in Utah, 1870–1896*, ed. Carole Cornwall Madsen (Logan, UT: Utah State University Press, 1997): 116–135.

5. "The Women of Utah," *New York Times*, Mar. 5, 1869, 6.

6. Thomas G. Alexander, "An Experiment in Progressive Legislation: The Granting of Woman Suffrage in Utah in 1870," in *Battle for the Ballot: Essays on Woman Suffrage in Utah, 1870–1896*, ed. Carole Cornwall Madsen (Logan, UT: Utah State University Press, 1997), 105–115.

7. Carole Cornwall Madsen, "Emmeline B. Wells: 'Am I Not a Woman and a Sister?'" *Brigham Young University Studies* 22, no. 2 (1982): 161–178.

8. Carole Cornwall Madsen, "Emmeline B. Wells: A Voice for Mormon Women," *The John Whitmer Historical Society Journal* 2 (1982): 11–21.

9. Emmeline B. Wells, *The Diaries of Emmeline B. Wells* (Church Historians Press, Sept. 5, 1894), https://www.churchhistorianspress.org/emmeline-b-wells/1890s/1894/1894-09?lang=eng#title6 [https://perma.cc/X4E7-T648].

10. "New England Woman's Tea Party," *The Woman's Journal* 4, no. 50 (Dec. 13, 1873): 396.

11. Carolyn C. Jones, "Dollars and Selves: Women's Tax Criticism and Resistance in the 1870s," *University of Illinois Law Review* 1994, no. 2 (1994): 265–310.

12. "Declaration of the Rights of the Women of the United States by the National Woman Suffrage Association," Jul. 4, 1876, https://ccdl.claremont.edu/digital/collection/p15831coll5/id/1111 [https://perma.cc/2UMD-LEFR].

13. Jones, "Dollars and Selves," 267–269.

14. Juliana Tutt, "'No Taxation Without Representation' in the American Woman Suffrage Movement," *Stanford Law Review* 62, no. 5 (2010): 1473–1512.

234 · Notes to Chapter 8

15. Emmeline B. Wells, *The Diaries of Emmeline B. Wells* (Church Historians Press, Nov. 23, 1895), https://www.churchhistorianspress.org/emmeline-b-wells/1890s/1895/1895–11?lang=eng#title24 [https://perma.cc/K92E-2NLA].

16. *Judge v. Spencer*, 15 Utah 242 (1897).

17. Emmeline B. Wells, *The Diaries of Emmeline B. Wells* (Church Historians Press, Dec. 23, 1895), https://www.churchhistorianspress.org/emmeline-b-wells/1890s/1895/1895-12?lang=eng#title24 [https://perma.cc/284Y-BJ5X].

18. While Wells flirted with activist tax protest, she was also interested in the progressive tax proposals of her day. On March 31, 1896, she recorded in her diary that she listened to Dr. Pratt speak about the "single tax," an issue she characterized as "very fascinating." "[A]s citizens," she wrote, "we should try to comprehend all these intricate problems and questions that are agitating the public mind and become able to talk of them in a way to help others." Emmeline B. Wells, *The Diaries of Emmeline B. Wells* (Church Historians Press, March 31, 1896), https://www.churchhistorianspress.org/emmeline-b-wells/1890s/1896/1896-03?lang=eng [https://perma.cc/9ZPT-34F4]. The "single tax" was a proposal by Progressive Era political economist and journalist Henry George. George believed that a high tax on the value of land, but not on improvements to land, would both reduce land speculation, providing individuals with access to affordable land, and would generate so much revenue that the government could eliminate other taxes and tariffs. His ideas gained significant national and international currency between about 1880 and 1897, putting the lectures Wells attended in Salt Lake comfortably within the modern discussion of poverty alleviation. Fred Nicklason, "Henry George: Social Gospeller," *American Quarterly* 22, no. 3 (1970): 649–664. According to the *New York Times*, Georgist land value taxes have gained new popularity and currency in the early 2020s. Conor Dougherty, "The 'Georgists' Are Out There, and They Want to Tax Your Land," *New York Times*, November 12, 2023, https://www.nytimes.com/2023/11/12/business/georgism-land-tax-housing.html [https://perma.cc/9LN2-QDB8].

19. Erik M. Jensen, "Did the Sixteenth Amendment Ever Matter? Does It Matter Today?" *Northwestern University Law Review* 108, no. 3 (2014): 799–824.

20. Conor Clarke, "*Moore*: The Overlooked Excise Power," *Tax Notes Federal* 181, no. 10 (December 4, 2023): 1759–1766.

21. "Brown Is Unsuccessful," *Evening Star*, Jul. 20, 1909, 4.

22. U.S. Constitution, Amend. XVI.

23. Tax Analysts, "Tax History Museum, 1901–1932: The Income Tax Arrives," http://www.taxhistory.org/www/website.nsf/Web/THM1901 [https://perma.cc/T6B2-6NTD].

24. Congressional Research Service, Library of Cong., S. Doc. No. 103–6, *The Constitution of the United States of America: Analysis and Interpretation* (1992), 34 no. 8, https://www.govinfo.gov/content/pkg/GPO-CONAN-1992/pdf/GPO-CONAN-1992.pdf [https://perma.cc/5XAX-VDEF].

25. "Senator King Replies to Smoot in Vigorous Talk at Democratic Meeting," *Ogden Standard-Examiner* (Oct. 27, 1926): 6.

Notes to Chapter 8 · 235

26. Kathleen Flake, *Politics of Religious Identity: The Seating of Senator Reed Smoot, Mormon Apostle* (Chapel Hill, NC: University of North Carolina Press, 2004), 39.

27. Milton R. Merrill, *Reed Smoot: Apostle in Politics* (Logan, UT: Utah State University Press, 1990), 146, 171–172.

28. Revenue Act of 1913, Ch. 16, § II.C., 38 Stat. 168–169.

29. First Presidency to Reed Smoot, Jan. 22, 1914, First Presidency General Authority correspondence, CR 1/176 (box 9—Smoot 1914).

30. Harvard S. Heath, ed., *In the World: The Diaries of Reed Smoot* (Salt Lake City: Signature Books, 1997), 208.

31. *Trinidad v. Sagrada Orden de Predicadores*, etc., 263 U.S. 578, 44 S. Ct. 204, 68 L. Ed. 458 (1924).

32. Douglas A. Irwin, "Tariff Incidence in America's Gilded Age," *Journal of Economic History* 67, no. 3 (2007): 582–607.

33. Matthew C. Godfrey, *Religion, Politics, and Sugar: The Mormon Church, the Federal Government, and the Utah-Idaho Sugar Company, 1907–1921* (Logan, UT: Utah State University Press, 2007), 1–3.

34. Congress also worried that, with waves of prohibition sweeping the country, it would be unable to rely on excise taxes on alcohol to continue funding government. Statement of Sen. Edward Dixon, 44 Cong. Reg. 3941 (1909).

35. "Sugar Bill Passed by House, 198 to 103," *New York Times*, Mar. 16, 1912, 6; "Senate Amends Sugar Bill," *Hanford Weekly Sentinel*, Aug. 1, 1912, 9.

36. Statement of Sen. Anthony Higgins, 26 Cong. Rec. 5587 (1894).

37. Thomas G. Alexander, *Mormonism in Transition: A History of the Latter-day Saints, 1890–1931* (Urbana, IL: University of Illinois Press, 1986), 80.

38. Judson C. Welliver, "The Mormon Church and the Sugar Trust: How 'Beet Sugar,' Fostered by the Government, Has Been Absorbed by the Trust to Protect Its Tariff," *Hampton's Magazine* 24, no. 1 (1910): 82–93.

39. Matthew C. Godfrey, "The Battle over Tariff Reduction: The Utah-Idaho Sugar Company, Senator Reed Smoot, and the 1913 Underwood Act," in *Utah in the Twentieth Century*, eds. Brian Q. Cannon and Jessie L. Embry (Logan, UT: Utah State University Press, 2009), 186–205.

40. "The Apostle's Claim," *Salt Lake Tribune*, Jun. 7, 1913, 6.

41. Douglas A. Irwin, *Clashing Over Commerce: A History of US Trade Policy* (Chicago: University of Chicago Press, 2017), 334.

42. It makes sense that supporting sugar beet would have been good for Utahns in general; in 1916, for instance, Utah produced more sugar beets per capital than any other state besides Colorado. That year, Utahns produced 1.1087 tons of sugar beets per person, as compared with the 1.5415 tons per capita raised in Colorado. The third-highest per capital producer of sugar beets was Idaho, with just over half a ton per person. And after Idaho, the per capital production of sugar beets dropped radically, with only four other states growing more than one-tenth of a ton per person. Sara Fisher Ellison and Wallace P. Mullin, "Economics and Politics: The Case of Sugar Tariff Reform," *Journal of Law & Economics* 38, no. 2 (1995): 335–366.

236 • *Notes to Chapter 8*

43. Ellison and Mullin, "Economics and Politics," 371.

44. "Lively Tilt on Minority Side of the Senate," *Salt Lake Tribune*, Aug. 28, 1913, 1.

45. "Senator Smoot on War Tax," *The Ogden Standard*, Oct. 13, 1914, 4.

46. Conference Report, April 1925, 53.

47. "Smoot Will Offer a Tax Bill of His Own Making," *Palatka Daily News*, September 19, 1921, 1. Interestingly, seven decades later, another religious organization would renew the call for a national retail sales tax. The Church of Scientology, at war with the IRS over its status as a church for tax purposes, proposed such a tax as a way to eliminate the IRS altogether. Bruce Bartlett, "FairTax, Flawed Tax," *Wall Street Journal*, August 25, 2007, https://www.wsj.com/articles/SB118800635034508655 [https://perma.cc/YK6C-S6XP].

48. "Legion Certain Congress Will Grant Bonus," *New York Tribune*, March 25, 1920, 4.

49. Norman Hapgood, "Sales Tax Dead, Save to Smoot, Hapgood Finds," *Washington Times*, June 14, 1921, 3.

50. Joseph J. Thorndike, "Timelines in Tax History: From 'Class Tax' to 'Mass Tax' During World War II," *Tax Notes Federal* 176, no. 12 (Sept. 19, 2022): 1816–1824.

51. Joseph J. Thorndike, "Should It Stay or Should It Go? Defending the Income Tax in 1948," *Tax Notes* 167, no. 13 (June 29, 2020): 2240–2244.

52. In fact, to help people understand that they needed to pay taxes and how to actually pay them, a Disney short featured Donald Duck paying his taxes. Robert Smith and David Kestenbaum, "Summer School 6: Taxes & Donald Duck," *Planet Money*, Aug. 12, 2020, https://www.npr.org/2020/08/12/901837703/summer-school-6-taxes-donald-duck [https://perma.cc/5T29-P9AQ]. If you have never had the pleasure of watching this short, I highly recommend putting this book down for about six minutes and watching "Donald Duck: The Spirit of '43," https://www.youtube.com/watch?v=XNMrMFuk-bo.

53. Romain D. Huret, *American Tax Resisters* (Cambridge, MA: Harvard University Press, 2014), 209.

54. Matthew L. Harris, "Breaching the Wall: Ezra Taft Benson on Church and State," in *Thunder from the Right: Ezra Taft Benson in Mormonism and Politics*, ed. Matthew L. Harris (Chicago: University of Illinois Press, 2019), 2.

55. Brian Q. Cannon, "Ezra Taft Benson and the Family Farm," in *Thunder from the Right: Ezra Taft Benson in Mormonism and Politics*, ed. Matthew L. Harris (Chicago: University of Illinois Press, 2019), 27.

56. Matthew L. Harris, *Watchman on the Tower: Ezra Taft Benson and the Making of the Mormon Right* (Salt Lake City, UT: University of Utah Press, 2020), 3–6.

57. Robert A. Goldberg, "From New Deal to New Right," in *Thunder from the Right: Ezra Taft Benson in Mormonism and Politics*, ed. Matthew L. Harris (Chicago: University of Illinois Press, 2019), 73.

58. Gregory A. Prince and Wm. Robert Wright, *David O. McKay and the Rise of Modern Mormonism* (Salt Lake City, UT: University of Utah Press, 2005), 280.

59. Harris, *Watchman*, 29.

Notes to Chapter 8 · 237

60. Ezra Taft Benson, Address, Oct. 4, 1968, in *Conference Report*, 19.

61. Tax Policy Center, "Historical Highest Marginal Income Tax Rates," Feb. 4, 2020, https://www.taxpolicycenter.org/statistics/historical-highest-marginal-income-tax-rates [https://perma.cc/W5AS-5EGR].

62. Scott Greenberg, "Taxes on the Rich Were Not That Much Higher in the 1950s," Tax Foundation, Aug. 4, 2017, https://taxfoundation.org/taxes-on-the-rich-1950s-not-high/ [https://perma.cc/W67R-FSFT].

63. Ezra Taft Benson, Address, Oct. 4, 1968, in *Conference Report*, 19.

64. Richard Pearson, "Ezra Taft Benson, Mormon Chief, Dies," *Washington Post*, May 31, 1994, https://www.washingtonpost.com/archive/politics/1994/05/31/ezra-taft-benson-mormon-chief-dies/820365c5-bf1c-4292-a369-0e0764af68ff/ [https://perma.cc/KPY8-2UU4].

65. Ezra Taft Benson, "A Vision and a Hope for the Youth of Zion," Apr. 12, 1977, https://speeches.byu.edu/talks/ezra-taft-benson/vision-hope-youth-zion/ [https://perma.cc/A685-CPQZ].

66. Huret, *American Tax Resisters*, 206–207.

67. David Briscoe, "Western Tax Rebels Pull Out All Stops in IRS Fight," *The Ogden Standard-Examiner*, May 6, 1973, 12.

68. D&C 101:77, 80.

69. Reed D. Slack, "The Mormon Belief of an Inspired Constitution," *Journal of Church and State* 36, no. 1 (1994): 35–56.

70. Briscoe, "Western Tax Rebels," 12.

71. Department of Workforce Services, "Utah Economic Data Viewer," https://jobs.utah.gov/jsp/utalmis/#/population/areaname/Statewide/periodyear/1974 [https://perma.cc/BV4Z-2HTL].

72. Francis Ward, "Tax Rebellion: Defiers of IRS Take the Fifth," *Los Angeles Times*, December 28, 1974, 10.

73. Briscoe, "Western Tax Rebels," 12.

74. "Tax Protestor Declared Guilty," *Salt Lake Tribune*, March 23, 1977, 10.

75. Vern Anderson, "Tax Protestor Not Sure About Prison Risk," *The Ogden Standard-Examiner*, August 19, 1977, 17.

76. Harold B. Lee, "Admonitions for the Priesthood of God," *The Ensign*, January 1973, https://www.churchofjesuschrist.org/study/ensign/1973/01/admonitions-for-the-priesthood-of-god?lang=eng [https://perma.cc/795W-HVZE].

77. Robert F. Bohn, "I Have a Question: What Can You Tell Me About the Federal Income Tax?" *The Ensign*, January 1976, https://www.churchofjesuschrist.org/study/ensign/1976/01/i-have-a-question/what-can-you-tell-me-about-the-federal-income-tax?lang=eng [https://perma.cc/AE8Y-KWX4].

78. Duston Harvey, "Church Crackdown on Tax Protestors, Evaders Gets Results," *The Daily Herald*, July 8, 1976, 25.

79. "Repents, Pays Taxes," *The Daily Spectrum*, May 26, 1978, 6.

80. As absurd as these frivolous arguments sound, they are common enough that the IRS devotes space on its website to addressing them. "The Truth About Frivolous

238 · *Notes to Chapter 8*

Tax Arguments," March 2018, https://www.irs.gov/pub/taxpros/frivolous_truth_march_2018.pdf [https://perma.cc/4TQX-J3XC].

81. *Smith v. Comm'r*, 38 T.C.M. (CCH) 213 (T.C. 1979).

82. "Stake President," Newsroom, https://newsroom.churchofjesuschrist.org/article/stake-president [https://perma.cc/3C3A-58N4]; "Mission President," Newsroom, https://newsroom.churchofjesuschrist.org/article/mission-president [https://perma.cc/ZM6Y-54X3].

83. First Presidency to All Stake and Mission Presidents in the United States, January 21, 1983, Lester E. Bush Papers, LDS Church First Presidency Materials, 1976–1981, Ms 685, Box 8, Folder 3. Special Collections, J. Willard Marriott Library, The University of Utah.

84. Michael Harold Paulos, "'Does Not Purport to Comprehend All Matters of Church Government': The LDS 'General Handbook of Instructions,' 1899–2006," *Journal of Mormon History* 38, no. 4 (2012): 200–225.

85. The church did plan to prepare and provide printed versions for those leaders in areas without consistent internet access. Peggy Fletcher Stack & David Noyce, "LDS Church Publishes New Handbook with Changes to Discipline, Transgender Policy," *Salt Lake Tribune*, February 19, 2020, https://www.sltrib.com/religion/2020/02/19/lds-church-puts-new/ [https://perma.cc/35A8-JMBP].

86. *General Handbook of Instructions* (Salt Lake City: The Church of Jesus Christ of Latter-day Saints, 1983), 75. This edition was not the first time the church had addressed income taxes in the *General Handbook of Instructions*. But it was the first time it addressed members' duty to pay their taxes; the prior version's section on income taxes informed local leaders that the church could be subject to income taxation on certain types of income. While the central church would take care of filing returns and paying taxes when due, local leaders needed to provide timely financial information to the church's financial department. *General Handbook of Instructions* (Salt Lake City: The Church of Jesus Christ of Latter-day Saints, 1976), 106.

87. *General Handbook of Instructions* (Salt Lake City: The Church of Jesus Christ of Latter-day Saints, 1989), 11–12.

88. *General Handbook of Instructions Book 1* (Salt Lake City: The Church of Jesus Christ of Latter-day Saints, 1998), 151.

89. *General Handbook: Serving in The Church of Jesus Christ of Latter-day Saints* § 38.8.44 (Salt Lake City: The Church of Jesus Christ of Latter-day Saints, 2021), https://www.churchofjesuschrist.org/study/manual/general-handbook/38-church-policies-and-guidelines?lang=eng#title_number247 [https://perma.cc/J9T6-P9ZA].

90. "Ultraconservatives Say Church Is Purging Them," *AP*, November 29, 1992, https://apnews.com/article/81040a276f4310f7934e6f855c268501 [https://perma.cc/B2HE-L4P6]; Anti-Defamation League, "James 'Bo' Gritz, https://www.adl.org/sites/default/files/documents/assets/pdf/combating-hate/Gritz-James-Bo-EIA.pdf [https://perma.cc/4ZG9-JBVD].

Notes to Chapters 8 and 9 • 239

91. Matthew Harris, "Ezra Taft Benson, Dwight D. Eisenhower and the Emergence of a Conspiracy Culture within the Mormon Church," *The John Whitmer Historical Association Journal* 37, no. 1 (2017): 51–82.

92. Mario S. De Pillis, "The Emergence of Mormon Power Since 1945," *Journal of Mormon History* 22, no. 1 (1996): 1–32.

93. Of course, while Gritz pointed to his stake president asking about his taxpaying as a reason for leaving the church, that was not his only reason. Among other things, he had been reprimanded for baptizing someone without hierarchical permission and, during his presidential campaign, had been told not to accept speaking invitations in church buildings. Still, questions about his taxpaying seem to have represented a final straw to him, an indication that the church "appears to be more controlled by the government than God." Paul Parkinson, "Gritz Says He's Leaving LDS Church," *Deseret News*, October 19, 1994, https://www.deseret.com/1994/10/19/19137185/gritz-says-he-s-leaving-lds-church [https://perma.cc/2PQ5-N8PF].

94. I.R.C. §§ 6671(b), 6672(a); *Monday v. United States*, 421 F.2d 1210, 1214–1215 (7th Cir. 1970).

95. The IRS lays out its criteria for what constitutes a necessary expense in its Internal Revenue Manual. I.R.M. 5.15.1.1 (2019), https://www.irs.gov/irm/part5/irm_05-015-001 [https://perma.cc/ZT5B-GK7L].

96. *Thompson v. Comm'r*, 140 T.C. 173 (2013).

Chapter 9. Polygamy and . . . Taxes?

1. Richard S. Van Wagner, *Mormon Polygamy: A History* (Salt Lake City: Signature Books, 1989), 3.

2. Van Wagner, *Mormon Polygamy*, 63.

3. Van Wagner, *Mormon Polygamy*, 85.

4. Sarah Barringer Gordon, *The Mormon Question: Polygamy and Constitutional Conflict in Nineteenth Century America* (Chapel Hill, NC: University of North Carolina Press, 2002), 202–203.

5. Gordon, *Mormon Question*, 219–220.

6. Ken Driggs, "Twentieth-Century Polygamy and Fundamentalist Mormons in Southern Utah," *Dialogue: A Journal of Mormon Thought* 24, no. 4 (1991): 44–58.

7. Gordon, *Mormon Question*, 235–236.

8. Driggs, "Twentieth-Century Polygamy," 45.

9. Gordon, *Mormon Question*, 236.

10. Aimee Groth, "The REAL REASON So Many Mormons Become Executives and Political Leaders," *Business Insider*, July 22, 2011, https://www.businessinsider.com/mormon-business-leaders-2011-7 [https://perma.cc/9HLL-8V6Z].

11. McKenzie Stauffer, "LDS Church Changes Baptism Policy for Children of Polygamists," *KUTV*, December 18, 2019, https://kutv.com/news/local/lds-church-lifts-policy-on-baptisms-for-children-of-polygamists [https://perma.cc/8VFH-EA5T].

240 · Notes to Chapter 9

12. Ken Driggs, "This Will Someday be the Head and Not the Tail of the Church: A History of the Mormon Fundamentalists at Short Creek," *Journal of Church and State* 43, no. 1 (Winter 2001): 49–80.

13. Stuart A. Wright and James T. Richardson, "The Fundamentalist Latter Day Saints after the Texas State Raid: Assessing a Post-Raid Movement Trajectory," *Nova Religio: The Journal of Alternative and Emergent Religions* 17, no. 4 (2014): 83–97.

14. Casey E. Faucon, "Marriage Outlaws: Regulating Polygamy in America," *Duke Journal of Gender Law & Policy* 22, no. 1 (2014): 1–54.

15. *Crimes Associated with Polygamy: The Need for a Coordinated State and Federal Response*, Hearing Before the S. Comm. on the Judiciary at 92, 95 (Testimony of Carolyn Jessop) (2008).

16. *Crimes Associated with Polygamy*, 89 (submission of Sara Hammon).

17. *Crimes Associated with Polygamy*, 50 (testimony of Dr. Dan Fischer).

18. *Crimes Associated with Polygamy*, 137 (affidavit of Marvin Fischer).

19. Samuel D. Brunson, "Taxing Polygamy," *Washington University Law Review* 91, no. 1 (2013): 113–168.

20. *Crimes Associated with Polygamy*, 52 (testimony of Dr. Dan Fischer).

21. Brunson, "Taxing Polygamy," 144.

22. Brunson, "Taxing Polygamy," 144.

23. Tim B. Heaton and Cardell K. Jacobson, "Demographic, Social, and Economic Characteristics of a Polygamist Community," in *Modern Polygamy in the United States: Historical, Cultural, and Legal Issues*, eds. Cardell K. Jacobson and Lara Burton (New York: Oxford University Press, 2011): 151–161.

24. Charles O. Rossotti, Natasha Sarin, and Lawrence H. Summers, "Shrinking the Tax Gap: A Comprehensive Approach," *Tax Notes Federal* 169, no. 9 (November 30, 2020): 1467–1475.

25. James Brooke, "Utah Struggles with a Revival of Polygamy," *New York Times*, August 23, 1998, 12.

26. US Department of Justice, "Los Angeles Businessman, Utah Fuel Plant Operators and Employees Sentenced to Prison for Billion-Dollar Biofuel Tax Fraud Scheme," press release, April 7, 2023, https://www.justice.gov/opa/pr/los-angeles-businessman -utah-fuel-plant-operators-and-employees-sentenced-prison-billion [https:// perma.cc/72UW-AQZK].

27. *United States v. Dermen*, No. 218CR00365JNPBCW, 2021 WL 515883 (D. Utah Feb. 10, 2021).

28. Nate Carlisle, "A Multi-Million Dollar Biofuel Fraud Began with a Cowboy Hat and a Slew of Seafood, Jacob Kingston Testifies," *Salt Lake Tribune*, February 6, 2020, https://www.sltrib.com/news/2020/02/06/multimillion-dollar/ [https://perma.cc/ VC9W-5AV9].

29. Samuel D. Brunson, "Taxing Utopia," *Seton Hall Law Review* 47, no. 1 (2016): 137–196. The New Testament details these Apostolic economics in Acts 4. As a result

of this communitarianism, none of the members of the community owner private property and all had access to the support they needed.

30. Timothy Miller, *Communes in America, 1975–2000* (Syracuse, NY: Syracuse University Press, 2019), 64–65.

31. "District Judge Rules in Favor of UEP in Hildale Property Dispute," *Provo Daily Herald*, March 5, 1992, B3.

32. Jennifer Dobner, "FLDS Question State Management of Trust," *Provo Daily Herald*, August 15, 2008, A8.

33. "Back Taxes Put Some FLDS Homes at Risk," *Provo Daily Herald*, October 18, 2009, C9.

34. "Former FLDS Members Ask Judge to Reconfigure Church Trust," *Provo Daily Herald*, February 20, 2005, B7.

35. *Wisan v. City of Hildale*, 330 P.3d 76 (Utah 2014).

36. Dobner, "FLDS," A8.

37. Jennifer Dobner, "Residents Lobby Utah in Sect's Land Fight," *Provo Daily Herald*, April 30, 2009, B8.

38. *Wisan v. City of Hildale*, 330 P.3d 76 (Utah 2014).

39. Nataly Burdick, "19 More FLDS Evictions; Retaliation Against Constable, UEP Consultant," *St. George News*, July 8, 2015, https://www.stgeorgeutah.com/news/archive/2015/07/08/nnb-short-creek-evictions#.YMuL3PKSlPY [https://perma.cc/4JSR-ZG68].

40. Utah Code Ann. § 59-2-1302(2)(a) (West).

41. "FLDS Homes at Risk," C9.

42. *Wisan v. City of Hildale*, 2014 UT 20, ¶ 7, 330 P.3d 76, 78.

43. Bushman, *Rough Stone Rolling*, 182–183.

44. John S. McCormick and John R. Sillito, *History of Utah Radicalism: Startling, Socialistic, and Decidedly Revolutionary* (Logan, UT: Utah State University Press, 2011), 10.

45. Samuel D. Brunson, "Taxing Utopia," *Seton Hall Law Review* 47, no. 1 (2016): 137–196.

46. I.R.C. §§ 11(a), 301(c)(1) (2018).

47. Harry J. Rudick, "Section 102 and Personal Holding Company Provisions of the Internal Revenue Code," *Yale Law Journal* 49, no. 2 (1939): 171–223.

48. It is, of course, possible that the communitarian group could deduct some or all of the amount it paid as salaries. To the extent it made non-salary distributions, however, those distributions would not be deductible but would generally still have to be included in the recipients' gross income.

49. Brunson, "Taxing Utopia," 158.

50. 80 Cong. Rec. 9074 (1936) (statement of Sen. Walsh).

51. Revenue Act of 1936, ch. 690, § 101(18), 49 Stat. 1648, 1675–76. The provision has remained in the federal income tax, virtually unchanged, until the present. I.R.C. § 501(d) (2018).

242 • *Notes to Chapter 9*

52. I.R.S. Priv. Ltr. Rul. 2013–100–47 (Dec. 11, 2012).

53. I.R.S. Priv. Ltr. Rul. 2013–100–47.

54. "Jury Finds Ex-Polygamist Leader Guilty of Polygamy," *Standard-Examiner*, March 28, 2012, https://www.standard.net/police-fire/courts/jury-finds-ex-polygamist -leader-guilty-of-bigamy/article_6a63f233-8143-5e0d-8409-67f5df8768a4.html [https://perma.cc/PJ4R-N3RB].

55. I.R.S. Priv. Ltr. Rul. 2013–100–47.

56. See *Bob Jones Univ. v. United States*, 461 U.S. 574, 586, 103 S. Ct. 2017, 2026, 76 L. Ed. 2d 157 (1983).

57. I.R.S. Priv. Ltr. Rul. 2013–100–47.

58. Ben Winslow, "Pro-Polygamy Group Strives to Educate," *Deseret News*, July 26, 2008, https://www.deseret.com/2008/7/26/20266009/pro-polygamy-group-strives -to-educate [https://perma.cc/WN8F-DBPZ].

59. Brunson, "Taxing Utopia," 180.

60. I.R.S. Priv. Ltr. Rul. 2013–230–25.

61. Patrick Q. Mason, "The Politics of Mormon History," *Dialogue: A Journal of Mormon Thought* 53, no. 4 (2020): 1–20.

62. Elizabeth H. Mills, "The Mormon Colonies in Chihuahua after the 1912 Exodus," *New Mexico Historical Review* 29, no. 3 (1954): 165–182; John B. Wright, "Mormon *Colonias* of Chihuahua," *Geographical Review* 91, no. 3 (2001): 586–596.

63. Thomas H. Naylor, "The Mormons Colonize Sonora: Early Trials at Colonia Oaxaca," *Arizona and the West* 20, no. 4 (1978): 325–342.

64. Wright, "Mormon *Colonias*," 587.

65. Karl Young, "Early Mormon Troubles in Mexico," *Brigham Young University Studies* 5, no. 3/4 (1964): 155–67.

66. Dale M. Valentine, "The Juarez Stake Academy" (master's thesis, BYU, 1955), https://scholarsarchive.byu.edu/cgi/viewcontent.cgi?article=6182&context=etd.

67. Barbara Jones Brown, "What the Media Isn't Saying About the History of Mormon Polygamy in Mexico," *Salt Lake Tribune*, November 8, 2019, https://www.sltrib .com/religion/2019/11/09/commentary-what-media/.

68. Mills, "Mormon Colonies," 168–169.

69. Wright, "Mormon *Colonias*," 587–588.

70. "Claims Mormons Chased Him Away," *Salt Lake Tribune*, May 10, 1912, 2.

71. "Mormons Are Threatened in Sonora," *El Paso Herald*, May 10, 1912, 1.

72. "Mormon Colonists Deny Story from Old Mexico," *The News-Advocate*, May 16, 1912, 4.

73. "Taxes Demanded on Mormon Properties," *The Ogden Standard*, December 26, 1914, 3.

74. "Price and Vicinity," *Eastern Utah Advocate*, December 31, 1914, 5.

75. "Mormons Drafted in Mex. Army? Consul Denies It," *El Paso Herald*, December 29, 1917, 17.

Notes to Chapter 9 · 243

76. Thomas Cottam Romney, *The Mormon Colonies in Mexico* (Salt Lake City: University of Utah Press, 1938), 246.

77. William Stockton, "A Mormon Colony Thrives in Mexico," *New York Times*, February 20, 1986, C1.

78. John C. Lehr, "Polygamy, Patrimony, and Prophecy: The Mormon Colonization of Cardston," *Dialogue: A Journal of Mormon Thought* 21, no. 4 (1988): 114–121.

79. Lori G. Beaman, "Church, State and the Legal Interpretation of Polygamy in Canada," *Nova Religio: The Journal of Alternative and Emergent Religions* 8, no. 1 (2004): 20–38.

80. Lawrence B. Lee, "The Mormons Come to Canada, 1887–1902," *The Pacific Northwest Quarterly* 59, no. 1 (1968): 11–22.

81. Yossi Katz and John C. Lehr, "Jewish and Mormon Agricultural Settlement in Western Canada: A Comparative Analysis," *The Canadian Geographer / Le Geographe Canadien* 35, no. 2 (1991): 128–142.

82. Cat Koo, "Polygamy in Canada: How Many Wives Can a Man Have?" *BBC News*, November 23, 2010, https://www.bbc.com/news/world-us-canada-11776534 [https://perma.cc/SY55-3KGM].

83. "Canadian Polygamist Sect Under Pressure," *NBC News*, May 15, 2008, https://www.nbcnews.com/id/wbna24620442 [https://perma.cc/C9MN-PFFY].

84. *Blackmore v. The Queen*, 2013 TCC 264 (CanLII), https://canlii.ca/t/g07w1, retrieved on 2021–09–03.

85. Ken MacQueen, "The Polygamy Tax Break," *Maclean's*, January 31, 2012, https://www.macleans.ca/news/canada/hell-fire-and-undeclared-income/ [https://perma.cc/LN8Z-8VJS].

86. Samuel D. Brunson, *God and the IRS: Accommodating Religious Practice in United States Tax Law* (New York: Cambridge University Press, 2018), 173.

87. Reverend Joseph K Wipf, Jacob K Wipf, Reverend Peter S Tschetter, Reverend John K Hofer and Reverend John K Wurz (Plaintiffs) v Minister of National Revenue (Defendant), 73 DTC 5558.

88. Reverend Joseph K Wipf, Jacob K Wipf, Reverend Peter S Tschetter, Reverend John K Hofer and Reverend John K Wurz (Appellants) v Her Majesty the Queen (Respondent), 75 DTC 5034.

89. Income Tax Act § 143 (R.S.C., 1985, c. 1 (5th Supp.))

90. *Blackmore v. The Queen*, 2013 TCC 264.

91. MacQueen, "Tax Break."

92. Daniel Styler, "Blackmore v The Queen: Separate Tax Treatment of Communal Religious Organizations Not Available to Polygamous Mormon Group," *theCourt.ca*, September 16, 2013, http://www.thecourt.ca/blackmore-v-the-queen-separate-tax-treatment-of-communal-religious-organizations-not-available-to-polygamous-mormon-group/ [https://perma.cc/X3CH-5J52].

93. Income Tax Act § 143(4).

244 · *Notes to Chapters 9 and 10*

94. *Blackmore v. The Queen*, 2013 TCC 264.

95. Alanna Smith, "Property Owned by Convicted Polygamist Winston Blackmore on the Block," *Calgary Herald* (Mar. 9, 2019), https://calgaryherald.com/news/local-news/property-owned-by-convicted-polygamist-winston-blackmore-on-the-block [https://perma.cc/G2HE-L4P4].

96. *R v Blackmore*, [2017] BCJ No 1447, 2017 BCSC 1288, 2017 CarswellBC 2023, 350 CCC (3d) 429.

97. Smith, "Property Owned by Convicted Polygamist."

98. *Reynolds v. United States*, 98 U.S. 145, 164, 25 L. Ed. 244 (1878).

99. *Comm'r v. Tellier*, 383 U.S. 687, 691, 86 S. Ct. 1118, 1120, 16 L. Ed. 2d 185 (1966).

Chapter 10. The Mormon Church's Lobbying

1. Terryl Givens, "How Mormons Became American," *Religion & Politics*, November 14, 2012, https://religionandpolitics.org/2012/11/14/how-mormons-became-american/ [https://perma.cc/ZC2L-33VR].

2. John Montague, "The Law and Financial Transparency in Churches: Reconsidering the Form 990 Exemption," *Cardozo Law Review* 35, no. 1 (October 2013): 203–266.

3. John Montague, "The Law and Financial Transparency in Churches," 203–266.

4. Hearings on the Subject of Tax Reform Before the H. Comm. on Ways & Means, 91st Cong. 12 at 181–182 (1969) (statement of Prof. Lawrence M. Stone, School of Law, University of California, Berkeley).

5. Samuel D. Brunson, "The Present, Past, and Future of LDS Financial Transparency," *Dialogue: A Journal of Mormon Thought* 48, no. 1 (2015): 1–44.

6. Summary of Statement of Dr. Ernest L. Wilkinson, President, Brigham Young University, on Behalf of American Association of Independent College and University Presidents, Bernard D. Jr. Reams, *Tax Reform 1969: A Legislative History of the Tax Reform Act of 1969. Public L 91–172 with Related Amendments,* Vol. 16 doc. no. 39 (Buffalo, NY: William S. Hein & Co., Inc., 1991), 15–23.

7. Brunson, "LDS Financial Transparency," 7.

8. I.R.C. § 6033(a)(3)(A)(i) (2018).

9. H. George Frederickson and Alden J. Stevens, "The Mormon Congressman and the Line Between Church and State," *Dialogue: A Journal of Mormon Thought* 3, no. 2 (1968): 121–129.

10. Charles M. Whelan, "Church in the Internal Revenue Code: The Definitional Problems," *Fordham Law Review* 45, no. 4 (1977): 885–928.

11. Robert R. King and Kay Atkinson King, "Mormons in Congress, 1851–2000," *Journal of Mormon History* 26, no. 2 (2000): 1–50.

12. Conference Report No. 91–782, 1969–3 C.B. 644, 649.

13. In October 2019, the Mormon church retired the term "auxiliary" in favor of the term "organization." "Changes Announced to Strengthen the Youth," Newsroom, October 5, 2019, https://newsroom.churchofjesuschrist.org/article/october-2019-general-conference-youth-organizations [https://perma.cc/Y2GA-ZL3K]. While the change

Notes to Chapter 10 • 245

in terminology will have no impact of the tax status of these auxiliaries/organizations, it does represent a step away from the tax history created by the church, albeit an inadvertent .

14. Gregory A. Prince and Wm. Robert Wright, *David O. McKay and the Rise of Modern Mormonism* (Salt Lake City: University of Utah Press, 2005), 157–158; Peter Wiley, "The Lee Revolution and the Rise of Correlation," *Sunstone* 10, no. 1 (January 1985): 18–22.

15. Quentin L. Cook, "Adjustments to Strengthen Youth," https://www.churchof jesuschrist.org/study/general-conference/2019/10/25cook?lang=eng [https://perma .cc/3ZU2-A8NK].

16. Torie Atkinson, "A Fine Scheme: How Municipal Fines Become Crushing Debt in the Shadow of the New Debtors' Prisons," *Harvard Civil Rights-Civil Liberties Law Review* 51, no. 1 (Winter 2016): 189–238.

17. Heather G. White, "Beyond a 'Bond-Aid' Approach: Building a Better Bond Law," *University of Pennsylvania Journal of Law & Public Affairs* 7, no. 2 (May 2022): 315–390.

18. Ross Rubenstein & Benjamin Scafidi, "Who Pays and Who Benefits? Examining the Distributional Consequences of the Georgia Lottery for Education," *National Tax Journal* 15, no. 2 (2002): 223–238. While some studies find the implicit tax of lotteries to be a proportional burden on households, most find that lotteries represent a regressive way of funding government. Ibid., 226.

19. Charles T. Clotfelter and Philip J. Cook, *Selling Hope: State Lotteries in America* (Cambridge, MA: Harvard University Press, 1989), 34–35.

20. Clotfelter and Cook, *Selling Hope*, 37–38.

21. James Alm, Michael McKee, and Mark Skidmore, "Fiscal Pressure, Tax Competition, and the Introduction of State Lotteries," *National Tax journal* 46, no. 4 (1993): 463–476.

22. Charles T. Clotfelter and Philip J. Cook, *Selling Hope: State Lotteries in America* (Cambridge, Mass: Harvard University Press, 1991), vii.

23. Brett Kittredge, "Mississippians Must Be 21 to Buy Lottery Tickets," *Mississippi Center for Public Policy*, November 18, 2019, https://mspolicy.org/mississippians-must -be-21-to-buy-lottery-tickets-2/ [https://perma.cc/5J23-WF55].

24. Brad Tuttle, "Why You Can't Buy Powerball Tickets in Some Seriously Gambling-Friendly States," *Money*, January 12, 2016, https://money.com/states-no-powerball -lottery-sales/ [https://perma.cc/SX4K-RUMX].

25. Justine Paradis, "You Asked, We Answered: Why is New Hampshire SO Against Having an Income Tax?" New Hampshire Public Radio, February 9, 2018, https://www .nhpr.org/post/you-asked-we-answered-why-new-hampshire-so-against-having -income-tax#stream/0 [https://perma.cc/YT9Z-3EJY].

26. Matthew B. Lawrence, "Addiction and Liberty," *Cornell Law Review* 108, no. 2 (2023): 259–344.

27. Clotfelter and Cook, *Selling Hope*, vii.

28. Charles T. Clotfelter and Philip J. Cook, "Implicit Taxation in Lottery Finance," *National Tax Journal* 40, no. 4 (1987): 533–546.

246 · *Notes to Chapter 10*

29. Tax Policy Center. "Lottery Revenue," June 18, 2020, https://www.taxpolicy center.org/statistics/lottery-revenue [https://perma.cc/22JS-BGSC].

30. Local governments raised another $1.1 trillion. Tax Policy Center. "State and Local Own Source General Revenue," June 18, 2020, https://www.taxpolicycenter. org/statistics/state-and-local-own-source-general-revenue [https://perma.cc/6EA2 -55LA].

31. Alm, McKee, and Skidmore, "Fiscal Pressure," 465.

32. Office of Legislative Research and General Counsel, "Utah's General Sales & Use Tax: Where Are We? How Did We Get Here? Where Are We Going?" September 2011, https://le.utah.gov/lrgc/briefings/SalesTaxBriefingPaper.Sept11.pdf [https:// perma.cc/779F-UNPA].

33. Office of Legislative Research and General Counsel, "A History of Property Tax in Utah," September 2010, https://le.utah.gov/lrgc/briefings/BriefingPaperProperty TaxHistorySept2010.pdf [https://perma.cc/H4R9-RA85].

34. Joel Campbell, "Property-Tax Shock," *Deseret News*, September 29, 1993, https:// www.deseret.com/1993/9/26/19067986/property-tax-shock [https://perma.cc/LT3B -AXYN].

35. Utah Const. art. VI, § 28.

36. Utah Const. art. XXIII, § 1.

37. Cherie Huber, "Lottery for Education?" *Davis County Clipper*, May 15, 1986, 1.

38. "Idahoans Say Yes to Lottery," *Provo Daily Herald*, November 5, 1986, 10.

39. "It Lacks Noise and Glitz, But Is Still a Haven for Gamblers," *Provo Daily Herald*, February 9, 1990, B6.

40. Huber, "Lottery for Education?"

41. David Buice, "When the Saints Came Marching In: The Mormon Experience in Antebellum New Orleans, 1840–1855," *Louisiana History: The Journal of the Louisiana Historical Association* 23, no. 3 (1982): 221–237.

42. In 1868, the Union-Pacific Railroad approached Brigham Young and offered him a contract to grade a fifty-four-mile stretch of road approaching the Great Salt Lake. Young accepted and organized associates to subcontract the work. The grading promised to provide up to $2.25 million for Young and other church members, a welcome infusion of cash. As it had done in other communities, however, after the grading was completed, the Union-Pacific defaulted on its obligations. Young, meanwhile, had advanced significant funds (both of his own and of the church) to subcontractors so that they could meet their payroll obligations. The railroad's refusal to pay, then, had a significant impact on both Young and the Mormon church. Craig L. Foster, "'That Canny Scotsman': John Sharp and the Union Pacific Negotiations, 1869–72," *Journal of Mormon History* 27, no. 2 (2001): 197–214.

43. Letter to BY: Brigham Young office files, 1832–1878 (bulk 1844–1877); General Correspondence, Incoming, 1840–1877; General Letters, 1840–1877; Ma-Mi, 1870; F. A. Mitchell letter; Church History Library, accessed May 19, 2021, https://catalog.churchofjesuschrist.org/assets?id=fc2e4429-f648-46f3-9242-4b1 aa0b3b257&crate=0&index=0.

Notes to Chapter 10 • 247

44. David Walker, *Railroading Religion: Mormons, Tourists, and the Corporate Spirit of the West* (Chapel Hill, NC: University of North Carolina Press, 2019), 78.

45. Adam R. Brown, *Utah Politics and Government: American Democracy Among a Unique Electorate* (Lincoln: University of Nebraska Press, 2018), 93.

46. "LDS Apostle Speaks Out Against Lotteries," *Provo Daily Herald*, January 7, 1987, 5. The Mormon church's opposition to gambling was reflected in my own childhood. In the mid-1980s my father, a practicing member of the Mormon church, bought a CD player. One of the first two CDs he bought was Billy Joel's *An Innocent Man*. (The other was Neil Diamond's *The Jazz Singer*.) I could—and did—listen to it as much as I wanted. Except for Track 1. My dad let me and my siblings know, in no uncertain terms, that we were not allowed to listen to the first song on the album. A good son, I obeyed and probably did not actually hear "Easy Money," Joel's first-person narrative of a hopeless—and helpless—gambler until the following decade.

47. "Did Church Cross Political Line?" *Provo Daily Herald*, September 14, 1988, 5.

48. Jim Robbins, "Force of Mormon Faithful Is Felt in Politics," *New York Times*, April 1, 1990, E5.

49. "Idahoans Say Yes to Lottery."

50. Tony Semerad, "Will Utah Ever Have a Lottery?" *Salt Lake Tribune*, March 15, 1992, A4.

51. "Sure Bet," *Utah Daily Chronicle*, January 6, 1992, 6.

52. Bryan Gray, "Principles Aside: Gorilla Wins in Silly Test," *Davis County Clipper*, March 31, 1992, 17.

53. Rod Decker & Larry D. Curtis, "Utahns Wanted Lottery, But Lawmakers Refused to Let Citizens Vote," *KUTV*, January 14, 2016, https://kutv.com/news/local/polls-said -utahns-wanted-lottery-but-lawmakers-refused-to-let-citizens-vote [https://perma .cc/8GVA-HLCP].

54. "Lotto Fever," *Daily Utah Chronicle*, March 5, 1993, 4.

55. William D. Oswald, "Are Lotteries Legitimate Means of Financing Public Needs?" *The Ensign*, February 1986, https://www.churchofjesuschrist.org/study/ ensign/1986/02/i-have-a-question/are-lotteries-legitimate-means-of-financing -public-needs?lang=eng [https://perma.cc/W6XA-NN9B].

56. Jeffrey C. Fox, *Latter-Day Political Views* (New York: Lexington Books, 2006), 37.

57. Angela Dills, Sietse Goffard, Jeffrey Miron, and Erin Partin, "The Effect of State Marijuana Legalizations: 2021 Update," Policy Analysis no. 908, Cato Institute, Washington, DC, February 2, 2021, https://www.cato.org/policy-analysis/effect-state -marijuana-legalizations-2021-update [https://perma.cc/EC4E-U2MW].

58. Larry D. Curtis, "Top LDS Leaders Urge Members to Vote Against Legalizing Marijuana," *2KUTV*, October 13, 2016, https://kutv.com/news/local/lds-leaders-urge -members-to-vote-against-legalizing-marijuana [https://perma.cc/PM85-V2VQ].

59. Utah was, unsurprisingly, not alone in declining revenue that would have come attached to gambling. About seventy years earlier, as Canada tried to figure out how to create a modern, post-World War I tax system, politicians there "couldn't bring themselves to endorse a state lottery or taxes on Sunday theatres—either from their

248 • *Notes to Chapters 10 and 11*

own moral objections or from an awareness of the electoral weight wielded by sabbatarians and opponents of gambling." Shirley Tillotson, *Give and Take: The Citizen-Taxpayer and the Rise of Canadian Democracy* (Vancouver: UBC Press, 2017), 50.

Chapter 11. Volunteer Missionaries and Paid Clergy

1. Stephen C. Harper, "Missionaries in the American Religious Marketplace: Mormon Proselyting in the 1830s," *Journal of Mormon History* 24, no. 2 (1998): 1–29.

2. Lucy Smith, *Biographical Sketches of Joseph Smith the Prophet, and His Progenitors for Many Generations* (Plano, IL: The Reorganized Church of Jesus Christ of Latter-day Saints, 1880), 160.

3. Harper, "Missionaries," 2.

4. Tancred I. King, "Missiology and Mormon Missions," *Dialogue: A Journal of Mormon Thought* 16, no. 4 (1983): 42–50.

5. "2021 Statistical Report for the April 2022 Conference," *Newsroom*, April 2, 2022, https://newsroom.churchofjesuschrist.org/article/2021-statistical-report-april-2022 -conference [https://perma.cc/R7NW-8RDT].

6. D&C 84:78.

7. Luke 10:1, 4.

8. Richard L. Jensen, "Without Purse or Scrip? Financing Latter-day Saint Missionary Work in Europe in the Nineteenth Century," *Journal of Mormon History* 12 (1985): 3–14.

9. Oliver Boardman Huntington, *Oliver B. Huntington's Journal*, Diary, MSS 162, November 6, 1846, pp. 32–33, accessed April 27, 2022, Courtesy, L. Tom Perry Special Collections, Harold B. Lee Library, Brigham Young University, Provo, UT 84602.

10. James Farmer, *Diary of James Farmer*, Diary, MSS 1433, July 28, 1852, p. 130, accessed April 27, 2022. https://contentdm.lib.byu.edu/digital/collection/MMD/id/57289/rec/2. Courtesy, L. Tom Perry Special Collections, Harold B. Lee Library, Brigham Young University, Provo, UT 84602.

11. Samuel D. Brunson, *God and the IRS: Accommodating Religious Practice in United States Tax Law* (New York: Cambridge University Press, 2018), 153.

12. James G. Duffin, *Journal of James G. Duffin*, Diary, MSS 1696, March 20, 1904, p. 24, accessed April 27, 2022, https://contentdm.lib.byu.edu/digital/collection/MMD/id/65861/rec/1. Courtesy, L. Tom Perry Special Collections, Harold B. Lee Library, Brigham Young University, Provo, UT 84602.

13. Claude William Hawley, *Claude William Hawley Diary*, Diary, MSS SC 1660, April 17, 1912, p. 132, accessed April 27, 2022, https://contentdm.lib.byu.edu/digital/collection/MMD/id/71302/rec/29. Courtesy, L. Tom Perry Special Collections, Harold B. Lee Library, Brigham Young University, Provo, UT 84602.

14. True Banheardt Harmsen, "Forever or Never," *Improvement Era*, April 1933, 326–327.

15. George F. Richards, "Valiant in the Covenants," *Improvement Era*, June 1943, 337.

Notes to Chapter 11 • 249

16. Jessie L. Embry, "Without Purse or Scrip," *Dialogue: A Journal of Mormon Thought* 29, no. 3 (1996): 77–93.

17. Bookcraft, "For Your Winter Reading Pleasure . . . 6 Important New Books!" advertisement, *The Improvement Era*, February 1962, 79.

18. First Security Bank, "Special Savings for your Son's or Daughter's Mission," advertisement, *The Improvement Era*, March 1969, 39.

19. Gordon B. Hinckley, "Tithing: An Opportunity to Prove Our Faithfulness," *Official Report of the One Hundred Fifty-second Annual General Conference of the Church of Jesus Christ of Latter-day Saints* (Salt Lake City: The Church of Jesus Christ of Latter-day Saints, 1982), 63.

20. Gordon B. Hinckley, "The Question of a Mission," *Official Report of the One Hundred Fifty-sixth Annual General Conference of the Church of Jesus Christ of Latter-day Saints* (Salt Lake City: The Church of Jesus Christ of Latter-day Saints, 1986), 52.

21. Rodney Stark, "The Rise of a New World Faith," *Review of Religious Research* 26, no. 1 (1984): 18–27.

22. Jerry Mason, "I Have a Question," *The Ensign*, March 1989, https://www.church ofjesuschrist.org/study/ensign/1989/03/i-have-a-question/i-have-a-question ?lang=eng [https://perma.cc/NMT3-UT6Q].

23. Jeffrey L. Kwall, "Subchapter G of the Internal Revenue Code: Crusade Without a Cause, *Virginia Tax Review* 5, no. 2 (1985): 223–286.

24. David J. Herzig and Samuel D. Brunson, "Let Prophets Be (Non) Profits, *Wake Forest Law Review* 52, no. 5 (2017): 1111–1161.

25. 55 Cong. Rec. 6728 (1917). Senator Hollis was particularly worried about the viability of colleges and universities. As a result of the war, he estimated that they would lose half of their students (and thus half of their tuition revenue). Without some sort of external funding, he doubted whether universities would be able to survive past the war. Ibid.

26. War Revenue Act of 1917, ch. 63, § 1201(2)), 40 Stat. 300, 330.

27. Revenue Act of 1921, § 214(a)(11), Stat. Ann., 1921 Supplement at 137.

28. Rev. Rul. 62–113, 1962–2 C.B. 10.

29. Rev. Rul. 62–113, 1962–2 C.B. 10.

30. Rev. Rul. 68–67, 1968–1 C.B. 38.

31. Rev. Rul. 62–113.

32. In the revenue ruling, the IRS also answered an additional question: whether parents of young volunteer missionaries could claim a personal exemption for the missionary. And because the IRS had held that reimbursements to missionaries did not constitute income, young missionaries earned less than the $600 threshold that would disqualify their parents from claiming a personal exemption. So parents of missionaries could continue to get the tax benefits of having dependents, even while those dependents were away on missions. Rev. Rul. 62–113.

33. Treas. Reg. § 1.6662–3(a) (as amended in 2003).

34. I.R.C. § 170(c) (2018).

250 · Notes to Chapter 11

35. "U.S. Court Rules Missionary Support is Tax-Deductible," *The Ensign*, April 1984, https://abn.churchofjesuschrist.org/study/ensign/1984/04/news-of-the-church/u -s-court-rules-missionary-support-is-tax-deductible?lang=eng [https://perma.cc/ NCY7-GJQW].

36. Brunson, "God and the IRS," 147–148.

37. *Davis v. U.S.*, 664 F. Supp. 468 (D. Idaho 1987); *Davis v. U.S.*, 861 F.2d 558 (9th Cir. 1988).

38. *Brinley v. Comm'r*, 782 F.2d 1326 (5th Cir. 1986).

39. Claire Y. Nash and James Parker, "A Case-Based Analysis of the Responsibility to Withhold and Pay Over Trust-Fund Taxes," *Journal of Taxation* 132, no. 6 (June 2020): 9–33.

40. Tejas N. Narechania, "Certiorari, Universality, and A Patent Puzzle," *Michigan Law Review* 116, no. 8 (2018): 1345–1408.

41. Brunson, "God and the IRS," 158.

42. *Davis v. United States*, 493 U.S. 953, 110 S. Ct. 362, 107 L. Ed. 2d 349 (1989).

43. "Davis v. United States." *Oyez*. Accessed May 6, 2022. https://www.oyez.org/ cases/1989/89–98 [https://perma.cc/EJR7-S5J6].

44. Greg Hill, "Funeral Speakers Laud Life of Rex E. Lee," *Church News*, March 23, 1996, https://www.thechurchnews.com/archives/1996–03–23/funeral-speakers-laud-life-of-rex-e-lee-134282 [https://perma.cc/7BTF-23X2].

45. Oral Argument, *Davis v. United States*, *Oyez*, March 26, 1990, https://apps.oyez.org/ player/#/rehnquist3/oral_argument_audio/18364 [https://perma.cc/8P2W-MXY7].

46. Oral Argument, *Davis v. United States*, *Oyez*, March 26, 1990.

47. Oral Argument, *Davis v. United States*, *Oyez*, March 26, 1990.

48. *Davis v. United States*, 495 U.S. 472, 110 S. Ct. 2014, 109 L. Ed. 2d 457 (1990).

49. Kathy Stephenson, "Serving a Mission for the LDS Church Will Cost More in 2020," *Salt Lake Tribune*, June 27, 2019, https://www.sltrib.com/religion/2019/06/27/ serving-mission-lds/ [https://perma.cc/4LCL-EB7F].

50. "Policy Equalizes Mission Expenses," *Church News*, December 1, 1990, https:// www.thechurchnews.com/archives/1990–12–01/policy-equalizes-mission-ex-penses-147871 [https://perma.cc/YL53-QB2J].

51. "Policy Equalizes Mission Expenses," *Church News*, December 1, 1990.

52. Church News Staff, "What Are the Countries With the Most Latter-day Saints?" *Newsroom*, August 4, 2021, https://newsroom.churchofjesuschrist.org/article/what-are -the-countries-with-the-most-latter-day-saints [https://perma.cc/N92K-DX2W].

53. *The Church of Jesus Christ of Latter-Day Saints Trust Board v. Commissioner of Inland Revenue* [2019] NZHC 52, https://forms.justice.govt.nz/search/Documents/pdf/jdo/59/ alfresco/service/api/node/content/workspace/SpacesStore/7db0de2e-be09–4d66– 8d33–90adfd479fe7/7db0de2e-be09–4d66–8d33–90adfd479fe7.pdf [https://perma. cc/5MML-52DT].

54. "Church Responds to New Zealand High Court Decision Regarding Donations to Support Missionaries," *Newsroom*, March 4, 2019, https://news-nz.churchofjesus

christ.org/article/church-responds-to-new-zealand-high-court-decision-regarding
-donations-to-support-missionaries [https://perma.cc/3ZXE-LA85].

55. *The Church of Jesus Christ of Latter-Day Saints Trust Board v. Commissioner of Inland Revenue* [2020] NZCA 143, https://forms.justice.govt.nz/search/Documents/pdf/jdo/ fc/alfresco/service/api/node/content/workspace/SpacesStore/7eae25aa-529b-4b66 -befe-5366d3621a12/7eae25aa-529b-4b66-befe-5366d3621a12.pdf [https://perma .cc/3H77-WZ2A].

56. M. Russell Ballard, "O Be Wise," *Official Report of the One Hundred Seventy-Sixth Semiannual General Conference of the Church of Jesus Christ of Latter-day Saints* (Salt Lake City: The Church of Jesus Christ of Latter-day Saints, 2006), 16.

57. Doug Andersen, "The Church's Unpaid Clergy," *The Newsroom Blog*, September 3, 2009, https://newsroom.churchofjesuschrist.org/blog/the-church-s-unpaid-clergy [https://perma.cc/NU9D-GRDX].

58. Peggy Fletcher Stack, "How Much Do Top Mormon Leaders Make? The Answer May Surprise You," *Salt Lake Tribune*, January 26, 2017, https://archive.sltrib.com/article .php?id=4800350&itype=cmsid [https://perma.cc/H4WD-STC8].

59. That is, on the pay stub, the amount withheld for OASDI (Old-Age, Survivors, and Disability Insurance) and FICA (Federal Insurance Contribution Act) is listed as $0.00. Apostle's Pay Stub, https://www.docdroid.net/GEbupXj/apostles-pay-stub -ssn-redacted-pdf [https://perma.cc/7LKL-CVGV].

60. I.R.C. § 3121(b)(8) (2018).

61. I.R.C. § 1402(e) (2018).

62. Melanie James, "Revisiting the Minister's Housing Allowance," *Journal of Taxation* (May 2018): 14–21.

63. Apostle's Pay Stub.

64. I talk about these, and other, special tax rules for religious individuals extensively in my previous book, *God and the IRS: Accommodating Religious Practice in United States Tax Law*.

65. Samuel D. Brunson, "T God Is My Roommate? Tax Exemptions for Parsonages Yesterday, Today, and (if Constitutional) Tomorrow," *Indiana Law Journal* 96, no. 2 (2021): 521–570.

66. I.R.C. § 107 (2018).

67. Treas. Reg. § 1.107–1(b) (as amended in 1963).

68. "Mission Presidents Leave Home Behind to Serve Throughout the World," The Church of Jesus Christ of Latter-day Saints, June 25, 2010, https://newsroom .churchofjesuschrist.org/article/mission-presidents-leave-home-behind-to-serve -throughout-the-world [https://perma.cc/JS8E-8LW3].

69. *Mission President's Handbook* (Salt Lake City: The Church of Jesus Christ of Latter-day Saints, 2006), 80–82.

70. Heber J. Grant, J. Reuben Clark, Jr., and David O. McKay to Gustave A. Iverson, March 3, 1943, Church History Library.

71. Jones, "Class Tax to Mass Tax," 695.

252 • *Notes to Chapters 11 and 12*

72. Heber J. Grant, J. Reuben Clark, Jr., and David O. McKay to Gustave A. Iverson, March 3, 1943, Church History Library.

73. Heber J. Grant, J. Reuben Clark, Jr., and David O. McKay to Gustave A. Iverson, June 3, 1943, Church History Library.

74. Alan L. Feld, "Fairness in Rate Cuts in the Individual Income Tax," *Cornell Law Review* 68, no. 4 (1983): 429–467.

75. National Taxpayer Advocate, "2011 Annual Report to Congress, vol. 2," 2011, 22, https://www.taxpayeradvocate.irs.gov/wp-content/uploads/2020/08/TAS_arc _2011_vol_2.pdf [https://perma.cc/URU4-ZBU2].

76. *Mission President's Handbook*, 82.

77. *Bulletin* (1990–2), 2.

78. *Bulletin* (1990–2), 2.

79. Brent A. Andrewsen, "Charitable Planning with Appreciated Property," The Church of Jesus Christ of Latter-day Saints Philanthropies, 2020, https://philanthropies .churchofjesuschrist.org/gift-planning/for-professional-advisors/gpc/newsletter/ winter-2020/charitable-planning-andrewsen [https://perma.cc/5KJG-M7XH].

Chapter 12. Tax Exemption as a Lever for Change

1. *General Handbook: Serving in The Church of Jesus Christ of Latter-day Saints* § 38.8.44 (Salt Lake City: The Church of Jesus Christ of Latter-day Saints, 2021), https://www .churchofjesuschrist.org/study/manual/general-handbook/38-church-policies-and -guidelines?lang=eng#title_number192 [https://perma.cc/525J-BTVS].

2. *General Handbook: Serving in The Church of Jesus Christ of Latter-day Saints* § 34.8.1.

3. Lilian V. Faulhaber, "The Hidden Limits of the Charitable Deduction: An Introduction to Hypersalience," *Boston University Law Review* 92 no. 4 (2012): 1307–1348.

4. *Statistics of Income—2019 Individual Income Tax Returns,* Internal Revenue Service Washington, D.C., 21, https://www.irs.gov/pub/irs-pdf/p1304.pdf [https://perma.cc/ F4CA-Z6X9].

5. Faulhaber, "The Hidden Limits of the Charitable Deduction," 1328.

6. US Department of Treasury, "Tax Expenditures," December 9, 2021, https://home .treasury.gov/system/files/131/Tax-Expenditures-FY2023.pdf [https://perma.cc/ 3HGL-HGM6].

7. Office of Management and Budget, *A New Era of Responsibility: Renewing America's Promise* (Washington, DC: US Government Printing Office, 2009), 29–30, https:// www.govinfo.gov/content/pkg/BUDGET-2010-BUD/pdf/BUDGET-2010-BUD.pdf [https://perma.cc/2BZG-TY96].

8. Office of Management and Budget, *A New Era of Responsibility.*

9. Suzanne Perry, "Obama's Plan to Reduce Charitable Deductions for the Wealthy Draws Criticism," *The Chronicle of Philanthropy*, February 26, 2009, https://www .philanthropy.com/article/obamas-plan-to-reduce-charitable-deductions-for-the -wealthy-draws-criticism/?cid=gen_sign_in [https://perma.cc/7YN4-C3MS].

Notes to Chapter 12 • 253

10. "Tax Reform Options: Incentives for Charitable Giving," Hearing Before the Committee on Finance, United States Senate, S. Hrg. 112–646 (Oct. 18, 2011), 2–4, https://www.finance.senate.gov/imo/media/doc/77208.pdf [https://perma.cc/Q8WG-PWYL].

11. "From John Adams to Massachusetts Militia, 11 October 1798," *Founders Online*, National Archives, https://founders.archives.gov/documents/Adams/99-02-02-3102 [https://perma.cc/3EAL-UWX2].

12. "Tax Reform Options," 9–10. Oaks also objected to characterizing the charitable deduction as a tax expenditure. While delving into the question of tax expenditures is well beyond the scope or purpose of this book, the concept is worth a quick explanation. Essentially, a "tax expenditure" is a tax provision that is the economic equivalent of government spending. Not all deductions are tax expenditures—some help arrive at a more accurate measure of income. For instance, if you own a bookstore, the employee salaries are a cost of earning money. Allowing a deduction is not subsidizing the bookstore for employing people. Rather, it is allowing them to subtract these necessary costs from their taxable income. By contrast, mortgage interest is a cost of personal consumption. It, like the cost of rent or the cost of food, does not represent a cost of earning money. Rather, it represents the government subsidizing homeownership. The government could provide that subsidy by directly paying a portion of mortgage interest or by allowing its deduction. Economically, both choices are identical. If not tracked, the government could use tax expenditures to disguise its spending. Bruce Bartlett, "The End of Tax Expenditures as We Know Them?" *Tax Notes* 92, no. 3 (July 16, 2001): 413–422. Tax expenditures, then, are "departures from a normal income tax," and determining what qualifies as a tax expenditure depends on how we define a normal income tax. Ellen P. Aprill and Lloyd Hitoshi Mayer, "Tax Exemption Is Not a Subsidy—Except for When It Is," *Tax Notes* 172, no. 12 (September 20, 2021): 1887–1896. The question of whether the charitable deduction is a tax expenditure, then, is not one of public perception, or even one of intuition, but rather a question of what a baseline income tax looks like.

13. Rev. Rul. 57–462, 1957–2 C.B. 157 (1957).

14. "Tax Reform Options," 28.

15. *Brown v. Bd. of Ed. of Topeka*, Shawnee Cnty., Kan., 347 U.S. 483, 74 S. Ct. 686, 98 L. Ed. 873 (1954).

16. *Brown v. Bd. of Educ. of Topeka, Kan.*, 349 U.S. 294, 75 S. Ct. 753, 99 L. Ed. 1083 (1955).

17. *Green v. Cnty. Sch. Bd. of New Kent Cnty., Va.*, 391 U.S. 430, 88 S. Ct. 1689, 20 L. Ed. 2d 716 (1968).

18. "Segregation Academies and State Action," *Yale Law Journal* 82, no. 7 (June 1973): 1436–1461.

19. Samuel D. Brunson and David J. Herzig, "A Diachronic Approach to Bob Jones: Religious Tax Exemptions After Obergefell," *Indiana Law Journal* 92, no. 3 (2017): 1175–1220.

254 · Notes to Chapter 12

20. *Green v. Kennedy*, 309 F. Supp. 1127 (D.D.C 1970).

21. IRS News Release, [1970] 7 Stand. Fed. Tax Rep. (CCH) ¶ 6790, July 10, 1970.

22. Rev. Rul. 71–447, 1971–2 C.B. 230.

23. *McCrary v. Runyon*, 515 F.2d 1082 (4th Cir. 1975), aff'd, 427 U.S. 160, 96 S. Ct. 2586, 49 L. Ed. 2d 415 (1976).

24. David J. Herzig and Samuel D. Brunson, "Let Prophets Be (Non)Profits," *Wake Forest Law Review* 52, no. 5 (2017): 1111–1162.

25. *Bob Jones Univ. v. United States*, 461 U.S. 574, 103 S. Ct. 2017, 76 L. Ed. 2d 157 (1983).

26. Aaron Haberman, "Into the Wilderness: Ronald Reagan, Bob Jones University, and the Political Education of the Christian Right," *The Historian* 67, no. 2 (2005): 234–253.

27. Herzig and Brunson, "Prophets." In fact, two of the very few non-school organizations to have their exemption application denied under this rule for reasons other than racial discrimination were fundamentalist Mormon organizations. In 2012, the IRS denied exemption to Principle Voices of Polygamy, a polygamy advocacy group, and the Fundamentalist Church of Jesus Christ of Latter-day Saints, asserting that polygamy violated public policy. I.R.S. Priv. Ltr. Rul. 2013–100–47 (Dec. 11, 2012); I.R.S. Priv. Ltr. Rul. 2013–100–47 (Dec. 11, 2012). See also Samuel D. Brunson, "Taxing Utopia," *Seton Hall Law Review* 47, no. 1 (2016): 137–196.

28. "Feminist Party Is Seeking to End Tax Freedom of Catholic Church," *New York Times*, July 1, 1972, 8. Florynce Kennedy, a Black lawyer and activist, formed the Feminist Party in 1971 as an alternative to the National Organization for Women and other mainstream feminist organizations. The Feminist Party opposed the Catholic Church's participation in abortion politics. "Flo Kennedy: 'The Feminist Party Street Walks,'" Harvard Radcliffe Institute, August 5, 2020, https://www.radcliffe.harvard .edu/news-and-ideas/flo-kennedy-the-feminist-party-street-walks [https://perma .cc/7NRK-PCFQ].

29. I.R.C. § 501(c)(3) (2018). That language was identical in the Internal Revenue Code as it existed in 1970, which would have been the language relevant to the Feminist Party's complaint. U.S. Congress. United States Code: Normal Taxes and Surtaxes, 26 U.S.C. §§ 1–1970. 1970. Periodical. https://tile.loc.gov/storage-services/service/ ll/uscode/uscode1970-00602/uscode1970-006026001/uscode1970-006026001.pdf [https://perma.cc/S5DB-TGFH].

30. Samuel D. Brunson, "Reigning in Charities: Using an Intermediate Penalty to Enforce the Campaigning Prohibition," *Pittsburgh Tax Review* 8, no. 2 (2011): 125–170.

31. Proposed Amendment to the Constitution of the United States, 86 Stat. 1523.

32. Martha F. Davis, "The Equal Right Amendment: Then and Now," Columbia Journal of Gender and Law 17, no. 3 (2008): 419–460.

33. O. Kendall White, Jr., "Mormonism and the Equal Rights Amendment," *Journal of Church and State* 31, no. 2 (Spring 1989): 249–267.

34. Mike Carter, "Mormon Lobby Carries Influential Stick in Utah," *Salt Lake Tribune*, July 1, 1999, 4A.

Notes to Chapter 12 · 255

35. D. Michael Quinn, "The LDS Church's Campaign Against the Equal Rights Amendment," *Journal of Mormon History* 20, no. 2 (Fall 1994): 85–155.

36. "Equal Rights Amendment," *Church News*, January 11, 1975, 16. [AVAILABLE HERE: https://newspapers.lib.utah.edu/ark:/87278/s6w71q8n/26324854]

37. "LDS Survive 150 Years of Difficulty," *Provo Daily Herald*, April 10, 1980, 23.

38. Neil J. Young, "'The ERA Is a Moral Issue': The Mormon Church, LDS Women, and the Defeat of the Equal Rights Amendment," *American Quarterly* 59, no. 3 (2007): 623–644.

39. Peter Gillins, "Sexual Hangups Explored," *Idaho Free Press*, October 24, 1975, 11.

40. Kay Mills, "Mormons, ERA Not Friendly," *The Montana Standard*, October 10, 1977, 10.

41. Sue Tester, "Mormons Defend Church's Stand Against ERA," *The Santa Fe New Mexican*, December 5, 1979, 8.

42. K. Deborah Taub, "Demonstrators Protest Actions of Mormon Church Against ERA," *Baltimore Sun*, August 31, 1980, 2.

43. "Mormon ERA Expulsions Growing," *The Dispatch*, February 28, 1980, 29. It is probably worth noting here that any assertion that the Mormon Church—or any other church—violated the constitutional separation of church and state evinces a misunderstanding of the Establishment Clause of the First Amendment. The First Amendment serves to constrain the government's ability to endorse or adopt religion; it does not prevent private actors from doing so. (There is a narrow exception where a private actor is performing government services.) The relevant legal question, then, was not whether the Mormon Church was engaged in politics, but whether its work to defeat the ERA amounted to more than an insubstantial part of its activities. "State Action and the Public/Private Distinction," *Harvard Law Review* 123, no. 5 (March 2010): 1248–1314.

44. "Medieval Ruling by Mormons," *Times Colonist*, January 2, 1980, 5.

45. Ruth Mellinkoff, *The Mark of Cain* (Berkeley: University of California Press, 1981), 76. This framing, predominantly by white Christians, did not represent the only racial characterization of the curse of Cain. Since at least the nineteenth century, some Black interpreters have flipped these assumptions, viewing a Black Cain whose curse led to white descendants (thus making whiteness the curse of Cain). Nyasha Junior, "The Mark of Cain and White Violence," *Journal of Biblical Literature* 139, no. 4 (2020): 661–673.

46. Joseph R. Stuart, "'A More Powerful Effect upon the Body': Early Mormonism's Theory of Racial Redemption and American Religious Theories of Race," *Church History* 87, no. 3 (2018), 768–796.

47. Chiung Hwang Chen and Ethan Yorgason. "'Those Amazing Mormons': The Media's Construction of Latter-Day Saints as a Model Minority." *Dialogue: A Journal of Mormon Thought* 32, no. 2 (1999): 107–128.

48. *Brown v. Bd. of Ed. of Topeka, Shawnee Cnty., Kan.*, 347 U.S. 483, 495, 74 S. Ct. 686, 692, 98 L. Ed. 873 (1954), supplemented sub nom. Brown v. Bd. of Educ. of Topeka, Kan., 349 U.S. 294, 75 S. Ct. 753, 99 L. Ed. 1083 (1955).

256 · *Notes to Chapter 12*

49. W. Brevard Hand, "Affirmative Action: La Mort de la Republique—A Second Cry from the
Wilderness," *Alabama Law Review* 48, no. 3 (Spring 1997): 799–860.

50. O. Kendall White, Jr., and Daryl White, "Abandoning an Unpopular Policy: An Analysis of the Decision Granting the Mormon Priesthood to Blacks," *Sociological Analysis* 41, no. 3 (1980): 231–245.

51. "Emergency Meeting Fails to Solve BYU Protest," *Tucson Daily Citizen*, October 18, 1969, 12.

52. Adam Epstein, "Utah and Sports Law," *Marquette Sports Law Review* 28, no. 1 (Fall 2017): 107–142.

53. Joe Watts, "Hallock Denies Charges of WAC Racism," *Provo Daily Herald*, October 22, 1969, 9.

54. "NMCLU Requests UNM to Withdraw from WAC," *Provo Daily Herald*, October 22, 1969, 9.

55. Mark L. Grover, "The Mormon Priesthood Revelation and the São Paulo, Brazil Temple," *Dialogue: A Journal of Mormon Thought* 23 no. 1 (1990): 39–53; D. Dmitri Hurlbut, "The LDS Church and the Problem of Race: Mormonism in Nigeria, 1946–1978," *International Journal of African Historical Studies* 51 no. 1 (2018): 1–16.

56. Matthew L. Harris and Newell G. Bringhurst, *The Mormon Church and Blacks: A Documentary History* (Urbana, IL: University of Illinois Press, 2015), 107.

57. *Grand Lodge-Free & Accepted Masons of Wisconsin v. Conta*, 84 Wis. 2d 701, 267 N.W.2d 375 (1978).

58. Lance Gurwell, "Critics Still Question 'Revelation' on Blacks," *Chicago Tribune*, June 2, 1988, 5.

59. Darron T. Smith, *When Race, Religion, and Sport Collide: Black Athletes At BYU and Beyond* (New York: Rowman & Littlefield, 2016), 96.

60. Matthew L. Harris, *Second-Class Saints: Black Mormons and the Struggle for Racial Equality* (New York: Oxford University Press, 2024): 201-202. Not every organization places such a premium on its tax exemption. After losing its tax exemption, Bob Jones University continued to ban interracial relationships. Finally, in 2000 the university lifted the ban. Even after it dropped the ban, though, Bob Jones University did not reapply for tax-exempt status until 2014, and did not regain its tax-exempt status until 2017. Herzig and Brunson, "Prophets," 1153; Nathaniel Cary, "Bob Jones University Regains Nonprofit Status 17 Years After It Dropped Discriminatory Policy," *Greenville News*, February 16, 2017, https://www.greenvilleonline.com/story/news/education/2017/02/16/bju-regains-nonprofit-status-17-years-after-dropped-discriminatory-policy/98009170/ [https://perma.cc/MPY2-XGTM].

61. *Baehr v. Lewin*, 74 Haw. 530, 852 P.2d 44 (1993), as clarified on reconsideration (May 27, 1993), and abrogated by *Obergefell v. Hodges*, 135 S. Ct. 2584, 192 L. Ed. 2d 609 (2015).

62. William N. Eskridge, Jr., "Latter-Day Constitutionalism: Sexuality, Gender, and Mormons," University of Illinois Law Review 2016, no. 4 (2016): 1227–1286.

Notes to Chapter 12 · 257

63. Robert Salladay, "Prop. 8 Lawyer Vetted First Gay Marriage Initiative With Mormon Leaders," *California Watch*, Jan. 29, 2010, https://web.archive.org/web/20110905050658/californiawatch.org/dailyreport/prop-8-lawyer-vetted-first-gay-marriage-initiative-mormon-leaders-926; Taylor G. Petrey, *Tabernacles of Clay: Sexuality and Gender in Modern Mormonism* (Chapel Hill: University of North Carolina Press, 2020), 152.

64. Jenifer Warren, "TV Ad for Anti-Gay Marriage Initiative Targets Latino Voters," *Los Angeles Times*, January 21, 2000, https://www.latimes.com/archives/la-xpm-2000-jan-21-mn-56317-story.html [https://perma.cc/9VHL-6U6P].

65. Gordon B. Hinckley, "Why We Do Some of the Things We Do," https://www.churchofjesuschrist.org/study/general-conference/1999/10/why-we-do-some-of-the-things-we-do?lang=eng [https://perma.cc/U3V9-Q3WP].

66. Scott L. Cummings and Douglas NeJaime, "Lawyering for Marriage Equality," UCLA Law Review 57, no. 5 (2010): 1235–1332.

67. "Catholics' Initiative Gifts Won't Spur Probe," *Santa Ana Orange County Register*, October 31, 1999, 3.

68. Jordan Lite, "Mormon-Backed Initiative Criticized," *Appeal-Democrat*, October 8, 1999, A3.

69. In re Marriage Cases, 43 Cal. 4th 757, 183 P.3d 384 (2008).

70. Katie Oliviero, "Yes on Proposition 8: The Conservative Opposition to Same-Sex Marriage," in *The Marrying Kind? Debating Same-Sex Marriage within the Lesbian and Gay Movement*, eds. Mary Bernstein and Verta Taylor(University of Minnesota Press, 2013), 167–216.

71. "California and Same-Sex Marriage," The Church of Jesus Christ of Latter-day Saints press release, June 30, 2008, https://newsroom.churchofjesuschrist.org/lds newsroom/eng/commentary/california-and-same-sex-marriage [https://perma.cc/RE63-QG4M].

72. Tony Semerad, "Utahns, LDS Church Spent More On Prop. 8 Than Previously Known," *Salt Lake Tribune*, February 9, 2009, https://archive.sltrib.com/story.php?ref=/news/ci_11666895 [https://perma.cc/3D4D-58RB].

73. Nicolas Riccardi, "Mormons Feel the Backlash Over Their Support of Prop. 8," *Los Angeles Times*, November 17, 2008, https://www.latimes.com/archives/la-xpm-2008-nov-17-na-mormons17-story.html [https://perma.cc/3PNN-VZPM].

74. Matthai Kuruvila, "Tax-Exempt Benefit Disputed in Prop. 8 Campaign," *SFGate*, November 28, 2008, https://www.sfgate.com/bayarea/article/Tax-exempt-benefit-disputed-in-Prop-8-campaign-3183401.php [https://perma.cc/RQ6R-TK4V].

75. Brian Galle, "The LDS Church, Proposition Eight, and the Federal Law of Charities," *Northwestern University Law Review* (Colloquy) 103 (2009): 370–379.

76. Jonathan Turley, "An Unholy Union: Same-Sex Marriage and the Use of Governmental Programs to Penalize Religious Groups with Unpopular Practices," in *Same-Sex Marriage and Religious Liberty: Emerging Conflicts*, eds. Douglas Laycock, Anthony R. Picarello, Jr., and Robin Fretwell Wilson (New York: Rowman & Littlefield Publishers, 2008): 59–76.

258 · *Notes to Chapter 12*

77. "We Are Undertaking the Biggest, Loudest and Most Comprehensive Challenge to a Church's Tax-Exempt Status in History," MormonTips.com, https://www.mormontips.com/-about [https://perma.cc/55G3-V8FA].

78. Jennifer Sinco Kelleher, "Mormon Critics Challenge Church's Tax-Exempt Status," *AP News*, August 16, 2018, https://apnews.com/c0ef623d31624dc0a49dbe51ef7150d3/Mormon-critics-challenge-church%27s-tax-exempt-status [https://perma.cc/Q2AJ-R6BU]; Letter from Rights Equal Rights to Commissioner John Koskinen, Aug. 16, 2018, https://0aad6db1-5b27-4638-af03-46fce61bdf13.filesusr.com/ugd/86a9f4_0c5aeef869464557b3ca81c81e146d80.pdf [https://perma.cc/VLZ3-PWVP].

79. Kelleher, "Mormon Critics."

80. Dennis Wyatt, "Faulty Logic Targets Mormons on Prop. 8," December 2, 2008, https://www.deseret.com/2008/12/2/20380737/faulty-logic-targets-mormons-on-prop-8 [https://perma.cc/YG87-S3JR].

81. Kathy Shaidle, "Payback for Proposition 8," *The Catholic World Report*, May 16, 2011, https://www.catholicworldreport.com/2011/05/16/payback-for-proposition-8/ [https://perma.cc/9H65-PDYZ].

82. "The Divine Institution of Marriage," Newsroom, https://newsroom.churchofjesuschrist.org/article/the-divine-institution-of-marriage [https://perma.cc/SD6U-L9PB].

83. Jason Swensen, "Church Commentary Defends Traditional Marriage," *Church News*, January 22, 2014, https://www.churchofjesuschrist.org/church/news/church-commentary-defends-traditional-marriage?lang=eng [https://perma.cc/CQU2-3HW6].

84. "Statement on the Signing of the US Respect for Marriage Act," *Newsroom*, December 13, 2022, https://newsroom.churchofjesuschrist.org/article/respect-for-marriage-act-signing [https://perma.cc/F232-3U37].

85. Respect for Marriage Act, 136 STAT. 2305, December 13, 2022.

86. While it is true that *Obergefell* requires all states to recognize same-sex marriages, in the wake of the Supreme Court overturning *Roe v. Wade*, proponents of the Respect for Marriage Act worried that *Obergefell* was also at risk. Thus, the Respect for Marriage Act protected same-sex marriage to the extent Congress had authority. *See* Anthony Michael Kreis (@AnthonyMKreis), "This is true but Congress could not impose on states a requirement to issue marriage licenses under their Section 5 powers if Obergefell was overturned. So, it doesn't do what many people think, but it does about as much as Congress could do," Twitter, November 16, 2022, https://twitter.com/AnthonyMKreis/status/1592997950678257664 [https://archive.md/6cOIN].

87. "President Oaks Explains the Church's Position on the Respect for Marriage Act," *Newsroom*, February 11, 2023, https://newsroom.churchofjesuschrist.org/article/president-oaks-church-position-respect-for-marriage-act [https://perma.cc/YF5K-9QCE].

88. "Answers to Common Questions: Understanding Religious Freedom," https://www.churchofjesuschrist.org/study/manual/religious-freedom/answers-to-common-questions?lang=eng [https://perma.cc/55Q2-2B8X].

Notes to Chapter 12 and Conclusion • 259

89. While the Mormon Church has generally complied with the tax law, in other financial areas, it has been less careful. In particular, it both allowed and encouraged Ensign Peak Advisors, its investment manager, to fail to file a required form, violating securities law and eventually facing public censure—and a fine—from the Securities and Exchange Commission. I discuss this failure further in the final chapter.

Conclusion

1. D&C 20:1.

2. Nathan B. Oman, "'Established Agreeable to the Laws of Our Country': Mormonism, Church Corporations, and the Long Legacy of America's First Disestablishment," *Journal of Law and Religion* 36, no. 2 (2021): 202–229.

3. Robert S. Wicks and Fred R. Foister, *Junius and Joseph: Presidential Politics and the Assassination of the First Mormon Prophet* (Logan, UT: Utah State University Press, 2005), 290.

4. Joseph Smith, Journal, 2 March 1842, The Joseph Smith Papers, accessed October 12, 2022, https://www.josephsmithpapers.org/paper-summary/journal-december-1841-december-1842/19 [https://perma.cc/WF3S-HTUS].

5. Joseph Smith, History Draft, 2 March 1842, The Joseph Smith Papers, accessed October 12, 2022, https://www.josephsmithpapers.org/paper-summary/history-draft-1-january-30-june-1842/7 [https://perma.cc/GJC5-HWZS].

6. "Introduction to State of Illinois v. JS for Assault and Battery," The Joseph Smith Papers, accessed October 12, 2022, https://www.josephsmithpapers.org/paper-summary/introduction-to-state-of-illinois-v-js-for-assault-and-battery/1 [https://perma.cc/8R4T-F8RZ]; Joseph Smith, Journal, 5 Sept. 1843, The Joseph Smith Papers, accessed October 12, 2022, https://www.josephsmithpapers.org/paper-summary/journal-december-1842-june-1844-book-3-15-july-1843-29-february-1844/91 [https://perma.cc/3MNY-NRE8].

7. "Journal, December 1842–June 1844; Book 3, 15 July 1843–29 February 1844," p. [52], The Joseph Smith Papers, accessed October 12, 2022, https://www.josephsmith papers.org/paper-summary/journal-december-1842-june-1844-book-3-15-july-1843-29-february-1844/58 [https://perma.cc/QPZ7-99FC].

8. "Introduction to State of Illinois v. JS"; Complaint, 1 August 1843 [*State of Illinois v. JS for Assault and Battery*], Joseph Smith Papers, accessed October 12, 2022, https://www.josephsmithpapers.org/paper-summary/complaint-1-august-1843-state-of-illinois-v-js-for-assault-and-battery/1 [https://perma.cc/LDH2-BL3F]. Information about this altercation appears to come primarily from William Clayton's diary; currently, however, his 1843 diary is unavailable to the general public, so I used the Joseph Smith Paper's summary as well as the primary documents that are available to paint a picture of this conflict.

9. Wicks and Foister, *Junius and Joseph*, 290.

10. "Great Meeting of Anti-Mormons!" *Warsaw Message*, September 13, 1843, 1–2.

11. John Joseph Wallis and Wallace E. Oates, "The Impact of the New Deal on American Federalism," in *The Defining Moment: The Great Depression and the American Economy*

260 · Notes to Conclusion

in the Twentieth Century, eds. Michael D. Bordo, Claudia Goldin, and Eugene N. White (Chicago: University of Chicago Press, 1998), 155–180.

12. Joel Slemrod and Jon Bakija, *Taxing Ourselves: A Citizen's Guide to the Debate over Taxes* (Cambridge, MA: The MIT Press, 2008), 16–17.

13. 17 CFR § 240.13f-1 (as amended in 2011).

14. Ensign Peak Advisors, Release No. 96951, February 21, 2023, https://www.sec.gov/litigation/admin/2023/34-96951.pdf [https://perma.cc/8HBA-SHAV]. For a broader discussion of the Mormon Church's violation of the securities law, *see* Sam Brunson, "The Church, the Investment Advisor, and the SEC," By Common Consent (February 21, 2023), https://bycommonconsent.com/2023/02/21/the-church-the-investment-advisor-and-the-sec/ [https://perma.cc/ED4M-YJFH].

Index

abatement, 54, 72–73, 76–78, 85
abortion politics, 185–86
Act of Toleration (1689), 10
Adams, John, 181
agriculture. *See* farmers and agriculture
alcohol, 7, 29
Amish, 144
Anthony, Susan B., 109
Anti-Mormon Party, 200
Apostolic churches, 29, 144
Arrington, Leonard J., 4, 191
assessment/assessors: and Brigham
    Young, 52; in Canada, 144; changes in
    administration, 8; different than collec-
    tor, 46–48; in Hawai'i, 87, 89; Jesse Hale
    works as, 17; and Joseph Smith, 18; in
    Mexico, 140; in Nauvoo, 28, 33, 41–43,
    56, 58; in Nevada, 83, 85; in New York,
    15, 90–93, 97, 102–3; and railroads, 111;
    for roads, 16, 58–59; signatures on scrip,
    50; and tithing, 68–79; in Utah, 60, 64,
    66, 154
audit, 65, 131, 143, 166, 187

Backenstos, Jacob, 48, 200
Bagby, Walter, 48, 199–200

Baker, Samuel, 42
Ballard, M. Russell, 173
banks, 14, 21–22, 29–30, 50, 65, 112, 147,
    153, 161–62
Baptists, 13, 87, 159; Evening Star Baptist
    Church, 104
Barnett, John T., 26, 33–34, 41–42, 52
Bennett, John C., 26, 33–34, 44
Bennett, Samuel, 42
Bennett, Wallace, 151–52
Benson, Ezra Taft, 116–18, 124
biofuels, 132
bishops (Mormon), 27–28, 51, 57–58, 65,
    67, 75, 120, 122, 133, 161. *See also* Presid-
    ing Bishopric (LDS)
Black Americans, 36, 131, 182–85, 189–91.
    See also race/racial
Blackmore, Winston, 143–47: Blackmore
    Farms Ltd., 148; J.R. Blackmore & Sons
    Ltd., 144
Blakeslee, George A., 93–94
Bob Jones University, 184–85
Bob Jones University v. United States, 182–85,
    188–91
bonds, 46, 60, 109–12, 156
Book of Mormon, 9, 17, 67, 87, 159–62

262 · Index

Boston Tea Party, 107, 109
Boy Scouts, 124–25
Bray, Karl, 119
Brigham Young University (BYU), 118, 167, 175, 193; American Association of Independent College and University Presidents, 150–51; civil rights protests, 190
Brigham Young University–Hawai'i, 88. *See also* Polynesian Cultural Center
Brinley family, 167
Brooklyn, NY, 90–104, 179, 196–97
Brosnan, Cornelius, 84
Brown, L.S., 119
Brown v. Board of Education, 182–83
Burch, Lynn, 145

Campbellites, 159
Canada, 134, 142–48; British Columbia Supreme Court, 148; Canadian Revenue Agency, 147–48
Capone, Al, 143
Carpenter, Liz, 187
cash: cash poor, 66, 75–76, 86; gold, 21, 23, 50–61, 66, 84–85; greenbacks, 84–85; scrip, 50–53, 65, 159–62; silver, 21, 23, 50–51, 85. *See also* currency
charity and charitable donations: and church tax exemptions, 149–50; deductions for, 163–71, 179–82; not income, 69–70; and lotteries, 153; and Mormon fundamentalists, 138–39; in New Zealand, 171–72; and the Polynesian Cultural Center, 89; and race, 184; taxation of passive income, 112; tax-exempt, 185; and tithing, 72
Chetlain, Augustus L., 68
Chickasaw (nation), 84
church and state (wall of separation between), 1, 8
Church of England (Anglicans), 10–11
Church of Jesus Christ (Original Doctrine), 148
Church of Jesus Christ of Latter-day Saints. *See* Mormon Church (Church of Jesus Christ of Latter-day Saints)
civil rights, 23, 109, 116, 183–84, 189–90, 197
Civil Rights Act (1964), 183, 189

Civil War (US), 30, 68–72, 79, 100, 110, 149
Clayton, William, 38, 48, 200
clergy (professional), 13–14, 87, 94, 173–78
Coe, Joseph, 48–49
Committee on Municipal Laws, 44–45
Communism, 116–18
Congregationalists, 10–13, 153, 164
Corporation of the Presiding Bishopric, 93, 96, 99–102. *See also* Presiding Bishopric (LDS)
corporations/corporate: and bonds, 111–12; and Brooklyn church building, 91–104; and charitable deductions, 163; disincorporation, 5, 74, 80, 128; income tax, 110; Kirtland Safety Society, 21; Mormon businesses, 113; of Nauvoo, 35; and payroll taxes, 124; of religions in New York, 17, 199; religious corporations, 94–97, 101–2; reorganization, 90; and same-sex marriage, 196; taxation of, 135–37; without dividends, 136
corporations sole, 93–94, 101–4
Corrill, Isaac, 27
Council of Fifty, 57
Coward, Mr., 171
Cowdery, Oliver, 18
currency, 20–21, 50, 84–85, 142; foreign currency, 171–73. *See also* cash

Davis, Bart, 166–70
Davis, James M., 52
Davis, William, 104
Davis v. United States, 170
debt, 15, 20, 27, 50, 76, 84–85, 153, 156, 160, 175
Declaration of the Rights of Women, 109
deductions (tax): and church charitable donations, 150; and fundamentalist Mormons, 139; and lotteries, 155; and missionary service, 163–70, 176–78; and race, 183–84; and same-sex marriage, 193; and Shakers, 70–71; uncapped charitable, 179–82
deeds, 27, 49, 93–94, 99–102, 134
Delano, Columbus, 75
democracy, 3, 26, 34, 40
Democrats, 53, 110–11, 114–15
Dent, John, 38–39

Index · 263

Dermen, Lev, 132
Deseret (state), 57–60, 62–65, 126, 140, 149, 151
Diaz, Porfirio, 140
disestablishment (of religion), 7, 11–14
dissenters, 10–12, 189
Doctrine and Covenants, 118, 123
dog tax, 31, 38–42, 90
Douglass, John W., 76–79
Duffin, James, 161
Dunham, Jonathan, 51
Dutch Reformed Church, 11

Eastern Orthodox Church, 94
Eastern States Mission, 91–92, 95, 98, 101–104, 176
Edmonds Act, 108
Edmonds-Tucker Act, 108
Eisenhower, Dwight, 116–17
Eldridge, Horace S., 59
Ellerbeck, T.W., 74
Emmons, Sylvester, 26
England: Church of England, 10–11; Corn Laws, 32; income taxes, 10, 30–33, 67; missionaries in, 30–32, 64, 160. *See also* Great Britain
Ensign Peak Advisors, 201–2
Episcopal Church: Williams Institutional Colored Methodist Episcopal Church, 103
Equal Rights Amendment (ERA), 185–88, 193; Mormons for ERA, 188
Eyring, Henry, 174

Farmer, James, 160
farmers and agriculture, 32–34, 39–40, 84, 131, 136–37, 143–44
Feminist Party, 185, 187
Feminists, 185–87
Fillmore, Millard, 59
Fischer, Dan, 130–31
Fischer, Marvin, 130
Foote, Warren, 82, 86
Ford, Thomas, 52
French settlers, 35
Fundamentalist Church of Jesus Christ of Latter-day Saints (FLDS), 129–39, 143, 146; Yearning for Zion Ranch, 129

Gibbs, George, 98–99
Grant, Heber J., 111
Grant, Ulysses S., 68–69
Great Britain, 7, 30–33, 38–39, 67, 107, 109, 143. *See also* England
Greene, John, 42, 51
Green Mountain Boys, 23
Grismore, John, 118
Gritz, James "Bo," 123–24

habeas corpus, 28
Hale, David, 17
Hale, Emma. *See* Smith, Emma Hale
Hale, Jesse, 17
Hale, Jonathan, 48, 50
Hammon, Sara, 130
Harris, George Washington, 52
Hatch, Orrin, 181–82, 188
Haviland, Mr., 96
Hawai'i, 81, 86–89, 153, 167, 192
Hawley, Claude, 161
Higgins, Anthony, 114
Hills, Gustavus, 33
Hinckley, Gordon B., 162, 193
Hollis, Henry, 163, 181
Hollister, O.J., 69, 72–77
Holy Land Experience, 89
Hooper, William H., 76–77
Hotchkiss, Horace, 47
Hunter, Edward, 61
Huntington, Oliver, 160
Hutterites, 144–47: Hutterite Rule, 144–47

immigrants, 30–32, 58, 67, 155
income taxes: in Britain, 7, 10; in Canada, 144–48; and exemptions, 80, 184; and farmers, 34, 39; and the Holy Land Experience, 89; and lotteries, 154; in Mexico, 140; Mormonism and, 201; and Mormon missions, 162–64, 168, 173–78; Mormon opposition to progressive taxation, 116–18; Mormon protests against, 118–26; and polygamy, 130–31, 135–40, 144–48; and the Presiding Bishopric, 63–64; and professional clergy, 173; and Reed Smoot, 110–15; and tithing, 68–80; in the United States, 105
Internal Revenue Code, 138–39, 166

264 · *Index*

Internal Revenue Service (IRS), 138–39; 1950 law, 103, 149; and *Bob Jones*, 182–85, 190; and church aid, 177; and church tax exemptions, 148–50; and employment taxes, 124; and the ERA, 185–88; and fundamentalists, 131, 137–39, 148; and Mormon missionaries, 164–73; and the Mormon racial restriction, 190; and the Polynesian Cultural Center, 88–89; and professional clergy, 173–74; and same-sex marriage, 193, 195; and section 501(c)(3), 138–39; and tax protests, 119–21, 124–26
Israelite House of David, 135–36
Iverson, Gustave, 176
Ivins, Anthony W., 142

James, Arlo, 155
Jefferson, Thomas, 1, 8, 34, 60, 155
Jeffs, Warren, 134, 143
Jessop, Carolyn, 130
Jews, 11, 96, 188
Johnson, Andrew, 68
Johnson, John, 19, 22
Johnson, Sonia, 188
Julian, George Washington, 108

Kalakana and Kapiolani, 87
Karger, Fred, 195
Kean, John, 110
Kelly, E.L., 93–94
Kimball, Heber, 30, 51, 57
Kimball, Hiram, 44–45
Kimball, Spencer W., 120, 186, 189
King, William H., 111
Kingston family, 131–32
Kirtland Safety Society Anti-Banking Company, 21–22, 30
Kirton, Wilford W., 166–67
Knight, Pete, 193
Knight, Vinson, 41–42
Kohn, Stuart, 97–102

Law, William, 26, 44
Law, Wilson, 41–42, 52
lay ministry, 19, 118, 121–22, 173, 179
Lee, Harold B., 119–21
Lee, Rex E., 167–69

Leno, Mark, 193
Lincoln, Abraham, 83
lobbying (Mormon Church): 193, 195, 201: and abatement, 77; and corporations sole, 93–94; and the ERA, 185–88, 193; and the federal income tax, 201; and lotteries, 152–58; post-theocracy, 60; and same-sex marriage, 195; and tariffs, 114; and tax exemptions, 149–52
lotteries, 152–58
Lyman, Francis, 69
Lyon, John, 104

Maloney, Francis, 119
Mann, S.A., 108
McBride, Reuben, 49
McFall, Hugh, 26
Methodists, 9, 13, 87, 103, 159
Mexico, 2, 140–43; Juarez Stake Academy, 140; Mexican Revolution, 141
ministers, 10–20, 32, 87–88, 125, 173–74
missionaries/missions: in Canada, 143; Eastern States Mission, 91–92, 95–98, 101–4, 176; in England, 30, 33, 64; and the ERA, 187; and foreign currencies, 171–73; government subsidies for, 162–71; in Hawai'i, 86–89; history of Mormon, 159–62; and the Muddy River Colonies, 82; in Nevada, 85; and race, 190; travel without purse or scrip, 159–61; Trust Board, 172; ward missionary funds, 170, 172. *See also* mission presidents
mission presidents, 91, 98, 121, 161, 170, 175–78
Mitchell, F.A., 156
Monson, Walter, 91–101
Morgan, J. P., 111
Morley, Isaac, 27
Mormon Church (Church of Jesus Christ of Latter-day Saints): cash-poor, 66, 75–76, 86; church courts (discipline), 59–62, 75, 80, 85, 119–24, 128; Church Handbook of Instructions, 122–25, 179; communalism, 133, 135, 137; exclusive jurisdiction, 60–61, 63; First Presidency, 26, 57, 92, 95–104, 111–12, 117, 121–24, 141–42, 176, 194, 196, 201; Gen-

Index · 265

eral Authorities, 95, 173–75; integrated auxiliaries language, 151; leaders as dual roles as religious and political leaders, 26; originally called Church of Christ, 7, 9, 14, 17–19, 159, 199; Quorum of the Seventy, 193; Restorationist, 13–14, 127, 133, 202; tax-exempt status, 91, 104, 179, 187–97, 201–2; as Tax Rebellion Movement, 121; Trust Board, 172; without purse or scrip, 159–61

Morrison, Arthur, 44

Muddy River Colonies, 82–86

National Organization of Women, 187–88

National Women's Political Caucus, 187

Native Americans, 5, 57, 64, 67, 82, 84

Nauvoo, IL: charter, 25, 28–30, 33–37, 41, 45, 49–56; City Council, 26–29, 33–38, 41–54, 64; Clerk of the Municipal Court, 47; Committee on Municipal Laws, 44–45; Committee of Ways and Means, 43; High Council, 27; poor fund, 52

Nauvoo Expositor, 53

Nauvoo Legion, 28, 36, 52

New Zealand, 171–73

Nibley, Charles W., 99–102, 114

Nielsen, Wendell Loy, 138

Oaks, Dallin H., 156, 181–82, 196

Obama, Barack, 180

Obergefell v. Hodges, 196

Oswald, William D., 157

Panic of 1837, 21, 30, 65

parsonage, 174

Partridge, Edward, 27

Perpetual Emigrating Fund for the Poor, 58

Philippines, the, 113

Pleasonton, Alfred, 79

police, 50–51, 143

polygamy: 1890 Woodruff Manifesto, 80, 128, 140; and the agricultural industry, 131, 137, 143–44; and Americanization, 149, 189; anti-polygamy movements, 74; in Canada, 134, 142–48; and communitarianism, 135–40; and disincorporation, 5, 72; early practice of, 127–28; and economics, 127; and fundamentalism,

129–32, 135–40, 143; in Hawai'i, 88; in Mexico, 140–42; plural wives as spiritual wives, 130; and private ownerships, 133, 135; renunciation, 80; and state taxes, 132–35; and tax exemption, 87; terminology, 128; and tithing, 69; treasurer, 38, 47, 50; and women's suffrage, 108. *See also* Fundamentalist Church of Jesus Christ of Latter-day Saints

Polynesian Cultural Center, 88–89, 195

Populist Party, 124

Pottawatomie, 64

Presbyterians, 13, 159

Presiding Bishopric (LDS), 61, 63, 78; Corporation of the Presiding Bishop, 93–96, 99–102, 114, 122, 201

Principle Voices of Polygamy, 139

pro bono, 166–67

Protestants, 10–13, 94, 96, 102; evangelicals, 159, 185

public nuisances, 29, 38–39

Quakers, 15, 153

Quorum of Twelve Apostles, 26–27, 30, 55, 111, 113, 116, 156, 160, 181, 186. *See also individual apostles by name*

race/racial: discrimination, 138, 183–85; interracial marriage, 36; and the Respect for Marriage Act, 196; segregation, 183, 189; and tax exemption, 189–91. See also *Bob Jones v. United States*

railroads, 84, 111–12, 156

Raksis, Elaine, 188

Randall, Jose, 141

Reagan, Ronald, 167

Rebbeck, Lydia, 93–94

Religious Corporations Law (NY), 94

Reorganized Church of Jesus Christ of Latter Day Saints, 93–94

Republican Party, 69, 110–11, 115

Respect for Marriage Act, 196

Revolutionary War, 11, 108–9

Rich, Charles, 34, 54, 57

Richards, Franklin, 92–101

Richards, George, 161

Richards, Henry P., 86–88

Richards, Willard, 31, 34, 38, 41, 51, 57

266 · Index

Rigdon, Sidney, 21, 26, 44, 47
Robinson, Lewis, 47
Rockefeller, John D., 111
Roman Catholic Church, 192–93, 196; and
clergy, 87–88; and corporations sole,
93–96; and same-sex marriage, 192–93,
196; and secularism, 3; and taxes, 11, 102;
and tax exemptions, 150, 185–88
Rushton, Edwin, 61

Salt Lake City High Council, 56–60
same-sex marriage, 192–96; Proposition 8,
193–96; Proposition 22, 192–94
Satan, 9
Scovil, Lucius, 155–56
Second Great Awakening, 9–10, 13–14, 199
secularism, 1, 3, 10, 27–28, 53, 59, 62, 67,
117, 121, 194
Securities and Exchange Commission
(SEC), 201
Shakers (United Society of Believers),
70–71, 75–76, 137
Sherman, John, 77
sheriffs, 48–49, 84–86
Sherwood, Henry, 50
Short Creek Raids, 129
silver, 21, 23, 50–51, 85
slavery, 35–37
Smith, Asael, 12–13
Smith, Don Carlos, 26
Smith, Emma Hale, 17, 55
Smith, George, 54
Smith, Gerald G., 104
Smith, Hyrum, 16–18, 26, 41, 47, 52–53
Smith, James and Jean, 121
Smith, Jesse, 12
Smith, John, 56
Smith, Joseph, Jr.: and abolition, 36; birth-
place, 7, 11; and communitarianism, 135;
death, 26, 55, 199–200; and habeas cor-
pus, 28; moves to Illinois, 25; and mis-
sionary work, 159; and the Mississippi
River, 44–45; and Nauvoo City politics,
26, 34, 42, 44, 48–49; and the *Nauvoo
Expositor*, 53; and New York taxes, 14–18;
Old Major (dog), 42; and polygamy, 88,
127–28; presidential campaign, 36; and

proposed dog tax, 41–42; and real estate,
48–49; and the Second Great Awaken-
ing, 9–10; temple theology, 37; and tith-
ing, 27–28, 78–80; and Zion, 29
Smith, Joseph, Sr., 12, 15–18
Smith, Joseph F., 91, 98–102, 111, 114, 128
Smith, Mary, 160
Smith, Samuel Harrison, 26, 42, 52, 159
Smith, Thomas S., 82
Smith, William, 26, 53
Smoot, Reed, 90, 110–18, 128
Spencer, Daniel, 49, 51
Spencer, John D., 110
Spencer, Orson, 38, 51
steamboats, 44–45
Steinem, Gloria, 187
Stone, Lawrence, 150
Stone, Louise, 161
suffrage. *See* voting
sugar, 32, 56, 91, 113–15

Taggart, Edwin, 70
Taggart, John P., 68–79
tariffs, 7, 14, 30–32, 105, 110, 113–16;
Smoot-Hawley tariff, 115; Wilson-Underwood tariff bill, 114
taxation/taxes: base, 22, 29–37; bread,
31–33; church, 10–14; collectors, 3, 7,
15, 17, 46–48, 52, 59–64, 69–73, 79–85,
100, 110, 141–42, 199–200; delinquency,
42–43, 48–49, 57–62, 66, 84–86, 125,
134; excise tax, 7, 33, 83, 89, 105, 110, 137,
153; in-kind payments, 16, 50, 65, 74–75;
itemized deductions, 180, 182; local, 7,
30, 63, 66, 105, 130, 171; Old Fort tax,
56; of marijuana, 158; payroll, 173–74;
poll, 12, 58, 63–64; progressive, 3, 43,
45, 91, 116–18; protest, 17, 32, 43, 48, 77,
83, 107–26; rates, 28–33, 115, 117, 154,
163; road, 14–20, 42–45, 50, 57–59, 65,
87; sales, 115–16, 148–49, 154–55; sin,
90–91; taxation without representation,
108–10; tax credits, 130, 132, 171–73;
universal, 7, 100; Victory, 176. *See also
specific tax types by name*
Taylor, Delbert G., 103
Taylor, John, 26, 33, 41, 52, 60–61, 140

Index • 267

temples (LDS): Kirtland, 20; Missouri, 22; Nauvoo, 28, 37–38; in New York, 96; and polygamy's end, 80; and race, 189–92; recommends, 120–25; and same-sex marriage, 194; Temple Lot, 35–38
theocracy, 3, 26–28, 37, 53, 59–62, 156
Thompkins, Arthur S., 95, 102
Thompson, George, 124–25
tithing: abandonment of, 79–80, 104; and charitable deductions, 180–82; in early Mormonism, 27–28; and funding of public works, 4; of labor, 65, 145; in Nauvoo, 26; pamphlets on, 122; savings for, 162; sermonizing on, 64–68; taxation of, 63–64, 68–80; and tax deductions, 125
trusts: charitable, 138–39, 169, 184; Church of Jesus Christ of Latter-Day Saints Trust Board, 172; and the Hutterite Rule, 144; and income taxes, 124; sugar, 114; trustees-in-trust, 70, 74; United Effort Plan Trust, 133–34, 138–39
Tsongas, Paul, 188

Universalism, 12–13
US Bureau of Internal Revenue, 68–79, 169, 174
US Congress: and charitable deductions, 168–69, 180–83; and church incorporation, 74; and the Civil Rights Act (1964), 183, 189; and clergy, 173–76; and currency, 84; and Deseret statehood, 57; and the ERA, 186; and federal income tax, 34, 70, 74–77, 80, 116; and the Israelite House of David, 136; Mormon missions, 162–63; Mormons in, 5; and polygamy, 108–13, 131–32, 137, 139; and state boundaries, 83; and tax exemptions, 149–52
US Constitution: church and state concerns, 2–5; and currency, 21; Establishment Clause, 1; and Ezra Taft Benson, 118; Fifth Amendment, 119; First, 125, 184–87; Fourteenth Amendment, 183; Free Exercise Clause, 184, 196; and income taxes, 110–11; and Missouri reparations, 23; and morality, 181–82; and Mormon tax protest, 118–22; Nine-

teenth, 187; and religious freedom, 139; Sixteenth Amendment, 105, 110–11, 118–21; and taxation of federal property, 35. See also Equal Rights Amendment (ERA); US Supreme Court; US Supreme Court decisions by name
US House of Representatives, 5, 69, 150–51; Committee on Ways and Means, 79, 150
US Justice Department, 145
US Senate, 5, 53, 110–11, 114–15, 128, 151–52, 188; Advisor to Senate Committee, 144; Committee on Finance, 77, 181; Judiciary Committee, 130. See also senators by name
US Social Security, 173–74
US Supreme Court, 5, 35, 112, 121, 138, 148, 167–70, 182–85, 188–92, 196; justices, 168–69
US Treasury, 69–70, 112, 174, 180
Utah-Idaho Sugar Company, 113–15

voting (suffrage): and the ERA, 186; and lotteries, 155–58; Mormon block vote, 53; Mormons lose right to, 5; National Woman Suffrage Association, 109; in Nauvoo, 36–37, 42, 64; and the Nauvoo temple, 37; and the Nineteenth Amendment, 187; Reed Smoot in Congress, 110–11; and religious taxation, 12; and same-sex marriage, 192–95; and taxation, 23, 66, 108–10

Wales, 48
Walsh, David, 136–37
Wardle, Lynn, 193
Warrington, Benjamin, 26
Wells, Daniel H., 34, 49, 54, 61, 63, 73–74, 77–78
Wells, Emeline Young, 110
Wells, Emmeline B., 108, 110
white Americans, 36, 67, 86, 116, 165, 183–84. See also race/racial
Whitmer, Christian, 18
Whitmer, John, 18
Wilkinson, Ernest L., 150–51
Williams, J.D., 188

268 · *Index*

Willis, William W., 56
Wilson, Woodrow, 105
Wise, Roland, 120
Women's Suffrage Association, 108; women's right to vote, 23, 108–10
Woodruff, Wilford, 26, 51, 80, 113, 128
World War I, 115, 163
World War II, 116

Young, Brigham: and communitarianism, 135; and England, 30–31; and federal taxation, 63–64, 79–80; and lotteries, 156; and missionaries, 160; and Nauvoo government, 26, 41–42, 50–52; and race, 189; sermons on taxation, 64–68; and Southern Utah settlement, 82, 86; and tithing, 68–79; and Utah's early years, 55–59; and women's consumption, 66
Young, Joseph, 84

Zion, 19, 26, 29, 38

SAMUEL D. BRUNSON is the Georgia Reithal Professor of Law and the associate dean for Academic Affairs at the Loyola University Chicago School of Law. He is the author of *God and the IRS: Accommodating Religious Practice in United States Tax Law*.

The University of Illinois Press
is a founding member of the
Association of University Presses.

Composed in 10.25/13 Marat pro
with Optima LT Std display
by Lisa Connery
at the University of Illinois Press

University of Illinois Press
1325 South Oak Street
Champaign, IL 61820-6903
www.press.uillinois.edu